The Banking Revolutions

Alberto León Cebrián

The Banking Revolutions
Self-published by Alberto León Cebrián
Edition, translation, cover, design and layout by Alberto León Cebrián
Printed in Spain

www.albertoleoncebrian.com

Dedicated to Maria, a person who inspires everyone who knows her, beyond words can describe.

To Elina, Teresa, Dolores, Maria, Pilar, Carmen, Vicky.

To Pedro, the professor who awakened my love for History.

«Old John D. Rockefeller and his 19th century fellow-capitalists were convinced of one absolute truth: that no great monetary wealth could be accumulated under the impartial rules of a competitive laissez faire society. The only sure road to the acquisition of massive wealth was monopoly: drive out your competitors, reduce competition, eliminate laissez-faire, and above all get state protection for your industry through compliant politicians and government regulation. This last avenue yields a legal monopoly, and a legal monopoly always leads to wealth. »

Anthony Sutton, *Wall Street & FDR*.

Gabriel—What is that for a mythical power which they had obtained?

Rakovsky —They had acquired for themselves the real privilege of coining money ... Do not smile, otherwise I shall have to believe that you do not know what moneys are ... I ask you to put yourself in my place. My position in relation to you is that of the assistant of a doctor, who would have to explain bacteriology to a resurrected medical man of the epoch before Pasteur. But I can explain your lack of knowledge to myself and can forgive it. Our language makes use of words which provoke incorrect thoughts about things and actions, thanks to the power of the inertia of thoughts, and which do not correspond to real and exact conceptions. I say: money. It is clear that in your imagination there immediately appeared pictures of real money of metal and paper. But that is not so. Money is now not that; real circulating coin is a true anachronism. If it still exists and circulates, then it is only thanks to atavism, only because it is convenient to maintain the illusion, a purely imaginary fiction for the present day.

G.— This is a brilliant paradox, risky and even poetical.

R.— If you like, this is perhaps brilliant, but it is not a paradox. I know - and that is why you smiled - that States still coin money on pieces of metal or paper with Royal busts or national crests; well, so what? A great part of the money circulating, money for big affairs, as representative of all national wealth, money, yes money - it was being issued by those few people about whom I had hinted. Titles, figures, cheques, promissory notes, endorsements, discount, quotations, figures without end flooded States like a waterfall. What are in comparison with these the metallic and paper moneys? . . . Something devoid of influence, some kind of minimum in the face of the growing flood of the all-flooding financial money. They, being the most subtle psychologists, were able to gain even more without trouble, thanks to a lack of understanding. In addition to the immensely varied different forms of financial moneys, they created credit-money with a view to making its volume close to infinite. And to give it the speed of sound ... it is an abstraction, a being of thought, a figure, number, credit, faith...

Jose Landowsky, *The Red Symphony*, 1952

A NEW APPROACH

The way we study History in the Contemporary Age is not so different from the way we did back in the Old Age. The first records of written History described in detail the lives of caesars, emperors, feudal lords or kings, and the essence that animated the narrative were the endless struggles and disputes of these autocrats for expanding their domains. Many of these warlords were lost in oblivion, and only a few of these great conquerors forged legendary empires. Today, as it happened then, History is analyzed mainly in terms of nations and chiefs of state.

As parliamentary systems spread across western world, with the Glorious Revolution of 1688, the American Revolution of 1776 and the French Revolution of 1789, absolute power of the monarchs diminished, and were gradually replaced by these new structures of power. Such a forces eventually dominated the social and political life of twentieth century. It prevails among historians a remarkable difficulty in dealing with the new dynamics of powers

Overcoming this historiographical methodology that has been valid for thousands of years is naturally a difficult issue, especially if we consider that the world has suffered more changes in the last century – social, political and scientific- than in the preceding five millennia. Many readers will appreciate how naïve is to think that the world we live in owes its direction to presidents', prime minister's or even parliaments, rather than corporations, financial institutions, multilateral organizations, political advisors, lobbies and other similar powers. The very same terms of nation or state seem to be obsolete terms in this new century, words close to disappear in a global world. We know the history of the twentieth century, but not the whole story. It prevails among many historians the habit of re-editing secondary and tertiary sources, rather than using first hand testimonies, the voices of the leading figures of their time.

In my previous book I exposed the history of one of these rising structures of power, the Freemasonry, and its influence on the revolutions of the end of the eighteenth century. These revolutions established the beginning of the Modern Age. This second book is a critical history of financial capitalism and explains the role of the several German and Anglo-Saxon banking houses in the development of the western world. No group is more relevant than the other, because money does not understand differences of religion, race or nation. The timeframe is approximately from 1850 to 1950. Both books deal with different topics, but there is an evident continuity in the time and matters dealt with. This second work is more suitable for any public, and there's no need to be a financial expert to enjoy the reading.

The book has a glossary and another complementary information at the end of it for an easier guidance of the familiar and economic relations described here. We start a new initiatory journey that will lead us to know the tycoons of the financial capitalism that forged the twentieth century.

THE CENTURY OF INVESTMENT BANKING

The major milestone in the History of Finance probably was laid when the coin replaced the bartering as a way of exchanging goods and services. The introduction of the first coins was known to take place in Asia during the 6th and 7th centuries BC. It was a simple means of payment, more useful for the trade than transporting the goods that had to be exchanged, food, animals or other properties. Currencies had then an intrinsic value of the precious metals in which these were minted.

Money lenders and the money changers have been the key figures in the world of finance were since biblical times, being both crafts related. The moneychangers, quite often Jews, kept gold and wealth of those who wanted to keep their money in a safe place. In exchange of a payment for their services they issued a receipt or any proof of payment of the ownership of the money taken under custody. The money they kept allowed them to issue loans to other customers, a service for which they also charged fees in concept of interest. Eventually the moneylenders realized that by using receipts, payment notes and other forms of "paper money" they could extend their credits beyond the reserves they kept. A moneylender could lend in paper a thousand florins, even if he only hoarded a hundred in deposit. By using this system they could lend ten times a money they had not, and perceive the interest fees on this non-existent money. Just in case someone got lost; a money lender could issue as many payment promises as he wanted, being able to create money out of thin air, and earning an interest for doing that. The system would work as long as others trusted the payment notes of the lender, but if several customers requested the exchange of paper for real money the money lender would be in trouble. It was a system based on confidence, that is, on credit. This is the origin of the fractional reserve banking that lasts until present day. Commercial banks no longer "create" paper money, and in fact paper money represents now a really small fraction of the money supply, being most of it hoarded in the virtual form of book entries in computers.

Jews were historically discriminated in Europe due to an irrational hate to their racial and religious condition, but their great skills in finance and their occasional use of usury -lending with a very high interest rates- is also a fact to consider. That did not make them very popular in the places where they settled. Jews simply had an advantage of centuries in the banking business over Christian and Islamic worlds, due to cultural factors, more specifically its religion. The Bible forbade the loans with interest, and so did later fathers of Christian theology like St. Thomas or St. Augustine. The teachings of the prophet Muhammad also warned in this regard. Jews were forbidden to lend with interest to their own people, but this did not apply to foreigners.

The Knights Templars emerged as the great financial power of Christendom in the Middle Ages, between the 12th and the 14th centuries. Long before the internationalized Jewish families appeared in the 18th century, the Knights Templars provided financial services in the East and the West. Knights Templars always kept an excellent relation with the Jews and were their protectors wherever they inhabited. The fall of the Order of the Temple marked the end of the Christian banking in Europe, and only after the Lutheran Reformation some Protestant countries, particularly the Calvinists, the financial activity reactivated. The Roman Church interpreted in the literal sense the beatitudes that preached the Kingdom of Heavens would be reserved to the poor, but Lutherans and Calvinists had a more materialistic views on life and believed those who were enriched in life were doubtlessly blessed by God. During the Middle Ages the Jews were converted, expelled from several countries or forced to live in ghettos. As Roman Catholic and more intensely Protestant bankers got involved in the same banking practices of his Jewish fellows, the hostile attitude towards Jews was softened.

By the mid-19th century, in England, France, Austria, Prussia and the states of the Italian peninsula there were powerful Jewish and Protestant families lending banking services to statesmen and citizens.

Switzerland became one of the most important financial centers of the world. The Old Swiss Confederacy was created in the 12th century by thirteen small states in the southwest of what is now Germany. Many Knights Templars found a haven there after the persecution of the order in France, and probably it's no accident that the national flag of the Helvetic country, the world financial center par excellence, is a white Greek cross on a red background, while the Templars used a red Greek cross on a white background.

The money lenders grew in relevance as centuries passed, and they increased their fortunes by keeping the equity of important bourgeois, princes and monarchs, making loans and investments with the capital obtained. At the end of the 18th century and in the early 19th century the power of these bankers was so immense that they could decisively influence in the battles of these European princes, as it happened in the Napoleonic Wars. This century marked the beginning of the big international banking, in coincidence with the diaspora of several Jewish families of bankers all over the economic capital cities of Europe. For their services they were ranked as Knights, Barons and Lords, achieving also political compensations.

In the 19th century the venerable Jewish and Protestant houses of investment occupied the seats of boards in the central banks of the United States and the European countries. The power to issue the currency of a country would allow them to manipulate the prices, create at will expansive periods of artificial wealth or credit crunches that could cripple the economy, generate or destroy jobs, and to a certain extent to elevate governments or depose them. The most important central banks in Europe were the Bank of England and the Bank of France, which emerged after the Glorious Revolution of 1688 in England and the French Revolution of 1789. In 1913 the same European banking families which laid the foundations of these institutions achieved a new success when they established a new central bank in the United States, the Federal Reserve. Their previous attempts in North America had given short lived results.

The 20th century gave birth to the Golden Age of financial capitalism. The banking aristocracy, which had competed in a handful of familiar firms, mastered the rules of the game of a free market economy. The bankers learnt that it was more fruitful to cooperate to protect their common interests rather than competition; price fixing was always preferable. The most profitable monopolies were those backed by the State protection; the bigger the government and the more regulations that kept competitors away from the market, the more wealth they would amass. They found their allies in the most unexpected ways of government, usually in totalitarian states. In the democratic governments they concealed their widespread control over the economy by means of a broad interpretation of the regulations. They avoided the emerging anti-monopoly laws by exchanging their partners in the boards of directors of other banks, creating complex societal structures, sealing their alliances with marriages of convenience and creating closed familiar networks.

In addition to the generous profits harvested related to the banking business itself, these families of aristocrats-bankers enjoyed benefits beyond the economic, in terms of influence. Owed to the servitude that the debt generated in the debtor they obtained seats in the board of directors of different corporations. This favored the creation of big trusts in all sectors across all industries and produced the same distortions in the free competence that they have caused in the world of business. Sovereign states, who were the most important clients of the investment bankers, also paid their fair share of power, always expressed in political seats in the subsequent governments, regardless their political allegiance. For instance, it is very rare to see a Secretary of Treasury in the United States that did not come from the world of private finance, or who did not have any stake in them. The diplomatic seats and those related to defense of the country were also very tasteful bites for the geniuses of the high finance.

Their experience in the old Europe proved them that an economy of stable growth could provide a generous but limited returns, but other scenarios provided a much more favorable environment: War and crisis multiplied the profits in an exponential way. Wars allowed banks to sell very easily the best product of a bank's portfolio, the debt. Any country would fall into debt until exhaustion to preserve its own existence as a nation. Regardless who was the on victorious side, the bankers would ensure the winner –also a debtor- would force defeated nation to pay the debts. The crises of the 20th century, mostly of a monetary or financial sort, became periods of reaping profits. Being the banking fraternity in command of central banks of the Western countries they were not only able to anticipate adverse economic cycles, but also to create them; the crises provided unsurpassed opportunities of buying, favored the enterprise mergers, facilitated the extinction of their rivals and reinforced their positions of oligopolistic leadership.

The first part of this work narrates the story of the great Anglo Germanic banking dynasties, and the second part describes their roles in the revolutions in the first half of the 20th century.

This is the story of how a handful of family firms of international banking hoarded all sources of wealth we know; paper money, oil, gold, diamond and raw matters. The story of how they exerted control over the finance and the industry. A control strong enough to manage the broad policies in the Western world, some of which led to the two world wars. This is a story you will not find in the textbooks.

PART I. THE ARISTOCRATS OF HIGH FINANCE

FORMER ROTHSCHILD - SCHIFF HOUSE

Placed in 148 Judengasse, Frankfurt.

THE HOUSE OF ROTHSCHILD

Who hold the balance of the world? Who reign
O'er Congress, whether royalist or liberal?
Who rouse the shirtless patriots of Spain?
(That make old Europe's journals squeak and gibber all.)
Who keep the world, both old and new, in pain
Or pleasure? Who make politics run glibber all?
The shade of Bonaparte's noble daring?
Jew Rothschild, and his fellow Christian Baring.
Those, and the truly liberal Lafitte,
Are the true lords of Europe. Every loan
Is not a merely speculative hit,
But seats a nation or upsets a throne.

Lord Byron, *Don Juan, Canto XII,* 1819.

Our story about the tycoons of the high finance begins in the Jewish ghettos of Germany in the mid-18th century. Some of the most prominent banking dynasties who ruled our recent history started there. Such a dynasties were closely linked by familiar and entrepreneurial bonds, and almost all of them had its origins in the city of Frankfurt. One of these families shone with its own light, the House of Rothschild. By the end of the 19th century they were the greatest financial power of Europe. The Rothschilds took its surname from the emblem on his home, *zum Roten Schild,* which in German meant "house of the red shield" [1]. The first known Rothschild, as mentioned by the

---

[1] Since the end of 18th century, and due to administrative needs, the Austrian, Russian and Napoleonic Empire, as well as some German states legislated the obligatoriety for the Jews to use hereditary surnames. Many of these surnames are related precisely with the activities that they practiced; Goldstein, Goldman o Goldberg ("goldsmith"), Silverstein ("silversmith"), del Banco ("banker"), etc.

funerary registries of Frankfurt, was Moses Rothschild, deceased in 1550[2].

Mayer Amschel Rothschild, born about 1743, became the architect of the wealth of the legendary House of Rothschild. The son of a merchant, since his childhood he assisted his father in the tasks of a moneychanger. He studied to be a rabbi, like many of his ancestors, but soon he knew his future, and that of his future generations, was in the world of finance. Mayer Amschel was widely known as the financial agent of William IX Hesse-Cassel, the biggest fortune of his time, which increased due to the American Independence War[3]. In 1812 the wealth of Mayer Amschel was estimated in 20 million dollars, an equity that would embarrass any European Prince[4].

Over the years Mayer Amschel sent his five male sons to the main capital cities of Europe: His son Mayer Amschel remained in Frankfurt to continue the familiar business there, Salomon Mayer settled in Berlin in 1815 and Karl Mayer went to Naples in 1821. None of them achieved a success like the other two brothers, Nathan Mayer, who settled in London, and James Mayer, who did the same in Paris.

London

Nathan Mayer Rothschild, who settled down in London, was the most industrious successor, increasing considerably the family power through *N.M. Rothschild & Sons*, founded in 1811. The German Prince Karl Theodor von Dalberg trusted his equity to Nathan Mayer, a money he used to finance the English side in the Napoleonic Wars. According to the Jewish Encyclopedia[5] the Rothschild acquired large amounts of gold to support the military campaign of the Duke of

[2] Cyrus Adler, *The Jewish Encyclopedia*, vol. X, Funk & Wagnalls, 1912, N.Y., p. 489.

[3] Cyrus Adler, *The Jewish Encyclopedia*, vol. X, p.p. 490-495.

[4] New York Times, May 19, 1878, *The Rothschild Family. The Greatest Financiers of the Age.*

[5] Cyrus Adler, *The Jewish Encyclopedia*, vol. X, p.p. 494-495.

Wellington against Napoleon Bonaparte; *The elector's money had been sent to Nathan in London, who in 1808 utilized it to purchase £800,000 worth of gold from the East India Company, knowing that it would be needed for Wellington's peninsular campaign. He made no less than four profits on this: (1) on the sale of Wellington's paper, (2) on the sale of the gold to Wellington, (3) on its repurchase, and (4) on forwarding it to Portugal.*

The reconstruction of Europe was even more lucrative than its destruction, and according to the Encyclopedia Judaica: *The French loan of 1816 of 850, 000, 000 francs yielded 10 per cent; and the Austrian loan of 50,000,000 gulden in 1815 yielded 9 per cent. As early as Feb. 5, 1817, the Rothschilds had taken up a Prussian loan of 1,500,000 gulden at 5 per cent; and by the end of the following year the brothers in their collective capacity were reported to be the richest firm in Europe…the loans issued by the Rothschilds during the years 1817 to 1848, as far as these can be definitely ascertained: they make a total of $ 654,847,200.*

In 1848 the power of only one of the Rothschild brothers, Nathan, was so immense that he could bankrupt the Bank of England with a snap of his fingers. The *New York Times* of May 19th of 1878 dedicated an article full of praise to the Rothschild family, which also told a story on how he jeopardized the Bank of England once[6]:

> «.The London firm [N.M. Rothschild], requiring a loan for a short time, made application to the Bank of England, offering securities therefor. The Governor declined, much to the surprise of Nathan Meyer, who at once summoned his bankers for a conference. The London firm change monthly their bank account from one to the other of the banks which they select to receive their deposit and cash their checks. At that time the amount of gold in the Bank of England was at the lowest point, and had a run been commenced it must have led to the suspension of the bank. Rothschild, well knowing this fact, gathered in all his balances from his several bankers, and, returning to the Bank of England,

[6] Aforementioned article of New York Times, May 19, 1878.

demanded specie for three times the amount held by that institution. The Governor, amazed at the position in which the bank was placed, hastily summoned the Directors, who at once resolved to convey to Rothschild the expression of their deep regret at the occurrence, and their hope that he would withdraw his demand for the specie[7]. This he [Nathan Rothschild] immediately did, because selfishness or vindictiveness was no part of his character.

Some years after, when the charter of the Bank of England required renewal, Rothschild expressed to the committee of the House of Commons his firm belief that the Government funds should never be committed to the custody of a private corporation without positive safeguard, since he could have bankrupted the Bank of England had he desired. »

The article of the *New York Times* enumerated then the many virtues of the Rothschilds and their dedication to humanitarian and philanthropic causes. We can take the aforementioned case as an example of the patriotism and the philanthropy that impregnated the actions of the House of Rothschild and their associates: The Bank of England refused to extend them a loan, and as a reprisal they threatened to unleash a bank run that could drown the British monetary system. A few years later the Rothschilds persuaded the British Parliament that the Bank of England was not a safe enough place to store the public funds, because speculators –like themselves- could easily make it fail. For that reason, they proposed to entrust them the

[7] In 1848 the British currency was backed by gold. Any citizen or institution could claim in the Bank of England the countervalue of his pounds sterling in gold. Naturally, the institution did not hoard gold enough to refund more than a fraction of the money issued, so that if a group of petitioners big enough claimed the exchange of pounds for gold, or if there were a panic caused by the coordinated effort of a group of bankers, as it was the case, the Bank of England would immediately fail.

funds to other hands, suggesting their own hands would be the most appropriate. Their proposal was attended some years later, and Alfred de Rothschild, grandson of Nathan Meyer, was director of the Bank of England during 20 years, from 1869 to 1889.

The British central bank was founded in 1694, six years after the Glorious Revolution that deposed the monarchy of Jacob II Stuart, and set up that of William III Orange. As professor Quigley affirms[8] some firms of private banking acquired a dominant position in the Board of Directors of the Bank of England: *Baring Brothers*, *N. M. Rothschild*, *J. Henry Schroder*, *Morgan Grenfell*, *Hambros* and *Lazard Brothers*, and these firms held its position even after the Bank of England was nationalized in 1946. That year the government returned to the English people the power to mint the currency, that until then had been in private hands.

Paris

The youngest son of the saga, James Mayer Rothschild, founded *Rothschild Frères* in 1817 in Paris with a great success. In order to realize the true power of the Rothschilds in France, we can trust the Jewish Encyclopedia which affirmed that *In the year 1848 the Paris house was reckoned "to be worth 600,000,000 francs as against 362,000,000 francs held by all the other Paris bankers."*

Solely the value of the House of Rothchild of Paris worth more than the rest of bankers together. The Rothschild arrived to France almost at the time the Bank of France was established, the year 1800 in Paris. Professor Quigley, in his history of civilizations *Tragedy and Hope* explained the coming of the central banking to France[9]:

> «At that date, financial power was in the hands of about ten or fifteen private banking houses whose founders, in most cases, had

---

[8] Carroll Quigley, *Tragedy and Hope. A History of the World in our Time*, The Macmillan Company, 1974, New York, p. 500.

[9] Carroll Quigley, *Tragedy and Hope*, p. 515. The following quotes p. 516.

come from Switzerland in the second half of the eighteenth century. These bankers, all Protestant, were deeply involved in the agitations leading up to the French Revolution. When the revolutionary violence got out of hand, they were chief forces behind the rise of Napoleon, whom they regarded as the restorer of the order. As a reward for his support, Napoleon in 1800 gave these bankers a monopoly over French financial life by giving them control of the new Bank of France.»

We find a surprisingly similar pattern in English and French revolutions: The Glorious Revolution of England in 1688 provided not only a change of an absolutist regime for other more liberal, but also in a collateral way led to the establishment of a central banking system in England a few years later. This system was headed by the Rothschilds and their associates. A century later Europe witnessed with perplexity the French Revolution in 1789, another change of regime much more radical, which produced an armed conflict which extended from Portugal to Russia, leaving two million deaths behind. The economic outcome of the French Revolution was similar, and only one year after the rise of Napoleon to power the Bank of France was created[10]. It's possible that both revolutions had more to do with a change of economic regime than social, indeed. Eventually, as Professor Quigley points out, the bankers turned Napoleon away:

«By 1811 most of these bankers had gone over to opposition to Napoleon because they objected to his continuation of a warlike policy. France at that time was still in the stage of commercial capitalism, and constant war was injurious to commercial activity. As a result, this group shifted its allegiance from Bonaparte to Bourbon, and survived the change in regime in 1815. »

[10] The masonic lodges, crowded by Enlightment philosophers and other personalities like the Duke of Orleans and Napoleon himself, were instrumental to handle the intellectual, political and economic elites of France.

When Napoleon ceased serving the banker's fostered revolution, to serve the interest of France -or maybe to serve himself- he lost the favor of the international bankers, who switched their allegiance and financed the English military campaign. Thanks to the money of the Rothschilds, and for a narrow margin, in 1815 Wellington crushed Napoleon's army in Waterloo, ending the imperialist dream of France. After the first wave of Swiss protestant bankers, a second wave of German bankers arrived to France:

> «Among these figures the chief bore the names Mirabaud, Mallet, Neuflize and Hottinguer. In the course of the nineteenth century, a second group was added to French banking circles. This second group, largely Jewish, was also o non-French origin, the majority Germanic (like Rothschild, Heine, Fould, Stern and Worms) and the minority of Iberian origin (like Pereire and Mirès). A rivalry soon grew up between the older protestant bankers and the newer Jewish bankers. This rivalry was largely political rather than religious in its basis. »

The group of Protestant bankers was led by the Mirabauds, and the Jewish Group, by the Rothschilds. Quigley explains that despite their rivalry, the cooperation between those houses known as the *haute banque*[11] was steady. From 1800 to 1936 the Rothschild were the dominant group in the Bank of France[12]:

---

[11] The *haute banque* or high finance is a term used to name the most ancient and reputable houses of banking of France. Quigley divide those houses in seven Jewish banks (*Rothschild, Stern, Cahen d'Anvers, Propper, Lazard, Spitzer* and *Worms*), a group of seven protestant banks (*Mallet, Mirabaud, Heine, Neuflize, Hottinguer, Odier* and *Vernes*), and a group of five catholic banks (*Davillier, Lubersac, Lehideux, Goudchaux* and *Demachy*). Quigley, *Tragedy & Hope*, p. 520.

[12] The first part of the quote, *Tragedy & Hope*, p. 56, the second, p. 520-521.

«In France, for example, in 1936 when the Bank of France was reformed, its Board of Regents (directors) was still dominated by the names of the families who had originally set it up in 1800; to these had been added a few more recent names, such as Rothschild (added in 1819); in some cases the name might not be readily recognized because it was that of a son-in-law rather than that of a son…

Three seats were held by the same families for well over a century. In the twentieth century the names of Rothschild, Mallet, Mirabaud, Neuflize, Davillier, Vernes, Hottinger, and their relatives were consistently on the board of regents. »

Under the *haute banque* and the Bank of France, the third economic power of France were the *banques d'affaires*, banking houses that offered their services to enterprises and were managed by a small number of families established before the mid-19th century:

«[13]In the third line of control of the French economy were the Investment banks called "banques d'affaires." These were dominated by two banks: the Banque de Paris et des Pays Bas set up by the Rothschild group in 1872 and the Banque de l'Union Parisienne founded by the rival block in 1904. These investment banks supplied long-term capital to industry, and took stock and directorships in return. Much of the stock was resold to the public, but the directorships were held indefinitely for control purposes. In 1931, Paribas held the securities of 357 corporations, and its own directors and top managers held 180 directorships in 120 of the more important of these. »

A reader erudite in financial matters might have recognized some of the most exclusive European boutique banking firms dedicated to

[13] Carroll Quigley, *Tragedy and Hope*, p. 521.

private equity management. Some of them still endure until today, keeping a low profile without loosing not a bit of relevance.

The French and English branches of the Rothschild family together with the *Hottinguer* house founded in 1845 a railroad company in Paris that connected France and Belgium, the *Compagnie des chemins de fer du Nord.* This enterprise centralized the operations of the French house until well advanced the twentieth century. Baron James de Rothschild was its first President.

United States

One of the biggest economic mistakes in the History of the Rothschild family was the purchase of Confederate bonds during the American Civil War, which was their second bet against the United States after having collaborated with William IX Hesse-Cassel. This investment caused them heavy losses and according to the Encyclopedia Judaica this closed them the market for decades, although this is only true in part. During some time the Rothschild did not work again in the United States on their own, but they did through agents. The most prominent was August Belmont. In 1829, at the age of thirteen, Belmont started as an apprentice with the Rothschild of Frankfurt, who became fascinated by the personality of the boy. The author Stephen Birmingham[14] affirmed that August Belmont was born in Germany as August Schönberg, but changed his surname for Belmont, both the German and the French meaning "beautiful mount". Belmont worked for the Rothschilds in Naples in the negotiations with the Papal Court, and later on in Havana. During the economic panic of 1837 he disembarked in New York, founding there *August Belmont & Co.*, and he became there one of the major bankers and a social figure of the high society of the city of skyscrapers.

---

[14] Stephen Birmingham, *Our Crowd*, p.p. 25, 35-36, *The Great Jewish Families of New York*, 1985, Futura Editions, first edition of 1967.

August Belmont was the main agent of the Rothschild in the United States until the age of *Kuhn & Loeb & Co.,* one of the most powerful houses of investment banking during the last years of the 19th century and the beginnings of the 20th, and acted as a link between the bankers of Frankfurt and New York.

By the end of that century *Kuhn & Loeb & Co.* only *J.P. Morgan & Co* was a rival that could match it. *Kuhn & Loeb & Co.* was the exclusive financial agent of the United States in Germany, while Morgan was for a long time the major American agent in England and France.

Jacob Henry Schiff, the man leading *Kuhn & Loeb*, came from one of the most prestigious families of the Jewish community of Frankfurt. The known origins of the Schiff family date back to 1370[15], and his biographer Cyrus Adler[16] states that the Schiffs are one of the longest-lived Jewish families whose origins can be traced, being one of the most prominent in their community. In Adler's words: *for over six hundred years there can be traced an unbroken line of rabbis, scholars, men of affairs, and communal leaders.*

Born in 1847 in Frankfurt am Main, he and his family dwelled in the mansion located in 148 of the ghetto known as *Judengasse* or "Jewish passageway", sharing their home with the Rothschilds[17]. The economic links between Schiffs and Rothschilds were very close, as Encyclopedia Judaica points out, Jacob Schiff *adopted the vocation of his father, Moses Schiff, one of the brokers of the Rothschilds in that city*[18].

In 1865, at the early age of eighteen years, Jacob Schiff left behind centuries of familiar History in Frankfurt and set the course to New York, where is career in banking soared. In 1875 Schiff began his work in *Kuhn & Loeb & Co.* and that same year he got married to the daughter of one of the founders of the firm, Therese Loeb. *Kuhn &*

---

[15] Jacob Cohen Zedek Schiff, born around 1370, seems to be the founder of the Schiff saga. *Cyrus Adler, Jewish Encyclopedia,* vol. XI, p. 96

[16] Cyrus Adler, *Jacob Schiff. A Biographical Sketch*, p. 4.

[17] Stephen Birmingham, *Our Crowd,* p. 175.

[18] *Jewish Encyclopedia* vol. XI, p. 96.

Loeb & Co. had been founded with the merger of two German Jewish fortunes, Abraham Kuhn and Solomon Loeb, being the second banker married to the sister of the first. Under the leadership of Jacob Schiff, the Rothschild's agent, *Kuhn & Loeb* became one of the most influential banks in history.

Paul and Felix Warburg, belonging to another German family of bankers far from negligible, joined later on to this syndication of great fortunes created in *Kuhn & Loeb*. The origins of the Warburg family, according to Cyrus Adler, can be traced back to a Venetian family of bankers known by the surname "Del Banco" [19]. Adler remarks that *the most prominent Jew in Venice in 1507 was a certain Anselmo Del Banco*. It was approximately at that time when the Del Banco family decided to immigrate to the German city of Warburg[20] due to the restrictions imposed on the Jews and the creation of a ghetto in the Republic of Venice. The Del Banco changed then their surname from their new German hometown.

---

[19] Cyrus Adler, *Felix M. Warburg in Memoriam*, Bulletin of the American Schools of Oriental Research, No. 68, Dec., 1937, p.p. 2-4. Meaning "from the bank".

[20] Literally meaning "city of war". A curious surname for the financiers of several wars and revolutions.

PAUL WARBURG

Banker of *Kuhn & Loeb & Co.* first Vice Governor of the Federal Reserve.

Three brothers made legendary the Warburg saga. Paul immigrated to America and married to Nina J. Loeb, the daughter of Solomon Loeb in 1895, the same year he was accepted as a partner in *Kuhn & Loeb & Co*[21]. Paul was the first promoter of a central banking system in United States, a project that came to life in 1913 as the Federal Reserve. He became Vice Governor of the Federal Reserve Bank of New York, the apex of the monetary and banking system of the country. Paul also reached the presidency of some of the most important banks of the country, like *Wells Fargo & Co.* in 1910 –a position Jacob Schiff "inherited" after the arrival of Paul Warburg to the Federal Reserve. And finally, Paul was President of the *International Acceptance Bank,* a bank he founded in 1921, and the *Bank of Manhattan,* which absorbed his bank in 1929.

His brother Felix Warburg became a partner in *Kuhn & Loeb & Co.* in 1895 after he married Frieda Schiff, the daughter of the president of the bank[22]. The third brother, Max Warburg, remained in Hamburg as their correspondent and counselor of the Kaiser Wilhelm II of Germany, and eventually became the second in command in the *Reichsbank,* the German central bank. Max was the last of the three brothers to immigrate to the United States in 1938, after the rise of the Nazis.

The last of the great partners of *Kuhn & Loeb* was Otto Kahn, who sealed his compromise with the firm by marrying Addie Wolff, the daughter of Abraham Wolff, another partner. Kahn was a member of the bank *Speyer & Co.* since 1893, and later he became a close associate and friend of Edward Harriman, a tycoon of the railroads who theoretically was one of his major rivals in the business. According to the biography authorized by his daughter Kahn acted as courier between *Kuhn & Loeb*, the Rothschild and their European associates [23]

---

[21] Stephen Birmingham, *Our Crowd*, p. 1.

[22] Cyrus Adler, *Jacob Schiff. A Biographical Sketch*, p. 62.

[23] Mary Jane Matz, *The Many Lives of Otto Kahn*, The McMillan Company, 1963, New York, p. 47. We must trust in the good faith of his daughter, Margaret Kahn-

«Kahn's annual European tour kept up Kuhn, Loeb's relations with the Rothschilds in London and Paris, with Baring's, Cassel and Fleming in London, Neuflize in Paris, the Deutsche Bank, and scores of other major European banks, including the branches of the Warburg firm, with which Kuhn, Loeb had maintained the closest ties since its founding.»

Judging by this kind of arranged marriages one would say women were only an asset in the balance of international bankers. Their role in the familiar business was limited to marry other bankers to have the family obtaining influence, prestige and security inside the banking fraternity. This diagram shows in detail the family relations between the founding partners of *Kuhn & Loeb & Co*:

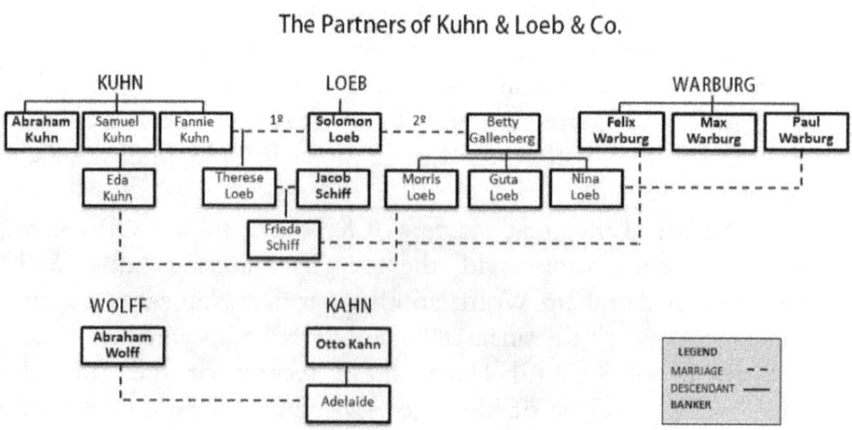

Ryan, owner of the commercial rights of the biography of his father Otto Kahn. Margaret was married, by the way, with the grandson of Thomas Fortune Ryan, one of the great bankers of his time.

The Frankfurt Syndicate

Both *August Belmont* and *Kuhn & Loeb & Co.* worked as the financial arms of the Rothschilds in the United States. There were also a crowd of financial houses who followed the familiar banking model developed by the Rothschilds, who worked side by side with them. These international houses of Jewish German descent spread their members across the world capital cities of finance, giving birth to the international banking system as we know it today. The branches of each family around the world worked together and also formed a community of interests with other houses of Frankfurt. This network flourished under the shadow of the tree of the Rothschilds. They interlocked their businesses by means of a web of economic relations, and as the Rothschilds, they reinforced it with bonds of blood.

The epicenter of that diaspora was Frankfurt, the capital city of the German finance, and not by accident the coat of arms of Frankfurt is a red shield, the emblem of the Rothschild family. In order to simplify concepts I called the network of banking families formed by the Rothschilds and the other German families orbiting around them "The Frankfurt Syndicate", although it never existed any organization of bankers formally established with such a name.

Among the most important sagas of Central European bankers that followed the Rothschilds there were the Lazards of Frauenberg in Austria, the Speyers of Frankfurt, the Goldmans and the Sachs of Trappstadt, the Sterns of Frankfurt, the Seligmans of Baiersdorf, the Lehmans of Rimpar, the Strauss of Ottenberg, the Oppenheim of Friedberg or the Guggenheims of Langanau, Switzerland, and a few non Jewish like the Schröders of Hamburg. All these families were part of a great diaspora from Germany to the financial centers of Europe and the United States during the XIX century[24].

---

[24] The pages at the end of the book include important information about these families and their relations.

The Frankfurt Syndicate

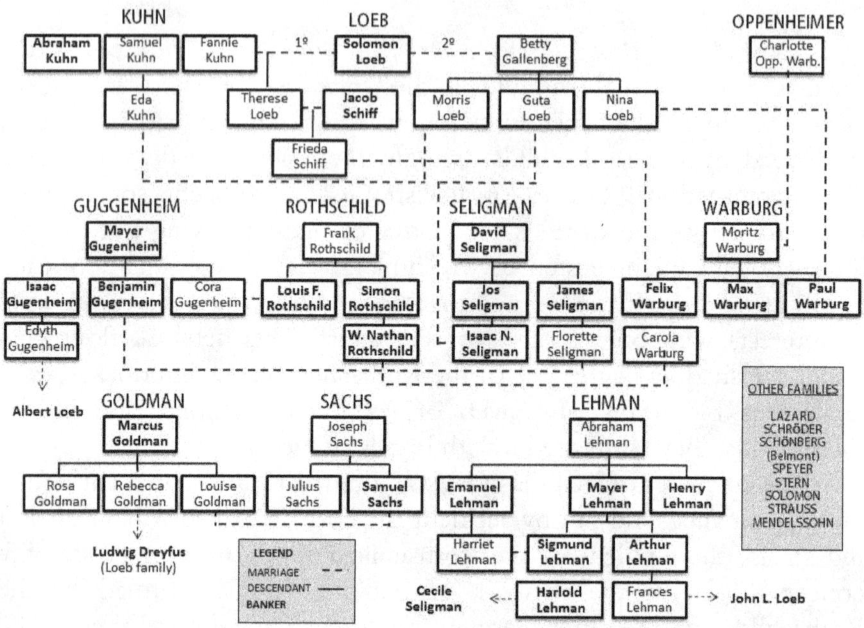

This graph only describes in part the complex network of familiar Relations in the Syndicate of Frankfurt[25].

Great American financiers like August Belmont and the partners of *Kuhn & Loeb* worked under the guidelines of the Rothschild in Europe, and Otto Kahn was his link.

In the United States there were also the Seligmans, known as the "American Rothschilds" [26], and, even if they have sometimes been presented as rivals, it would rather seem that both families divided up the entire market of American debt for almost a century. For instance, during the American Civil War (1861-1869), the Seligmans bet for

[25] Based mainly in the aforementioned work by Birmingham and *The Warburgs* by Ron Chernow, Random House, 1993, New York.

[26] Stephen Birmingham, *Our Crowd*, p. 17.

Lincoln and against the Confederate Army –and therefore, against the Rothschild-. Joseph Seligman had so much power in the Lincoln administration that he persuaded him to appoint him as the leader of the Union Army[27]. During the Lincoln and Johnson terms, the Seligmans enjoyed excellent relations with every Secretary of Treasure like Chase, Fessenden and McCulloch.

For that reason, when Grant became president of the United States, Seligman expected that he could return the favor[28]:

> «When their old friend from Watertown days, Ulysses S. Grant, took Presidential office in 1869, they had every reason to look forward to the same preferential treatment. »

Grant knew how to compensate Joseph Seligman, the patriarch of the family, by offering him the position of Secretary of the Treasury, but he declined. In 1869 George Sewall Boutwell took this office, but he turned to be an obstacle for the interests of the bankers. In the first bonds issuance, he stubbornly rejected to accept a rate of interest above 4.5%, even if the previous issuances were issued at the rate of 5%. This greatly annoyed Joseph Seligman, who thought the new bonds would not be sold in Europe at the rate proposed by Boutwell. Seligman asked for a second opinion to his European associates[29].

> «To support his thesis, Joseph cabled his brother Henry in Frankfurt, asking him to canvass leading German bankers to see how they felt about the Boutwell plan. In Paris he asked William to sound out the formidable "Haute Banque" group –Hottinguer, Mallet, Marcuard, and De Neuflize. The brothers' wires came back; the European bankers felt as Joseph did: Boutwell's "cheap" bond

---

[27] Stephen Birmingham, *Our Crowd*, p. 84.

[28] Stephen Birmingham, *Our Crowd*, p.p. 114.

[29] Stephen Birmingham, *Our Crowd*, p.p. 114-116.

would not sell in Europe; 5 per cent was the lowest sensible figure.»

The fact that Seligmans and Rothschilds were in opposite sides during the American Civil War was no obstacle to present a united front with the old Frankfurt bankers and the *haute banque* of Paris. Joseph Seligman did not make contact only to sound out their opinion, but rather to agree a minimum acceptable price with his European partners. Boutwell's first issuance was completed took some more time, but the following issuances were successfully sold at 4.5%.

The Rothschilds kept doing business with the Seligmans after the war. The Encyclopedia Judaica confirmed the power of the Frankfurt bankers of the American economy by the end of 19th century[30]:

> «In 1879 the Seligmans, with the Rothschilds, took over the whole of the 8150,000,000 bonded loan of the United States. They have been financial agents for the Navy and the State Department of the United States since 1876. »

The members of the Frankfurt Syndicate usually financed both sides of the conflict, ensuring that regardless the outcome, both sides would honor their debts. Lehmans and Seligmans for instance, linked by their bloodlines, financed opposite sides during the Civil War[31]:

> «In London, Emanuel Lehman and Joseph Seligman encountered one another, each with his supply of bonds, two salesmen for two warring powers. Their manner toward each other was cool, reserved. Though both men were loyal to their respective causes in the "unholy rebellion", as it was called. They were not really in the business of fighting a war. They were in the business of making money. »

---

[30] Cyrus Adler, *Encyclopedia Judaica, vol. XI*, p.p. 165-169.
[31] Stephen Birmingham, *Our Crowd*, p. 88.

The Speyers were another family very proficient in the business of making money, and closely linked to important American banking houses like *Kuhn & Loeb* itself. Jacob Schiff, when he arrived to New York was hosted by a friend from Frankfurt named William Bonn, a banker of *Speyer & Co*[32]. Another partner of *Kuhn & Loeb*, Otto Kahn, also began his career in *Speyer & Co*[33]. The bustle of these bankers between rival firms was quite frequent.

Finally, other surnames like Lehman, Goldman and Sachs forged two of the most powerful firms in the last century: *Lehman Brothers* established in 1850 and *Goldman Sachs,* in 1869. Lehman played an infamous role in the 2008 crisis, and Goldman Sachs has become the most influential bank of the 21th century.

Probably most of the commercial relations of the Frankfurt bankers did not take place in the offices placed in the exclusive square formed by Wall Street and Broadway, but in the vicinity of the Emanu-El synagogue, a few blocks above, where many Jewish tycoons attended frequently.

The families of Frankfurt opened a new era of international banking in the 19th century. As New York replaced it as the center of global finance, the German families moved where the money was. In that century there were many displacements of Jewish population, usually from the East to the West. From the ghettos of the Tsarist Russia many Jews moved to Germany, while German Jews also moved to Switzerland, Belgium, Netherlands, Luxembourg and France.

* * *

If the genealogy of the Syndicate of Frankfurt is remarkable, the genealogy of the Rothschilds is even more astonishing. Far from mixing with other families, most of their early members married to other

---

[32] Stephen Birmingham, *Our Crowd*, p. 177.

[33] Mary Jane Matz, *The Many Lives of Otto Kahn*, p.13

Rothschilds as if they wanted to perpetuate the purity of their bloodline. As the Encyclopaedia Judaica points out:

> «The number of marriages between cousins in the later history of the family is remarkable, especially in the second and third generations after the five brothers had gone to five different capitals. Altogether of fifty-eight marriages contracted by the descendants of Mayer Amschel Rothschild to date (1905), no less than twenty -nine, or exactly one-half, have been between first cousins[34]. »

The breed and its purity are serious issues for the Jews since biblical times. The Old Testament describes the lineage of its characters so in detail that you could trace the ancestry of some of them for more than twenty generations. It's also true that Jews are not prone to marry *gentiles* or non-Jews, even in modern times, although endogamy is not a usual practice.

The genealogical issue also has a more practical interpretation, and it consists on concentrating the most wealth possible in a handful of individuals. The medieval aristocracy in Europe, for instance, used to arrange marriages only inside their own noble equals. In combination with the right of primogeniture -the inheritance of the familiar fortune solely by the first-born child- it helped to extend and perpetuate the power of these aristocratic bloodlines, generation after generation. These practices of the medieval nobility had its continuation in the families of Central European Jewish bankers, who set up closed familiar networks directed by only one heir. The financiers of Frankfurt, gathered under the scepter of the Rothschilds, inaugurated in the 20th century a new feudal age where they were the princes of finance, and the serfs were the nations enslaved by the debts. The Protestant Anglo-Saxon bankers also participated in practices of this kind.

---

[34] Cyrus Adler, *Encyclopedia Judaica, vol. X,* p. 497.

In 1913 a New York Times article appraised the fortune of the Rothschilds in 2.000 million dollars[35], a massive fortune at that time. But today it's unusual to find them in the press; they do not appear in lists of millionaires published by newspapers, in the chronicles of the high society, and they do not appear in the list of directors of great corporations. This silence is owing to the control exerted by the banking industry over the media, and to the active effort of the Rothschilds to avoid being noticed in the public scene, particularly after they were dispossessed of their real estate and art collections by the Nazis in Austria[36] and the Republic of Vichy in France[37].

Frankfurt and the World Mining

The Rothschilds and their associates of Frankfurt controlled in the last century an important part of the market in the world mining and in the trade of raw materials. The Rothschild, Oppenheim and Guggenheim families have been among the most successful in those industries. The Rothschild, for instance, were involved in the *gold fixing*, the process for setting the prices of gold worldwide, almost since arrival of Nathan Mayer to London in 1805. The London gold bullion had been led by another Jewish house, *Mocatta & Goldsmith*, established in 1671, three years before the *Bank of England* began operating[38] .

Nathan Mayer became known in the gold market when he started the shipments of gold to the Duke of Wellington to finance the

[35] New York Times, June 26, 1913, *How the Rothschild Fortune of 2.000.000.000 was Made*.

[36] New York Times, May 17, 1915, *Seize Rothschild Estate, Austrian also take property of Britons, French and Russians*.

[37] New York Times, November 7, 1942, *Vichy gets Rothschild Estate*.

[38] Moses Mocatta was agent of the Bank of England, which allowed him to mantain a preferential relation in the *East India Company*. Between 1731 and 1840 *Mocatta & Goldsmid* became the exclusive oficial broker of the Bank of England. The bank of Mocatta has been the most long-lived institution in the *London Bullion Market*, and is still a member in the price fixing committee.

Napoleonic Wars. In 1855 the Rothschilds owned one of the four gold refineries authorized by the *London Bullion Office*, which was the office of the Bank of England that minted gold bars and fixed its price. After several changes in the *gold fixing* system, in 1919 the Bank of England decided that a committee of five banks would set the price of gold in the offices of *N.M. Rothschild & Sons,* in number 24, St. Swithin's Lane. The *gold fixing* remained in the house founded by Nathan Mayer Rothschild until 2004, the year that *N.M. Rothschild & Sons* sold the seat held in the committee.

The Rothschilds also developed an important mining activity. In 1873 the French branch of the house, *Rothschild Frères,* bought the state mines of *Rio Tinto* in Cadiz. *Rio Tinto* nowadays extracts aluminum, copper, iron and precious ores like gold and diamonds. It also mines energetic resources like coal and uranium. The mining activities of the Rothschild in the Belgian Congo are mentioned later on in this book.

The Oppenheim family, a surname derived sometimes in Oppenheimer, were also mining tycoons. The Oppenheimers were bonded with the Warburgs -Charlotte Oppenheim was the mother of Paul, Felix and Max Warburg- and also with the Rothschilds. In 1888 *N.M. Rothschild & Sons* financed *De Beers Consolidated Mining*, the world monopoly of diamonds of the Oppenheims in South Africa created by Sir Cecil Rhodes. In the last years the suspicions of the company involvement with the industry of blood diamonds in South Africa and practices of price fixing has darkened its public image.

In 1917, almost 30 years after the foundation of *De Beers*, and with the money of the American bank *J.P. Morgan & Co.*, Sir Ernest Oppenheimer created one of the biggest mining holdings in the world, *Anglo American.* Sir Ernest Oppenheimer, his son Harry Oppenheimer and his grandson Nicky Oppenheimer switched for long periods in the presidency and vice presidency of both companies. The Rothschilds had also an important stake at *De Beers*: the last patriarch of the family, David René de Rothschild, presided over the board of directors until a few years ago. In 2011, after a few years of economic decline, *De Beers* was absorbed by *Anglo American*, a company of extraction of iron, copper, nickel, manganese, phosphates and coal, in addition to precious ores like platinum and diamonds. We discover, therefore, that two of the most important mining holdings in the world, *Anglo American PLC* and *Rio Tinto* have been in the hands of the Rothschild for as much time as we can trace. The other holding, *BHP Billiton*, had no know relation with the Rothschilds and their associates.

And finally we have the Guggenheims, intermarried with the Rothschild and other German families like the Seligmans, Strauss or Loebs. Some of these relations are analyzed at the end of the book. Before becoming successful bankers the family consolidated their wealth in the mining business. According to the website of Guggenheim Partners, the family worked in the extraction of very diverse mineral resources, and *by the end of World War I, the family business controlled more than 80% of the world's supply of silver, copper and lead*[39].

The Guggenheim surname is linked also to the patronage of art, and they are best known by their museums in New York and Bilbao. The cultural patronage has been a common practice among bankers, for instance Otto Kahn was director of the *Metropolitan Opera* of New York, J.P. Morgan, sponsored the *Metropolitan Museum of Modern Art*. It's not unusual either to find these bankers in key positions in museums, universities, foundations and all kinds of cultural forums.

---

[39] *Guggenheim Partners*, Heritage, web visited in February 2012.

ALEXANDER HAMILTON

First Secretary of the Treasury, and President of the *First Bank of the United States.*

PHILADELPHIA

North America after the Independence

From the old Europe we look back at the origins of the banking industry in the United States. Founded in 1682, Philadelphia was for many years the most densely populated of the Thirteen Colonies, and it was the capital city of the United States until Washington achieved the capital status in 1790. New York, on the meantime, became the most important city, and eventually surpassed both cities as a financial center of the country. Philadelphia still holds a remarkable place in the history and in the minds of North Americans, due to its foundational meaning. Its name means "fraternal love" in Greek, and it was one of the main spots of revolution in the War of Independence. The city hosted the Continental Congresses of 1774 and 1775, where the people joined to settle the political organization of the Colonies, who had declared their independence from the British metropolis.

Since the independence of the country, the financial powers of Frankfurt did everything in their hands to centralize the issuance of currency, establishing a central banking system in the European fashion. In the early history of the American nation there was a decentralized issuance system, where each commercial bank could issue money backed by their own silver reserves. The money issued in silver coexisted with the paper currency that was easier to transport, although every American could go to a bank and exchange a dollar paper for its equivalent in silver. The money backed by precious metals was a good system to control the money supply, and therefore the inflation. The metal used in the United States was the silver, much more abundant that the gold, used in Europe, and this would make difficult to destabilize the economy, in case a small group of financiers or foreign countries wanted to do so. That was the legacy that the Founding Fathers gave the United States, but the old European bankers had different plans for the New World.

Before the Colonies minted its own Silver dollars, the most usual currency were the Spanish coins of 8 *reales* that were in legal tender until 1857. The American dollars were coined in silver since 1794 until 1873, the year when the United States Treasury ceased using this precious metal. In 1900 the United States joined the gold standard, more widely extended in the world, although the dollar was no longer convertible since a few decades ago.

The precious metal standard has been discarded nowadays in most countries, being replaced by fiduciary money or "fiat" in Latin. That means the paper money is not backed by gold, silver or any metal, but solely by the trust in the country of issuance and in its government. That is to say, an American dollar today worth no more than the paper in which it is printed. And in fact most of the money supply worldwide is not even printed, but in the form of credit and bookkeeping entries in computer systems, as advanced before. By decoupling the value of the paper from any tangible asset the financial economy dissociated from the real economy, causing economic bubbles and a situation of permanent inflation. The first step towards the fiat money implied the creation of a private central bank in the United States.

Alexander Hamilton and the First Bank

In 1791 there was a major change in the economic organization of the United States, when the first Secretary of the Treasury, Alexander Hamilton, persuaded the first President George Washington for the creation of the *First Bank of the United States*, the first private central bank of the country.

Alexander Hamilton, one of the Founding Fathers of the United States, was born in Charlestown, in Nevis, a Caribbean island. A man of modest origins, Alexander and his brother became orphans at a very early age, and thanks to the charity he could travel to the Thirteen Colonies. His achievements were remarkable: he enrolled in the War of Independence as a soldier and left as Washington's chief of staff aide, he was a delegate to the First Continental Congress of 1774, he revised the *Articles of Confederacy*[40] and was the main contributor and supervisor of the *Federalist Papers*[41], one of the fathers of the United States Constitution and first Secretary of the Treasury in 1789. Few Americans achieved such a success like Alexander Hamilton did, an orphan with no background before his arrival to the American Colonies.

Hamilton helped founding the *U.S. Mint,* the *Revenue Cutter Service* or the maritime customs control and the *First Bank of the United States,* the first central bank of the United States. He also participated in the creation of the *New York Evening Post,* the oldest journal of the United States. Hamilton was married to Elizabeth Schuyler, the daughter of Philip Schuyler, another delegate of the *First Congress* and undoubtedly he was the optimal candidate for a President of the United States, and he would have been unless an extramarital relation had been known. Apparently his political rival Thomas Jefferson was the man behind the leak of the dark secret of Hamilton.

As a first Secretary of the Treasury of the United States, Hamilton proposed by the end of the 18th century the creation of a central bank under the name of *Bank of the United States.* His idea was forming a bank of issuance of currency, privately owned and in a monopolistic fashion, and for that purpose he exerted all the pressure he was capable of. The objective of the Bank was to stabilize the American currency and promote the trade. Hamilton summarized his plan in a few guidelines:

---

[40] The United States were briefly ruled by the *Articles of Confederation and Perpetual Union* approved in the Continental Congress of November 15th of 1777. Those were replaced by the Constitution during June 21th of 1788 and signed by the first President George Washington.

[41] The Federalist Papers of 1788 were a collection of essays written by Alexander Hamilton, James Madison and John Jay, promoting the elaboration of a Constitution for the United States. James Madison, fourth President and one of the Fathers of the Constitution, was never as a supporter of the creation of a central bank.

Letter of Alexander Hamilton to Robert Morris, 1780[42].

Article 1st: The plan I would propose is that of an American bank, instituted by authority of Congress for ten years under the denomination of The Bank of The United States.
2nd: A foreign loan makes a necessary part of the plan; but this I am persuaded we can obtain if we pursue the proper measures. I shall suppose it to amount to 2,000,000 £ Sterling. This loan to be thrown into the Bank as a part of its stock.
3rd: A subscription to be opened for 200,000,000 of dollars and the subscribers erected into a company called the company of the Bank of the United States.
4th: The Government to guarantee this subscription money to the proprietors at the rate of one for twenty; that is to engage at the dissolution of the Bank to make good to them the sum of ten millions of dollars in lieu of the 200.000.000 subscribed, payable in Spanish milled dollars[43] or a currency bona fide equivalent to them.
5th: The taxes raised in money annually to be thrown into stock[44].
6th: All the remaining paper to be called in (at the option of the possessor) and bank-notes issued in lieu of them for so much Sterling payable to the bearer in three months from the date at 2 per Cent an[num] interest…
7th: All the money issued from the bank to be of the same denomination and on the same terms.
8th: The Bank to furnish Congress with an annual loan of two millions sterling if they have occasion for it at 4 Cent interest.
9th: The whole, or such part of the stock as is judged necessary, to be employed in commerce, in the manner and on the terms which shall be agreed upon from time to time between the Company and a Board of Trade

---

[42] Alexander and Elizabeth Hamilton, *The Official and Other Papers of Major-General Alexander Hamilton, vol. I*, Wiley & Putnam, 1842, New York p.p. 403-406.
[43] The Spanish silver coin of eight reales.
[44] Hamilton notes: "The taxes are made to increase every year for the three years, because the money in circulation increases and consequently the people can afford to pay more."

to be appointed by Congress.
10th: The Bank to issue occasionally by permission of Congress such sums as may be thought safe and expedient in private loans on good securities at six per Cent interest.
11th: The government to share one half of the whole stock and profits of the Bank.
12th: The Bank to be managed by the trustees of the company under the inspection of the Board of Trade, who may have recourse to the company books whenever they think proper, to examine the state of its affairs.

These were the statutes that Hamilton proposed for the creation of the Bank of the United States, and most of his premises were accomplished, being granted a twenty year concession, instead of the original ten years requested. On February 25, 1791, the President George Washington signed the bill that the Congress had approved, establishing therefore the *First Bank of the United States.* Alexander Hamilton, who so thoroughly had fought for the creation of the bank was appointed its President.

The source of the capital for funding the bank is unknown, although probably the loan of two million of Sterling Pounds never took place and the capital was lesser, a fifth that amount. Hamilton proposed as a model the Bank of England, and the loan he wanted to get from London would convey a considerable obligation to the British metropolis, dependency of which the country had been freed twelve years before with the War of Independence. Nevertheless Hamilton seemed to take for granted the English loan (Art. 2nd), as long as it was in the "proper" terms, as Hamilton said, proper for the European lenders, we presume.

Besides its original monetary purpose, Hamilton established the bank as an institution of economic control with powers beyond the Congress. The bank was allowed to issue loans to the Government –so the Government could lend money to itself, and half of the interest paid would go to private hands- (Art. 7th). It also enabled the use of public funds in a discretionary fashion, for private ends, such as the promotion of trade (Art. 9th) and investments (Art. 10th). The statutes he proposed also enabled the bank to collect taxes that would be gradually increased, anticipating Hamilton an inflation of the economy after the set-up of the new bank. The bank he championed was, in a few words, a countrywide system of central economic planning, held in the hands of private institution.

The administration of the Bank of the United States would only be supervised –not controlled or coordinated- by an advisory body, the Board of Trade (Art. 12th), whose members would be elected by the Congress. The profits of the bank would be shared between the Government of the United States and the shareholders of the bank, equally divided. A genuine bargain for the American people, excepting that the mint of currency is a right naturally reserved to sovereign states, and that those states do not have any need to share its profits with any private capital corporation. In short, the creation of the *First Bank of the United States* granted a private institution a monopoly over the currency, the credit and the economy of the country bypassing the Congress. Thomas Jefferson, the third President of the United States, and at that time Secretary of State[45] proved to be one of the most firm voices against the bank of Alexander Hamilton:

> «I consider the foundation of the constitution as laid on this ground, that "all powers not delegated to the United States by the constitution, nor prohibited by it to the States, are reserved to the States or to the people." (Twelfth amendment.)… The incorporation of a bank, and the powers assumed by this bill, have not, in my opinion, been delegated to the United States by the constitution. »

[45] Thomas Jefferson, *Memoirs, Correspondence and Private Papers of Thomas Jefferson,* vol. IV, 1791, Library of the Congress of the United States, p. 536.

Jefferson expressed his concern with the role of the banks in the young American nation, in a letter to John Taylor in May of 1816:

> «[46]I sincerely believe, with you, that banking establishments are more dangerous than standing armies. »

Alexander Hamilton, Secretary of the Treasury and the right hand of George Washington, was an influential man, but not enough to undertake such a gigantic task as the foundation of the *First Bank* without of the European banking aristocracy. The invisible hand behind the First Bank belonged to the Rothschild family, according to Gustavus Myers[47]:

> «Under the surface, the Rothschilds have long had a powerful influence in dictating American financial laws. The law records show that they were powers in the old Bank of the United States August Bemont and Company were their American representatives. In 1873 it was estimated that $ 375,000.000 of American railroads securities were held abroad, chiefly by foreign bankers. »

The Struggle of Federalists and Republicans

By the end of the decade of the 1790's, the vision on what direction should the new nation take was divided into two diametrically opposed sides. On one hand there were the Federalists headed by Hamilton, and on the other hand the Republicans represented by Jefferson. The Federalists proposed for the United States a strong federal government, centralized, at the expense of a lesser power for the

---

[46] Thomas Jefferson, *Memoirs, Correspondence and Private Papers of Thomas Jefferson, vol. IV*, p. 288.

[47] Gustavus Myers, *The History of the Great American Fortunes, vol. III*, Charles H. Kerr and Company, 1910, Chicago, p.p. 183-184.

states, with a central banking system in the English fashion, and a preferential relation with the British metropolis. The term "Federalist" applied also to those who proposed the ratification of a Federal Constitution, and later on was used to the supporters of the President George Washington. Hamilton was the foremost representative among the Federalists, establishing the Federalist Party in 1792.

The republican appeared as a coalition of opponents to the vision of Hamilton, under the leadership of Thomas Jefferson. Their conception of the nation was closer to the French Republic, sustained on the individual rights rather than the power of the state and opposed to the creation of a central bank.

Alexander Hamilton was associated with the Vice President of the United States, Aaron Burr, for many years. In 1799 he helped him founding the *Manhattan Water Company*, a company founded with the purpose of providing the isle of Manhattan with pure and clean water. The city had suffered several epidemics due to the poor conditions of the water pipelines. Burr raised two million dollars for that end, and arranged to make a provision in the contract that would allow him to set up a bank with the surplus capital of the *Manhattan Water Company*. Burr committed a minimum amount of money to sanitize the pipes of Manhattan and spent most of the capital founding the *Bank of the Manhattan Water Company,* which opened its doors on September 1st 1799, in the number 40 of Wall Street. In 1808 the *Bank of Manhattan* sold the water services to remain focused in the banking business. In 1842 the system had to be rebuilt through the Old Croton Reservoir after countless health and epidemic issues. Long time after, in 1929, a merger with the *International Acceptance Bank* turned Paul Warburg into the new head of the *Manhattan Bank*.

By the time that Aaron Burr's *Bank of Manhattan* appeared, Hamilton's *First Bank of The United States* was the most important bank of the country, developing not only the tasks of a central banking but also those of a commercial bank. Only a handful of European firms like the Barings[48], the Rothschilds and *Brown Brothers & Shipley* could be a rival in United States to Hamilton's *First Bank*. Hamilton not only pioneered the central banking in the United States, but also the commercial banking in the United States. He was one of the founders of the *Bank of North America* in 1781, and also in the *Bank of New York* in 1784 in collaboration with Alexander Mc Dougall e Isaac Roosevelt[49].

The creation of Burr's *Bank of Manhattan* had a double meaning: It broke the monopoly of Hamilton in the banking industry of the United States and also ended the financial dominance of the Federalists, represented by Hamilton. The *Bank of Manhattan,* created by Burr, also contributed to the displacement of the economic center of gravity of the country from Philadelphia to New York. These and other rivalries led Hamilton to engage in a gun duel with Burr, who was then Vice President of the Unite States. During the duel Hamilton received a shot in the stomach and died the next morning, on July 11, 1804. He had been challenged to a duel twelve times before, but he always declined until then. His 19 year old son died in a duel in 1801, defending his father's honor, and it is thought that Hamilton failed the shot on purpose, stricken by the grief of his son's decease.

The concession granted to the *First Bank of the United States* expired in 1811 and was not renewed, but again in 1816 the financial powers urged the Government to establish the *Second Bank of the United States.*

---

[48] A banking house founded in 1761 by a wool merchant named Sir Francis Baring. The *Barings Bank* was the eldest commercial bank of London, which in 1802 was refounded as *Baring Brothers & Co*. It remained open until 1995, the year it failed. The Barings were a German Christian family.

[49] These were the first and third oldest bank of the United States. Isaaac Roosevelt was the great-uncle of President Theodore Roosevelt and the great-grandfather of President Franklin Delano Roosevelt.

ANDREW JACKSON
7th President of the United States.

Nicholas Biddle and the Second Bank

After the *First Bank* was liquidated, the country lived without a central bank for four years, but a few tycoons and bankers like John Jacob Astor, David Parish, Stephen Girard, Jacob Barker, John C. Calhoun and Alexander Dallas lobbied relentlessly for reestablishing the central banking in the United States.

In February 1814 Congressman Calhoun proposed a Law for the creation of a second National bank with no success. In April a Tennessee Congressman requested the formation of a committee for researching into the possible creation of a central bank, but the proposal failed again. In October Secretary of Treasury Alexander Dallas made another proposal with the same purpose that was rejected again in the Congress. In 1815 and 1816 they tried to enact similar laws but failed after President Madison vetoed those twice. Madison finally had to surrender to the pressure and signed into law the creation of the *Second Bank* in April 10th, 1816.

The *Second Bank* got a new grant for twenty years, working with similar features to the *First Bank*. It was a better business for the shareholders than its predecessor: only five of its twenty five directors were selected by the President and confirmed by the Senate, and 80% of the market stock remained in private hands[50]. In practice, the bank was free from any kind of governmental supervision.

The director of the *Second Bank*, a politician and banker named Nicholas Biddle, enjoyed full powers on that institution. He answered this way to the attempts of Washington to influence over the election of its board of directors[51]:

---

[50] Website of the Bank of the Federal Reserve of Philadelphia, *The Second Bank of the United States, A Chapter in the History in Central Banking*, December 2010.

[51] Nicholas Biddle, *The correspondence of Nicholas Biddle dealing with national affairs*, 1807-1844, Houghton Mifflin Court, 1919, Boston, p. 72.

«We are obliged to receive and glad to receive nominations from any respectable quarter, & always treat them with respect — but you must not suspect that any particular consideration is given to nominations from Washington. With Washington, in its character as the seat of Government, the Bank has no concern. It has in fact nothing to do with the Government except that in administering the national finances, it will give its aid cordially and sincerely to every administration. But with no administration will it have any political connection.

Nor would the Influence of the President and all the Departments put together be sufficient to appoint a single Director who was not considered qualified for his trust. This Independence forms the point of honor with the Bank.»

The letter showed the annoyed tone in which the President of the *Second Bank* objected to the interference of the public officials of the Government in a private business –the issuance of the American currency-. Biddle was by then the most important banker of Philadelphia, with a familiar pedigree that could be traced several generations ago. His brother Thomas founded the *Thomas Biddle & Co.* bank, one of the oldest investment banks of the country with *Jay Cooke & Co.* (the first bank was created in the early 19th century, and the second, some years later, in 1863). His uncle Edward Biddle was a prominent politician, a Delegate of the First Continental Congress as it was Alexander Hamilton.

Despite the main reason of the existence of the *Second Bank* was the stabilization of the economy and the suppression of the monetary panics, 1819 unleashed the biggest financial of crisis known at that time. It happened primarily due to the rampant number of loans granted by the bank, together with the outflow of gold out of the country. During the lifetime of the *Second Bank* there were also the crises of 1825 and 1833-34. The historian of the great American fortunes, Gustavus Myers, questioned the honor of the President of the *Second Bank*[52].

«Perhaps the foremost banker in the United States in the first four decades of the nineteenth century was Nicholas Biddle, that proud aristocrat and founder of a family of aristocrats. He was long president of the once all-powerful Bank of the United States, and was held up to the whole country as an illustrious example of the position to which any able and well-regulated youth could attain.

Yet he was accused of being a thief, an embezzler, a malefactor in law. After his retirement from the presidency of the Bank of the United States, that institution brought a civil action against him and the cashier, John Andrews, for the restitution of $400,000 which they were charged with stealing from the bank in 1836. This theft, it was further specifically charged, was concealed by fraudulent entries, burning of vouchers and by other methods. By the time the suit came up in court in 1844, Biddle had died, but the action was pressed against Andrews. His answer was a general denial, but Judge Parsons decided that he was convinced that the claim for recovery was one which could be enforced, and he overruled Andrews' demurrer. »

By the time the new bank took the first steps, in 1822, a man named Andrew Jackson appeared in the first line of politics. The son of an impoverished family of Scottish Protestants who emigrated to the United States, and with only twelve years old, Jackson enlisted in the militia that fought the English forces in the War of Independence. He was wounded and captured during the war, and he received a saber slash in the face which also affected some of his fingers, as a punishment for his refusal to clean the boots of his British captors. His captivity severely impaired his health for life, having suffered malaria and smallpox. In 1815 Jackson led the American troops in a new battle with the British, the Battle of New Orleans, from which he emerged victorious as one of the greatest heroes of American history. Jackson

[52] Gustavus Myers, *History of the Great American Fortunes, vol. III,* p.p. 185-186.

joined then the recently formed Democrat Party and was its candidate in the 1824 elections, although he was not victorious in his first attempt. In the next elections of 1824 he achieved the presidency against John Quincy Adams, who sought the reelection.

Jackson's political campaign and his mandate had as a pivotal point the annihilation of the *Second Bank*, an objective he achieved at the expense of a high personal risk. Jackson suffered an attempt of assassination in 1835, the first attack against a President of the United States, and he survived because both guns of the aggressor failed, in a surprising stroke of luck. In a letter of Jackson to the Vice President Martin van Buren –who later became President too- he confessed: *The bank, Mr. Van Buren, is trying to kill me, but I will kill it*[53]. Andrew Jackson carried out his threat: In 1832 he vetoed a new grant for the *Second Bank*, and in 1833 he withdrew all the funds of the Government in that institution. In 1836 the 20 years grant of the *Second Bank* ended, and those were not renewed. Andrew Jackson was the last President who cancelled the full amount of the American public debt in January 1835[54], providing the foundation for the future prosperity of the United States[55].

---

[53] John C. Fitzpatrick, *Annual Report of the American Historical Association, vol. II, The Autobiography of Martin van Buren*, Washington Government Printing Office, 1920, Washington, p. 625. Three of the four presidents assasinated in United States challenged the financial power. Due to the high linterest rates demanded to finance the Civil War, 16th President Abraham Lincoln issued the Greenbacks, some dollar bills not backed by any precious metal. He died of a gunshot in 1865. Garfield, the 20th President, spoke against inflationary policies conducted an investigation into the Gold Panic of 1869 while in the Banking and Currency Committee. His presidency lasted 200 days, he died because of two shots in September 1881. In June of 1963, the 35th President Kennedy signed Executive Order 11110, which allowed the United States government to issue silver-backed bills, giving the country the possibility of issuing its own currency. On November 22, 1963, he was killed by at least one shot. The only exception is the assassination of the 25th President William McKinley in 1901, with no known financial connections.

[54] Bureau of the Public Debt, United States Department of Treasury, web revised

JOHN PIERPONT MORGAN

In company of his son John Pierpont Morgan Jr., also known as Jack.

THE EMPIRE OF MORGAN

Peabody and the Age of Merchant Bankers

John Moody, the financial analyst of Wall Street and founder of *Moody's*, the first financial rating company of America, researched in his work *The Masters of Capital*[56] about the origins of the legendary banking house of John Pierpont Morgan. The most famed banker of all time began his career in banking under the shadow of a British merchant named George Peabody, and as many modern investment banks, the firm of *J.P. Morgan & Co.* was born as a bank for trade or a "merchant bank".

> «The great financial houses of Wall Street, which are today most closely identified with the organization and control of the great corporate enterprises of the country, nearly all started as firms engaged in the dry-goods or clothing business. Not only the Morgans, but the Brown Brothers, Kuhn, Loeb and Company, the Seligmans, and other old private banking houses of New York, began in this way [...]
>
> In the year 1811, a sixteen-year-old dry-goods clerk, George Peabody, was thrown out of employment by the burning of his brother's little store in the old town of Newburyport, Massachusetts. He then went with an uncle to Georgetown, D. C. (since incorporated with Washington), and opened a small retail dry-goods store there. After some years he moved to Baltimore and established branches in Philadelphia and New York.
>
> Finally, in 1837, at the age of forty-two, he went to London and founded there the merchant banking house of George Peabody and Company, which later became J. S. Morgan and Company [...]

[56] John Moody, *Masters of Capital. A Chronicle of Wall Street*, Yale University Press, 1919, New York, p.p. 4-11.

In London and in parts of England, he bought British manufactures for shipment to the United States; and the ships came back freighted with every kind of American produce for sale in England. To that lucrative account, however, was added one far more lucrative.

The merchants and manufacturers on both sides of the Atlantic, who transmitted their goods through him, sometimes procured from him advances on account of the goods in his possession long before they were sold... Thus he became a banker as well as a great merchant, and ultimately much more of a banker than a merchant...

When Peabody took up his residence in London, European capitalists were already competing for the opportunity to exploit American enterprises.

Strong foreign houses were forming financial connections between London and New York. The Rothschilds had sent August Belmont to represent them in New York in the same year that Peabody had settled in London. The Barings had married into a Philadelphia family in the early years of the century and were also financially interested in the United States. Peabody, nevertheless, set out to be the chief representative of America in England...

When Peabody retired, in 1864, Junius S. Morgan became the head of the business. Morgan was another Yankee dry-goods trader — a member of the firm of J. M. Beebe and Company of Boston — who had been taken into partnership by Peabody ten years before. He was now about fifty-one and was fully capable of carrying on the high traditions of the Peabody firm — doing international commercial banking, holding deposits of customers, and buying and selling securities. The firm placed considerable issues of American railroad bonds in London and negotiated a loan to Chile. The name of George Peabody and Company ended with the death of Peabody, according to his own wish. But the business was carried on without interruption under the name of J. S. Morgan and Company.

Junius Morgan had a son, John Pierpont by name, born in Hartford, Connecticut, in 1837. »

Peabody, whom John Moody describes as the "the chief representative of America in England", seems to be the first link between Morgan and the Rothschilds. In 1838 Morgan and Peabody established *Morgan, Grenfell and Co.* in London. The Grenfell surname appears quite frequently in the board of the Bank of England, as it is the case of Lord Catto, one of the Governors of the central bank. John Moody tells us that George Peabody, who died with no heirs, handed over control over of his enterprises to Junius Morgan and his son, who in 1854 founded *J.S. Morgan & Company* in London.

The banking house of Morgan has been one of the most important of History, and undoubtedly the most influential in the United States. The historian of great American fortunes, Gustavus Myers, links the massive increase of wealth of the Morgans to his appointment as financial representatives of the Government[57].

«Junius S. Morgan became a partner of George Peabody in the banking business. When the Civil War came on, George Peabody and Company were appointed the financial representatives in England of the United States Government. Synchronously with this appointment their wealth suddenly began to pile up; where hitherto they had amassed riches by stages not remarkably rapid, they now added many millions within a very few years.»

The firm of Junius Morgan, the father of John Pierpont Morgan, changed its name several times. In the United States the Morgans started in business with other partners in *Duncan, Sherman and Company*,

[57] Gustavus Myers, *The History of the Great American Fortunes, vol. III*, p.p. 149-150.

a company he left to establish *Dabney, Morgan and Company*, in 1864 with other partners in New York. Some years later John Pierpont Morgan associated with the Drexels, another important milestone in this story.

The Drexels and the Monopoly of the American Debt

After the death of George Peabody, Morgan joined forces with Anthony Joseph Drexel and his brother Joseph William Drexel in *Drexel, Morgan & Co.* The Drexels were a Protestant family coming from Dornbirn, in Austria. That was the most powerful banking family of Philadelphia, except for the Biddles, a family they joined when the nephew of the President of the *Second Bank,* Nicholas Biddle, married the daughter of Anthony Joseph Drexel. The two big houses of Philadelphia sealed their alliance by means of a marriage, in the Frankfurt fashion. Gustavus Myers continues[58]:

> «Morgan's next partnership was as a member of the firm of Drexel, Morgan and Company. He began to be conspicuous in very large transactions. One of these was the floating of the $260,000,000 U. S. Government bond issue of 1877. Avoiding plunging into detail, which would be intricate at best, suffice it to say that this bond issue was generally regarded, and not without full reason, as one of the very worst cases that had ever been known of the people being betrayed over to a few bankers. The selling of the bonds was apportioned among these banking houses: August Belmont, the Rothschilds, J. and W. Seligman Brothers, and Drexel, Morgan and Company, the last named acting for themselves and for the firm of J. S. Morgan and Company in London. This syndicate at once sold the bonds at an advance of from one to four per cent, above the price which they had paid to the Government. The profits of the syndicate reached into the tens of millions of dollars. Drexel, Morgan and Company alone were

[58] Gustavus Myers, *The History of the Great American Fortunes, vol. III*, p. 189.

credited with "making" a clear profit of $5,000,000. Their function consisted in nothing more or less than acting as licensed speculative middlemen for a Government which could have disposed of the bonds without intermediaries. »

Myers recounts how a public bonds issuance of 260 million dollars was allotted single-handedly to three banks of the Frankfurt Syndicate - the Rothschilds, their American agent August Belmont and *J & W Seligman and Co.* - together with the Morgans. The bankers earned a fortune, from one to four percent only for selling bonds that the government could have sold on its own.

The financial group of Drexel and Morgan, established in the United States during the sixties, quickly made his way through the American market of debt, as agents of the Rothschilds in collaboration with Jay Cooke, a banker affiliated to *Jay Cooke and Company* in Philadelphia[59].

«Jay Cooke estimated that by 1869 at least a billion dollars' worth of United States bonds were held abroad, of which a large proportion were held in South Germany. This large investment had established a new and powerful business interest in America — the Jewish bond dealers, with foreign connections in the great European money center of Frankfort[60]. With this new group of financial merchants Cooke had naturally allied himself, since the greatest source of English capital was only to be tapped through the Drexel-Morgan interests.

A keen contest arose between the Cooke interests and (with their German Jew backing) and the Drexel- Morgan interests to secure the contracts for the government financing. In this contest Cooke and his party won and then carried through an extraordinarily difficult operation so successfully that the

[59] John Moody, *Masters of Capital*, p. 16-17.

[60] Obviously, the Rothschilds and their associates.

Rothschilds offered themselves as Cooke's associates in future enterprises. But the Morgan interests kept after the business, and subsequently, in combination with Levi P. Morton[61], secured a half interest in the government refunding operation of 1873, involving a sale of $300,000,000 of bonds — an enormous transaction for those days. Later, in the fall of the same year. Jay Cooke and Company failed and this left the field in the United States for great financial operations entirely in the hands of the Drexel-Morgan-Morton associates. »

The fail of Jay Cooke left as August Belmont, *Drexel & Morgan & Co.* and Levi P. Morton as American partners of the Rothschilds. Despite their veto in the United States the Frankfurt family kept on doing big money. By the mid-seventies, the Rothschilds decided to enter directly in the American market and summoned the patriarch of the Seligmans to invite them to the exclusive group of financiers who monopolized all the bond issues of the United States. [62]. The Seligmans had supported the Union Army of Lincoln, and they enjoyed excellent Relations with the Secretary of Treasury, which would open the doors of the market to the Rothschilds to work again with the American Government without middlemen.

«In the autumn of 1874, Baron Rothschild summoned Isaac Seligman to his office to give him a piece of news. Some $55 million worth of the United States bonds were to be offered for sake, and, the Baron suggested, the issue might be backed by a combination of the three houses – the House of Rothschild, the House of Morgan, and the House of Seligman. For the first time,

---

[61] Levi P. Morton was a prominent banker held positions in several public offices. This Morgan partner was named American Ambassador in France during the Garfield term (1881-1885), Governor of New York (1895-1896) and Vice President during the Harrison term (1889-1893).

[62] Stephen Birmingham, *Our Crowd*, p. 157.

August Belmont would act as an agent for both the Rothschilds and J & W Seligman & Company. Needless to say, Isaac accepted. The Seligmans were now participating in the most powerful financial combination in the history of banking.

At last the Seligmans were able to consider themselves the Rothschilds' peers. The Seligman-Belmont-Morgan-Rothschild alliance, furthermore, was so successful that by the end of the decade there were complains in Wall Street that "London -and Germany- based bankers" had a monopoly on the sale of United States bonds in Europe- which they virtually did.»

In 1876 *Drexel & Co.* took part in a 300 million bond issue of the Treasury, at a 4.5% interest. That banking syndicate was led by the Rothschilds, and again in 1878 the Secretary of the Treasury John Sherman awarded a 50 million issue to the old folks[63] The banks in charge were the *First National Bank*, *August Belmont & Co.*, *Morton, Bliss & Co.*, *J.W. Seligman, Drexel, Morgan & Co.* in New York and their correspondents in London *N.M. Rothschild & Sons*, *Seligman Brothers* and *J.S. Morgan & Co.* All these banks had something in common; they belonged to the Morgan or Rothschild groups. The Treasury organized a new issue of bonds in 1879 with the same banks managing the loan.

In 1868 Drexel and Morgan opened an office in Paris under the name of *Drexel, Harjes & Co.*[64]. Some years later, in 1886, the French Morgans meet *J.W. Seligman* in leading the American banking syndicate that financed the Panama Canal[65]. This very same year concluded the works of the Suez Canal, an operation directed by Lionel Nathan de Rothschild, the head of the English branch of the Rothschilds[66].

---

[63] New York Times, April 12, 1912, *Resumption a Certainty.*

[64] The French branch of Morgan was known as *Drexel, Harjes & Co.*, first, then *Morgan, Harjes & Co.*, and finally *Morgan et Cie*.

[65] New York Times, July 1, 1893, *Anthony Drexel is Dead; Philadelphia's Greatest Banker Stricken with Apoplexy.*

[66] The Rothschild Archive, *Lionel de Rothschild and the Suez Canal*, web revised in

We find that Morgan did not build his fortune from scrap, as some biographers try to make us think, but he inherited a considerable estate from his father Junius S. Morgan, a estate he enlarged enormously when he became the protégé of the Anglo Germanic banking aristocracy; the Rothschilds, the Peabody, the Grenfells and the Drexel-Biddles. This aristocracy was in control of the European and American economies, both in the public and private sides, keeping his firm grip over commercial and central banking business. As owners of the debt of nations their prestige grew exponentially, receiving as an award for their services, honors, public positions and titles of nobility. Some journalists referred to them with disdain as "the robber barons".

The Morgans took advantage of their privileged position in the public sector to make business with a great success, but sometimes not very ethically. Gustavus Myers tells how it was one of the first Morgan operations, when they resold the American Government their own rifles by six times the value of its purchase[67]:

> «On August 5, 1861, a notification (was sent) to General Fremont, commanding at St. Louis, (reporting) that he had five thousand new carbines, in perfect condition, and inquiring whether Fremont would take them. From Fremont's headquarters came word to ship them to the army headquarters at St. Louis at once. During all of this time the carbines had remained at the arsenal in New York City. Upon receiving Fremont's order, Morgan paid the Government the sum of $17,486 at the rate of $3.50 a carbine. The rifles were shipped direct from the arsenal to St. Louis. And what was the sum charged upon the Government for them? The bill made out to Fremont called for the payment of $22 a piece for the consignment.

May 2016.

[67] Gustavus Myers, *The History of the Great American Fortunes, vol. III*, p.p. 171-173. Quoting Reports of Committees, Second Session, Thirty-seventh Congress, 1861-62, vol. II : XIV-LXXLI.

This was one of the many army contracts popularly and officially regarded as scandalous in the highest degree; one of the select Congressional Committees of 1862 lost no time in the investigating of it. After making a full inquiry this committee reported:

Thus the proposal actually was to sell to the Government at $22 each 5,000 of its own arms, the intention being, if the offer was accepted, to obtain these from the Government at $3.50 each… It is very evident that the very funds with which this purchase was effected were borrowed on the faith of the previous agreement to sell. The Government not only sold one day for $17,486 arms which it had agreed the day before to repurchase for $109,912 – making a loss to the United States of $92,426 – but virtually furnished (Morgan) the money to pay itself the $17,486 which it received.

The committee further reported that the rifles were so bad that it was found that they would shoot of the thumbs of the very soldiers using them. »

In 1870 the London correspondent of the Morgans, *J.S. Morgan & Co.* subscribed a loan to France valued in 250 millions, probably the most important financial operation of this kind in the country. The reputation of the Morgans grew at both sides of the Atlantic Ocean, and by the middle of that decade the United States had issued more than 850 million dollars in bonds, placed in the markets solely by Morgan and his German associates.

Far from showing his gratitude to the American Treasury, in 1894 the Morgans did the same gamble that the Rothschild did with the Bank of England 46 years before[68]:

«In 1894 the Government had been drawn into handing over two bond issues of $50,000,000 each to these bankers. Their profits, it is estimated, reached tens of millions. With the advent of

[68] Myers, *The History of the Great American Fortunes, vol. III*, p.p. 221-224.

the year 1895 the United States Treasury was again emptied of gold. Where had the gold, which the Government had purchased only a short time previously at usurious rates, gone? The reports of the large banks gave the answer. By the end of January, twenty-six banks in New York City had in their vaults a hoard of $65,000,000 in gold. Presently [1910] the amount totaled $129,000,000, all told. The Government shrieked in helplessness; President Cleveland was reported as saying privately that "the banks have got the country by the throat."

At the appropriate moment a syndicate of bankers appeared in the open and magnanimously offered to supply gold to the Government in exchange for bonds. This syndicate was composed of J. P. Morgan and Company, August Belmont and Company, representing the Rothschilds: James Speyer, the National City Bank and four other extremely powerful national banks.

The situation, then, was this: The syndicate had squeezed the Unitd States treasurt of its gold; it had then compelled a bond issue, and declared that it alone could supply the required gold.»

According to Myers, Morgan emptied the gold reserves of the American Treasury, leaving the country vulnerable to a financial panic, and then he offered himself to sell his own gold, together with the Rothschilds and other bankers. He proved, as the Rothschild did, that "selfishness or vindictiveness was no part of his character". Senator of Colorado, Charles S. Thomas also claimed that the panic of 1893 was deliberately created by the bankers. He quoted a memorandum allegedly issued by the *American Bankers Association*[69]:

«"It was a panic," he said, "deliberately produced in this country for the purpose of doing away with a statute of the United States the operation of which was objectionable to the great financial powers of the country." The statute in question was the

[69] New York Times, May 31, 1913, *Senator Thomas on Panics.*

Sherman act for the compulsory purchase of silver by the Treasury, repeal of which Mr. Thomas declared to be "the most colossal tragedy of the nineteenth century.[70]" In support of his contention Senator Thomas declared that eight days after the inauguration of President Cleveland in 1893 this circular was sent to the National Banks in the United States:

> "Dear Sir: The interests of National bankers require immediate financial legislation by Congress. Silver, silver certificates, and Treasury notes must be retired, and the National banknotes upon a gold basis made the only money. This requires the authorization of $500,000,000 to $1,000,000,000 of new bonds as a basis of circulation. You will once retire one-third of your circulation, and call in one-half of your loans. Be careful to make a money stringency felt among your patrons, especially among influential business men. Advise an extra session of Congress for the repeal of the purchase clause of the Sherman law, and act with other banks in your city in securing a large petition to Congress for its unconditional repeal, as per accompanying form." »

The authorship of that memorandum presented by Senator Thomas was denied by the *American Bankers Association.*

Morgan and the Age of Trusts

Alongside his financial success, Morgan extended his operations into many industrial sectors. The most important, the railroads, would central for the economic and industrial development of the United

[70] The Sherman Act obliged the government to periodically purchase silver, and it was intended to strengthen the silver reserves of the Treasury, protecting the American banking system from panics such as the one created by Nathan Rothschild in the Bank of England.

States during the following twenty or thirty years. In 1879 Morgan got into the business when the greatest railroad tycoon, William Henry Vanderbilt, president and main shareholder of the *New York Central and Hudson River*[71] turned to him for help. Vanderbilt was under investigation by the authorities in relation with his railroads monopoly in the country, and with the mysterious amassing of 100 million in just a decade. Morgan then quietly sold a part of Vanderbilt's stock in the *New York Central* in England in order to divert the attention of the tycoon and save him from being prosecuted. The operation appeared in the American and British newspapers afterwards, and five years later, in 1884, the expected American railroad crash took place. When this happened Morgan took advantage of the occasion to enter himself into the railroad business[72]:

> «Thus, before the panic of 1893, the firm of Drexel, Morgan and Company built up its reputation as the financier and reorganizer of mismanaged properties and in this respect stood in a unique position among American bankers. The great Jewish security merchants had as yet little hold on American railways. The Rothschilds were content to remain a close ally of Morgan rather than a competitor, so far as the American field was concerned.
>
> Kuhn, Loeb and Company had not yet become a railroad power. The Speyers were strong but not masterful. The Seligmans, who had been prominent in the government refunding operations, had not become a leading house of issue for railway securities. »

The railroad re-organization consolidated the first of the industrial trusts of the Morgan group, and it was not the last one. Every time Morgan got into an industry he expelled all the competitors and formed

---

[71] His father, Cornelius Vanderbilt, is considered the second richest man of all time, only preceded by John D. Rockefeller. This operation is also mentioned in Gustavus Myers en *History of American Fortunes, vol. III*, p. 191.
[72] John Moody, *Masters of Capital*, p. 27.

an unbeatable monopoly which fixed the price without any opposition. In Wall Street they spoke ironically of the "morganization" of one or another industry. Morgan did not only re-organized the railroad business, but he also controlled and consolidated in a decisive way all the American industries of his time; the coal, steel, the electricity and the agricultural machinery, in addition to the banking and insurance services. Actually J.P. Morgan formed almost all the American trusts of the 20th century, excluding of course, the oil monopoly created by John D. Rockefeller.

While Morgan and others made a fortune in the railroads, a report of the Interstate Commerce Commission[73] exposed that from 1888 to 1907, no less than 53,406 employees lost their lives in the railroads, and more than 800,000 were crippled or handicapped. That was the modern life of slavery of American railroads where *Kuhn & Loeb*, Morgan, Vanderbilt, Gould, Harriman and others forged their economical empires. Most of their employees were immigrants who worked long working days in drudgery and in exchange of a miserable salary.

When the unavoidable railroad crash of 1884 hit, many companies had to reduce prices until placing them in the verge of bankruptcy. Morgan did not like at all the competition unauthorized by him, or rather any sort of competition, and sent a memorandum to all businessman of the railroads to make an alliance to avoid competition and self-regulate the growth of the industry[74].

> «On January 2, 1889, a circular marked "Private and Confidential" was issued by the three banking houses of Drexel, Morgan and Company, Brown Brothers and Company, and Kidder, Peabody and Company[75]. The most painstaking care was

[73] Gustavus Myers, *History of the Great American Fortunes, vol. III*, p. 189.

[74] Gustavus Myers, *History of the Great American Fortunes, vol. III*, p. 203.

[75] *Kidder, Peabody & Co.* was a company created in 1865 by Francis H. Peabody, with Henry P. Kidder and O.W. Peabody. Francis H. Peabody was the fourth cousin once removed of George Peabody, co-founder of the Morgan empire, and one of

exercised that this document should not find its way into the press, or otherwise become public. Indeed, extraordinary measures were taken to surround its contents with every precaution of secrecy.

Why this fear? Because the circular was an invitation, tacitly understood as a command, to the great railroad magnates to assemble at Morgan's house, No. 219 Madison avenue, and there form, in the phrase of the day, an iron-clad combination. The plan was to make a strict compact which would efface competition among certain railroads, and unite those interests in an agreement by which the people of the United States could be bled even more effectively than before. For the sake of appearance, in case the nature of the undertaking should leak into public print, the promoters garnished over their real purposes with a string of diverting phrases. Their sole aim, so they pleasantly indicted it, was an association "to maintain public, reasonable, uniform and stable rates."»

In a meeting in his mansion in 219 of Madison Avenue, surrounded by the most prominent banking and railroad tycoons, John Pierpont Morgan announced[76]:

«I am authorized to say, I think, on behalf of the [banking] houses represented here [...] that they will not negotiate, and will do everything in their power to prevent the negotiation of, any securities for the construction of parallel lines, or the extension of lines not approved by that executive committee. I wish that distinctly understood. »

The message, distinctly understood, was an ultimatum of Morgan to avoid any sort of competition in the railroads, and a call to cease the

---

the directors of *U.S.Steel*. New York Times, September 23, 1905, *Francis H. Peabody Dead*.

76 Gustavus Myers, *History of the Great American Fortunes*, p. 211.

development of any new lines unless those were authorized by him. Not even the President of the United States had such a tremendous power to enforce, or even to formulate such a statement, but Morgan did, and the threat was directed to railroad managers as well as bankers who dared to stand in front of him. He actually could fix and regulate the size of the industry, because he controlled the credit of the country needed for the railroads' survival and for any new developments.

Soon Morgan arrived into the coal market, an option which produced natural synergies with the railroads. His entry in the market was marked by the bankruptcy of most independent operators, with dishonorable means, according to Myers. At the time of his arrival, from 1892 to 1893 the coal production was reduced from 50,000 to 40,000 tons, as the Interstate Commerce Commission pointed out. In the light of the intentional reduction of the supply of the coal, the prices consequently surged[77].

The next industry that attracted the almighty banker's attention was the electrical sector. In 1892 *Drexel, Morgan & Co.,* led the banking Syndicate that financed the creation of *General Electric,* that appeared from the merger of *Edison General Electric Company* -where Morgan was already a major stockholder- with the *Thomson-Houston General Electric.* With *General Electric* a new monopoly was born, which electrified the entire country thanks to the alternating current invented by Tesla, the forgotten genius.

In 1902 Morgan formed the trust of the agricultural machinery when he created *International Harvester*[78]. The aggregate of his stock gave him control over the 85% of the buoyant market of the farm equipment; *International Harvester* represented 60% of total business, *John Deere* the 17% and *Case* the 8%[79].

---

[77] Gustavus Myers, *History of the Great American Fortunes, vol. III*, p. 217.

[78] *International Harvester* was other of the big trusts formed by Morgan after the merger of *McCormick Harvesting Machine Company, Deering Harvester Company, Milwaukee Harvester Company, Plano Harvester Company* and *Warder*, and *Bushnell and Glessner*.

1902 was a memorable year for the House of Morgan, as it also achieved control over the steel industry in the United States. John Pierpont Morgan acquired the biggest company of the country, the *Carnegie Steel Company*, at the price of 300 million dollars, refunding it as the *U.S. Steel Corporation.* Some years later it was known that only the assets of the steelmaker equaled the price paid by Morgan, and the capitalization was more than three times the price paid[80]. The reason why Carnegie gave away his company remains a mystery, but the banker did not waste the chance to fleece thousands of investors[81].

> «The profits made by Morgan were instantaneous and gigantic. The stock obtained by him he was able to sell at the market price of about 50. By October, 1902, Morgan and his immediate partners in the syndicate had already distributed $40,000,000 in profits. From whom did these stockjobbing profits come? From a host of middle class investors throughout the world.
>
> Lured on by the glowing prospectuses of the Steel Trust, and certain that the money that they put in would produce large dividends, and the stock would rise in value, they literally scrambled to pay over their money for the stock. After the process had been exhaustively worked by the manipulators, the price of common stock was gradually beat down, until, in 1904, it sank to 834. Hordes of middle class investors were ruined; the magnates had transferred their money to their own pockets. »

The list of stockholders of the *U.S. Steel Corporation* provided in the annual shareholders' meeting of 1910, unveiled as important holders the British branch of *J.P. Morgan* & Co., the Rothschilds and Luke H. Cutler, who was widely known as a John D. Rockefeller's agent[82].

---

[79] Anthony Sutton, *Wall Street and FDR*, p. 140.

[80] Gustavus Myers, *History of the Great American Fortunes, vol. III*, p.p. 262-286.

[81] Gustavus Myers, *History of the Great American Fortunes, vol. III*, p. 263.

[82] Gustavus Myers, *History of the Great American Fortunes, vol. III*, p. 286.

Among all the philanthropists tycoons, it seems that only Carnegie was really committed to the cause. His obituary in the *New York Times,* August 12, 1919[83] mentioned an estate of approximately 500 million dollars, of which 350 went to charitable contributions. Myers, however, denounced that the *Carnegie Steel Company* hired immigrants –sometimes minor children- at an average salary of 1.60 dollars a day. The conditions of the Carnegie factories were subhuman; the working times exceeded seventy two hours a week in overcrowding, lack of illumination and ventilation, with high temperatures and deafening noise, caused a high mortality among workers. Those who survived suffered severe illnesses derived from the harsh conditions of the job. Carnegie was an archetypical case of what Charles Dickens called "telescopic philanthropy"; he was a man delivered to the cause of helping the ailing mankind, but incapable of caring about his neighbors.

The fame of Morgan transcended boundaries, and there was no day in which newspapers published an ode to the feats of "Morgan the Magnificent", "Captain Morgan" or "the Corsair", as he was depicted. Most of them, by the way, were under his control. What has been told so far is only a fraction of the vicissitudes of Morgan.

The Money Trust

In 1912 the Congressman of Louisiana, Arséne Pujo formed a committee to investigate if a small group of financiers, the so called "Money trust", were in control of the main companies of the country, hampering the competition in many industries. Samuel Untermyer was named to conduct the hearings. Untermyer was a well-known member of Wall Street, a lawyer in the office of *Guggenheimer, Untermyer & Marshall,* in 37 Wall Street, together with his half-brother Randolph Guggenheimer[84]. He was one of the foremost contributors in the

---

[83] New York Times, August 12, 1919, *Andrew Carnegie Dies of Pneumonia in his 84th Year.*

[84] New York Times, September 4, 1912, *Untermeyer Quits the Firm: Wants to Give*

campaign of Woodrow Wilson, and a Delegate of the Democratic National Convention in 1904, 108, 1912, 1916, 1932 and 1936.

In June 1913 the *New York Times* published some of the conclusions of the Pujo Committee directed by Untermeyer. The official report affirmed the financiers exerted their domain across several industries of the country through interlocked directorates; installing a number of directors in the board of a big number of companies, many of which were in direct competition with each other[85]:

> «We define a money trust as an established identity and community of interest between a few leaders of finance, which has been created and is held together through stock-holding, interlocking directorates, and other forms of domination over banks, trust companies, railroads, public service and industrial corporations, and which has resulted in vast and growing concentration and control of money and credits in the hands of a few men.
>
> The three dominant personalities in this community of financial interests have been J. Pierpont Morgan, who is now in his seventy-sixth year, and spends much of his time in Europe; James E. Stillman, who is in his sixty-third year, and lives in Europe, and George F. Banker, who is in his seventieth year, and is now the most active man in the group.
>
> The five institutions which these men and their associates dominate and which are regarded by the committee as the superstructure of the money trust, are J. P. Morgan and Co., the First National Bank, the National City Bank, the Bankers' Trust Company, and the Guaranty Trust Company. By means of community or identity of interest and through interlocking directorates these five institutions are shown by the testimony to be potentially affiliated with or in control of banks and trust

Younger Members a Chance.

85 New York Times, June 12, 2013, *Say Money Trust is Disclosed.*

companies, insurance companies, transportation, producing and trading companies, and public utility corporations. Together have 341 Directors in 112 corporations having aggregate resources or capitalization of $22,245,000,000[86], distributed as follows:

One hundred and eighteen Directors in thirty-four banks and trust companies, having total resources of $2,679,000,000 and total deposits of $1,983,000,000.

Thirty Directors in ten insurance companies having total assets of $2,293,000,000.

One hundred and five Directors in thirty two transportation systems having a total capitalization of $11,784,000,000 and a total mileage of 150,200, without counting express companies and steamship lines.

Sixty-three Directors in twelve public utility corporations having a total capitalization of $2,150,000,000. »

No congressman or senator but Untermeyer were allowed to make any questions, and he didn't inquire into the interlocking directorates or the gold transfers that caused the previous monetary panics, or the relations of the Money Trust with the European bankers. Untermeyer's report only urged to a greater federal regulation but it did not find any illegal behavior, partly because the commission had no legal powers. Nevertheless, the hearings forced the bankers to travel to Washington every session for months. Neither the President leaving, William Howard Taft, nor the incoming, Woodrow Wilson, seemed to care much about the findings of the committee.

---

[86] In 1913 the capitalization of the New York Stock Exchange was $26.500.000.000. The "Money Trust" thus, exercised control over 84% of the listed securities of the country.

The Dawn of the House of Morgan

During the last part of his life, the health of John Pierpont Morgan quickly worsened, partly because of the pressure of the hearings of the Pujo Committee, of which Morgan was supposed to be the ringleader. Morgan died alone in a hotel of Rome, in March 27, 1913. Despite all his economic accomplishments, he passed away in not such a comfortable economic position as one could expect for the greatest tycoon in the history of the United States, excluding maybe, John D. Rockefeller, of course. Modern historians valued the personal fortune in some 80 million dollars, in addition to the 50 million in which his fine art collection was appraised, and which went later to the *Metropolitan Museum of Art.*

Even this value seems an exaggeration of his real wealth, in the light of his last will, published in the *New York Times*[87]. Morgan only left his relatives some 20 million in cash, including some provisions for the St. George church, for his household workers, and his employees at *J.P. Morgan.* He also mentioned his artwork collection, his mansion in New York and his real estate properties in Madison Avenue, Manhattan. Regarding his stock on other enterprises, his last will mentioned the fund created by his father Junius Morgan in 1867, whose value was not made public. Where was the estate of the man who subdued the economy of the country in the panics of 1894 and 1907, who threatened all the railroad tycoons, who bought Carnegie his steel monopoly at the price of 300 million without even bargaining? When Morgan died, Carnegie exclaimed astonished, while witnessing the Corsair's art collection "And to think, he wasn't even a rich man![88]"

The author Eustace Mullins suggests the doubts about his wealth might be in the obituary of Baron Alphonse de Rothschild, the man leading the familiar empire, and one of the governors of the governors

---

[87] New York Times, April 20, 1913, *The Full Text of the Will of J.P. Morgan.*

[88] Stephen Birmingham, *America's Secret Aristocracy,* Little, Brown and Company, 1987, Toronto, p. 207.

of the Bank of France, from 1854 until his death. The article stated that Baron Alphonse owned 60 million in American stock, despite no economic activities of the Rothschilds were known in the United States[89]:

> «The House [of Rothschild] has also had considerable dealings in American securities through the Belmonts, J. Pierpont Morgan, and John W. Gates… It is estimated that with the other heads of the family Baron Alphonse de Rothschild had at the time of his death $60,000,000 invested in American securities. The Belmonts have been the Rothschilds' American agents or many years…»

Is it possible that Morgan's money was in fact the money of Frankfurt? Another clue about the estate of the House of Morgan can be found in the work of Gustavus Myers[90]:

> «In 1873 it was estimated that $375,000,000 of American railroad securities were held abroad, chiefly by foreign bankers. The Final Report of the Industrial Commission in 1902 estimated (see page 404 of that report) the amount of these securities held by foreign banking houses and others abroad at about $3,100,000,000.»

The relations of the Morgans with the American Rothschilds were excellent. For instance Robert S. Pririe, President of *L.F. Rothschild & Company,* and a Senior Director *Bear Stearns*[91], frequently meet Morgan in a secret and exclusive club named "The Zodiac". Its members were twelve of the most influential men of the country in the most diverse fields[92].

---

[89] New York Times, May 27, 1905, *Head of the Rothschilds' Paris House is Dead. Baron Alphonse Unexpectedly Succumbs to Bronchitis.*

[90] Gustavus Myers, *History of the Great American Fortunes, vol. III*, p.p. 183-184.

[91] One of the largest investment banks by the end of the 20th century, founded in 1923 by Joseph Ainslee Bear, Robert B. Stearns and Harold C. Mayer.

[92] *America's Secret Aristocracy*, p.p. 204-209. Each of his members held the name

It is an unlikely fact that Morgan had died as a "poor" man, or that his economic empire had simply vanished. The most probable option is that his fortune was stored in the form of gold or precious metals, whose trail is more difficult to trace. But there's also a chance that Morgan was only a front for the operations of the Rothschild in the United States, and that all his operations were performed with the money of the Frankfurt Syndicate, whom his father had collaborated since he joined the business of George Peabody in London. If this were the case old Morgan wouldn't have been the genius of finance that he was supposed to be, but a discreet administrator in the service of the Rothschild family.

When his father passed away, John Pierpont Jr. acquired control of the business, but the mighty star of the House of Morgan faded away after the death of the Corsair. His niece, Henry Sturgis Morgan, was more successful than his son, and founded in 1935 with Harold Stanley and the Drexels the investment bank *Morgan Stanley*, nowadays one of the most important players of Wall Street.

In 1933 the Glass-Steagall Act was enacted[93], and the House of Morgan was divided into *J.P. Morgan & Co.*, a commercial bank, and *Morgan Stanley*, an investment bank. In 1995 the *J.P. Morgan* bank absorbed *Chase Manhattan Bank,* which was founded by Aaron Burr, the third Vice President of the United States. And finally, during the crisis of 2008, the Treasury adjudicated to *J.P. Morgan* the failing *Bear Stearns*

---

of one of the twelve constellations of the zodiac, being Morgan the brother "Libra". Other members not named in Birmingham's book were J.P. Morgan Jr. and several architects of the Federal Reserve like Nelson Aldrich, Henry P. Davison and Benjamin Strong. The registries of their meetings are still kept in the *Morgan Library & Museum*.

[93] The Glass-Steagall act of 1933 was enacted to stop the financial speculation that caused the Crash of 1929 and the Great Depression. Some of it's main reforms included the compartmentalization of commercial banking and investment banking, making a firewall to protect the the savings of Americans from the dangers of high risk investments. This law was repealed in 1999 and few doubt that it's supression became one of the main causes of the crisis of 2008.

bank at the price of $ 2 per share, although the final price was risen to $ 10 [94]. By that time *Bear Stearns*, one of the top four investment banks, was in financial distress, but one year before the bank's price was thirteen times the adjudication price, so anyone might think the shareholders were not very happy with the arbitrary decision of the Secretary of the Treasury. At the time this work was written J.P. Morgan was the biggest bank of the United States.

---

[94] New York Times, June 9, 2008, *More Executives Leave Bear Stearns After Its Sale to JPMorgan*.

THE HOUSE OF MORGAN

1837 Birth of *George Peabody and Company* (London).
1838 *Morgan, Grenfell & Co.* (London).
1864 *J.S. Morgan & Company* (London).
1864 *Dabney, Morgan and Company* (New York).
1867 The French branch is opened *Drexel, Harjes & Co.,* later *Morgan, Harjes & Co.* en 1895, and then *Morgan et Cie.* en 1926 (Paris).
1871 *Drexel, Morgan and Company* (New York).
1895 *J.P. Morgan & Co.* acquires *Chase Manhattan Bank* (New York).
1935 Former partners of *J.P. Morgan* founded *Morgan Stanley* (New York).
2008 The Treasury adjudicates *J.P. Morgan & Co.* one of the top investment banks of Wall Street, *Bear Stearns.* (New York).

JOHN DAVISON ROCKEFELLER

The founder of *Standard Oil* and his son John D. Rockefeller Jr.

THE ROCKEFELLER DINASTY

The Rockefellers[95]

In 1859, ten years after the gold fever started in California, a different fever began: the "black gold". Petroleum was already a known product, but it had not consolidated yet as a new energy source. A merchant of Cleveland, Ohio, named John Davison Rockefeller, began in 1860 a company with other two partners and only a few hundreds of dollar as startup capital. Rockefeller, who managed the company, insisted his partners to re-invest the money on the business. Unlike all his rivals, he knew a large reserves of capital was a crucial element to ensure the success and survival of the company. During the sixties the three partners hoarded a great reserve of capital, and in 1867 they ceased turning to banks to grow. In 1870 they formed the *Standard Oil Company of Ohio,* a company with a capital of a million dollars.

In the seventies, many oil operators resorted to Wall Street for capital, but the banks were too busy financing other business of greater growth like the railroads, which allowed the Rockefellers to buy some of their rivals at a good price. During these years, the *Standard Oil* managed to fix a very low tariffs which left his competitors out of the market[96]. Nevertheless, they didn't need the railroads for a long time because they soon started connecting their refineries by means of oil pipelines.

In 1875, five years after the creation if the *Standard Oil,* the enterprise had increased its capitalization from one to thirty five millions, and in 1881 it was forty millions. By 1890 the *Standard Oil* had bought almost all of its competitors and it had delivered dividends of eleven million dollars.

---

[95] Almost the entire chapter is based on *Masters of Capital* by John Moody.

[96] More specifically Myers points out that "The Standard Oil Company had built up its power largely by reason of the secret railroad rebates and discriminations." Myers, *History of the Great Fortunes* vol. III, p. 197.

The *Standard Oil* not only was able to finance its growth with its own capital, but it also used that capital as financial arm for making other investments. The headquarters of the business moved from Ohio to New York in 1822, in the office of 26 Broadway. Its new banking unit was in full growth mode, and Wall Street was the financial center of the United States.

The *Standard Oil* achieved control of 90% of the oil business in the United States until 1911 the Supreme Court ruled it's fragmentation into several companies of smaller size based on the Sherman Antitrust Act. That measure was very ineffective, because the resultant companies ended up in the hands of the same major shareholders and directors of the original *Standard Oil.* During the period that the *Standard Oil* remained active, between 1882 and 1911, it distributed 751 million in dividends. After it's dissolution, from 1911 until 1921, the aggregate of enterprises following the fragmentation of the oil conglomerate delivered the shareholders more than 923 million in cash and 283 million more in shares, having quadrupled their value in that decade[97]. John D. Rockefeller died in 1937 keeping an estimated fortune of about 1,500 million dollars[98]. In terms of value updated by inflation it is the biggest fortune in the history of the United States, and probably the biggest fortune earned -non-inherited- in the world.

City Bank

City Bank was known in its time as one of the most solid financial institutions of the United States. It's President since 1855 was Moses Taylor. Before that he was the agent of John Jacob Astor, one of the American magnates *par excellence*, and one of the most infamous, who made his fortune in the fur trade first, and in the real estate later on.

---

97 New York Times, December 25, 2001, *Standard Oil Value up to $3,276,027,243; Quadrupled in the Decade Since the Supreme Court Ordered Dissolution.*

98 New York Times, May 24, 1937, *Financier's Fortune in Oil Amassed in Industrial Era of 'Rugged Individualism'.*

Taylor shared Rockefeller's belief that a large reserve of capital was key to success, so that when the frequent panics came the bank could bear it and get strengthened out of every crisis. Moses Tylor died in 1882 as one of the major personal fortunes of the United States, and by then the *City Bank* was the biggest financial institution of its class. Percy R. Pyne came after him and in 1891, and afterwards James Stillman, who had orbited also around the Astors.

The Rockefellers were already involved in the banking business when in 1885 William Rockefeller became the Director of *Hanover Bank*, where he established a durable friendship with Stillman, one of the directors of the bank. The arrival of Stillman to *City Bank* en 1891 almost tripled the deposits, from twelve million dollars up to thirty one in 1893. This happened to a great extent due to the money of the Rockefellers flowing to the bank and the *City Bank,* which became known as "the *Standard Oil* bank"[99]. William Rockefeller, following the fashion of the banking aristocracy of Frankfurt, married James Stillman's daughter, Elsie. The son of the couple, James Stillman Rockefeller, in turn married in 1925 with Nancy Carnegie, granddaughter of the brother of Andrew Carnegie, the steel magnate.

By 1893 the business of the Rockefellers spread across other raw materials as the iron mines of *Lake Superior Company*, while Henry Rogers, the Vice President of the *Standard Oil,* created the giant of the industry of American copper when he formed the *Amalgamated Copper Company,* which merged afterwards with the *Anaconda Copper Company.* Stillman's *City Bank* channeled funds of this operation that according to Moody was supported by the money of the Rockefeller family, and costed 150 million dollars. In 1909 Stillman left the presidency of *City Bank* and was replaced by Frank Vanderlip, one of the founders of the Federal Reserve of the United States.

---

[99] John Moody, *Masters of Capital*, p. 64.

THE ROCKEFELLER DINASTY

1799 The *Manhattan Company*, antecessor of *Manhattan Bank,* was established.
1812 Founded *City Bank of New York.*
1877 Founded *Chase National Bank.*
1885 William Rockefeller is appointed Director of *Hanover Bank.*
1891 The Rockefeller heavily invest in *City Bank.*
1930 *Chase Bank* acquired *Equitable Trust* an asset of the Morgan group. John D. Rockefeller Jr. remained as a major shareholder.
1952 James Stillman Rockefeller was appointed President of the *City Bank.*
1955 Merger of Rockefeller's *City Bank* and Morgan's *First National Bank*, forming the *First National City Bank.*
1955 *Chase Bank* acquired the *Bank of Manhattan* to form *Chase Manhattan Bank.*
1960 David Rockefeller became President of the *Chase Manhattan Bank.*
1976 Reorganization of the *City Bank* into the *Citibank* and the *Citigroup* holding.
1991 *J.P. Morgan* acquired the *Chase Manhattan Bank.*

Edward H. Harriman

Edward H. Harriman, born in 1848, was the son of an Episcopalian priest turned into bank clerk. He began his work as a Wall Street broker, until in 1870 he could buy his own seat in the New York Stock Exchange. By 1880 Edward Harriman was a renowned expert in the railroads business, and in 1897 he secured his position acquiring one of the most important lines of the country, the *Illinois Central*, which had more than 5.000 miles long.

From 1887 till 1894 Morgan and Harriman were competing for the Purchase of some Railroad lines without a clear winner, and when in 1895 the shareholders of the *Union Pacific Railroad* desperately sought for the reorganization of the line, Morgan declined and Harriman decided to go for it. But he clashed with *Kuhn & Loeb & Co.*, which then had some experience in the railroad business, stood in his way.

Jacob Schiff of *Kuhn & Loeb* enjoyed a privileged position, being able to obtain the necessary funds from his German allies at a 5-6 per cent interest rate –the Rothschilds-, while Edward Harriman could get the money in the United States at a rate of 3.5 or 4 per cent –the Rockefellers-. Both titans reached an agreement; Jacob Schiff took *Union Pacific* for *Kuhn & Loeb* and Edward H. Harriman became his President. When in 1897 Harriman and *Kuhn & Loeb & Co.* agreed the reorganization of the *Union Pacific*, they did it through *City Bank*, the Rockefeller's bank, in an operation that required the disbursement of 45 million in cash[100].

The acquisition of the *Union Pacific* is an important milestone in our History. When William Rockefeller and James Stillman joined forces with *Kuhn & Loeb & Co.*, they forged a visible alliance between the aristocrats of Frankfurt and the tycoons of New York. Additionally, the operation opened the doors for the Harriman family to a very exclusive banking fraternity, made by the six or seven families of financiers most important of history. Edward Harriman became a friend and mentor for Otto Kahn of *Kuhn & Loeb,* and replaced in leading the railroad business when Harriman passed away. The Harrimans were representatives of the Rockefeller group for many years[101].

In the early twentieth century the railroad business was a reflection of the rest of the American industries, which were divided into two economic blocks; on one hand the Harriman group, backed by the money of *City Bank, Kuhn & Loeb* and the Rockefellers, and on the other hand the tycoon James J. Hill, supported by the *First National*

---

[100] John Moody, *Masters of Capital*, p.p. 65-66.

[101] As stated by Myers (*History of the Great American Fortunes*, vol. III, p. 234) "The belief prevailed that Harriman, [was] representing the Standard Oil oligarchy and Moody "Harriman was still closely associated with the Rockefeller and City Bank interests." (*Masters of Capital*, p. 100. See also p.p. 66-67, 104.)

Bank of the Morgan group. However, the competition between the two bocks was rather doubtful.

Edward Harriman kept hoarding railroad properties and in 1900 he bought a 45% stake in the *Southern Pacific Company*, until then a property of the Huntington, magnates of the railroad in decline. During those years a growing concern appeared among the American people and some politicians regarding the formation of trusts that prevented the free development of the industries. In February 1907, the Interstate Commission of Commerce began an investigation of Harriman's *Union Pacific*, due to his inflated participations in the stock of his rivals. The Commission suspected Harriman was in the process of building one of the biggest monopolies of the country. *Kuhn & Loeb* bitterly protested the movement of the President Theodore Roosevelt, which time ago was a friend and champion of Harriman. Jacob Schiff himself, the head of *Kuhn & Loeb,* wrote infuriated to the President to complain for the abuse received by his *protégé*[102].

> «Kahn was not alone in resenting the tenor of the investigation. Jacob Schiff wrote angrily to President Roosevelt on March 4, 1907:"...The purpose of the investigation appeared so evident, namely, to break down not only Mr. Harriman, but with him those who in one way or another have been associated with him... that I cannot but protest the methods which were employed in the endeavor to accomplish this."»

His faithful friend Otto Kahn, even if he was troubled by the prosecution of Harriman, recognized the fact that[103]:

> «Harriman's action in piling up interest upon interest was his one serious mistake in his management of the Union Pacific, and almost proved to be his undoing. »

---

[102] Mary Jane Matz, *The Many Lives of Otto Kahn*, p. 36.
[103] Mary Jane Matz, *The Many Lives of Otto Kahn*, p. 35.

The case of Harriman, like Morgan's, were clear examples on how three or four tycoons could control an entire industry by means of interlocking directorates. The "anti-trust" President, Theodore Roosevelt, surrendered to Schiff's influence, and as it happened in the Money Trust investigation of Morgan, everything came to nothing.

After Edward Harriman's early decease in 1909, the Rockefeller-*Kuhn & Loeb* block controlled a great part of the American railroad mileage, particularly the south, east and central areas; *Illinois Central, Union Pacific, Southern Pacific, Saint Joseph & Grand Island*, and *Central Georgia Railway*. Harriman also served until 1905 as the director in the *Denver & Rio Grande*, which belonged to another railroad tycoon named George Gould, while Gould was in the board of Harriman's *Union Pacific*[104]. On the opposite side, the group of Hill and the Morgans had enough by controlling the rest of the system; in the North, *Great Northern* and *Northern Pacific,* and in the Midwest, *Chicago, Burlington & Quincy*. Both blocks shared practically the entire mileage of the United States, and as far as we know there was a very soft rivalry between the aforementioned blocks, if any. Professor Sutton summarized the role of the Morgan-Rockefeller duopoly that controlled the entire American economy at the beginning of the twentieth century:

> «[105]Before World War I, the financial and business structure of the United States was dominated by two conglomerates: Standard Oil, or the Rockefeller enterprise, and the Morgan complex of industries-finance and transportation companies. Rockefeller and Morgan trust alliances dominated not only Wall Street but, through interlocking directorships, almost the entire economic fabric of the United States. Rockefeller interests monopolized the petroleum and allied industries, and controlled the copper trust, the smelters trust, and the gigantic tobacco trust, in addition to having influence

[104] Mary Jane Matz, *The Many Lives of Otto Kahn*, p. 41.

[105] Anthony Cyril Sutton, *Wall Street and the Bolshevik Revolution*, Claireview Books, p.p. 49-50.

in some Morgan properties such as the U.S. Steel Corporation as well as in hundreds of smaller industrial trusts, public service operations, railroads, and banking institutions. National City Bank was the largest of the banks influenced by Standard Oil-Rockefeller, but financial control extended to the United States Trust Company and Hanover National Bank as well as to major life insurance companies-Equitable Life and Mutual of New York.

The great Morgan enterprises were in steel, shipping, and the electrical industry; they included General Electric, the rubber trust, and railroads. Like Rockefeller, Morgan controlled financial corporations - the National Bank of Commerce and the Chase National Bank, New York Life Insurance, and the Guaranty Trust Company. In the early part of the twentieth century the Guaranty Trust Company was dominated by the Harriman interests. When the elder Harriman (Edward Henry) died in 1909, Morgan and associates bought into Guaranty Trust as well as into Mutual Life and New York Life. In 1919 Morgan also bought control of Equitable Life, and the Guaranty Trust Company absorbed an additional six lesser trust companies. Therefore, at the end of World War I the Guaranty Trust and Bankers Trust were, respectively, the first and second largest trust companies in the United States, both dominated by Morgan interests. »

In the financial sector, after a number of mergers, three out of the four or five biggest institutions of the country belonged to the Morgans and Rockefellers. In the rest of the industries of the country the level of competition between the two economic superpowers was similarly scarce. The interests of Morgans and Rockefellers also converged in the metallurgical industry. In 1901 Morgan's *U.S. Steel* acquired the *Lake Superior Company* mines, which belonged to their "rivals", the Rockefellers. The *New York Times* reported the merger[106];

[106] New York Times, March 17 1901, *Standard Oil and U.S. Steel in Harmony.*

«The [Lake Superior] company is a property is distinctively a Rockefeller-Standard Oil property. The deal is regarded in Wall Street as peculiarly significant, in that it indicate clearly the Standard Oil interests are working in harmony with Mr. Morgan in the Steel Trust's development. »

Brown Brothers Harriman

We step back in time to the age of the "merchant bankers". In 1800 an Irish merchant named Alexander Brown with his four sons William, George, John and James established *Alex Brown & Sons* in Baltimore, United States. Alexander Brown started a mercantile business similar to the Junius Morgan and George Peabody enterprise, importing Irish linen to England and exporting cotton and tobacco back to the United States.

In 1810 his elder son, William Brown, founded *William Brown & Co.* as its correspondent in Liverpool, and in 1825 William Brown associated to Joseph Shipley, expanding business into other zones of Europe under the name of *Brown, Shipley and Company,* a firm which exists nowadays[107]. As it happened with other merchant banks, the credit business ended up eclipsing the mercantile business and finally it became a firm exclusively dedicated to financial services. In 1863 a partner named Mark Collet opened the London office of *Brown, Shipley & Co*, and in 1887 he became the Governor of the Bank of England, establishing a lasting relationship between both institutions. His grandson, Lord Montagu Norman[108], followed his steps, becoming a Director in *Brown, Shipley & Co.*, and also he headed the English central bank from 1920 until 1944. Another prominent member of this

---

[107] *Brown Shipley & Co.*, History, website revised in January 2014.

[108] Norman's biography written in 1940 explains that "There is a formal understanding that a director of Brown, Shipley should be in the Board of the Bank of England". As quoted by Eustace Mullins in *Secrets of the Federal Reserve*, Bridger House Publishers, Carson City, 1991, p. 49.

banking house was Edward Heath, who became Prime Minister of England from 1970 to 1974.

Meanwhile, in 1818 a new entrepreneurship of the Brown Brothers, John and James, started the business in Philadelphia, which still was an important financial center. That business was *Brown Brothers & Company*, and in 1825 it also opened a branch office in New York, where James Stillman Rockefeller –the grandson of William Rockefeller and James Stillman- was another of its illustrious members. In 1931 the American branch of the Browns joined the heirs of Edward Harriman's, Averell and Roland, to form a new alliance: *Brown Brothers Harriman* was the company resulting from the merger of *Brown Brothers & Co.* (1825), *W.A. Harriman* & *Co.* founded by Averell (1922), and *Harriman Brothers & Co.,* founded by Averell and Roland (1927).

The Harriman influence was intensely felt in the American policy of the first half of the twentieth century. Averell Harriman, before he reached the peak of success in business world was a foremost politician, who held positions as Secretary of Commerce, Ambassador in the United Kingdom, Ambassador in the Soviet Union and Governor of the State of New York. He also was a member of the National Recovery Administration of Roosevelt, the National Defense Advisory Commission, and the Office of Production Management[109]. He took advantage as a public officer, to obtain profits doing business with the Nazi Germany and the Soviet Russia. His brother Roland Harriman was a member of the Board of Governors of the Red Cross in 1947 and President of the American Red Cross from 1950 on. The most remarkable merit the Red Cross awards is in fact the "Harriman Award".

In 1931 Prescott Bush was one of the founding partners of *Brown Brothers Harriman*, where his father in law George Herbert Walker also worked. Prescott, who had started in *W.A. Harriman & Co.* in 1926 became a partner of that firm in 1931. Roland Harriman graduated in

---

[109] *Brown Brothers Harriman*, History, website revised in January 2014.

Yale in the same year Prescott Bush, the patriarch of the second most important presidential dynasty, did[110].

Prescott Bush, who started in the railroads and steel businesses, was during the World War I the public officer in charge of the coordination and assistance to military contractors, which allowed him to discretionally select the weaponry providers and other suppliers. Prescott Bush secured his position in *Brown Brothers Harriman* in 1921, by marrying the daughter of his boss, George Herbert Walker. Prescott, who entered in *W.A. Harriman & Co.* in 1926, was named partner in 1931. The Bush family held a position close to the exclusive circle of bankers due to their participation in the business of the Harriman, and held also close personal and political relations to the Rockefellers, particularly with Senator Nelson Rockefeller.

BROWNS AND HARRIMANS

1800 Alexander Brown opens *Alex Brown & Sons* (Baltimore).
1810 His son William Brown opens *William Brown & Co.* (Liverpool).
1825 *William Brown & Co.* becomes *Brown, Shipley & Co.*
1863 *Brown, Shipley & Co* opens a new office (London).
1818 Two of the sons of Alexander Brown, James and John, joined to form *Brown Brothers & Company* (Philadelphia).
1825 James opens a new branch of *Brown Brothers & Company* (New York).
1922 William Averell Harriman creates *W.A. Harriman* & *Co.*
1927 Roland and William Averell establish *Harriman Brothers & Co.*
1931 The firms of the Browns and the Harrimans join forces to establish *Brown Brothers Harriman & Co.*

---

[110] They also meet at the macabre masonic society of Yale *Skull & Bones*. Sutton, who studied the society (*America's Secret Establishment*, p.p. 20-22.) stated that Averell and Roland Harriman were initiated, like Prescott. His grandson George W. Bush, in an interview with Tim Russert in *Meet the Press,* in Feb 7, 2004, admitted that his membersip in *Skull & Bones* was *"so secret* we *can*'t *talk* about it".

PART II. THE BANKING REVOLUTIONS

WILSON'S REVOLUTIONS: THE FEDERAL RESERVE AND WORLD WAR I (1918-1921)

Bankers Trust

The Morgan Empire was analyzed in the first part, its European connections and its sway over the American industry. We briefly return to that story to know his circle of trust and its banking structure. Moody provides an accurate picture of the financial panorama of the early XX century, an economic landscape ruled by Morgan.

> «[111]The three great New York banks which, it is understood, Morgan then long controlled, were the First National, the National Bank of Commerce and the Hanover National. Their immense resources may be realized from these facts: The First National has a capital of $10,000,000, deposits of $113,000,000, and a surplus of $18,600,000. The National Bank of Commerce has a capital of $25,000,000, deposits of $170,000,000, and a surplus of $15,000,000. The Hanover National has a capital of $3,000,000, deposits of $82,000,000 and a surplus of $10,000,000. Since then, as we shall see, Morgan has extended his control over a vast number of other banks, virtually forming a Money Trust. »

The acquisition of *Guaranty Trust*, *Mercantile Trust*, *Equitable Trust*, *Morton Trust* and *Fifth Avenue Trust* allowed him to influence directly a capital of ten or twelve thousand million dollars of that time, scattered in very diverse industries across the country. [112]

---

[111] Gustavus Myers, *The History of the Great American Fortunes, vol. III*, p. 265.
[112] Gustavus Myers, *The History of the Great American Fortunes, vol. III*, p.p. 306-307

Some of the most powerful, bankers of the country joined to create the flagship of the banking apparatus of the Morgan Empire. *Bankers Trust Company*, known as "Morgan's Bank" was established in 1903 and among its twenty initial shareholders there were William H. Porter, Vice-President of the *Chemical National Bank*, John F. Thompson and Henry P. Davison of the *First National Bank,* and George W. Perkins and Thomas W. Lamont, both partners of *J.P. Morgan & Co.*[113]

In 1905 Morgan also held control over the three biggest insurance companies of the country: *Mutual Life Insurance Company*, the *Equitable Life Insurance Company* of Thomas F. Ryan and *New York Life Insurance Co.*[114] John Pierpont Morgan had the monopoly over almost all the industries of the country; banking, insurance, industry, media, etc.

In the last years of Morgan's life, a group of six strong men was growing in relevance inside its banking empire. When he passed away Davison, and later Lamont, succeeded him.

Thomas W. Lamont: Thomas Lamont was a New York banker, co-founder of *Bankers Trust* in 1903 and a partner in *J.P. Morgan & Co.* since 1911. Lamont was an American representative in the Paris Peace Conference that followed the Second World War in 1919 where he was assigned the task of calculating the German payments to the Allied nations. An outspoken socialist while a devote fascist, he took part in the negotiation of the Dawes and Young plans of 1924 and 1929 for structuring the payments of the German debt. Such plans are listed among the main causes of the rise of National Socialism in the Second World War.

George F. Baker: The president of the *First National Bank* was one of the biggest fortunes in the history of the United States, more than twice the old J.P. Morgan.

---

[113] Thomas W. Lamont, *Henry P. Davison. A Record of a Useful Life*, p.55.

[114] John Moody, *Masters of Capital*, p. 150.

Henry P. Davison

Thomas W. Lamont

George F. Baker

Benjamin Strong

William Boyce Thompson

James Stillman

BANKERS TRUST CIRCLE

Baker is an example on how the bankers formed their own golden circle inside the high society of New York. He was a friend and neighbor of Morgan, who lived a few houses away in the exclusive area of Madison Avenue[115]. His son George F. Junior married the grandniece of Anthony Drexel, and his niece married the niece of Jacob Schiff. Baker built his fortune with the *First National Bank,* which he founded in 1863 with the banker John Thompson, and his sons Samuel and Frederick F. Thompson, together with other partners of *Jay Cooke & Co.*, one of the oldest investment banks of the United States.

> «[116]The First National Bank of New York had been founded in 1863 by two brothers, John and Frederick Thompson, with whom Mr. Baker had been in association at Jay Cooke & Co. »

When Samuel Thompson retired in 1877, George F. Baker was unanimously chosen as the new President of *First National Bank*, which was by then one of the biggest institutions of the country. The history of the Thompsons deserves a brief mention. In 1864 the *New York Times* published a letter in which Secretary of the Treasury Salmon P. Chase expressed his gratitude to *Jay Cooke & Co.* for the services rendered to the government, having sold over 600 million dollars of the American debt issued during the civil war[117]. *Jay Cooke & Co.*, one of the first representatives of the Rothschilds in the country, failed due to the panic of 1873, wiping away the savings of many investors, but Baker and the Thompsons kept a preferential relation with the Treasury afterwards, when they founded a new bank, the *First National Bank*[118]. Probably, it was by no accident that when John Thompson decided to

---

[115] New York Times, July 17, 1911, *Edith Kane to Wed George F. Baker Jr.*

[116] *Henry P. Davison, the Record of a Useful Life*, p. 48.

[117] New York Times, April 9, 1864, *The Five-Twenty Loan-Jay Cooke & Co. Letter from Secretary Chase.*

[118] Harvard Business School, *Baker Family. Baker Family Papers*, web revised 2016.

create another bank in 1877, the *Chase National Bank*[119], he named it after the Secretary of Treasury that did so much for him and for Baker.

The *First National* and *Chase* banks eventually become part of the Morgan and Rockefeller empires. In 1930 the *Chase,* a Rockefeller's property, acquired Morgan's *Equitable Trust*, creating the biggest bank in the world, leaving George F. Baker was one of the main shareholders:

> «The Chase-Equitable merger not only created the world's largest bank in terms of assets and deposits but also gave the Rockefeller family, which controlled Equitable, a strong connection to Chase. The Rockefellers have been associated with Chase ever since. »

Later, in the 90's, there was a lot of mergers and acquisitions in the banks Morgans and Rockefellers owned (see annexes), such as *Hannover Bank*, *Manufacturers Trust* and the *Chemical Bank*, culminating in the merger of *J.P. Morgan* and the *Chase Manhattan Bank* in 1999. The story of the institutions that came after *Jay Cooke & Co.* reveals that most the banking mergers that took place in the century after the liquidation of that institution did not change at all the property of the banks of the country, but instead gave a false impression of change or competition among the players of the financial panorama in the United States.

Henry Pomeroy Davison: Davison worked in small banks until his career took off in 1891 with the Astors in the *Astor Place Bank*. From there he got access to two of the banks under control of George F. Banker; in 1894 the *Liberty National Bank*, that he eventually presided, and later on in the *First National Bank,* whose vice-presidency he achieved in 1902[120]. Davison was one of the co-founders of *Bankers*

---

[119] *The History of J.P Morgan Chase & Co. 200 Years of Leadership in Banking*. Web revised in September 2014. This info and the next quote from p.p. 4 and 9.

[120] Thomas W. Lamont, *Henry P. Davison, the Record of a Useful Life*, p.p. 43, 47. Garret A. Hobarth, a board member of *Liberty National Bank* was Vice President under the term of McKinley. (*The Record of a Useful Life*, p. 46).

Trust in 1903, and a senior partner of J.P. *Morgan & Co.* in 1909[121]. It was his own idea to create *Bankers Trust,* the "banker's bank", and he was the most active member in the trip to Jekyll Island.

Henry P. Davison was widely known as the founder and first President of the International Red Cross (1919-1922) and Managing Director of the Council of the American Red Cross (1917-1919)[122]. The American Red Cross, created in 1881 by a nurse from Massachusetts named Clara Barton, grew in relevance from 1905 on, by getting a grant from the United States Congress to perform humanitarian and relief duties on its behalf[123]. Under the presidency of Davison the American Red Cross became the greatest firmament of banking stars the world has ever known.

William Boyce Thompson: Colonel Thompson was a mining developer, founder in 1916 of the *Newmont Mining,* one of the biggest mining companies of the world. Boyce Thompson had worked with the Guggenheim, and from time to time as agent of Morgan. Thompson married his daughter Margaret with Anthony Joseph Drexel Biddle Jr., creating solid bonds with the Drexels, the old partners of Junius Morgan. Boyce Thompson was one of the first directors of the Federal Reserve Bank of New York in 1914, a Director in the *Metropolitan Life Insurance,* and a Delegate of the Republican National Convention in 1916 and 1920. This Renaissance man, banker, politician and mining developer appears later on in our story as one of the big capitalists behind the rise of the Bolsheviks.

Benjamin Strong: In April 1904 Benjamin Strong was included in the list of partners of *Bankers Trust.* Strong had been working for Morgan and Davison for years, with Paul Warburg as Vice-President[124]. The relations of Frankfurt and the Morgan group kept on being splendid.

---

[121] Thomas W. Lamont, *Henry P. Davison, the Record of a Useful Life,* p. 117.

[122] The War Council of the Red Cross was a body created by Wilson in 1917 to coordinate the operations of the Red Cross in World War I.

[123] Thomas W. Lamont, *Henry P. Davison, the Record of a Useful Life,* p. 265.

[124] Thomas W. Lamont, *Henry P. Davison. A Record of a Useful Life,* p. 59-60.

The Panic of 1907

The Panic of 1907, the greatest ever seen hitherto, began in mid-October with the collapse of the *Knickerbocker Trust Company*, one of the most prominent banks of New York, under control of Fritz Augustus Heinze, the copper king of Montana, and Charles W. Mores, owner of the ice trust in America.

The crisis began in October 21, 1907, when the *National Bank of Commerce* announced it would decline payments of the checks of the *Knickerbocker Trust Company*, allegedly due to the high chances of a default of that bank. *Knickerbocker Trust* had used shares of the *United Copper*, also in the hands of Fritz Heinze, as a collateral or guarantee of payment, while his brother Otto Heinze had been speculating with the value of its shares. The consequences of these risky operations were disastrous for the *United Copper*, and dragged *Knickerbocker Trust* into a bigger problem. The crisis of confidence spread across the country. The interbank lending suddenly stopped and some other minor bank panics and bankruptcies followed.

The least known part of the story of 1907 is perhaps the fact that the *National Bank of Commerce,* the bank that unleashed the panic by rejecting the checks, was a Morgan's bank, who had a particular interest on seeing the overturn of Morse and Heinze, because they were seen as rivals, outsiders to the Money Trust with an important participation in banks and other industries. The Rockefellers had also their own reasons to tear down Heinze, precisely in relation to old disputes in the copper industry.

According to Congressman Wright Patman, President for ten years of the Committee on Banking and Currency, House of Representatives[125]:

[125] Wright Patman, *A Primer on Money,* Subcomittee on Domestic Finance, Committee on Banking and Currency, House of Representatives, 88th Congress, 2nd Session, 1964, p.p. 56, 57.

«It was not, however, until the panic of 1907 that the public generally began demanding banking reforms and investigations to see what was wrong. That panic had its origins in a sort of financial warfare between two of the country's large, private money groups. Specifically, the so-called Standard Oil group set about to break a bank, the Mercantile National Bank in New York City, in which a rival financial power, one Mr. Heinze, was heavily involved. The Standard Oil people had developed a personal animosity toward Heinze over a contest for control of copper mining in Montana. Heinze won this battle and forced the Standard Oil people to buy his copper interests at what was considered an exorbitant figure — some $10.5 million.

Heinze used the proceeds of this sale to acquire control of the Mercantile National Bank, and then proceeded to make heavy investments of the bank's funds in the stocks of a new and more or less fictitious copper company. The Standard Oil people, aware of the risky enterprise in which Heinze was engaged, quietly invested large sums in these same stocks, then dumped the stocks on the market at a crucial moment, breaking both the price of the stocks and Heinze's bank. »

The crisis worsened in November 2. A brokerage firm named *Moore & Schley* had used its shares in the *Tennessee Coal, Iron & Railroad Company*[126] as a collateral in a similar scheme to which Heinze used with *Knickerbocker Trust.* Using shares as a collateral was a relatively common practice, but the market crash put the company against the ropes. Morgan rushed to this new bailout, together with his partners and James Stillman, an agent of the Rockefellers[127]:

126 As its very name implies, an industrial enterprise in the business of coal, iron and Railroad, thus, a rival of all industries where Morgan was strong.

127 Thomas W. Lamont, *Henry P. Davison, the Record of a Useful Life*, p.p. 73-74.

«The elder Mr. Morgan hurried home from Bar Harbor. This was in October, 1907. At once he organized a rescue party, the three chief figures of which were himself, George F. Baker, and James Stillman of the National City Bank. The story of their indefatigable work has been frequently told, but not so often that of the younger men upon whom fell the heavy task of carrying out the policies which their elders laid down. Of this younger group, George W. Perkins, a partner in the Morgan firm, and Harry Davison, the vice-president of the First National Bank, were the most active. »

The Corsair had already "rescued" the country during the Panic of 1893, when the bankers forced the repeal of the *Sherman Act,* ending thus the Government's silver reserves, to supply later his own, at an exorbitant price. And also in the panic of 1907, willingly or not, he had a leading role in the outbreak and the resolution of the crisis.

Despite the fact that it was a national interest issue, Morgan's associates alone[128] audited the books of *Knickerbocker Trust* and determined it was insolvent. Morgan decided 25 million would be needed to save *Knickerbocker Trust* and other 25 million for the *Tennessee Coal, Iron & Railroad Company* [129]. Stillman of *National City Bank* and Baker of the Morgan group were in charge of selling a part of the assets of *Knickerbocker Trust,* which re-opened in March 1908. The situation of the *Tennessee Coal* was different, firstly because the company was not known to be in financial distress and secondly it was not a problem of the American people, and if it was a problem at all, it should be solved between the shareholders and the creditor banks. But maybe Morgan thought it would be an excellent trophy for his collection, a perfect complement for the *U.S. Steel*, his steel trust.

---

[128] Lamont does not mention any intervention of the government to appraise the financial condition or in the sale of the *Knickerbocker Trust* or the *Tennessee Coal.*
[129] Thomas W. Lamont, *Henry P. Davison, the Record of a Useful Life*, p.p. 76-78.

The Morgan-Rockefeller Group -the Money Trust represented by J.P. Morgan itself and James Stillman- was the main beneficiary of the Panic of 1907. Morgan, who triggered the crisis when he rejected the paper of *Knickerbocker Trust*, one of its main competitors, achieved a full victory by acquiring it at the price fixed by himself, and he got rid of another competitor, the *Mercantile National Bank*. Amid the financial hysteria, and maybe unexpectedly, he also took a grip on one of his most important industrial rivals, the *Tennessee Coal, Iron & Railroad*. The Rockefellers settled an old dispute with Heinze in the copper industry with the downfall of *United Copper*, a direct competitor of his trust, the *Anaconda Copper Company*. The Heinze-Morse block, the only who rivalled the Money Trust, never recovered after the panic of 1907.

There was only one obstacle for Morgan to put his hands on the *Tennessee Coal, Iron & Railroad*. Theodore Roosevelt's Sherman Antitrust act prevented the acquisition of one of the main competitors of Morgan, who already dominated these industries. On November 4th President Theodore Roosevelt saw himself in a crossroad, having to decide if he should allow Morgan's *U.S. Steel* to acquire the *Tennessee Coal*. This purchase infringed the antitrust laws he himself had signed. A few hours after the opening of the stock market Roosevelt capitulated and the *Tennessee Coal* became part of his showcase of hunting trophies, enlarging his monopolies in the industries of steel, coal and railroads. Teddy Roosevelt always boasted to be the scourge of the trusts, but Gustavus Myers affirmed that image was not adjusted to reality[130]:

> «An overbearingly potent and heroic "great man" Roosevelt appeared... For what? If history tells the tale aright it will tell how he begged campaign funds from the very trust magnates whom he pretended to flout; how, in a critical moment in the national election of 1904, he so despaired of success that he was forced to appeal to Morgan, Harriman and their fellow magnates for a fresh

---

130 Gustavus Myers, *History of the Great American Fortunes, vol. III*, p.p. 245-246.

and immediate infusion of funds. The world does not revere a loser, unless he be a great one, and for a great cause. In considerable degree, Roosevelt fought the fight of a rapidly-decaying cause, that of the middle-class, a cause doomed to fall ignobly, and rightly so. On the surface he seemed the "big man" of the day; in point of fact, he was vanquished by such magnates as Morgan, Harriman and Rockefeller…at basis, Roosevelt, despite his pretenses, was an instrument of the trust magnates. »

Theodore Roosevelt, who publically proclaimed his scorn for the monopolist tycoons, in 1902 assigned Morgan the operation of the payment of the Panama Canal, valued in 40 million dollars. Then, in 1904, he received from the bank of Morgan no less than 150.000 dollars for his re-election campaign[131]. So, as anyone could expect, Theodore Roosevelt approved the acquisition of the *Tennessee Coal* and the confidence return returned to the New York Stock Exchange, which was euphoric that day. It was rather useless, because the market lost half of its value in the next few months. Morgan bought in 45 millions a company valued in 1.000 millions[132].

Despite the fact that Morgan and his bankers controlled the mass media, they persuaded very few Americans this time. The people had seen too frequently the same trick once and again. A few years later Morgan, Baker and others had to testify in a committee presided by Senator Arsene Pujo, who investigated the Money Trust.

The Panic of 1907 brought alongside another collateral effect. On October 27 the city of New York had to ask Morgan for help, admitting the city of skyscrapers would declare insolvent unless the Mayor was able to get some twenty or thirty millions before November began: The draught in the interbank money market made impossible the renewal of the credits for the city. Morgan invited then the Mayor

---

[131] Ron Chernow, *The House of Morgan*, Ed. Simon & Schuster, 1991, Nueva York, p.p. 111-112.

[132] Ron Chernow, *The House of Morgan*, p. 128.

and some other public officers to his library, where he drafted on his own hand a few lines that fitted in half a sheet of paper, extending a loan valued in thirty million dollars. So it was narrated by Thomas Lamont[133].

> «It was on a Sunday, October 27, in that year, that it developed that New York City was facing a financial crisis. Something like thirty million dollars of short term obligations were coming due, and there was no prospect of renewing them. The money market was completely disorganized. The rates for call money were fluctuating wildly, and, on one or two days, the renewal rate on the New York Stock Exchange had run up as high as 150% per annum. But the moment that the elder Mr. Morgan had heard the story from Mayor McClellan and the other City officials, he undertook to meet the danger.
>
> He thought over the problem for a full forty-eight hours. Then he invited the Mayor and other City officials to his library. After a brief discussion, Mr. Morgan sat down at his desk, picked up a pen and began to write.
>
> Fifteen minutes or so passed. Then he gathered the loose sheets and handed them to his banking associates present, George F. Baker and James Stillman, and to his counsel, F. L. Stetson. The writing constituted a draft of a contract. Under its terms Mr. Morgan agreed to furnish the City with the thirty million dollars required. The contract that he had drawn was so complete in both substance and form that it was accepted at once by the Mayor and his legal advisers, as well as by the bankers. »

The improvised contract was immediately accepted by the Mayor of New York, who could do nothing but tilt his head, begging for mercy as a defeated animal. The newspapers that told the feat failed to explain that Morgan, representing himself, and Stillman for the

[133] Thomas W. Lamont, *Henry P. Davison, the Record of a Useful Life*, p. 86.

Rockefeller group, constituted themselves practically the entire American banking system, the same system that closed the doors to the city a few days earlier, and only that system could reopen these doors to credit. Morgan carefully macerated the fear and unrest of the Mayor of New York for two days and then staged the bailout of the city, solving the problem by only drafting barely fifteen lines in a piece of paper.

One of the immediate consequences of the panic in May 1908 was the creation of a monetary committee focused on studying the causes of the recent crisis headed by Senator Nelson W. Aldrich. Aldrich, who had married his daughter Abigail in 1901 with the unique male heir of the legendary John D. Rockefeller, was an unbeatable choice to preside over a committee devoted to limit the excesses of the American banking industry. The degree of control of the banks over politics at the beginning of the twentieth century was almost absolute. The committee led by Aldrich spent thousands of dollars to reach a conclusion that shouldn't be a surprise to anyone: a new central bank should be established, and not in the hands of the people, but in private hands instead. Recent history has repeatedly disproved the idea that a central bank could better protect the country from panics or crisis.

The creation of the Federal Reserve did not avoid, but was rather one of the chief causes, of the Crash of 1929 and the Great Depression. Nobody knew until many years later that the decision of creating a central bank was not made by the Congress or the Senate or the President, but by Senator Aldrich and a handful of bankers who went on a secret trip to Jekyl Island in 1910.

The Trip to Jekyll Island, 1910

The Federal Reserve System is not Federal; it has no reserves; and it is not a system at all, but rather, a criminal syndicate.

Eustace Mullins, *Secrets of the Federal Reserve.*

The establishment of the Federal Reserve System in 1913 was one of the most important events in the History of the United States. The creation of a new central bank was the product of a decision taken by a few man in a secret reunion in Jekyll Island, a private resort in the State of Georgia. These men, representing the major financial institutions of the country, met a night of November 1910 in the train station of Hoboken, New Jersey. There they started the trip to Jekyll Island in a sealed train car, with the blinds closed, seeking privacy in a discreet place to discuss the issue far from the public opinion.

Henry Davison was a senior partner of *J.P. Morgan & Co.*, co-founder of *Bankers Trust* and Vice President of the *First National Bank.* Paul Warburg, the man who most publicly spoke for a system of central banking was a partner of *Kuhn & Loeb* and a delegate of Frankfurt. And Frank Vanderlip, President of *National City Bank,* was the main agent of the Rockefeller family. There were also some assistants and Senator Nelson Aldrich, who months ago promoted the "Aldrich Plan", a failed project that preceded the "Federal Reserve Act". When they arrived to Brunswick station they met a group of journalists who expected to publish any story about some of the most powerful man of the planet gathering in a train, but Davison approached them and he persuaded them to avoid publishing anything of what they saw. The bankers knew their hand should not be seen in the Federal Reserve. The monetary Panic of 1907 was still very vivid in the minds of the American people and any law from Wall Street would spark a public outrage, especially if it was related to a new central bank.

The meeting lasted nine days and it barely appeared in any newspaper. The story of the Federal Reserve was virtually unknown to the American people until Eustace Mullins published *Secrets of the Federal Reserve* in 1952. The Jekyll Island club was at the beginning of the twentieth century what the Bilderberg Club is today; one of these private discussion forums where the most influential men of the country gather to direct the world policy in a more or less informal way. *The Times*, in the Obituary of George F. Baker published in 1931 stated:

> «[134]The exclusive Jekyl Island Club lost one of its most distinguished members with the death of George F. Baker at New York tonight… When the famous Jekyl Island Club was formed the combined wealth of its charter members was said to represent one-sixth of the world's total accumulation. The original roster included Vanderbilts, Astors, Goulds, Rockefellers, Morgans, Bakers, Mills and others of that rank. »

The story of the secret trip can be reconstructed from the memoirs of the protagonists. The biography of Henry Davison names five individuals Davison himself, Nelson Aldrich, Paul Warburg, Frank A. Vanderlip and Abram Piatt Andrew[135]. The excuse for the secret meeting was a duck hunt, although probably these days none was taken down.

> «[136]Aldrich's biography which appeared in 1930, writes entertainingly of the so-called Jekyl Island trip which was made In November of 1910…
>
> Davison realized, just as the experienced Senator Aldrich had realized, that the elaborate Investigations and the report of the Monetary Commission would go for little, unless some practicable

---

134 New York Times, July 2, 1931, *Jekyl Island Club Loses Leader in Banker*.

135 Thomas W. Lamont, *Henry P. Davison, The Record of a Useful Life*, p.p. 96-97.

136 Thomas W. Lamont, *Henry P. Davison. The Record of a Useful Life*, p. 97.

scheme for American banking and currency reform were evolved from the work of the Commission. Yet how was such a plan to be worked out? Davison's ready and resourceful mind gave an answer to Senator Aldrich's Insistent question on this point He would gather together a few tried and experienced banking men, and together with the Senator they would journey to the remote Jekyl Island Club, off the southeastern corner of Georgia. There without interruption, they would spend a week or ten days together and thresh out a plan. Senator Aldrich eagerly accepted Davison's suggestion and left him to make up the party.

Davison invited on this "duck-shooting" trip Paul M. Warburg, then of Kuhn, Loeb & Co., a thorough and experienced student of the art and science of banking; Frank A. Vanderlip, the head of a great banking institution, and himself widely versed in both domestic and international banking and as well a clear draftsman; and Dr. Piatt Andrew, the special assistant to the Monetary Commission and an economist of standing. These four together with Senator Aldrich proceeded quietly to Jekyl Island, and when they returned, after ten days of protracted and indefatigable discussion and labor, there was a "Plan" in hand. »

Paul Warburg, some months before dying explained the story of his trip. In his recall he mentioned a sixth man, Arthur B. Shelton:

«[137]The small party, consisting of Senator Aldrich, Mr. Shelton, secretary, and Professor A. Piatt Andrew, special assistant of the Monetary Commission, Davison, Frank A. Vanderlip, and myself, set out on its trip to Jekyl Island in November, 1910. It spent a week in complete seclusion and privacy, and it developed and formulated then and there the first draft of what later became known as the Aldrich Bill. »

---

[137] Thomas W. Lamont, *Henry P. Davison. The Record of a Useful Life*, p. 98.

Benjamin Strong[138], who held the seat of Governor during 14 years, till the day of his death, was not ignorant of the plan. He wrote:

> «[139]Throughout all the discussion that preceded the organization of the Federal Reserve System Davison's attitude and labors were most constructive. At that time I was being urged to resign the presidency of the Bankers Trust Company and to governor of the Federal Reserve Bank. Davison was a supporter of the Owen-Glass plan. Although he had preferred the Aldrich plan. It was, In fact, Harry and Jack Morgan who finally urged upon me that the organization of the Federal Reserve Bank of New York was a duty which I could not escape and should not decline. »

During the atypical elections of 1912, the main candidates to the presidency held in their program a monetary reform. Taft and the Republican Party prepared the Aldrich Plan, while Woodrow Wilson and the Democrats presented the Federal Reserve Act. Both paid the utmost care to avoid mentioning that both reforms had identical aims and only diferred in the title and the wording. Congressman Charles Lindbergh, father of the famous aviator, denounced in 1911 the true object of the Aldrich Plan, a project presented by his own party[140]:

> «Wall Street brought on the 1907 panic and got the people to demand currency reform; brought the Aldrich-Vreeland Currency bill forward. And of if it dares will produce another panic to pass the Aldrich central bank plan. We need reform, but not at the hands of Wall Street.»

---

[138] He replaced Henry Davison as Vice President of the *First National Bank* and as Vice President of *Bankers Trust Company*.

[139] Thomas W. Lamont, *Henry P. Davison. The Record Of A Useful Life*, p. 102

[140] New York Times, 9 July 1911, *Wants a Bank Inquiry. Republican Insurgent Sees Something Behind Aldrich Plan.*

The Aldrich Plan of the Republicans, and the Federal Reserve of the Democrats, had the same goal of establishing a third, private and definitive central bank. The plan of Senator Aldrich was never voted because the Republicans lost control of the Congress in 1910 and the Oval Office in 1912. The Democrats simply took the project of central banking at the same point where Aldrich left it. Congressman Carter Glass and Senator Robert L. Owen gave their name to the law to avoid any sort of suspicion, although Senator Aldrich was behind the new law, this time under the wrapping provided by the Democrat Party.

The Owen-Glass Act, by which the Federal Reserve was established, was passed in the Congress in September 18, 1913, and in the Senate in December 19 without a consensus in both houses. On December 22 such discrepancies were solved with an unprecedented speed and the act was approved in both houses. A high number of senators and congressman had already started their Christmas holidays, believing –erroneously- that such a differences would not be discussed until January, at least. Most politicians didn't even had the chance of reading it and whoever did would hardly infer its meaning, as the text was written in a deliberately misguiding style. There was no mention at all of a private central bank, but several federal banks, and the text repeated several insubstantial and ambiguous remarks in a banking jargon unintelligible for the average citizen, including vague expressions such as "mobilization of credit", "rediscount of commercial paper" or "currency elasticity". The Act mentioned supervision and the bait for congressman was an attached provision to limit the power of the Money Trust and regulate the interlocked directorates, which gave some sort of apparent respectability to the Act. But this provision was discussed in a different voting, and unlike the *Federal Reserve Act* it was not passed. The secrecy of the operation is clear in the testimony of his chief architect, Paul Warburg, who later on dared talk about a conference with Senator Aldrich, avoiding a mention to the trip to Jekyll Island:

«[141]The results of the conference were entirely confidential.

Even the fact that there had been a meeting was not permitted to become public. »

It was almost impossible to found headlines about the Federal Reserve Act in the main journals of the country, in the following days. Most of these papers, under control of the Money Trust, avoided any mention about a law of such a magnitude, and in the few cases where the act was named nothing led to believe a third private central bank was about to be established. In December 18 the *New York Times* only repeated some of the same abstractions contained in the Owen-Glass Act, including some statements inconsistent with the truth, such as the the law would promote the gold standard. There were no gold reserves in the Federal Reserve, and the system did not held any relation with the gold standard. Its twenty five pages hide a unique and unequivocal project; to create a new and private central bank.

---

[141] Paul Warburg, *The Federal Reserve System, Its Origin and Growth, vol. I*, p. 60, MacMillan, 1930, New York.

THE FIRST BOARD OF GOVERNORS OF THE FEDERAL RESERVE, 1914

Left to right, Paul Warburg of *Kuhn & Loeb*, Vice Governor, J.S. Williams, W.H.G. Harding and A.C. Miller. Below, C.S. Hamlin, William McAdoo, son in law of Woodrow Wilson and Secretary of Treasury, and Frederick Delano, uncle of Franklin Roosevelt.

The Federal Reserve, 1914

The international bankers put their utmost care in disguising their true motives. They avoided using the name of a central bank and they devised a secret plan with the purpose of avoiding the Americans to establish any relation with Wall Street. They designed a system initially made of four banks but later came up with the idea of twelve banks, in order to arrange the system as if it was federal and not centralized, although only the Bank of New York was operational in reality. As author Eustace Mullins points out, the other eleven banks were just expensive mausoleums to maintain the appearance of a decentralized and public system.

As opposed to the general belief, the Federal Reserve is not a public entity but a private entity[142], and it's not a source of capital but a source of credit. Congressman Wright Patman pointed out that [143] "every dollar in existence represents a dollar of debt owed by an individual, a business firm, or a governmental unit." This meant in practice that the shareholders of the Federal Reserve, that had the monopoly over the printing of American currency, would automatically obtain annual interest on every dollar issued, making use of a right of issuance never delegated by the Constitution of the United States, as Thomas Jefferson pointed out.

The Federal Reserve of 1914 had Benjamin Strong of *Bankers Trust* as Governor and Paul Warburg of *Kuhn & Loeb* as Vice Governor. The board, made of seven members, included politicians as William McAdoo, the Secretary of Treasury married with the daughter of President Woodrow Wilson, and Frederick Adrian Delano, the uncle of the future president Franklin Delano Roosevelt.

How many riches did the bankers amassed due to the grant as a monopoly over the printing of American money? The Federal Reserve,

---

[142] It develops a public interest function, but as a private entity.
[143] Wright Patman, *A Primer on Money*, p. 17.

entirely in the private hands of its "member banks" proved to be such a profitable business as they expected. According to Thomas Lamont:

> «[144]It may not be amiss to set down here a few figures, just to show the importance and primacy of the workings of the Federal Reserve Bank of New York. The Bank opened its doors for business on November 16, 1914, with a paid-in capital of $3,321,950; on December 31, 1928, shortly after Benjamin Strong's death, its capital was $50,123,950, surplus $71,281,905, deposits $988,776,865, reserves $738,738,422, chiefly gold against notes issued. These figures give some little idea of the material growth of the institution during the fourteen years of Benjamin Strong's administration. »

The dramatic increase in the profits in just fourteen years is not strange at all, if we consider that every dollar issued by the Federal Reserve for the United States is not capital but credit, and the rate of interest is charged to the American people. As notes in legal tender before 1914 were removed from the market, and replaced with Federal Reserve notes, the interest collected by shareholders –called "member banks" in the Federal Reserve jargon- grew proportionally.

In April 1914 the twelve banks of the Federal Reserve had issued shares worth 74,740,800 dollars, a capital entirely acquired by a small group of American banks[145]. Eustace Mullins suggested the operation was closed by paying only a fraction of the money and cancelling the remainder with mere accounting entries, in what is known as paper issued against paper[146]. At the end of the day the Federal Reserve was able to issue bank notes *ad infinitum.*

If the Federal Reserve was by no means a public institution, who were its owners? As in the case of the *First Bank* and the *Second Bank of*

---

144 Thomas W. Lamont, *Henry P. Davison. The Record of a Useful Life*, p. 61.

145 New York Times, April 30, 1914, *Take Reserve Bank Stock.*

146 Eustace Mullins, *The Secrets of the Federal Reserve*, p. 36.

the United States, and despite being granted by the Government a state monopoly on a subject of public interest, nowadays the stock allocation is a complete mystery undisclosed for Americans, as its accounting in detail is not available to the public. We know each of the twelve regional banks issued their own shares, and we know that the Federal Reserve Bank of New York, the apex of the system, issued 203.053 shares[147]. Provided the Federal Reserve has never made public the list of its owners or "member banks", we can consider the version of Eustace Mullins, which by the way is the only one known today. This was the shareholder structure of the main bank members of the Federal Reserve in the fifties[148]:

* 30,000 shares *National City Bank*: being its largest shareholders *J.P. Morgan & Co.,* the Rockefeller family, some of its agents as James Stillman, the heirs of Moses Taylor, and the brothers Pyne, Percy and Moses Taylor, the last of them the President of *First National City Bank*.

* 21,000 shares *National Bank of Commerce*: A bank whose largest shareholder was Morgan, run by corporations as *Equitable Life*, *Mutual Life*, *J.P. Morgan & Co.*, *Kidder, Peabody & Co.*, and individuals like J.P. Morgan Jr., E.J. Berwind (mining developer and a Morgan's partner), George F. Baker (President of the *First National Bank*), Thomas Fortune Ryan (*Equitable Life*), and Henry P. Davison (*First National Bank, Bankers Trust*); by different agents of Frankfurt as Paul Warburg, Jacob Schiff or Levi P. Morton; and other investors as Mary W. Harriman, the widow of E.H. Harriman or William Waldorf Astor, Viscount of Astor.

* 15.000 shares *First National Bank*: a bank whose foremost shareholders were George F. Baker, his son George Baker Jr., *J. P. Morgan & Co.*, Henry P. Davison and Mary C. Thompson, the widow

147 *Annual Report of the Comptroller of the Currency, vol. I,* Washington Government Printing Office, 1915 p. 155, Federal Reserve Bank of St. Luis.

148 Eustace Mullins, *Secrets of the Federal Reserve*, p. 34. The breakdown of the major shareholders is based on an article of the New York Times, 23 September 1914, *Banks' Stock Full of Surprises*.

of Frederick F. Thompson, the co-founder of *First National Bank* and the *Chase National Bank.*

* 6.000 shares *Chase National Bank:* mostly under control of George F. Baker and the Thompson family, founders also of the *First National Bank.*

* 6.000 shares *Marine Midland*, a bank later acquired by *HSBC* in 1999, no known relations with the banks that we deal with in this work.

We find that the banks after the Federal Reserve were in the hands of a dozen bankers and their heirs, names we see repeatedly in this book as J.P. Morgan, Henry Davison, Moses Taylor, James Stillman, Thomas F. Ryan, Frederick Thompson and E.H. Harriman. Also the Rockefellers and to a lesser extent some members of *Kuhn & Loeb* like Paul Warburg or Jacob Schiff.

Mullins renders account of more than a third of the stock issued by the Federal Reserve of New York -78.000 of the 203.053 shares-, and seems to solve the question of who controls today the Federal Reserve. In the fifties four banks shared almost the entire stock at sight. After *J.P. Morgan* acquired some of the banks mentioned here, at the end of twentieth century (see annexes), 92.2% of the stock known of the Federal Reserve -35.4% of total stock- remained in the hands of a single banking institution: If the remaining two thirds we don't know followed a similar pattern we could deduct that the Federal Reserve is today a subsidiary of *J.P. Morgan.*

WOODROW WILSON

28th President of the United States, Governor of the State of New York, President of the Princeton University, awarded the Nobel Peace Prize.

Woodrow Wilson

«In fact, the Virginian, Woodrow Wilson, left an unsurpassed legacy to the nation; he gave us the income tax, World War I, and the Federal Reserve Act. No other President can claim to have saddled his unfortunate fellow countrymen with so many crushing burdens. »

Eustace Mullins.

Thomas Woodrow Wilson, born in 1856, was the son of Scottish-Irish immigrants. Wilson studied Law in the University of Virginia and later in the John Hopkins. He started a career in the academic world as a lector in the Cornell University in 1886 and then wrote some books on political science until in 1902 was elected to preside over the prestigious Princeton University. After that he took the leap to politics with the Democrat Party, and he was elected as Governor from 1911 until 1913 in the State of New Jersey, the *Standard Oil*'s feud.

In the presidential elections of 1912 William Howard Taft was the candidate of the Republican Party, aiming for the renovation of his first presidential term, and on the other hand there was Wilson, for the Democrats. Taft's reelection was taken for sure; he was already in the White House and he was quite charismatic politician, while Wilson was a Princeton academic unknown to the public, a withdrawn man, without great communication capabilities and in general with not much appeal to the people.

All the odds were in favor of Taft but the elections of 1912 were very atypical. The ex-President Theodore Roosevelt, predecessor of Taft in the office and a fellow member of the Republican Party, publically manifested his unrest with Taft and his own party, and despite his political career was more than finished, he decided to render a last service to Jacob Schiff by founding the Progressive "Bull Moose" Party, an excision of the Republicans. This inserted a new arithmetical variable in the elections, by dividing the votes of the Republican Party in two. Teddy Roosevelt not only lost but also caused the disgrace of his old fellow Taft, who lost his re-election to Wilson. The results were as follows:

Woodrow Wilson, Democrat Party 41.8%
Theodore Roosevelt, Progressive Party 27.4%
William Howard Taft, Republican Party 23.2%
Eugene Victor Debs, Socialist Party 6%

The problem with Taft was that he proved to be incapable of taking forward the Aldrich Plan, the great project of centralized banking of the international bankers. Wilson made it possible a few years later. Among the most positive aspects of the Wilson's terms, he made regulations on the child labor, the women's suffrage and the labor reduction to 8 hours in the railroads. He also tried to reduce the power of the trust in the *Clayton Antitrust Act* of the 1914 but his success was as limited as it was the *Sherman Antitrust Act.*

In the second term, in 1917, Wilson showed his most militarist aspect when he declared war on the Central Powers, and when he approved two laws, the *Trading With The Enemy Act* and the *Espionage Act.* The first one restricted the trade with the enemy and the second punished any insubordination or interference with the war operations or even with the recruitment, with prison or even death penalty. The powers of the *Espionage Act* weakened the American civil liberties and extended from 1918 until 1920, widening the range of offences to forms of expression considered disloyal with the government, the institutions and the armed forces. In practice it enabled the government during the periods of war to jail any dissident, objector or anyone who publically declared his opposition to the war. It was a law in conflict with the constitutional freedom of expression (the First Amendment). The sentences could be of five to twenty years in jail.

Wilson also created in 1917 the War Industries Board to centralize the expenditure and the direction of the war budget, and the Committee on Public Information, and euphemism that hid the first

Western office of military propaganda, founded solely to influence and promote a positive opinion to the American people in favor of the Great War. Paradoxically enough, in 1919 Woodrow Wilson received the Nobel Peace Prize thanks to the entry of the United States in the European Great War. Wilson had been reelected by a narrow margin in the 1916 elections under the slogan "he kept us out of war".

The introductory quote in this section faithfully reflects some of the milestones of the Wilson terms: he pretended to be the scourge of the Money Trust, but when he became president he awarded the bankers with a third and definitive central bank, almost a hundred years after the creation of the *Second Bank*. He based his electoral campaign of his second term solely in the American neutrality in World War I, but soon after his reelection he embarked the country into the Great War, sending the very bankers he despised to manage the emerging American war machine.

In fact Wilson kept the country away from the war during his first term because the economic system at that time would have made it impossible to embark in a big scale war, but the international financiers had already planned the entry of the United States in the war long time ago. In 1913 Wilson created a new tax on the personal income to the Americans by approving the Income Tax, and in 1914 he set up the Federal Reserve, a central and that would allow the government to indebt at levels never seen before. The European economies were depleted at that time for the military effort, and probably without the American intervention, the final of the war would have been an early armistice of the powers in conflict. However, the new fiscal system and the Federal Reserve allowed the United States to insufflate more credit in an economically exhausted Europe.

The Men of Wilson

«Since I entered politics, I have chiefly had men's views confided to me privately. Some of the biggest men in the United States, in the field of commerce and manufacture, are afraid of somebody, are afraid of something. They know that there

is a power somewhere so organized, so subtle, so watchful, so interlocked, so complete, so pervasive, that they had better not speak above their breath when they speak in condemnation of it[149]*.»*

Woodrow Wilson, *The New Freedom.*

«[150]*We have restricted credit, we have restricted opportunity, we have controlled development, and we have come to be one of the worst ruled, one of the most completely controlled and dominated, governments in the civilized world — no longer a government by free opinion, no longer a government by conviction and the vote of the majority, but a government by the opinion and the duress of small groups of dominant men. »*

Woodrow Wilson, *The New Freedom.*

The speeches of Wilson prior to his presidency, conveyed the idea for the American people the firm idea that Wilson was not only a brainy academic of Princeton, but also a pragmatic man, a man of character, able to stand up against the trusts like Theodore Roosevelt. This legend of a great president has even aggrandized as time goes by. A glance to his government cabinet, particularly during the second term, allows us to see how objectionable is that view. The team that led Wilson to win the elections included people like Henry Morgenthau Sr., Edward Mandell House and William Mc. Adoo.

Henry Morgenthau Sr., had been Financial President of the Democrat Party in the campaigns of Wilson during 1912 and 1916, and he also supported Wilson's campaign with relevant sums of money from his own pocket. Grateful for that, Morgenthau Sr. was appointed as Ambassador of the United States in the Ottoman Empire, by the time of the Young Turks Revolution[151]. In 1919 he took part in the

---

[149] Woodrow Wilson, *The New Freedom. A Call for the Emancipation of the Generous Energies of a People*, Doubleday, 1913, New York, p.p. 13-14.
[150] Woodrow Wilson, *The New Freedom*, p. 201.

Paris Peace Conference as counselor for Eastern Europe and Middle East, and in several chairs related to relief management, including the Red Cross. Morgenthau's son kept having a crucial role in the Democrat Party some years later, by launching the electoral career of Franklin Delano Roosevelt.

William McAdoo and Colonel Edward Mandell House were the chief campaign advisors of Wilson. McAdoo was a lawyer, President of the *Hudson-Manhattan Railroad*, a railroad enterprise controlled by *Kuhn & Loeb*, and he eventually became Director of the United States Railroad Administration. We can infer that his personal and economic interests coincided with those of the railroad tycoons as Morgan, Harriman, Khan or Schiff. In 1912, the year of Wilson's reelection, McAdoo was Vice President of the National Democrat Committee. During Wilson's term he was Secretary of the Treasury and later he was awarded a position in the board of governors of the Federal Reserve. McAdoo married in 1918 with the daughter of the President, Eleanor Randolph Wilson.

Among all the supporters Wilson had during his political career, Edward Mandell House stood out. He was a businessman of Texas. The heir of a cotton empire who became something similar to a modern political advisor. House helped four of his protégés becoming governors of the State of Texas, and then he achieved the presidency for Woodrow Wilson. House only worked as counselor for his protégés, rejecting any official chair.

During Wilson's mandate, Colonel House unofficially developed the functions of a Secretary of State and a general advisor of Foreign Affairs, being the person of highest trust and consideration of Wilson, acting frequently as his personal emissary. By reading House's papers one realizes that Wilson was no more than a puppet, and House was the true strong man in his administration. House was the mastermind

---

[151] A revolutionary Turkish party which deposed sultan Abdul Hamid II in 1908. During their regime, at least a million Armenian Christians were murdered. See New York Times, December 15, 1915, *Million Armenians Killed or in Exile*.

who persuaded Wilson for the creation of the Federal Reserve, working closely with the international bankers and Senator Aldrich, and took on behalf of Wilson some of the most important decisions of the twentieth century.

The opening speeches of Wilson are not exempt from hypocrisy; Wilson knew well the existence of a handful of men that composed a discreet economical elite that silently run the country. Upon his arrival to the White House he place many of these man at the very heart of his government.

Coronel House

«Mr. House is my second personality. He is my independent self. His thoughts and mine are one. If I were in his place I would do just as he suggested… If any one thinks he is reflecting my opinion by whatever action he takes, they are welcome to the conclusion. [152]*»*

Woodrow Wilson on E.M. House, *The Private Papers of Col. House.*

House, the second personality of Wilson, was the son of a family of immigrants of Dutch origin named Huis. His father, a cotton merchant, was one of the richest man of Texas. House lived thanks to the huge rent provided by the cotton plantations he inherited, and devoted an important amount of his time and money to advise politicians. House actually did not make any military career, but he got his rank of Colonel as an honorary title granted by one of his political protégés from Texas. In 1911 Woodrow Wilson was his personal choice for the United States presidency. He was not a candidate who initially thrilled the Wall Street tycoons, due to some assertions he did during the campaign, but House managed to make them change their minds and revert these opinions. House wrote:

---

[152] Charles Seymour, *The Intimate Papers of Colonel House, Behind the Political Curtain, vol. I*, Houghton Mifflin Company, 1926, Boston, p. 114.

«[153]I took lunch with Colonel Harvey yesterday… he told me that everybody south of Canal Street was in a frenzy against Governor Wilson and said they were bringing all sorts of pressure upon him to oppose him. He said he told them he had an open mind, and that if they could convince him he was a dangerous man he would do so.

He said that Morgan was particularly virulent in his opposition to Governor Wilson. I asked him what this was based upon, and he said upon some remark Governor Wilson had made in Morgan's presence concerning the methods of bankers and which Morgan took as a personal reference.

He told me that he believed that any amount of money that was needed to defeat Governor Wilson could be readily obtained. He said he would be surprised if they did not put $250,000 in New Jersey alone in order to defeat delegates favorable to his nomination.

We are going to try to devise some plan by which we can use this Wall Street opposition to Governor Wilson to his advantage. »

House mentioned the former hostility of Morgan, and quite obviously, the money of New Jersey he spoke belonged to the Rockefellers and the *Standard Oil of New Jersey*. Two fortunes and influential powers as those would be enough to turn the campaign in favor of one candidate or another.

A psychological profile of Wilson, as understood from the papers of House and other sources, reveals his insecurity and his tendency to evade from reality. For that reason he was extremely dependent on House. George Wickersham, the Attorney General of the United States under Taft's term, served in other public positions under the terms of Wilson and Hoover. He privately expressed their doubts about the character of the President:

---

153 Charles Seymour, *The Intimate Papers of Colonel House, vol. I*, p. 51

Mr. George W. Wickersham to Mr. E. S. Martin (forwarded to Colonel House). New York, February 3, 1914

«My dear Mr. Martin,

Your editorial for February 11 is very sane. The trouble with Mr. Wilson is that he lives in an imaginary world. He fancies that a thing should be so, and it *is* so. Which is all very well until a large enough number of people begin to inquire, "Is it so?" Then, like "the unsubstantial fabric of a vision" vanishes. Unlike it, it *does* leave a mark behind.

Yours faithfully,

George W. Wickersham[154]»

House was not only Wilson's chief advisor and confident, but he was also the attorney of the trusts, and the "King Solomon" to whom the American tycoons came when they needed help. The great monopolists took for granted that the usual way of settle their conflicts was getting closer to any influential politician of Washington, and during the times of Wilson's mandate that man was House. For instance, in 1914 the patriarch of the Speyers came to him with the hope that Wilson could fix an increase in the railroad rates, very concerned because the free market could harm the profitability of their industry.

Mr. James Speyer to Colonel House. New York, March 12, 1914

«My dear Colonel House:

I am glad you are coming back soon! I am satisfied that the gentlemen in Washington do *not* realize the seriousness of the

154 Charles Seymour, *The Intimate Papers of Col. House, vol. I*, p. 132.

financial situation through the general impairment of railroad credit. The Interstate Commerce Commission shows no disposition to hurry its decision, as to an advance in rates; on the contrary, they have again extended time for hearings and are asking more questions, etc. Meantime gross and net earnings are declining and the weaker roads like the Southern Railway, Chesapeake and Ohio, etc., cannot sell their bonds except at bankruptcy figures, *if* at all. I can only repeat that in my opinion, which I do *not* express publicly, we are face to face with the possibility not of *one* but of *several* receiverships of the big railroad systems...

Something must be done and done soon, in a big and courageous way, to stop these attacks by Government agencies, both Federal and State, if disaster is to be averted. We need a practical and constructive policy and measures...

James Speyer[155]»

In March 22, 1913 House diaries told the visit of Henry Clay Frick, the partner of Andrew Carnegie and President of the *Carnegie Steel Company*. He was known as one of the most hated and cruelest businessman of the United States, for his tyrannical character and the brutal repression he uses against the trade unions[156].

«March 22, 1913: Mr. Frick came at eleven. He wished to know whether I thought it was possible to settle the United States Steel corporation suit outside the courts. He declared that he came of his own initiative and no one knew he was doing so. He wanted

---

[155] *The Intimate Papers of Col. House, vol. I*, p. 133.

[156] The strike of Homestead in 1892 was notorious. Frick dispersed a crowd of steel workers by sending 300 armed detectives of the Pinkerton Detective Agency. A pitched battle started, and many agents of the Pinkerton Agency and demonstrators were killed or injuried. The Governor sent thousands of military forces to restore order until the mining operations back to normal.

the matter kept confidential, excepting the president and Attorney-General… I promised to mention the matter and to see what could be done…[157]»

House spoke about this issue with Wilson, but the President dealt with the issue refusing a special consideration, and referred him directly to the Attorney General. Wilson did not embrace entirely the Wall Street interests yet, and still held the naïve belief that it was him, and not the tycoons, who ruled over the United States. The thoughts of Wilson and House was not one, as Wilson himself had stated, but Wilson's thoughts were actually House's thoughts.

The Papers of House: A Chronology of the Federal Reserve

«More than fifty years ago the Morgan firm decided to infiltrate the Left-wing political movements in the United States. This was relatively easy to do, since these groups were starved for funds and eager for a voice to reach the people. Wall Street supplied both. The purpose was not to destroy, dominate, or take over but was really threefold: (1) to keep informed about the thinking of the Left-wing or liberal groups: (2) to provide them with a mouthpiece so that they could "blow off steam," and (3) to have a final veto on their publicity and possibly on their actions, if they ever went "radical"[158]. »

Carroll Quigley, *Tragedy and Hope.*

The most comprehensive perspective about the origins of the Federal Reserve is provided by Colonel House, a true ambassador of the bankers in the White House. His participation on the creation of the Federal Reserve traces back at least to 1911 and it's proven in detail in his private papers. These are extracts of the documents of House.

---

[157] *The Intimate Papers of Col. House, vol. I,* p.p. 128-129.
[158] Carroll Quigley, *Tragedy and Hope*, p. 938.

November 25 1911, Letter of House to William Jennings Bryan[159].

«He [Wilson] is also opposed to Aldrich plan, but I think you are both wrong there. You will have to convert me the next time I see you.

I am inclined to think that Aldrich is trying to give the country a more reasonable and stable system. It also seems to me a long way in advance of the money trust which now dominates the credit of the nation. [160]»

The cynicism of House in criticizing the Money Trust was out of measure, and as we will be able to see later on, it was Morgan himself who wrote the plan of the Federal Reserve with his own hand. Expressing the opposite of what he thought was the usual way for House to probe the opinion of the other person without exposing his own real motives.

The banker's plan necessarily had to be brought up at a parliamentary level, and House established contact with some politicians to be his voice in the Congress. He found in Congressman Carter Glass the most suitable spokesperson for enacting the Federal Reserve Act in Washington.

November 28, 1912, letter of House to Wilson.

«I had a most interesting hour with Mr. Glass. He candidly confessed that he knew nothing about banking or the framing of a monetary measure. I congratulated him upon this, for I told him that it was much better to know nothing than to know something wrong. He, too, indicated a willingness to do everything in his power to give as speedily as possible a sound economic bill, and upon lines advised by you…[161]»

---

[159] Bryan was the first Secretary of State of Woodrow Wilson.

[160] *The Intimate Papers of Col. House, vol. I,* p. 50.

Glass, who confessed not knowing a damn about banking and currency was named for Wilson as the President of the Committee on Banking and Currency 1913-1918, and Secretary of the Treasury 1915-1920. He gave his name to the two most important laws for the monetary system and for the financial regulation in the United States: He signed the *Owen-Glass Act* of 1913, which allowed the creation of the Federal Reserve in the Wilson term, and twenty years later, he enacted the *Glass-Steagall Act* of 1933, during Franklin D. Roosevelt term, which intended to correct the financial problems that caused the Crash of 1929 and the Great Depression. Congressman Carter Glass was a man who recognized his complete ignorance in such a matters, but he knew how to dance a waltz at the sound set by the international bankers. They prepared the laws to their taste and gave Wilson those ready to be signed[162]:

July 26, 1911, letter of Colonel House to senator Colbertson.

«Dear Senator,

> …I think Woodrow Wilson's remark that the money trust was the most pernicious of all trusts, is eminently correct. A few individuals and their satellites control the leading banks and trusts companies in America. They also control the leading corporations.»

Again, the cynicism in the words of House about the Money Trust was shameful. House also used this strategy with other politicians, trying to persuade them of the eligibility of Wilson, presenting him, when it suited his interests, as a President able to face the power of Wall Street. Wilson's discourse was probably more honest and innocent

---

[161] *The Intimate Papers of Col. House, vol. I,* p. 94.

[162] *The Intimate Papers of Col. House, vol. I,* this quote p. 159, next one p.p. 160-161, and the remaining four excerpts extracted from p. 161.

than House's, and it's almost certain that he didn't knew about the trip of the financiers to Jekyll Island.

The papers of House continue to point out how House supplied Wilson information and research material to forward the banking reform. Obviously, he only handed over reports that supported the interests of the bankers:

> «Colonel House was indefatigable in providing for the President the knowledge that he sought. He collected in his study the banking laws of every nation of Europe. He gathered reports and abstracts from college professors of economics and banking. But he laid chief stress upon his frequent conferences with the bankers themselves, especially those who had had practical experience in drafting previous bills for Republican Administrations. »

House based his information in previous Republican laws, and here he made a very clear reference to the Aldrich Plan.

December 19, 1912.

> «I talked with Paul Warburg over the telephone regarding currency reform. I told of my Washington trip and what I had done there to get it in working order; that the Senators and Congressmen seemed anxious to do what Governor Wilson desired and that I knew the President-elect thought straight concerning the issue. »

February 26, 1913.

> «I went to the Harding dinner[163] and talked with the guests invited to meet me. It was an interesting occasion. I

[163] W.P.G. Harding was Executive Director of the War Finance Corporation (1918-

first talked to Mr. Frick, then with Denman, afterwards with Otto Kahn.[164]»

March 13, 1913.

«Vanderlip and I had an interesting discussion regarding currency reform. »

March 27, 1913.

«Mr. J.P Morgan, Jr. [his son Jack Morgan], and Mr. Denny, of his firm, came promptly at five. McAdoo came about ten minutes afterwards. Morgan had a currency plan already formulated and printed. We discussed it at some length. I suggested that he should have it typewritten and sent to us today.»

This was an admission of magnitude; the law that gave life to the Federal Reserve had been a dictum of old Morgan. In fact the entire plan was typewritten to avoid any suspicion that it was Morgan who wrote it. He wanted to give a strike of personal authority by presenting a draft handwritten, as when he saved the city of New York, but House wisely advised that the document should not so focused on his figure, as this would bring problems to pass the law.

March 24, 1913.

«I had an engagement with Carter Glass at five. We drove in order not to be interrupted… I urged him not to allow… the Senate Committee to change what we had agreed upon in any of the essential features. He promised to be firm. I advised using

---

1919) and Governor of the Federal Reserve Board (1916-1922).

[164] *The Intimate Papers of Col. House, vol. I*, p. 161. *Ibid.* for next two quotes.

honey so long as it was effective, but, when it was not, I would bring the President and Secretary of Treasury to his rescue.

I spoke to the President about this after dinner and advised that McAdoo and I whip the Glass measure into final shape, which he could endorse and take to Owen as his own…

The Currency Bill was brought into the House of Representatives early in the extra session, its main features unchanged from the first drafts decided upon by the President, McAdoo, and the Chairmen of the House and Senate Committees. The initial difficulties threatened by certain elements in the party which tended toward economic freethinking, were safely passed[165]. »

This entry in the diary is interesting, because it becomes evident that the Owen-Glass Act only belonged to Senator Carter Glass in the name and the signature. House warned Glass about the possible existence of any freethinker congressman who might interfere with the law, trying to protect the public interest of the American people.

October 31, 1913.

«Paul Warburg was my first caller and he came to discuss the currency measure. There are many features of the Owen-Glass Bill that he does not approve. [166]»

November 17, 1913.

«Paul Warburg telephoned about his trip to Washington. He is much disturbed over the currency situation and requested an interview, along with Jacob Schiff and Cleveland H. Dodge… He had a feeling that the President knew what he was doing and did

[165] *The Intimate Papers of Col. House, vol. I*, p.p. 161-162.

[166] *The Intimate Papers of Col. House, vol. I*, p.p. 164-165, next quote p.p. 165-166.

not need any more advice than he was getting from the channels he himself selected. I told him I shared this view and that, since all the experts disagreed, it left one in doubt as to what to do.

Mr. Schiff and Mr. Warburg came in a few minutes. Warburg did most of the talking. He had a new suggestion in regard to grouping the regional reserve banks, so as to get the units welded together and in easier touch with the Federal Reserve Board. Mr. Schiff did not agree as to the advisability of doing this. He thought the regional reserve banks should be cut down to four and let it go at that. »

Paul Warburg phoned House, probably concerned about Wilson's doubts, and added he did not think any other information should be provided to the President unless that he proposed. Needless to say, because House already delivered him the information that Paul carefully had selected.

February 21, 194, letter of Colonel House to the President.

«Any recommendation made by members of Congress should be prima facie evidence of unfitness, and I would not take any suggestions from that quarter without the most careful Investigation. What I mean is that their recommendations would be political, and therefore largely worthless[167]. »

House warned Wilson to hermetically seal the law against the interference of the politicians, these meddlers, representatives of the American people. The banker's plan was masterfully executed, and even Jacob Schiff congratulated Jacob Schiff personally for the services rendered:

December 23, 1913, letter of Jacob Schiff to Coronel House.

---

[167] *The Intimate Papers of Col. House, vol. I*, p.p. 169-170.

«My dear Colonel House,

I want to say a word of appreciation to you for the silent, but no doubt effective work you have done in the interest of currency legislation and to congratulate you, that the measure has finally been enacted into law…

Jacob H. Schiff[168]»

In addition to the burden of a new central back over the shoulders of the American people, Wilson created an income tax over the families, a measure enforced by an amendment of a doubtful legality. With the Federal Reserve and the income tax the international financiers provided the United States with the economical machinery needed for the country to enter in the Great War. Taxes, debt and inflation were necessary tools for finance a public expenditure of such a magnitude[169]. The only thing missing was a *casus belli,* a reason to persuade the American people of the imperative need to go to war.

Hamburg America Lines: A Plot in Four Parts, 1914

At the beginning of the twentieth century Europe was a melting pot of imperialist ambitions. The greatest rivalry, which confronted

---

168 *The Intimate Papers of Col. House, vol. I,* p. 174.

169 While Paul Warburg laid the monetary foundations for the Great War in United States, Max settled the fiscal basis for the development of the German militarism. Max thought the Reich suffered a disadvantage against Russia, Britain or France because it lacked a tax base. In 1907 he gave a speech in a The Germans Bankers' Association under the suggestive title of *Financial Preparedness for War*, where he estimated the cost of a hypothetical European war in 22.000 million marks a year. His conclusion was that Germany was unprepared for war, and in 1909 he persuaded the Hamburg Chamber of Commerce to support a formal declaration requesting a rise in the taxes to the Kaiser. Niall Ferguson, *High Financier. The Lives and Time of Siegmund Warburg*, Penguin Books, 2011, Londres, p. 17.

Germany and France, could be traced back to the war they fought in 1870, which ended with the defeat of Napoleon III. The fragile balance of powers stood still until the colonial quarrels of both powers over Morocco appeared, first in 1905, and again in 1911. The latest crisis, was very close to hasten the World War I in three years[170]. In 1908 the Austro-Hungarian Empire annexed Bosnia and Herzegovina, and the tensions in the area only increased after the Balkan wars of 1912 and 1913. The war was only a matter of time.

In June 28, 1914, the heir of the Austro-Hungarian throne, the Archduke Franz Ferdinand and his wife were assassinated in Sarajevo by a nationalist Serbian group called Black Hand. A month later the Austro-Hungarian Empire declared war on Serbia and the system of secret alliances of the European powers established at the end of the nineteenth century caused the conflict to reach a worldwide scale. Russia, linked to Serbia by a treaty, started to mobilize troops and Germany declared war in return. France, which was bonded to Russia by another treaty, declared war to Germany, who decided to invade Belgium as the shortest route to France. Great Britain was indirectly linked to France and also Belgium and together with Great Britain came many countries under English influence like Canada, Australia, New Zealand, India or South Africa, and then Japan, bonded also by treaties. Everything took place in less than a month.

---

[170] Wilhelm Regendanz, the Executive Director of *Hamburg Morocco Society,* founded by Max Warburg, was the main figure in the Second Moroccan Crisis. In 1911 he informed the German government that the French were trying to hoard large deposits of copper and fertile agricultural fields in the south of Morocco. Regendanz also complained about the aggressions suffered by German colonists by natives. The fact of the matter is that only kilometers of desert existed, with no value at all and no German inhabited there, but the false claims caused a formal complain of the Kaiser against France. He further sent a warship and started a major diplomatic crisis which was a prelude for the World War I. See Ron Chernow, *The Warburgs*, p.p. 144-147 and Niall Ferguson, *High Financier*, p. 16.

The block consisting in the German Empire, the Austro-Hungarian Empire, the Ottoman Empire and the Kingdom of Bulgaria was known as the Axis powers. The opposite block, known as the Entente Cordiale[171], was composed of a Group of countries led by Serbia, Russia, France, Great Britain, Belgium, Canada, Australia, New Zealand, India, South Africa and Japan. At a later stage Italy (1915) and the United States (1917) joined the Entente countries.

Maybe only incidentally, the German Kaiser Wilhelm II, the British King George V, and the Russian Tsar Nicholas II were grandchildren of Queen Victoria. The three aristocratic cousins embarked all their subjects in a battle that would leave million victims in Europe.

The entry of the United States into World War I changed the course of the conflict and gave that country a worldwide supremacy that lasts until today. Textbooks give credit to the theory that the sinking of the merchant vessel *RMS Lusitania* 1915, by a German submarine, was the chief reason for the United States to declare war on Germany. More than a hundred North American passengers died there, but the sinking of the ship was probably the last relevant factor of a series of provocations that increased tensions between the United States and Germany since 1914. This chain of errors proved to be fatal for Germany.

Since the beginning of the military conflict in 1914, the Anglo German line *Hamburg-America Line* o *HAPAG*[172], as it was known by his German acronym, was the main *agent saboteur* of the Kaiser in American soil, even before that Germany and United States became enemy powers in 1917. The activities of *Hamburg-America Line* included attaching limpet mines attached to almost twenty American ships, a plan to deplete the ammunition supply of the Allied forces and the

---

171 The Franco-British led block in World War I has been usually known by historians as the "Entente Cordiale", but at the time of the entry of the United States in the military conflict, the term "Allies" was indistinctively used.

172 *Acronym of Hamburg-Amerikanische Packetfahrt Actien Gesellschaft.*

participation in a coup in Mexico with the sole purpose of forcing the country to declare war on USA.

The story of *HAPAG,* an Enterprise involved in all espionage and sabotage activities of Germany in American soil, is particularly relevant to our story because Felix Warburg happened to be one of the directors in the American board[173], and his brother Max Warburg was a director in the German board. Ron Chernow, the acclaimed biographer of the finance tycoons like J.P. Morgan or John D. Rockefeller pointed out in his biography of the Warburgs that: *"In 1901 Kuhn Loeb bought a few million HAPAG shares, and five years later M.M. Warburg joined the banking consortium that financed the firm."* It is hard to believe that the illicit activities of *HAPAG* were unknown to the two German bankers, being both directors at opposite sides of the Atlantic Ocean. The situation eventually became so scandalous that in 1918 Paul Warburg had to renounce to his seat in the vice presidency of the Board of Directors of the Federal Reserve[174]. The alleged reason was the expiration of his term, but the real reasons behind the decision were more related to his participation in the Board of *HAPAG,* and the fact that his brother Max was the Kaiser's main advisor was an open secret. And it was also a well-known fact that Max was also a partner of the Kaiser in the shipping line, as Chernow suggests: *"[Káiser William] provided benevolent protection for the firm and was even rumored to be a large stockholder[175]."*

This was not an obstacle for him to run again the Federal Reserve from the shadows, in a more discreet position in the Advisory Council of the bank, since 1921 to 1926. Albert Strauss of *J.W. Seligman & Co* replaced him as Vice Governor[176].

---

[173] New York Times, February 16, 1915, *Two Edged Inquiry. Senate Will Investigate McAdoo and Trust on Ship Bill.*
[174] New York Times, August 10, 1918, *Warburg Now out of the Reserve Board.*
[175] This and previous fragment from Ron Chernow, *The Warburgs,* p.p. 105 & 107.
[176] New York Times, August 23, 1918, *May Succeed Warburg, Albert Strauss of Seligman Firm Considered for the Reserve Board.*

The economic activities of *HAPAG* spread out to Morgan and the Harrimans through several cooperation agreements in certain traffics. Two German banks, *Deutsche Bank* and *Disconto-Gesselschaft,* were also key figures in the Kaiser's secret operations in America. The *HAPAG* spies conspired in American soil in four different lines of investigation.

The first mission entrusted to the spy-bankers consisted in organizing the smuggling of United States with Germany, using the fleet of *HAPAG* as supply vessels for the German army. When War started, the United States were declared a neutral power, which was not entirely truthful. Great Britain remained as a preferential commercial partner, and an essential part of the plan of the Entente countries was based on the naval blockade of supplies to Germany. United States took part in that strategy by dramatically restricting trade with the Central Powers at the beginning of the war.

Not everyone inside the United States seemed to comply with the trade restrictions: *HAPAG* monopolized the traffic between the United States and Germany by means of smuggling goods via some countries in the North of Europe. As soon as 1914, four months after the war started, the British intercepted a vessel called *Fram,* freighted by *Hamburg-America Line*[177] in the Shetland islands. The vessel was full of coal, provisions and oil paste routed to Norway, where it would be reshipped to Germany. Then came the *Somerstad*, the *Lorenzo* and the *Berwind,* all of them property of *Hamburg-America Line* and all of them detained under suspicion of contraband with the Germans[178]. In December the *President*[179], freighted by *Hamburg-America Line,* escaped from the port of La Habana with the lights off and avoiding the port formalities, presumably full of supplies for the Germans. That same month the *Dacia*[180] was intercepted in Port Arthur under suspicion of shipping goods to Germany. The ship, as the others, was freighted by

177 New York Times, November 23, 1914, *The Fram Seized By British Patrol.*

178 New York Yimes, February 27, 1915, *Shiftcharge Against Hamburg-American.*

179 New York Times, December 3, 1914, *Hamburg Liner Flees from Havana.*

180 New York Times, December 29, 1914, *Says E.N. Breitung Got Hamburg Liner.*

HAPAG, and its shipowner was the German banker Edward N. Breitung.

The most striking case was the ship *Hamburg*[181], property of the German shipping line and freighted (hired) by the American Red Cross with the purpose of transporting medical supplies and sanitary staff to the war zone. The ship was renamed as the *Red Cross*, and its American flag was replaced by the German with the authorization of the Congress. It was painted in white and they placed a Red Cross in the hull of the vessel. A request for relief was loudly sent by the Morgan offices in France, requesting donations valued in 250.000 dollars for the construction of a hospital in Paris. Among the signatories there were Junius S. Morgan III, one of the heirs of J.P. Morgan and a Director in *Guaranty Trust*. There were also August Belmont and Jacob Schiff, two well-known agents of the Rothschilds.

After the *Red Cross* was freighted, a doctor named Brown-Landone warned in a Canadian paper that the vessel set sail without a part of the medical supplies and that the Red Cross was a pro-German agency[182]. He affirmed that the Red Cross sent the German soldiers the donations handed over by an association of British women, whose original aim was to aid the British wounded soldiers. Also, Brown-Landone complained that the Red Cross spent 67.000 dollars in the transport of a medical material that other lines had voluntarily offered their ships to do it for free. The Red Cross had discretionally assigned the transport to a German agency as *Hamburg-America Line* without any tender. Finally, the physician pointed out that the true President of the Red Cross was not Woodrow Wilson but Jacob Schiff. The *New York Times*, commenting on Brown-Landone statements, published a refutation in favor of Schiff, acknowledging the banker was one of the 67 original founders of the American Red Cross, but denied Schiff had developed other task than treasurer.

---

[181] New York Times, September 1, 1914, *Red Cross Engages the Liner Hamburg.*

[182] New York Times, January 24, 1915, *Red Cross Refutes Toronto Charges; Denies Dr. Brown-Landone's Statement That British Aid Went to Germans.*

Had the bankers taken advantage of the good faith of the American people? Had *Kuhn & Loeb*, the Rockefellers and the Morgans used the Red Cross as a vehicle to conduct their own private business? Based on what we know about the Red Cross, *Hamburg-America Line*, and the bankers behind both institutions the statement of Brown-Landone is believable; the Red Cross might have helped the bankers to take advantage of the funds for relief, using those in their own profit, for making arbitrary assignments to their own companies, evading the American neutrality by avoiding any kind of border controls, and side with one faction or the other in an armed conflict.

By 1916 the activities of *Hamburg-America Line* in American soil were well known by the public, appearing in countless pages of American newspapers until 1917. These cases did not help to improve the German image in the country in the United States. On January 2, the *New York Times* published a comprehensive report about the German operations. The journal described the smuggling operations as follows[183]:

> «The alien machine in America began to operate the moment Germany declared war on the Allies. As a matter of fact, evidence in the possession of the Department of Justice proves that the machine was oiled even before the war was actually declared…
>
> In the Atlantic and the Pacific at that time were a dozen or more German cruisers and commerce raiders. These ships had to be supplied if they were to continue operations, and the German agents decided that New York, Norfolk, New Orleans, San Francisco and other American ports were "splendid bases" for the purposes in hand…
>
> A fleet of fourteen ships was acquired. The auxiliaries were loaded with supplies for the German raiders, and Dr. Buenz and

---

[183] New York Times, January 2, *Matching Wits with the Teuton Plotters; Tireless, Fearless, and Efficient, the United States Secret Service Agents Have Followed Devious Trails and Uncovered Many Conspiracies.*

his associate "managers" applied for clearance papers and submitted to the Collectors of Customs what were supposed to be bona fide manifests of the cargoes. The clearances were for various ports in the South Atlantic and the Pacific. »

Karl Buenz, the director of *HAPAG* in the United States eventually went to jail with much more serious charges than simply smuggling with countries at war.

The second part of the *HAPAG* plan consisted on the sabotage of as many merchant ships as possible. In 1915 the police revealed a plan of the Germans to obstruct the supply of Allied materials as much as possible, by adhering limpet mines to critical parts of the American ships[184]. The ringleader of this thread was a German Lieutenant in the reserve called Robert Fay, who admitted he was sent to the United States by officers of the Kaiser's secret service. Max Breitung, the nephew of the banker Edward N. Breitung provided most of the 30.000 dollars used in the sabotage of American ships with the purpose of stopping the abundant American exports of ammunition to the Allied forces. The *New York Times* so explained the sabotaje plot[185]:

> «The "ship fires", which in practically every instance followed an explosion of varying intensity… and up to the present time the cargoes of twenty-three vessels, all carrying supplies to the Allies, have been damaged… The fact that many of the ships were liners and carried large numbers of innocent passengers did not deter the plotters. »

Robert Fay proudly recognized to be part of the plot, and confirmed Karl Boy-Ed, the Naval Attaché of the German Embassy, and Franz von Papen, the Military Attaché, were well aware of his

---

[184] New York Times, October 26, 1915, *Men Higher Up Sielded?: Fay Admits the Kaiser's Secret Service Sent Him to America.*

[185] New York Times, January 2, 1916, *Matching Wits with the Teuton Plotters.*

plans. The investigation exposed high ranking members of the Embassy as masterminds of the plan, such as Heinrich Albert, Attaché of the German Ambassador, and Paul Koenig, a sort of private detective in the payroll of *Hamburg-America Line*, a company in the center of all the conspiracy threads of the plot in United States. Koenig as informally known as the "police chief of *HAPAG*", provided information to the Germans about the supplies the Americans was selling to their enemies. The Military Attaché, von Papen, explained many years later in his memoirs the undercover activities of the *HAPAG* spies in the United States:

> «[186]The Hamburg-Amerika Line had employed a private detective named Paul Koenig in their New York harbor offices, and as their liners were no longer running, he was recommended to me. He was a completely reliable and the most intelligent fellow to whom I assigned the task of obtaining all possible information concerning shipments of war material to Europe. In this he was most successful, and I was able to keep the General Staff constantly posted as to their quantity and nature…
>
> He had a number of agents working for him, most of whom were unknown to me, but neither he nor they at any time received orders to carry out acts of sabotage. »

It is a striking fact, to begin with, that a private Corporation as *HAPAG* needed intelligence agents in the staff, and it is even more surprising that their American directors, as Felix Warburg, were ignorant about all that.

The third part of the German plot consisted in depleting the ammunition and explosives supply of United States, which was a neutral country on paper, but in reality exported huge amounts of military material to the Entente countries. This part took place by financing labor unions that promoted strikes in American ammunition

[186] Franz von Papen, *Memoirs*, Andre Deutsch, 1952, London, p. 36.

factories and creating a ghost company named *Bridgeport Projectile Company*, whose only aim was to block the production of American military powder and explosives by any means. Most German people thought –quite accurately- that the United States was the great beneficiary of the war, selling huge amounts of supplies and ammunition to the British. The fictitious company, created by German spies, for instance bought all available supply of powder and phenol, raw matters needed for the production of ballistic projectiles and explosives respectively.

The directors of the *Bridgeport Projectile Company* were Carl Henyan, an old agent of *Hamburg-America Line* and Hugo Schmidt, from *Deutsche Bank*[187]. The letters of Dr. Heinrich F. Albert, Economic Attaché of the German Ambassador, proved the company had been created to break the supply chain of the Entente countries. The problem was that such materials could not be exported to Germany or be used in a productive way. The *Bridgeport Projectile Company* also hindered the supply of plates or molds needed to produce bullets and projectiles. It signed contracts with producers, including exclusivity clauses that later failed to fulfill. The *Bridgeport* then had to pay high penalties due to the breach of contract, but so they managed to delay the production for the Entente countries during months. In other words, the bizarre plan of the *Bridgeport Projectile Company* was simply to spend the money of the Kaiser in subsidizing –more or less undercover- certain American military companies in exchange for not sending material to the Entente countries. This was probably known fact by the American factories and maybe by the government. Von Papen mentioned in his memoirs some years later:

> «[188]As far as I knew, there was only one factory manufacturing gun barrels, and only two major concerns manufacturing explosive

[187] New York Times, November 17, 1915, *Tied Up Munitions By German Trick*.
New York Times, August 18, 1915, *Gompers Confirms Foreign Tampering*.
New York Times, January 28, 1916, *Von Papen Sought Munitions Here*.

powder, the DuPont Powder Company and the Aetna Powder Company. The flood of new contracts could only be met by building additional plants.

Without any clear indication of how long the war might last, the Americans were not inclined to take undue commercial risks…

I was kept well informed of this, because most American banks employed German-Americans, who provided us with very full information about all these transactions without even having to ask for it…

The plan was relatively simple. An American friend, Mr. George Hoadley, was given a contract to build a large factory for the production of guns and ammunition, to be called the Bridgeport Projectile Company. It was to work, to all outward appearances, as an American company, and accept contracts from the Allied Powers. Every firm in the United States making machine tools, hydraulic presses and rolling mills for the manufacture of war material was given enough orders by our company to keep them occupied at full capacity for a couple of years at a maximum rate of delivery. When the allies finally settled their price difficulties in the spring of 1915 and started to place their orders, they found that all the contractors with the equipment to build the necessary factories were fully booked with orders. Our secret had been well kept, and the general belief was that other American firms had bought up the machinery in order to produce for Allied accounts. I suppose in these days Mr. Hoadley might very well be called before the Committee for Un-American Activities, but he was a perfectly good American patriot who did not see why his country's neutrality should benefit only one side in the conflict. »

In fourth place, and finally, the group of German spies conspired to start an armed conflict between Mexico and the United States. Here Germans played both sides, seeking on one hand to get close to the

---

[188] Von Papen, *Memoirs*, p.p. 37-38.

Mexican President Venustiano Carranza, and financing on the other side a *coup d'état* against him, headed by General Victoriano Huerta. This plan was an extension of the other three lines of work, seeking the depletion of the ammunitions and military resources of the Entente, trying to start a war with the neighbor country. The group of *HAPAG* here tried to spread the conflict to other two neutral countries, United States and Mexico.

Frank Dagobert Johannes von Rintelen, a naval intelligence officer who was also involved in the gunpowder plot, was in charge of the Mexico mission. Von Rintelen was member of a prominent German banking family, having served in *Deutsche Bank* and *Disconto-Gesellschaft*, another big bank. The *New York Times* article January 2, 1916 continues as follows[189]:

> «April, 1915, was the "big month" of the "Grand Conspiracy." In that month there arrived in New York Captain Franz von Rintelen if the Imperial German Navy, an intimate of Prince Henry of Prussia...
>
> Von Rintelen came to America with unlimited financial credit. His was the "great mission" of all, for to him had been entrusted the task of instigating strikes in the munition plants engaged in filing orders for the Allies. If he failed to "pull the strikes," he was to switch to the task of engineering American intervention in Mexico, the theory being that if the army had to cross the Rio Grande the United States would need all the ammunition and guns manufactured in this country...
>
> The amount of money used in the effort to tie up the munition plants will probably never be known, although the government has an itemized history of one account of $500,000 that von Rintelen deposited with a certain downtown trust company...

---

[189] New York Times, January 2, 1916, *Matching Wits with the Teuton Plotters.*

Von Rintelen did not wait to find out whether the strike part of his mission would fail before starting work on the Mexican section of his program. He selected General Huerta as the man to lead the New Mexican revolution, and was ready to finance him with a fund estimated at about $12,000,000, with as much more held in reserve. There was a meeting in the Fifth Avenue hotel, attended by various Mexicans who had been prominent during the days of Diaz and Huerta, and the plans of the revolution were agreed upon…

In June all was ready and Huerta left New York ostensibly for the "San Francisco Exposition," but in reality for the blood-soaked fields of his unhappy country. He got as far as Newman, N.M. where the United States took him in hand, locked him up in jail, and ordered him prosecuted for plotting on American territory a revolution that from the very first had never had a chance of getting beyond El Paso. Huerta comes to trial in San Antonio this month.

Thus ended the "mission" of Captain Franz von Rintelen. »

The double game of the Germans became evident in January 1917, when the British intercepted a communication of the German Ministry of Foreign Affairs Arthur Zimmerman to the Ambassador in Mexico, Heinrich von Eckhardt. The telegram he sent, known as "Zimmerman's telegram", gave instructions to offer Mexican President Carranza a covenant against the United States, inviting Mexico to reconquer New Mexico, Texas and Arizona. Zimmerman did not only sent a message to his Embassy by an insecure channel, but also, once the British made it public, he made the mistake of acknowledging it's authorship. He could have simply denied the allegations claiming it was a stratagem of the British intelligence. Von Papen also remembered this incident, but protested this episode was only an exaggeration of the Entente countries. Germany had stockpiled lots of military materials in American soil that could not be exported to Germany, so they thought they could get rid of it by creating a conflict between Mexico and the United States:

> «[190]We found ourselves with increasing quantities of explosives on our hands, and sought some means of disposing of them which would still deny their use to the Allies. We were able to sell a certain amount of this material to Mexico as a normal commercial transaction. I know it has been suggested that this was all part of a long-term plot that reached its culmination with the famous Zimmermann telegram in 1917, proposing a Mexican declaration of war on the United States, but I am afraid that this is too convenient an assumption. We were also engaged in trying to get rid of this mass of useless war material by shipments to other neutral powers, such as Norway, Sweden and Spain, and it cannot be claimed that there was any intention of getting them to declare war on the Entente Powers.»

The German Embassy as in charge of distributing all the funds for the *HAPAG* and Von Rintelen operations. Well aware that the transfer of big sums of money from Germany to the United States, the Economic Attaché Heinrich Albert, decided to use a channel nobody could suspect, the Red Cross. In order to hide the origin of the money the German spies used funds of relief donations delivered to the Red Cross and repaid the equivalent in German reichsmarks.

> «[191]The financing of all these measures came under Herr Albert, who was the financial adviser to the Embassy. The supply of funds presented no particular difficulty. Immense sums had been collected by the German Red Cross, and this money could not be transferred in the normal way, Berlin was advised from time to time of the amount collected, and the Reichsmark equivalent

[190] Von Papen, *Memoirs*, p. 39.
[191] Von Papen, *Memoirs*, p. 39.

was placed at the disposal of the Red Cross in Germany. We were able then to use dollars in the United States. »

In summary, the plan devised by the Military Attaché von Papen and *HAPAG,* together with the corporate spy network of the Warburg brothers, consisted in wasting huge amounts of German money to sabotage certain American industries and put other working to the max. Instead of investing the Kaiser's money in their own military industry or devote their intelligence resources to other Allied countries, the von Papen spies wasted a fortune provoking a neutral power like the United States, and they made mistakes over mistakes in a catalogue or errors unparalleled in the history of espionage. If we are able to see beyond the conflict between several powers unexpectedly drawn into war, it is easy to understand that the conflict benefitted only the international bankers, who would see the debt of nations piling up. Simultaneously, the companies under their control increased the production frenetically; the copper trust of *Anaconda Copper Mining* (Morgan-Rockefeller) saw the orders of copper-made bullet and projectiles shells piling up – funded, by the way, by the ill-fated German government-. The iron, another basic raw material for the war industries was extracted by mining companies like the *Lake Superior Iron,* and processed by the *United Steelworks* (both trusts belonging to the Morgan-Rockefeller block). And finally, the companies resulting of the split of the *Standard Oil* (Rockefeller) would gladly supply fuel or kerosene to the mechanized Allied force.

The family that reaped the biggest profits in war, tangentially mentioned in this book, was the du Pont. During World War I their company *E.I. du Pont de Nemours* was the exclusive manufacturer of powder for military materials in the United States, and its plants produced 40% of the ammo of the entire Allied army[192]. Its president

---

192 William H.A. Carr, as quoted by Ferdinand Lundberg, *The Rich and the Super-Rich*, Bantam Books, 1969, New York, p. 174-176. Nowadays the DuPonts put together one of the greatest familiar fortunes of the World.

Pierre S. du Pont invested heavily on the giant automobile manufacturer *General Motors* before the entry of the United States in the war, and the bulk of the planes and the American tanks was also built by that company. The du Ponts held the majority of the stock in *General Motors* until 1957, the year they had to get rid of their shares due to the Clayton Antitrust Act. By that time they had reaped huge profits from the two great wars. The du Pont were, in last place, an authorized provider for the Army, through his firearms manufacturing company *Remington.*

It is self-evident that the sinking of the *RMS Lusitania* appeared as an isolated incident, even admissible in the context of an international conflict. The United States could also tolerate some acts of contraband and sabotage, but stirring a revolution in Mexico to start a war with United States was a challenge the country could not ignore. It revealed the fact that Germany would do anything to weaken the country. A few months after the Mexican plot was known United States declared war on Germany. The textbooks use to omit the most interesting parts of the story and the only *casus belli* seems to be the sinking of the *RMS Lusitania.*

Before the appearance of the careless German spies, United States was a country of non-interventionist tradition, with no interest in the territorial ambitions of the old continent. Only the persistent provocations of the *HAPAG* spies changed the public opinion of an important part of the people towards an intervention in that war, the biggest known so far.

Formal accusations were made, and several officers and employees of *HAPAG* went to trial and were convicted, including Karl Buenz, general manager of the line in the United States, who died in prison in 1918 at the age of 75[193]. Max Breitung, the nephew of the banker Edward N. Breitung, was detained for the duration of the war [194]. Paul

---

[193] New York Times, September 16, 1918, *Karl Buenz Dies in Atlanta Prision.*

[194] Max Breitung is the nephew of the Jewish German banker Edward N. Breitung. New York Times, 25 de enero 1918, *Max Breitung Interned.*

Koenig, known as "the *Hamburg-America Line's* police chief" pleaded guilty of buying information to *National City Bank* about the Allies purchases and was investigated in relation with the falsification of the affidavits of the witnesses that allegedly saw weapons in the *RMS Lusitania*[195]. It is not known if Koenig finally was imprisoned. Lieutenant Robert Fay, held accountable for the sabotage of several vessels, was convicted to an 8 years sentence. He escaped the prison of Atlanta a few days after his imprisonment, but was captured again two years later in Madrid and extradited to the United States[196]. Despite his serious crimes against the country Von Rintelen was not prosecuted due to his diplomatic immunity and only spent a few years in prison out of American soil. Neither Paul nor Felix Warburg were examined in relation with the murky activities of the German line in the country.

In December 1915 the espionage case of the Germans reached the high ranking members of the German Embassy as Franz von Papen, as the Military Attaché, and Captain Boy-Ed, Naval Attaché. He was never under trial due to their condition of foreign diplomats, although they were recused and expelled from the country[197].

The magnitude of the German operation in the United States became known gradually. The *New York Times* quoted official sources to affirm about Karl Boy-Ed, the Naval Attaché of the German Embassy: *"The trial showed that Captain Boy Ed directed the expenditure of more than three quarters of a million dollars in the financing of the enterprise against 'American neutrality*[198]*.'"*

The huge economic and military effort performed by Germany against a neutral power was hardly justifiable from the strategical point of view, unless as the article pertinently points out, the objective of the

---

195 New York Times, April 7, 1917, *Eight Taken There as German Spies.*

196 New York Times, August 16, 1918, *Fay Captured in Spain.*

197 New York Times, December 4, 1915, *Statements by Boy-Ed and Von Papen; Both Say They Have Merely Done Their Duty; Other Important Dismissals May Follow.*

198 New York Times, January 2, 1916, *Matching Wits with the Teuton Plotters.*

German spies was to involve the United States in a war against Germany. And, for what reason would the *HAPAG* spies would want that? That was exactly the opposite to the interests of Germany, and even America, but probably the banking spies did not work on the premise of national but supranational interests, those of multinational enterprises like *Deutsche Bank*, *Disconto-Gesellschaft* and *Hamburg-America Line,* among others. Those were their own interests.

The full picture of the conspiracy was clearer when the British authorities intercepted Franz von Papen in Falmouth, and despite his diplomatic status they did not hesitate to search in his luggage. A number of revealing documents of the Military Attaché von Papen came into light[199], the most important was the checkbook which unveiled the big unknown, who paid the bills? Von Papen himself was in charge of the financing of the German operations in America, in representation of German ambassador von Bernstorff. The checkbook showed the connection of all conspirators, and all conspiracies merged into *HAPAG*; The smuggling, sabotage, espionage, revolution and even the possibly false affidavits that caused Germany to attack the *Lusitania.* It was known then that Koening was in the payroll of von Papen, and among his informants there was Frederick Scheindl, a clerk of the *National City Bank* who secretly provided information to the Germans about the Allied transactions.

Letting Franz von Papen go proved to be a fatal error for the United States, although this could also be part of the plan of the international bankers. Von Papen became Chancellor of Germany in 1932 and from that office he played a key role in the rise of Adolf Hitler to power. He was part of the first cabinet of the Nazi government and he was Ambassador in Austria later. It was acknowledged in the trials of Nuremberg but nevertheless he was not convicted, again.

[199] New York Times, January 16, 1916, *Von Papen Paid Check to Koening; Hamburg-American Line's Secret Service Chief Is Found Named on Seized Papers.*

HAPAG retained its relevance in Germany after the war. Albert Ballin, the President of the shipping line from 1886 to 1918, committed suicide just before the 1918 armistice, it was said, due to the sinking of his shipping empire. Wilhelm Cuno, successor of Ballin, left the Company from 1922 till 1923 to become the Chancellor of Germany, the seat the chief of spies Franz von Papen held only a few years later. During the brief period of Cuno as chief of the German government, the Belgian occupation of the Ruhr and the hyperinflation of 1923, the worst case known in the Western world. After Cuno was in office, leaving behind a country in ruins, he came back to his comfortable position in the German line. We find man related to the espionage in the World War I like Cuno and von Papen, leading the German inter-war government and driving the country again to a new World War.

In regards to *HAPAG*, its clandestine activities did not cease until three years after those were known, and by then the country had already declared war on Germany. At the end of 1917 the *Hamburg-America Line* building was raided and its good seized by the Government of the United States under the Trading with the Enemy Act, and the offices were used as headquarters of the maritime operations of the Allied forces. The raid of the *HAPAG* offices offered another unexpected turn in the investigation [200]:

> «Strangely enough, before the decision was reached to seize this property under the Trading with the Enemy act, which provides for the administration of enemy property, the United States Government had made arrangements to hire part of two floors in this buildings for the quarters of the Port War Board. In other words, the United States Government was hiring some of its most important war offices directly from the Kaiser, who is personally one of the largest stockholders in the Hamburg American Line. The contract had even been signed by which the

---

[200] New York Times, November 9, 1917, *Hamburg-American Office Seized*.

Emperor of Germany became the landlord for the War Department of the United States. »

The *New York Times* article reveals an unheard of fact: before the raiding of the *HAPAG* facilities, American military authorities were planning to rent space in the Kaiser's building, to establish a center of naval communications between the United States and the Allied countries. The joint American-Allied operations base would be placed therefore right at the side of the German espionage center, the offices of *HAPAG*.

Max Warburg was a director of *HAPAG* in Germany until the Nazis removed him from the board of directors in 1933. In the United States his brother Félix Warburg was a director of *HAPAG*, and Paul Warburg was appointed as head of the War Finance Corporation, an institution he himself had created to manage the military financing of the United States[201]. The course of the war was undoubtedly in the hands of the Warburgs, but it's difficult to determine under which flag did they place their loyalty.

The Warburg brothers were not the only connections of *HAPAG* with the bankers: In 1902, long before the war started, *HAPAG* signed a cooperation agreement with Morgan's *International Mercantile Marine* de Morgan to achieve the monopoly of the Atlantic North[202]. And in 1920 the shipping line of the German spies had the privilege of being the first company to re-establish all the maritime traffics between the United States and Germany that were cancelled during the First World War, by means of an Alliance with Harriman as their counterparts in the United States[203]. That was not the first time *HAPAG* and the

[201] "Mr. [Paul] Warburg was the author of the plan organizing the War Finance Corporation". New York Times, 10 agosto de 1918, *Warburg Now Out of the Federal Reserve Board.*

[202] New York Times, May 10, 1912, *German Lines' Pool With Morgan Ended.*

[203] New York Times, June 6, 1920, *Harriman Line in Great Sea Merger.*
New York Times, October 10, 1920, *Germans Welcome Harriman Ship Deal.*

Harrimans worked together. In 1917 the Warburgs achieved too the monopoly over the transport in the Bolshevik Russia, with their entrepreneurship *Deutsche-Russian Transport* or *DERUTRA,* as described later in this book.

The Sinking of the Lusitania, 1915

Since the war started the fundamental pillar of the British strategy consisted on a commercial blockade of Germany. This proved to be a very successful decision during the war.

At the beginning of the war Germany avoided targeting neutral merchant ships, especially those from the United States, which was the chief trade partner of the British. Some German strategists like Ludendorff strongly advocated for retaliation to the British blockade and in February 1915 they decided to start the "unrestricted submarine warfare", a change in strategy that allowed German submarines to attack any enemy or neutral ship approaching the coasts of Great Britain. The sinking by a German torpedo of one of these merchant ships the *RMS Lusitania,* was considered by many as a tipping point in World War I, because the support of the United States brought a new hope to the Entente countries.

Days before the sinking by a submarine the German Embassy in the United States published official announcements in American newspapers, warning civilians to refrain from traveling on passenger ships entering conflict zones, and very specifically referred to the *RMS Lusitania.*

The American government, on the other side, did not issue any warning regarding the danger that its own citizens could face. The alerts issued by the Germans suggest that they suspected about the shipment of military supplies to Britain, and they were planning to attack the ship.

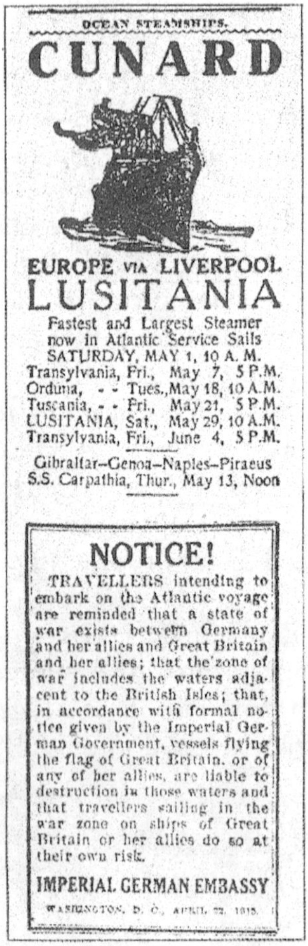

It is easy to assume that the American authorities were informed in advance of German intentions.

Despite the German announcement in the American press, on May 7, 1915 the 45,000-tonne English liner RMS Lusitania entered conflicting waters carrying civilian passengers and cargo. In response, a German submarine torpedoed the English ship off the coast of Ireland, sinking it and causing more than a thousand casualties, a part of which were American citizens. Although the submarine launched a single torpedo, it was a second explosion of unknown origin that caused the ship to capsize.

A spokesman for the German government, Bernhard Dernburg, denounced that the ship was carrying 260,000 pounds of brass, 60,000 pounds of copper, 189 boxes of military equipment, 1,271 boxes of ammunition and 4,200 boxes of cartridges[204]. The sinking, according to Dernburg, was justified and within the international legality represented by the Laws of The Hague.

The German Ambassador von Bernstorff personally explained to Woodrow Wilson that he had several

---

[204] New York Times, May 9, 1915, *Sinking Justified, Says Dr. Dernburg.*

witnesses who signed affidavits, claiming to have seen or heard information about the *Lusitania* carrying arms[205]. The ship could have sailed with two cargo manifests, one authentic, containing the camouflaged military material, and the other one false, presented to the American port authorities. It is practically impossible to prove the existence or not of arms and ammunition for the Allies in the *RMS Lusitania*, but this is in fact an accessory matter, being the essential fact that its collapse was the *casus belli* for the United States to enter the war. And apparently there were both German and American interests determined to involve the United States in the conflict.

Gustav Stahl was one of the main German witnesses of the alleged shipment of arms but the American investigators affirmed that "Stahl never within a mile of the Lusitania, much less on board that ship"[206]. Paul Koenig, the "*HAPAG* chief of police" was investigated in connection with the purchase of false affidavits from the *Lusitania*[207]. The shipping company, through its investigator Paul Koenig could have provided the German ambassador Von Bernstorff with false information about the supposedly existing military cargo of the *Lusitania*. If this were true, *HAPAG* would not only be conspiring against the United States, but also against its own country, Germany, embarking it on a war against a neutral country that would change the course of the destiny of the nation.

Why would the German spies make the Kaiser believe that the *Lusitania* carried military supplies for the Allies if this were not true? Perhaps the real objective of *HAPAG* was to make the United States declare war on Germany, in view of how ineffective and discreet their operations in a neutral country had been, as well as dangerous. Kaiser Wilhelm II had entrusted Germany to banker Max Warburg, director of *HAPAG* in Germany, while Wilson entrusted the fate of his country to

---

205 New York Times, June 3, 1915, *Affidavits About Lusitania Guns.*

206 New York Times, June 12, 1915, *Seek Men Higher Up In Affidavit Case.*

207 New York Times, Dec 18, 1915, *Conspiracy Started Here.*

his brothers Paul and Felix. The Kaiser, Wilson, or maybe both of them had been deceived.

There was a natural interest among the Allies, and even within certain economic sectors in the United States, to provoke the American entry into the armed conflict. The papers of Colonel House constantly link him to the Warburgs and other international bankers, and the strangest passage of his writings refers precisely to the sinking of the *Lusitania*. Colonel House knew perfectly well the danger of the ship and the American passengers traveling on that fateful day in May. His personal diaries suggest that House and others knew in advance of its collapse, and intended to use it with the aim of generating anti-German sentiment in the United States. House traveled in the *Lusitania* only a few months before, and on the day of the tragedy, he recorded some very explicit notes in his diary:

> «[208]On the morning of May 7, House and Grey drove out to Kew. "We spoke of the probability of an ocean liner being sunk" recorded House, "and I told him if this were done, a flame of indignation would sweep across America, which would in itself probably carry us into the war." An hour later, House was with King George in Buckingham Palace. "We fell to talking, strangely enough," the Colonel wrote that night, "of the probability of Germany sinking a trans-Atlantic liner... He said, "Suppose they should sink the *Lusitania* with American passengers on board..."
>
> That evening House dined at the American Embassy. A dispatch came in, stating that at two in the afternoon a German submarine had torpedoed and sunk the *Lusitania* off the southern coast of Ireland. Many lives had been lost. »

Hours before the collapse of the *RMS Lusitania*, Colonel House, the President's right-hand man and the ambassador of the international bankers, spoke with the King of England and his Foreign Minister

[208] Charles Seymour, *The Intimate Papers of Col. House, vol. I*, p. 432.

about the possible -rather certain- collapse of the Lusitania, as a possible catalyst event for the entry of the United States into war. This strange and "unfounded" hypothesis was formulated House hours before the sinking, and then went to dinner at the American Embassy to have the first news. It is evident, as we know by his own writings, that he was confident of the sinking of the vessel before it occurred. It also follows that House himself may have been interested in it, and the idea that House organized the incident with the help of the Warburgs it is by no means discarded. The second explosion could be fueled by ammunition that was transported, but it is also possible that someone wanted to make sure that the ship disappeared in the cold English waters.

Max and Felix, co-owners of *HAPAG*, could have been part of a double betrayal of Germany and the United States, buying false statements from the Lusitania and preparing for their destruction, as part of a continuing effort to provoke the conflict between the two countries. Meanwhile Paul, who had worked with House at least since the founding of the Federal Reserve, organized the American war finances by putting men of his trust at the head of the War Finance Corporation. Max in Germany and Felix in the United States directed the activities of subversion of *HAPAG* from the boards of directors of their respective countries. Undoubtedly, the bankers did not lack economic motivations[209]. President Wilson thought that Paul and Felix Warburg were his main asset in intelligence and that Max was a double agent in the service of the United States, while the Kaiser trusted Max and his brothers in New York to ensure the Germany the victory. The two statesmen placed their trust in the great service that the Warburgs seemed to lend to their own country.

The bankers-counselors-spies put themselves at the head of the intelligence services on both sides, and any sensitive information that

---

[209] During the war close to thirteen million men died on the different countries for injuries and illness. Only in two battles of 1916, Verdun and Somme, the losses were 1.7 millions. Quigley, *Tragedy & Hope*, p. 255.

came to the governments at war would before fall into their hands. Their motivations were more economic than patriotic. Some of the bankers at the head of Western secret services were:

- Sir William Wiseman (partner in *Kuhn & Loeb)* acted as "*head of the British Intelligence Service in the United States*[210]". He was the chief liaison officer between the British and American espionage services.
- Max Warburg, (*HAPAG, M.M. Warburg & Co.*) was the Kaiser's chief advisor. He boasted the influence he exerted over the emperor: *"The Kaiser thumbed the table violently and shouted, 'Must you always be right?" but then listened carefully to Max's view on financial matters.* [211]" Some sources also point to Max Warburg as chief of German espionage. Bankers like Franz von Rintelen (*Deutsche Bank, Disconto-Gesellschaft*) o Hugo Schmidt (*Deutsche Bank*) were protagonists in the cases of espionage and sabotage in the United States, along with Max and Edward Breitung. They were also involved were important *HAPAG* members such as Carl Henyan, Paul Koenig and Karl Buenz.
- Paul Warburg (*Kuhn & Loeb & Co., HAPAG*) was a close adviser to Wilson, he directed monetary policy in the United States from the Federal Reserve and organized war finances from the War Finance Corporation.
- Bernard Baruch, a Jewish broker from Wall Street, was assigned by Wilson to head the Military Industries Board. He managed the spending of millions of dollars of American taxpayers without any public merit except being one of the main economic contributors of the Democratic Party. Roosevelt, a man who also knew how to be

---

[210] Charles Seymour, *The Intimate Papers of Col. House, Into the World War, vol. III* Houghton Mifflin Company, 1928, New York, p. 88. This is also corroborated by *Secrets of the Federal Reserve*, p.90 and an article in *Time*, October 17, 1955.

[211] Eustace Mullins, *Secrets on the Federal Reserve*, p.p. 86-87, quoting the memories of Max Warburg de 1936. He also quotes a report of the Navy's Secret Service that defines Max as the "Leader of the espionage system of Germany."

grateful, assigned him to the Military Mobilization Board during World War II.

Von Papen and *HAPAG* devised a plan that would only bring misfortune to Germany, spread the conflict to other countries and benefit a financial and industrial elite. The Warburg convinced both sides of their allegiance by winning victories for each other, although in reality they did not work for any nation, but in their own interest and that of the cartel of international bankers. Lengthening the war as long as possible would push the indebtedness of the countries in war to the limit and maximize their benefits. Any of the services that the *HAPAG* spies would have rendered to Germany would be worthless in comparison with the ominous turn that the entry of the United States would give to Germany's fate. Members of the German embassy, such as von Papen, disagreed with the faction represented by von Rintelen and thought, quite reasonably, that using German resources to provoke the United States was a rashness contrary to the interests of Germany.

It turned out that involving the Americans was not an easy task and it still took another two years for President Wilson to declare war on Germany after obtaining the approval of the Senate. This happened on April 6, 1917. Until 1917 the United States had been a power apart fom the conflicts of the European princes and there was a generalized rejection of the idea of participating in the Great War. The arms industry would also welcome the entry into the United States war with open arms, and the banking *establishment*, since the war provides a blank check to any president to indebt his country for several generations. Professor Carroll Quigley explained the importance of the United States entry in war and the factors that made it possible:

> «[212]The most important diplomatic event of the latter part of the First World War was the intervention of the United States on the side of the Entente Powers in April 1917. The causes of this

---

212 Caroll Quigley, *Tragedy and Hope*, p.p. 249-250.

event have been analyzed at great length. In general there have been four chief reasons given for the intervention from four quite different points of view. These might be summarized as follows: (1) The German submarine attacks on neutral shipping made it necessary for the United States to go to war to secure "freedom of the seas"; (2) the United States was influenced by subtle British propaganda conducted in drawing rooms, universities, and the press of the eastern part of the country where Anglophilism was rampant among the more influential social groups; (3) the United States was inveigled into the war by a conspiracy of international bankers and munition manufacturers eager to protect their loans to the Entente Powers or their wartime profit from sales to these Powers; and (4) Balance of Power principles made it impossible for the United States to allow Great Britain to be defeated by Germany. Whatever the weight of these four in the final decision, it is quite clear that neither the government nor the people of the United States were prepared to accept a defeat of the Entente at the hands of the Central Powers. »

Quigley also refers to the propaganda campaign exercised by the Entente countries against Germany, and the circumstances surrounding the sinking of the *RMS Lusitania*:

«[213]...German submarines were acting in retaliation for the illegal British blockade of the continent of Europe and British violations of international law and neutral rights on the high seas... Americans had lent the Entente billions of dollars which would be jeopardized by a German victory... The important fact was that Britain was close to defeat in April 1917, and on that basis the United States entered the war...

The *Lusitania* was a British merchant vessel "constructed with Government funds as [an] auxiliary cruiser,... expressly included in

[213] Caroll Quigley, *Tragedy & Hope*, p.p. 250-251.

the navy list published by the British Admiralty," with "bases laid for mounting guns of six-inch caliber," carrying a cargo of 2,400 cases of rifle cartridges and 1,250 cases of shrapnel, and with order to attack German submarines whenever possible. Seven hundred and eighty five of 1,257 passengers, including 128 of 197 Americans, lost their lives. The incompetence of the acting captain contributed to the heavy loss, as did also a mysterious "second explosion" after the German torpedo struck.

The propaganda agencies of the Entente Powers made full use of the occasion. *The Times* of London announced that "four-fifths of her passengers were citizens of the United States" (the actual proportion was 15.6 percent); the British manufactured and distributed a medal which they pretended had been awarded to the submarine crew by the German government; a French paper published a picture of the crowds in Berlin at the outbreak of war in 1914 as a picture of Germans "rejoicing" at the news of the sinking of Lusitania. »

Erich Ludendorff

The importance of elements foreign to the battlefield in the First War has been a matter of discussion for years. The German army high command was composed mainly of the Kaiser Wilhelm II, Marshal Paul von Hindenburg and the head of the German General Staff on the eastern front, Erich Ludendorff, the true military strategist. After the defeat, Ludendorff developed the "stab in the back" theory, promoting the idea that Germany did not fail because of its inferiority on the battlefield but because of an aggregate of factors, which perhaps he himself did not fully understand. Such factors included the dominance of the media by the countries of the Entente, the spread of Bolshevism in Germany -the Spartacist Revolution of 1918- and even the sinister international influence of the Masonic lodges, led by the Mother Grand Lodge in England. In his post-war memoirs Ludendorff referred to the "dark conspiracy":

«[214]In the last stages of the war, and quite openly from the beginning of 1918 onward, propaganda worked ever more clearly for the social revolution, side by side with the political revolution. The war was painted as being waged by the upper ten thousand at the expense of the workers, and the victory of Germany as the workers' misfortune.

The enemy propaganda, and Bolshevism, which aimed at a world revolution, were working for the same ends in Germany. England gave China opium, our enemies gave us the revolution, and we accepted the poison and distributed it, as the Chinese distribute opium.

While the enemy propaganda was doing increasing harm to the German people and the army and navy, it also succeeded in maintaining the determination to fight in its own countries and armies, and in working against us in neutral countries.

Responsibility for the war, the Belgian atrocities, the ill-treatment of prisoners, our political immorality and treachery, our mendacity and brutality, the arbitrary Government of Prussianized Germany, the enslavement of the German people, all these reproaches were cleverly invented, for the purposes of the campaign of lies against us…

"To threaten countries with the aid of revolution has for many years been the policy of England," said Bismarck sixty years ago… Our political leaders apparently failed to observe the influence of the present Entente countries on the press of the world…

Even the Masonic lodges of the world, as had long been planned by England, worked with the whole mysterious strength of this most powerful of all secret societies in the service of the Anglo-Saxon, and thus, for us, of international politics. Only the national lodges in Prussia remained free of this influence. »

---

[214] Erich Ludendorff, *Ludendorff's Own Story, vol. I*, Harper, 1919, Nueva York, p.p. 428-435.

Ludendorff claimed that the objective of the Anglo-Saxon world at the beginning of the war was the economic annihilation of Germany, and the war was only a means to that end. A man of the general's confidence transmitted a conversation he had with the American consul general, who confessed to him about the *Lusitania* incident that:

> «[215]That was only the match that set fire to the straw, and it has been fully exploited as propaganda... Germany was undoubtedly the most industrious country in Europe before the war. We in America and England saw to what an exalted height Germany was climbing, and realized that in a few decades she could reach the pinnacle of power and be in a position to dictate, not only to Europe, but to the whole world. She had become a menace and we in America recognized the fact. For this reason we tackled the problem and thought we understood it.
>
> We are convinced that our people will take the lead after the war. It is we who are going to dictate, not only to Germany, but to the whole of Europe. The nations will expect great things from us, above all, peace. And they will get it, but on our conditions and at our price! »

It is evident that the testimony of Ludendorff, as an interested party, has a relative value. It is worth remembering, however, that it was not the Prussian expansionist yearnings but the assassination of the heir Franz Ferdinand, together with a series of inopportune secret treaties, what caused the conflict. It is equally true that Germany was on the way to becoming a great world power, and that the United States benefited from the conflict and emerged as the world's leading power ahead of old empires such as Germany, England, France or Russia. Finally, Germany violated the international laws of freedom of the seas by sinking the *Lusitania*, but only because England had been doing so since

---

[215] Erich Luddendorff, *Ludendorff's Own Story, vol. II*, Harper, 1919, N.Y., p. 18.

the beginning of the war, through the naval blockade to the Central Powers.

The power of international bankers seemed to be above the very General Staff even in times of war. Ludendorff recalled that Max Warburg, the Kaiser's right-hand man, initiated peace talks with the countries of the Entente without even bringing it to his attention:

> «[216]Colonel von Haeften had just been visiting foreign countries in order to discuss questions relating to propaganda. Without my knowledge he established communication with a subject of one of the enemy countries, who was acquainted with the objects and intentions of the authorities in London and Washington, and made me a verbal report on the subject. The terms then demanded of us were so severe that only a defeated Germany could have acceded to them. The Colonel further informed me that Conrad Hauszmann, then Reichstag Deputy, who has since confirmed this statement, and Herr Max Warburg-Hamburg had also tried to negotiate peace, but without success.
>
> The Government never informed me of these events, though it must have known of them. »

The experiences and reflections of Ludendorff, one of the most respected military in his country after the war, are very interesting to understand the point of view of many Germans after the war. Almost all the ideas contained in Hitler's *Mein Kampf* were formulated years before in the works of Ludendorff. His participation in the rise of Nazism goes far beyond the support given in the failed coup of 1923. The general, already of advanced age, projected in Adolf Hitler the young leader he wanted for Germany. It is evident that his hopes were betrayed, because in his last days he disavowed Hitler.

[216] Erich Ludendorff, *Ludendorff's Own Story, vol. II*, p. 226.

WAR COUNCIL OF THE AMERICAN RED CROSS

On top Henry Davison from *Bankers Trust* and *J.P. Morgan*, Grayson M-P Murphy, Director of *Anaconda Copper Mining* and *Guaranty Trust*, Charles D. Norton, Vice President of *First National Bank*, Edward N. Hurley, Chairman of U.S. Shipping Board. Below, Robert W. de Forest, Presidents Wilson and Taft and Eliot Wadsworth, Vice President of Exec. Committee of Red Cross.

The American Red Cross War Council, 1917

1917, the year United States entered the First World War, decisively marked the growth of the Red Cross throughout the world. That was the year it began to draw the attention of Wall Street tycoons. Politicians and bankers saw the strategic, military and economic potential of centralizing in a single agency the entire apparatus of war relief. This was an aspect of the war probably as profitable, in economic terms, as the military one.

In 1917 Wilson created the War Council of the Red Cross, and made sure all his banker cronies had a privileged position. All the interests described in the work were represented in this committee: There were men of the Morgan group such as Henry P. Davison, Grayson M-P Murphy and Charles D. Norton[217]. August Belmont, full time assistant in Washington[218], and Jacob Schiff, treasurer of the Red Cross in New York, were the delegates of the Frankfurt bankers. Most of the money used for the construction of the splendid offices of the American Red Cross -located one block away from the White House- came from the Rockefeller Foundation[219], who contributed $ 100,000, and E. H. Harriman also contributed generously. Franklin W. M. Cutcheon, a lawyer friend of Davison, was the general secretary and Stockton Axson, Wilson's brother-in-law, was elected secretary[220].

The Red Cross was an institution exclusively under the control of international bankers, and among the original war council it was impossible to find a single professional from the healthcare sector or specifically related to non-governmental organizations. Democratic President Wilson and former Republican President Taft maintained a

---

[217] Thomas W. Lamont, *Henry P. Davison. The Record of a Useful Life*, p. 275.
[218] Thomas W. Lamont, *Henry P. Davison. The Record of a Useful Life*, p. 277.
[219] Rockefeller Foundation, Our History, website revised in February 2015. Also Thomas W. Lamont, *Henry P. Davison. The Record of a Useful Life*, p. 271.
[220] Thomas W. Lamont, *Henry P. Davison. The Record of a Useful Life*, p. 270.

symbolic presence only to give respectability to the institution, ensuring that no one would interfere with their activities.

The next step was to create a special war fund to alleviate the consequences of the conflict. The American people contributed with initial donations of 114 million, which in a short time exceeded 400 million[221]. The international bankers were able to capitalize even the most altruistic feelings of the American people.

Their position in the Red Cross helped them to whitewash their deteriorated image and allowed them to assign funds discretionally for the purchase of products and services to their own companies, since they themselves approved all purchases. The Rockefeller donation, for example, of $ 100,000, was possibly not a significant expenditure, compared to its ability to directly influence a $ 400 million fund of public donations. Bankers discovered in charitable institutions, foundations and universities a perfect refuge for their surplus capital, which provided them with respectability, fiscal benefits, and influence to carry out their economic and political agenda.

The War Industries Board

In classical Rome, in times of war, the Senate could grant full powers to a general, allowing a dictatorship for a limited period. During the First World War in the United States that man was Bernard Baruch, to whom Wilson granted almost unlimited powers in the Military Industries Board[222]. Baruch was a Wall Street Jewish broker who had no previous experience in the military sector, was appointed to lead the American arms industry, making purchases and multi-million dollar allotments without his position even being approved by Congress. Moody, the great Wall Street columnist says:

---

221 Thomas Lamont, *Henry P. Davison. The Record of a Useful Life*, p.p. 270, 281.

222 According to Mullins, *Secrets of the Federal Reserve*, p.p. 25-26, the contribution of Col. House (35,000 $) to the Wilson campaign was only surpassed by that of Bernard Baruch (50,000 $).

«[223]Strangely enough, one of the first appointees to go from Wall Street to an important Washington post belonged to precisely the class which had incurred the President's distrust. Bernard Baruch all his life had been primarily a Wall Street operator — a very successful one, it is true, but a man who had had absolutely no business training in the "constructive" sense. Even Wall Street itself gasped when it learned that the President had made Baruch the head of the War Industries Board, and, as such, the man who would do most of the purchasing in this country for the United States and the Allies. It is an evidence of the flexibility of the Wall Street temperament that Baruch, despite his lack of practical experience, made a success of his job. When the war ended, this official was buying war materials at the rate of $10,000,000,000 a year and was unquestionably the greatest "buyer" the world has ever known. »

Baruch was one of the main contributors to the Wilson campaign, and later helped liberally Franklin Roosevelt. The Wall Street broker was not the only controversial appointment of Wilson, who mixed equally in the government interests of Frankfurt, Morgan, and Rockefeller, who had as the main point in their agendas putting the United States into the war[224]:

«Wilson's other two conspicuous appointments from Wall Street at first aroused great approval. After the collapse of the aircraft programme, he placed in charge of this work John D. Ryan, President of the Anaconda Copper Mining Company. But perhaps the Wall Street man who scored the greatest triumph was Charles M. Schwab. Wilson experimented disastrously for more than a year with the Shipping Board, the repeated failures of which almost disheartened the American people and their allies. All this

[223] John Moody, *Masters of Capital*, p. 177.
[224] John Moody, *Masters of Capital*, p. 178.

time there was one man, and one man only, ideally fitted for the task. »

Wilson put a handful of magnates, delegates of international financiers, to lead the American war industry. The head of military aviation was John D. Ryan, president of the *Anaconda Copper Mining*, the giant American copper trust, whose property was mostly held by William Rockefeller and his son Percy. Previously the French Rothschilds also maintained a considerable stock. During the war, Ryan left the direction of the Rockefeller copper empire to serve as general director of the Red Cross Assistance Program.

In the First Great War, the military conflict was still not essentially mechanized or motorized as it was the second and later wars, and copper was a fundamental raw material for the production of ballistic munitions. Again and again we see characters like Ryan, leading with one hand the military industry and with another the humanitarian organizations in charge of the reconstruction of countries that they previously reduced to ashes.

Charles M. Schwab, in charge of the American naval industry, was another *wallstreeter* who had been at the forefront of the steel monopoly first known as the *Carnegie Steel Company*, and then reconverted by Morgan into the *U.S. Steel*. While working under Carnegie, Schwab he was involved in a public procurement fraud in the armoring of US Navy[225]. Later, in the time of Morgan, he organized the *United States Shipbuilding Company*, a major naval company where Myers claims that he cleaned out the pockets of numerous investors:

---

[225] The costs of production was around $200 per each ton of steel plate. Carnegie sold it to the Russian government at the cost of $249, while he charged the American government $520 to $700 per ton. A report of the Congress accused Schwab of fraud and falsificaction. Gustavus Myers, *History of the Great American Fortunes, vol. III*, p.p. 253-254. The quote that follows *ibid.* p.p. 260-261.

«On his own hook, he and his associates issued false prospectuses, decoyed investors, fraudulently made a gift to themselves of $55,000,000 in securities, and otherwise committed such fraud upon fraud, that after the company had gone into bankruptcy the receiver denounced the whole transaction as "an artistic swindle."»

Schwab was president of *Carnegie Steel* and of the *U.S. Steel* of Morgan, and eventually also led its main competitor, *Bethlehem Steel.* Both corporations would be very pleased that Charles Schwab managing American naval spending in the war. Baruch, Ryan and Schwab, these three specimens of Wall Street were Wilson's choices to lead the military, air and naval industry in the war.

Take for example iron, one of the most prized raw materials during the war in any of its forms, especially transformed into steel. Baruch mentions as one of the Board's achievements the fact that its price remained under control, although he recognized that the profits of some steel corporations were gigantic:

«[226]It has been estimated that this regulation of steel prices saved more than a billion dollars. The steel industry also did a superb job of production; but there is no question that profits, especially of the great integrated companies, were still excessive. »

It is easy to understand why the big corporations got the best part of the business in the war: Their managers allocated the spending of the military programs of the government. At the beginning of the war an American general sent a memorandum to President Wilson where he estimated that some 3,000,000 tons of steel would be needed to renew the fleet, which at the price of 155 dollars per ton was a business of 5,000 million dollars. Colonel House's papers prove that industrial

---

[226] Bernard M. Baruch, *The Public Years*, p. 71.

sectors vital to war, such as naval production, could only be set in motion with Morgan's approval:

> «[227]Unfortunately for the shipbuilding programme, the relations between the Shipping Board and the Emergency Fleet Corporation did not prove harmonious, conflicts of authority and policy developed, and after months of wasted effort a complete reorganization was necessary. It was not until the following spring that American shipyards, under the driving leadership of Mr. C.M. Schwab, began to launch tonnage with the necessary speed. »

Here is another clear example: During the war, the United States had decided that the purchases of all the Allies would be centralized in a single institution, and there was only one financial group on the face of the earth able to carry out such a colossal task: *J.P. Morgan & Co.* But some countries among the Allies seemed not to be happy with the allocation of all allied purchases to a single American company:

> «[228][The Allies] realized clearly the unfortunate effects of British delay in arranging for a purchasing organization to take the place of that which had been carried on by J.P. Morgan and Company. »

After the discrepancies of the Allies by the monopoly of *J.P. Morgan & Co.*, Treasury Secretary McAdoo, Wilson's son-in-law and one of the members of the Board of Governors of the Federal Reserve, announced a change in the organization, albeit only on the surface:

> «[229]Formal agreements were signed today by the Secretary of the Treasury, with the approval of the President, on behalf of the

[227] Charles Seymour, *Intimate Papers of Colonel House, vol. III*, p.p. 20-21.
[228] Charles Seymour, *Intimate Papers of Col. House, vol. III*, p. 109.
[229] Charles Seymour, *Intimate Papers of Col. House, vol. III*, p. 122.

United States, and by the representatives of Great Britain, France and Russia for the creation of a commission with headquarters at Washington, through which all purchases made by those Governments in the United States shall proceed. It is expected that similar agreements will be signed with representatives of other allied governments within the next few days.

The agreements name Bernard M. Baruch, Robert S. Lovett, and Robert S. Brookings as the Commission. These gentlemen are also members of the recently created War Industries Board of the Council of National Defense, and will thereby be able thoroughly to coordinate the purchases of the United States Government with the purchases of the Allied Powers. »

The Allies replaced *J.P. Morgan* by a triumvirate composed of Bernard Baruch, the Wall Street broker in charge of the Military Industries Board, Brookings, also a member of the Board and in charge of the Price Setting Committee, and Lovett, related to the empire of the railways of the Harriman.

During the war Bernard Baruch was known as the Czar of American industry. Although he recognized that his conferred powers were very limited on paper, in practice he exercised them quite beyond his scope:

«[230]How did we in the WIB [War Industries Board] go about controlling the industrial output of the United States?... The most important instrument of control was the power to determine priority – the power to determine who gets what and when…Through the use of priority rulings, WIB was able to direct, restrain, or stimulate war production as the ever-changing situation required. »

[230] Bernard M. Baruch, *The Public Years*, p.p. 59-60.

The definition given by Baruch was equivalent to absolute economic power, not limited to American military industries. The Board could determine which companies obtained production inputs and at what price; metals, cotton, oil, rubber, chemicals or any other basic raw materials:

> «[231]In the three years before we entered the war, prices in the United States had skyrocketed as a result of frantic buying by the Allies. The average price of metals more than tripled, chemical prices had almost doubled, and food prices were nearly fifty per cent… Congress refused to enact any price control legislation…Despite this cautious and uncertain approach to the control of prices, and despite the fact that WIB had no direct responsibility for prices, we managed to exercise control over them by a broad interpretation of our duty and a judicious use of our priority power. In fact, after we entered the war prices were kept pretty well in check. Usually WIB could effect agreement on prices by negotiation. When a producer seemed bent on holding up the government, the reference to our priority order, the power to deprive him of his raw materials, was usually sufficient to encourage reasonableness. In extreme cases we threatened to wield our commandeering power. »

Baruch, who changed his Wall Street speculator career for one of those honorary "one dollar a year" jobs in Washington did not go home empty-handed. As the war was coming to an end at the end of 1917, and according to his own memories, he got rid of the numerous actions that he maintained in the American military industry, and he bet down in the *U.S. Steel*, anticipating the fall of the exorbitant profits the steelmaker harvested during the war. Congress investigated the use of privileged information for Baruch, Treasury Secretary McAdoo, Secretary of State Lansing, German ambassador von Bernstorff, and

---

[231] Bernard M. Baruch, *The Public Years*, p. 66.

Paul Warburg. Baruch, who earned $ 476,168.47 and liquidated his shares at the right time, was presented at his appearance as "speculator and investor" [232]. As it had happened with the Money Trust, the case ended without consequences for those involved. Major General Smedley Butler explained in 1935 that the only objective of United States the First World War was the profit of certain national economic interests.

> «[233]Fortunes would be made. Millions and billions of dollars would be piled up. By a few. Munitions makers. Bankers. Ship builders. Manufacturers. Meat packers. Speculators. They would fare well.
>
> Yes, they are getting ready for another war. Why shouldn't they? It pays high dividends…
>
> The normal profits of a business concern in the United States are six, eight, ten, and sometimes twelve percent. But war-time profits -ah! That is another matter- twenty, sixty, one hundred, three hundred, and even eighteen hundred per cent -the sky is the limit…
>
> Take our friends the du Ponts, the powder people –didn't one of them testify before a Senate committee recently that their powder won the war[234]? Or saved the world for democracy? Or something? How did they do in the war? They were a patriotic corporation.
>
> Well, the average earnings of the du Fonts for the period 1910 to 1914 were $6,000,000 a year. It wasn't much, but the du Ponts managed to get along on it. Now let's look at their average yearly profit during the war years, 1914 to 1918. Fifty-eight million dollars a year profit we find! Nearly ten times that of normal times, and

---

[232] Bernard M. Baruch, *The Public Years*, p.p. 35-38.

[233] Smedley Butler, *War is a Racket*, Round Table Press, 1935, New York. Ebook.

[234] The Nye Committee of 1934 investigated the role of the ammunition makers and other financial and industrial interests in WWI.

the profits of normal times were pretty good. An increase in profits of more than 950 per cent.

Take one of our little steel companies that patriotically shunted aside the making of rails and girders and bridges to manufacture war materials. Well, their 1910-1914 yearly earnings averaged $6,000,000. Then came the war. And, like loyal citizens, Bethlehem Steel promptly turned to munitions making. Did their profits jump -or did they let Uncle Sam in for a bargain? Well, their 1914-1918 average was $49,000,000 a year!

Or, let's take United States Steel. The normal earnings during the five-year period prior to the war were $105,000,000 a year. Not bad. Then along came the war and up went the profits. The average yearly profit for the period 1914-1918 was $240,000,000. Not bad.

There you have some of the steel and powder earnings. Let's look at something else. A little copper, perhaps. That always does well in war times. Anaconda, for instance. Average yearly earnings during the pre-war years 1910-1914 of $10,000,000. During the war years 1914-1918 profits leaped to $34,000,000 per year. »

The Wall Street tycoons were simultaneously the adjudicators of government military tenders and the contractors who benefited from these contracts. They self-awarded themselves with millions of dollars of public funds through their network of trusts. Therefore, it is not strange that some of the greatest American fortunes in history were born after World War I.

THE "BIG FOUR" AT THE PARIS PEACE CONFERENCE OF 1919

Left to Right David Lloyd George, Prime Minister of Great Britain, Vittorio Emanuelle Orlando, Prime Minister of Italy, Georges Clemenceau, Prime Minister of France and Woodrow Wilson, President of the United States.

The Paris Peace Conference, 1919

> «[235]It was natural that, during the war, President Wilson should look to House for advice on every matter that touched American relations with the Allies and especially on all problems of war aims. He selected him as chief of the organization for preparing the American case at the Peace Conference, appointed him head of the American War Mission to Europe for the coordination of military and industrial efforts, asked him to draft a constitution for a league of nations, and again sent him to Europe as American representative on the [Allied] Supreme War Council when it arranged the armistice with Germany. At the Peace Conference, House was Commissioner Plenipotentiary, and, because of his intimate personal relations with European statesmen, was constantly used by the President to conduct the most delicate negotiations. During Wilson's absence from Paris and his illness, the President selected him to take his place on the Supreme Council. »

In early 1919 the Allies held preliminary meetings in Paris to negotiate the conditions of peace. Among the figures gathered in Paris, the so-called "big four" stood out, the heads of state of the greatest Allied powers; Woodrow Wilson as President of the United States, Lloyd George as Prime Minister of Great Britain, Georges Clemenceau as Prime Minister of France and Vittorio Emanuele Orlando as Prime Minister of Italy. The Central Powers, the stone guests at the Paris Conference did not arrive until May, only to shut up and sign all the conditions imposed by the Allies.

In Paris there were many more important issues on the table than simply ending the war; To calculate reparations that Germany would pay, to redesign the world borders, to satisfy the territorial appetites of the participants, to recognize the new regime of the Bolsheviks, to

---

[235] Charles Seymour, *Intimate Papers of Colonel House, vol. III*, preface.

create a new world order represented by the League of Nations, and of course to solve the "Jewish question". The issue of reuniting the Jewish people in Palestine, although it had little to do with the war, was the first question of magnitude to be addressed, and practically the only one in which there was a unanimous consensus:

> «[236]*Jan. 5,* The question of establishing the Zionists in Palestine is one of the earliest subjects to take form in Conference circles. Rabbi Stephen Wise of New York has been here in conference with Colonel House; he has already seen Mr. Balfour at the British Foreign Office, and is waiting for a conference with the President on his return from Italy. Dr. Wise is Chairman of the American Zionist Organization, of which Justice Brandeis of the United States Supreme Court is Honorary President. A group of the foremost British Zionists are also here conferring with the British and other delegates.
>
> Following his talk with Balfour and Colonel House- and later with Tardieu[237], of the French delegation- Dr. Wise wrote out a statement which discloses that a very definite plan is now under way, to accomplish:
>
> First — a mandate to Great Britain as the trustee over Palestine.
> Second — a mandate to France as the trustee over Syria.

---

[236] Charles T. Thompson, *The peace conference Day by Day*, p.p 72-73. This book was the oficial publication of the American delegation in Paris. The policies for Turkey and Midle East after the war were established by House under the terms proposed by Wise. See *The Intimate Papers of Colonel House, vol. IV*, p. 199.
[237] Count Artur James, Lord of Balfour was the British Prime Minister from 1902 to 1905, and in 1919 he was part of the *Foreign Office* or British Foreign Office. Tardieu was the assistant of the French Prime Minister George Clemenceau, and some years later he himself was elected President of France.

Third — a mandate to the United States as the trustee over Armenia.

This is the first we have heard of "mandates" before the Peace Conference. »

The official diaries of the American delegation of the Paris Conference, prefaced by Colonel House, reveal that Rabbi Wise was one of the silent protagonists of the armistice negotiations in Paris in 1919. The very concept of "mandates" after the First World War was the idea of the Zionist leader.

The first step towards the creation of the State of Israel was to establish a mandate in Palestine under British control, where the first Jewish settlements founded by the Rothschilds and their associates were created. Rabbi Wise claimed for England the protectorate over Palestine:

«[238]Great Britain should be given, and, I believe, will be given, the Mandatory of Trusteeship over Palestine, which trusteeship Great Britain, I have reason for saying, will not accept save by the common consent of such disinterested peoples as our own. Great Britain's trusteeship over a Jewish Palestine will be because of the summons, or mandate, of the League of Nations, and for the sake of the Jewish people and the Jewish Commonwealth which they are in time to realize. "In all this," said Dr. Wise, "it is no secret that the President, Colonel House and Secretary Lansing have long watched with friendly interest the development of the Zionist movement. In this they have represented the judgment of the American people, including a vast majority of American Jews, and they will interpret that judgment with generosity and vision."»

---

[238] Charles T. Thompson, *The peace conference Day by Day*, p.p 73-74

The Zionists also had the British support. Halfway through the war, in 1917, British Foreign Secretary Lord Balfour made a formal statement in favor of the interests of Zionism, in a letter addressed to Baron Lord Lionel Rothschild, one of the most prominent British Zionists, and the Zionist Federation. The so-called "Balfour Declaration" expressed the sympathy and support of Great Britain for the creation of a Jewish state in Palestine. Colonel House recalled in his papers a conversation he had with British Prime Minister Lloyd George, whose interests coincided fully with those of the Zionists:

> «[239]November 20, 1917: I pinned George down to British war aims. What Great Britain desires are the African colonies, both East and West, an independent Arabia, under the suzerainty of Great Britain; Palestine to be given to the Zionists under British or, if desired by us, under American control; an independent Armenia and the internationalization of the Straits...»

Stephen S. Wise[240], the ubiquitous rabbi and self-appointed representative of the interests of world Jewry, a priori a voiceless with no formal position but as tourist in the American peace legation, proposed a partition project for the Ottoman Empire and the "big four" complied to the letter: the mandate on Palestine was granted to Great Britain, France was given the mandate on Syria and Lebanon, and the only part that was not carried out was the American mandate on

---

[239] Charles Seymour, *Intimate Papers of Col. House, vol. III*, p. 235.

[240] Stephen S. Wise co-founded the American Zionist Organization and was it's Honorary Secretary, following the path marked by Theodore Herzl, the "father" of Zionism. He was delegate in the Second Zionist Congress in Basilea in 1898, and he worked closely with Brandeis and Frankfurter. He founded in 1922 the Jewish Institute of Religion and took part with Untermeyer in the Jewish Boycott to Germany. Wise inspired in 1936 the creation of the World Jewish Congress with Nahum Goldmann and Leo Motzkin. He was its founder and President until 1949, the year of his death.

Armenia for disagreements with the Ottoman Empire. This ancient empire ended up disintegrating in the midst of internal conflicts after the Revolution of the Young Turks, to end up reduced to modern Turkey, a country with a territorial extension less than half of what it had in 1908. At that time Henry Morgenthau Sr., a well-known Zionist, was the American ambassador in the Ottoman Empire.

The Zionist movement achieved a complete success in World War II, when they forced the British to abandon their mandate over Palestine, giving rise to the modern State of Israel.

The promises made by the Allies to the Arab peoples, particularly those of the British regarding the creation of a united Arabia, were simply betrayed. The Bolsheviks published in 1915 the secret agreements between Great Britain and France for the distribution of the Middle East after the war, the most important being the Sykes-Picot treaty. It was revealed at the wrong time that the Franco-British plan for the Middle East consisted in disintegrating the Arab people in several states under the influence of France and Great Britain, instead of creating a large Arab state as promised, in exchange for their support. The distribution of the territory after the war was made without taking into account religious, ethnic, geographical, political or any other considerations. Probably the world powers thought that it would be very easy to continue exercising colonialism over a handful of small, divided and confronted states rather than over a united Arab world.

The current preferential relation of American diplomacy with the State of Israel –almost a relation of subordination to the newly born state- has its origin mainly in the first government of Woodrow Wilson.

His administration was crowded with characters from the Jewish world, with positions very close to Zionism, which in itself would have no political interest, if it were not because it generated a major conflict of interest. By swearing in and taking office in an elected American government, these officials and politicians acquired the duty to serve the people of the United States, and not the interests of Jewish nationalism.

STEPHEN S. WISE

Rabbi and leader of the Zionist Organization of América.

Baruch was one of the first great Zionists of the United States, and in Wilson's office more and more Zionists made their way into the organization of the Democratic Party, and they extended their political influence also in the later republican mandates. Rabbi Stephen S. Wise, the leader of international Zionism, was very active in peace negotiations during the First and Second World Wars. Other prominent Zionists within the government were the Morgenthau and Lehman families, Samuel Untermeyer, and the judges Louis Brandeis, Benjamin Cardozo or Felix Frankfurter, members of the Court of Appeals and the Supreme Court of the United States.

When Wilson went to the Peace Conference in Paris in 1919, he was lauded as the savior of Europe. Never any dignitary was received as the President in his visit to Europe. At the port of Brest, before disembarking from the presidential vessel, the USS George Washington, he received several warships firing salvoes in his honor, in a deafening spectacle of smoke and gunpowder. A crowd of men, women and children was waiting for him, chanting his name and carrying American flags. The banners displayed read "Hail the champion of the rights of man", "Honor to the apostle of international justice", and even a perhaps premature "Honor and welcome to the founder of the League of Nations." [241] Every European nation he visited revered like a living god, the man who had brought peace to the old continent.

Wilson took with him his own guidelines for peace, formulated in fourteen principles. It was a historical document known as the "fourteen points of Wilson." On the same, Clemenceau ironized that "the good God was enough only ten commandments." The most important point of his peace program was precisely the League of Nations. In a speech of the fourteen points Wilson pointed out that the League of Nations, a project of world governance, was much more than

---

[241] Gene Smith, *When the Cheering Stopped. The Last Days of Woodrow Wilson*, William Morrow & Company, 1964, p.p.37-38.

a consequence of the First World War, it was one of its causes. The very objective of the war had been the creation of a League of Nations:

> «[242]A League of Nations was the fundamental war aim; the rest were only machinery to provide a clean foundation for it. »

However, nothing in the program of the League of Nations was a product of Wilson's mind. His official biographer and Pulitzer Prize, Ray Stannard Baker -he dedicated more than twenty volumes to Wilson, to publish his documents, biography and legacy- sentenced:

> «[243]One fact arises above all others in studying those interesting documents: practically nothing –not a single idea- in the Covenant of the League was original with the President. His relation to it was mainly that of editor or compiler, selecting or rejecting recasting or combining the projects that came in to him from other sources. He had two great central and basic convictions: that a league of nations was necessary; that it might be brought into immediate existence. In voicing these he felt himself only a mouthpiece of the people of the world. »

The League of Nations, like the other thirteen points that made up Wilson's post-war project, actually came from the mind of a discreet Texas colonel[244].

---

[242] Charles Seymour, *Intimate Papers of Col. House, vol. III*, p. 349.

[243] Charles Seymour, *Intimate Papers of Col. House, vol. IV*, p. 4 quoting *Woodrow Wilson and World Settlement*, vol. I, p. 214.

[244] Charles Seymour, *Intimate Papers of Col. House, vol. IV*. According to House documents Wilson entrusted the Colonel the mission to bring the League of Nations to life (p.8). The Texan Colonel sent Wilson a draft with 23 articles (p.p. 27-36), of which President validated 18, which later reduced to 14. Not even the "Fourteen Points" came out of Wilson's mind, those were House's idea instead.

To whose interests did the League of Nations serve? Some important exponents of world Zionism pointed out in the 1922 congress that the League of Nations itself was a Jewish idea in itself, and a fundamental step forward in the Zionist project[245]:

> «"The League of Nations is a Jewish idea, and Jerusalem someday will become the capital of the world's peace" declared Dr. Nahum Sokolow, Chairman of the Zionist Executive Committee, at a special meeting of the Zionist Conference today... "What we have achieved after a struggle of twenty-five years we owe to the genious of our immortal leader, Theodor Herzl, who laid the foundation stone of our movement."
>
> It was decided at the meeting to send messages of congratulation to Max Nordau, one of Herzl first followers, the Earl of Balfour and Baron Edmond de Rothschild, the last named being the founder of the first Jewish colony in Palestine.»

Wilson spent the last years of his life campaigning for the League of Nations, a supranational body devised to become a kind of collegiate world government. On February 14 Woodrow Wilson left the conference that would define the future of Europe to promote the League of Nations in his own country. He took a train to Brest, and then embarked on the *USS George Washington* back to America. He left in Paris his nominal Secretary of State -Robert Lansing- and the real one -House- to finalize the details of the negotiations, under the assumptions set by Wilson himself.

The conference officially began on January 19, 1919. Although previous meetings had already taken place in the previous weeks, the disagreement on most issues was absolute. From the first moment the pretensions of the Italian Prime Minister Orlando were ignored, and the

245 New York Times, August 28, 1922, *Dr. Sokolow Tells Zionist Congress Jerusalem Will Be International Peace Capital.*

distance of the French position and that of the British and American delegations was remarkable:

> «[246]Clemenceau… had had a meeting with Lloyd George and the President all afternoon. I asked how they had gotten on… "Splendidly, we disagreed about everything."»

On February 19, Clemenceau was shot in his car on his way to see House and Lord Balfour. He received one shot in the shoulder and another in the chest, but he survived[247]. The author was a French socialist named Emil Cottin, sympathizer of the Bolshevik cause. Cottin was released in 1924 and died fighting as a volunteer in the Spanish Civil War on the Republican side.

With two of the main protagonists out of the chessboard, Clemenceau and Wilson, the weight of the negotiations would fall on Colonel House, as the main emissary of the American delegation, and on Lloyd George, of the English delegation. Needless to mention Lord Balfour and Great Britain were heavily indebted with Colonel House, who had changed the course of the war in favor of the Allies by forcing the American entry into the war by rigging the Lusitania incident. House, the agent of the international bankers and subtle master of persuasion, would be able to lead the peace negotiations alone with the unconditional support of the English delegation.

Much to everyone's perplexity, the octogenarian Clemenceau was recovered four days after his attack, on February 23, and back at the conference. On March 14, Wilson returned to Europe[248] without the pomp of his previous European visit, already visibly tired and ill. His project of the League of Nations had failed in his country, being rejected in both houses. The Americans had won their freedom after several wars, and refused to relinquish their sovereignty to give it to a

---

[246] Charles Seymour, *Intimate Papers of Col. House, vol. IV*, p.377.

[247] Charles T. Thompson, *The Peace Conference Day by Day*, p. 218.

[248] Charles T. Thompson, *The Peace Conference Day by Day*, p. 243.

bureaucratic apparatus like the League of Nations. Despite that, Wilson remained adamant in his demand that a provision be included on the League of Nations in the Peace Treaty. And this was done, although few countries took seriously the project of a statesman who was not able to convince to his own country.

On April 4 Wilson was so ill that he could not attend the negotiations, he was said, a victim of nervous tension in recent months and a cold. Actually his physical situation was much deteriorated and nobody had occasion to see him during his convalescence[249]. In the next two days a great bewilderment was created in Paris when it was learned that Wilson had given orders to the then Secretary of the Navy, Franklin Delano Roosevelt, so that the presidential ship could return to Brest to pick him up. He wanted to return to the United States, apparently fed up with the slowness of the negotiations and the refusal of the British and French to stick to his Fourteen Points, although the real reason was the aggravation of his physical condition[250]. Finally Wilson remained at the conference after a couple of days of rest.

Thomas Lamont of *J.P. Morgan*, the man who calculated the German reparations, and Norman Davis, a New York banker from the same group, presented the figures to the participants in the conference[251]. The payment of Germany would be one hundred billion German marks of gold distributed in an initial stretch of twenty thousand million from 1919 to 1921, another forty thousand million until 1951, and the remaining forty thousand million when the commission deemed it appropriate. This was the point that marked the beginning of World War II; the reparations that Germany would never be able to pay, and that made it a country subordinated to international bankers for an entire generation.

The preliminary negotiations of the Allies extended much more than initially expected, and the climate at the beginning of the

---

[249] Charles T. Thompson, *The Peace Conference Day by Day*, p.p. 285-291.

[250] Gene Smith, *When the Cheering Stopped*, p.p. 48-49.

[251] Charles T. Thompson, *The Peace Conference Day by Day*, p.p. 300-301.

Conference was one of weariness. On April 23, Wilson made some harsh statements in which he accused Vittorio Emanuele Orlando, the Italian Prime Minister, of being the chief cause of the stalemate in the peace negotiations[252]. The Italian case was strange; before war broke out Italy was bound to help the Central Powers by a treaty that did not comply, and yet in 1915 Italy entered the war on the side of the Entente. That year the Italians signed the London Pact with Great Britain, Russia and France agreeing their entry into the war in exchange of extensive territorial concessions in the Balkans, Turkey and Austria. The London Pact was secretly crafted, but a Bolshevik newspaper made it public in 1917. After Wilson's harsh public statements, the Italian legation headed by Prime Minister Orlando threatened to leave the conference and mobilize 200,000 men on the Yugoslav border if necessary. Two days later the Italians left the conference without carrying out their threat. They returned from Paris with empty hands, and this was another cause of the rise of Italian fascism, and therefore of the Second World War.

Five months after the negotiations began in Paris, on May 30, the German delegation led by Count Brockdorff-Rantzau arrived in Versailles. The vanquished powers were removed from the peace negotiations, waiting for the Entente countries to make all decisions about the future of Europe. The train in which they arrived was stoned, and the protests against his legation took place during his stay in Paris[253]. The official German delegation consisted of about 50 senior officials, delegates, commissioners and experts, and another 200 were auxiliary personnel, journalists, interpreters, officials, etc. Among the most select members of the legation of the Paris Peace Conference we find a considerable number of bankers, the real protagonists of the negotiations in Paris[254]:

---

[252] Charles T. Thompson, *The Peace Conference Day by Day*, p.p. 321-327.
[253] Charles T. Thompson, *The Peace Conference Day by Day*, p.p. 348-349.
[254] Charles T. Thompson, *The Peace Conference Day by Day*, p.p. 349-350.

- Max Warburg: Director of the banking family firm *M.M. Warburg & Co.* and Director in two other companies relevant in our story, *Hamburg-America Line* and *I.G. Farben.*
- Carl Melchior: Banker of *M.M. Warburg & Co.*, and a member, some years later of the *Bank of International Settlements.*
- Wilhelm Cuno: He replaced Albert Ballin in the presidency *Hamburg-America Line* and he would be the Chancellor of Germany.
- Baron Kurt von Schröder: This banker was a notorious member of the Nazi Party. He organized the meeting of Von Papen and Hitler which allowed the second to achieve the chancellorship.
- Emil George Von Strauss: General Manager of *Deutsche Bank*, and a member of more than 30 boards of other corporations. Von Strauss had close personal relations with Hitler and the Nazism, although he was never affiliated to the Nazi party.
- Franz Urbig: A banker linked to several banking houses, chiefly to *Deutsche Bank.*
- Karl Bosch: A German industrialist, Nobel in Chemistry in 1931 and co-founder of *I.G. Farben*, the Company that became one of the main financial sponsors of the rising Nazi Party. He was also accountable for the fabrication of the *Zyklon B* gas used in the German concentration camps.

On the American side there were prominent Morgan agents such as Davis and Lamont, as well as Bernard Baruch or Colonel House, in charge of the delegation[255]. Mullins includes Albert Strauss from *J & W Seligman*[256]. John Foster Dulles, Rockefeller's lawyer and then Secretary of State was also part of Baruch's group[257]. The Dulles brothers were nephews of Secretary of State Robert Lansing[258]. Professor Quigley

[255] Charles T. Thompson, *The Peace Conference Day by Day*, p.p. 96 and 266.
[256] Eustace Mullins, *Secrets of the Federal Reserve*, p. 109.
[257] U.S. Department of State, John Foster Dulles, website revised in 2014.
[258] U.S. Department of State, Robert Lansing, website revised in 2014.

noted the exacerbated presence of bankers-advisers at the Paris Conference:

> «At all of these meetings, as at the Peace Conference itself, the political leaders were assisted by groups of experts and interested persons, sometimes self-appointed. Many of these "experts" were members or associates of the international -banking fraternity. At the Paris Peace Conference the experts numbered thousands and were organized into official staffs by most countries, even before the war ended. These experts were of the greatest importance. They were formed into committees at Paris and given problem after problem, especially boundary problems, usually without any indication as to what principles should guide their decisions. The importance of these committees of experts can be seen in the fact that in every case but one where a committee of experts submitted a unanimous report, the Supreme Council accepted its recommendation and incorporated it in the treaty. In cases where the report was not unanimous, the problem was generally resubmitted to the experts for further consideration. »

On June 16, the Germans offered a counter-proposal they considered equitable, claiming that the terms of peace established were economically unviable for their country. Such claims were quickly dismissed by a letter from the French Prime Minister Clemenceau that clarified that the terms were not negotiable:

> «The protest of the German delegation shows they fail to understand the position in which Germany stands today... the treaty in its present form must be accepted or rejected. The allied and associated powers require a declaration from the German delegation within seven days as to whether they are prepared to sign this treaty as now amended... notification that the armistice will terminate and that the allied and associated powers will take such steps as they think needful to enforce their terms. [259]»

The Allies only had to wait four days for the Germans to accept. Max Warburg, present in the German delegation, appeared not to be able to obtain clemency for Germany from Colonel House, the faithful friend of his brother Paul. On June 29, the *USS George Washington* sailed again, taking Wilson, House and the rest of the American legation back to America. None of the participating countries, winners or losers in the war, left Paris satisfied, with the only exception of the Zionists.

The economist Lord Maynard Keynes, one of the assistants to the Conference of Peace, summed up the failure of Wilson in solving the conflicts of the old continent, and to lay a bases for the world-wide stability[260]:

> «When President Wilson left Washington he enjoyed a prestige and a moral influence throughout the world unequalled in history. His bold and measured words carried to the peoples of Europe above and beyond the voices of their own politicians. The enemy peoples trusted him to carry out the compact he had made with them; and the Allied peoples acknowledged him not as a victor only but almost as a prophet...
>
> The disillusion was so complete, that some of those who had trusted most hardly dared speak of it. Could it be true? They asked of those who returned from Paris. Was the treaty really as bad as it seemed? What had happened to the President? What weakness or what misfortune had led to so extraordinary, so unlooked-for a betrayal?
>
> The disillusion was so complete, that some of those who had trusted most hardly dared speak of it. Could it be true? They asked of those who returned from Paris. Was the treaty really as bad as it seemed? What had happened to the President? What weakness or

---

259 Charles T. Thompson, *The Peace Conference Day by Day*, p.p. 395-397.

260 John Maynard Keynes, *The Economic Consequences of the Peace*, Harcourt, Brace & Howe, 1920, New York, p.p. 38-43.

what misfortune had led to so extraordinary, so unlooked-for a betrayal? ...

It was commonly believed at the commencement of the Paris conference that the President had thought out, with the aid of a large body of advisors, a comprehensive scheme not only for the League of Nations, but for the embodiment of the Fourteen Points in an actual treaty of peace. But in fact the President had thought out nothing; when it came to practice his ideas were nebulous and incomplete. He had no plan, no scheme, no constructive ideas whatever for clothing with the flesh of life the commandments which he had thundered from the White House.

He not only had no proposals in detail, but he was in many respects, perhaps inevitably, ill-informed as to European conditions. And not only was he ill-informed -that was true of Mr. Lloyd George also- but his mind was slow and unadaptable. The President's slowness amongst the Europeans was noteworthy.... There can seldom have been a statesman of the first rank more incompetent than the President in the agilities of the council chamber. »

The psychological profile that Keynes elaborated on Wilson in 1919 was very similar to that made by Wickersham years before, although in fairness to Wilson, he was already seriously ill during the Peace Conference, and would die shortly thereafter. Wilson was possibly a man of good feelings, an idealist somewhat prone to fantasy, overwhelmed by the responsibilities of his office and dominated by his circle of advisors.

During his first marriage Wilson maintained a relationship with a married woman named Mary Peck, whom he met on a trip with his wife to Bermuda. The real extent of the relationship between Wilson and Peck is unknown to everyone except the two protagonists, and may not have passed an innocent friendship by correspondence. Wilson[261]

[261] Wilson sent Peck more than 200 letters and delivered 7.500 of his own pocket

claimed that his behavior was irreproachable and that his first wife, Ellen Axson, was aware of and involved in her friendship with Mary Peck.

In 1915, a year after his first wife Ellen Axson passed away, Wilson married again with Edith Galt. Some members of his party feared that if Wilson got married so soon, or if some inappropriate aspect of his relationship with Mary Peck came to light, his popularity could plummet before the 1916 election. Gene Smith, biographer of the last few years of Wilson, claimed that Colonel House and his son-in-law William Gibbs McAdoo[262] devised a plan to make him desist from the idea of marrying his second wife, Edith Galt:

> «McAdoo and House worked up a scheme that McAdoo carried out. Lunching with his father-in-law, McAdoo said that an anonymous letter had been received. The letter (which existed only in the minds of McAdoo and House) said Mrs. Peck was talking about the $7,500 and showing the President's letters to all interested comers. The President, as expected, was horrified…
>
> Later it would be whispered that she bought off Mrs. Peck with giant sums and that Louis Brandeis was appointed to the Supreme Court because he was the intermediary who carried the money; later it would be said Colonel House took Mrs. Peck to Europe to get her out of the way and that she was on a regular salary from McAdoo's Treasury Department in order to insure her silence… »

---

to alleviate her economic situation. This information and the following quote in Gene Smith, *When the Cheering Stopped. The Last Days of Woodrow Wilson*, p.p. 20-23.

[262] McAdoo, Secretary of the Treasury and one of the members of the board of governors of the Federal Reserve was married to Eleanor Randalph Wilson, 26 years younger.

Curtis Bean Dall, the son-in-law of future President Franklin Delano Roosevelt also spoke of the participation of some Wall Street members in such a murky affair[263]:

> «It appeared that Mrs. Peck's son allegedly got into some financial difficulties in Washington. He needed about $30,000 to get straightened out, but Mrs. Peck did not have that sum of money handy. She allegedly retained Samuel Untermeyer, a powerful New York lawyer, to represent her and help raise the money for her son. The events allegedly proceeded something like this: An appointment was made at the White House and Mr. Untermeyer called upon President Wilson and presented his client's case, saying that his client needed money and that for the sum of $250,000 she would return to President Wilson certain letters, or else dispose of them to others.»

According to the story told by Dall, Wilson offered Untermeyer $ 100,000, if that satisfied his client, Mrs. Peck. Untermyer would have responded with a counteroffer:

> «No, Mr. President, that would not satisfy my client, but I have just had an idea ... and, well, perhaps, it might be developed into a happy solution. If you indicate to me that you will consider appointing Mr. Louis Brandeis to the Supreme Court, I will then discuss this unfortunate matter of the letters with friends of mine. They might be able to then arrange to settle this matter to the benefit of all parties concerned. »

In 1916 Brandeis was appointed by Wilson for the Supreme Court and ratified by the Senate. Neither Dall nor Smith seem to have a very solid base to link Zionists as Samuel Untermeyer and Louise Brandeis

---

263 Curtis Bean Dall, *FDR. My Exploited-Father-in-Law*, Institute for Historical Review, 1967, California, p.p. 140, 141.

to the alleged blackmail of Mary Peck, but the participation of McAdoo and House in fabricating the story of blackmail is corroborated by several sources. Mary Peck never intended to use correspondence with the President. A few years after the incident she had a cordial meeting with Wilson and his second wife, denying her participation in any sort of blackmail, and she stated that she had never tried to misuse his correspondence. In fact, her old friend spent the previous years in a very difficult economic position. This story shows the degree of control that characters close to the Federal Reserve such as House and McAdoo were able to exercise over Wilson.

The popularity of Wilson went through its lowest point at the end of his term, inside and outside his country, but his political stature was enlarged over time thanks to the following generations of historians, who remembered him as the savior of Europe. However, Wilson's only noteworthy decision in the conflict was his formal declaration of war on Germany, breaking thus his main electoral promise. Other major policies launched during his presidency, such as the Federal Reserve or the League of Nations, were actually devised by other. Not even the fourteen points that bore his name were his idea. Those emerged, like all his other policies, from the machinations of a silent Texan colonel unknown to history, notwithstanding one of the most influential men of the first half of the 20th century.

After Wilson suffered a series of brain strokes in late September 1919 which deteriorated his health irreversibly, he delegated the negotiations to Edward Mandell House and his circle of assistants. In October Wilson suffered a new stroke that left him paralyzed and half blind on the left side for some time, barely being able to walk with a cane. For several months his condition was concealed from the public, but by February 1920 it was already known.

Wilson then faced the consequences of his second presidential term. Few of the master lines of its fourteen points were put into practice and practically none of the participants in the Conference, not even among the Allies, were satisfied in their aspirations. The Central Powers were victims of an ultimatum that established unacceptable territorial and economic conditions. In the Middle East the promise of a united Arabia was not fulfilled and the Ottoman Empire was broken up in several countries. The agreements signed with Italy nor the hopes of Japan were fulfilled either[264] causing a discontent that led both countries to fight on the German side in the next war; Wilson was not even able to materialize his primary goal, the League of Nations, the cause for which he had fought so hard.

At the end of his term, Wilson felt betrayed by House, Lansing, McAdoo and his other aides, who had negotiated unaffordable concessions for him. It was too late to solve his errors. He was confined in his home and his wife refused to receive his old friends and collaborators. He even fired Gordon Auchincloss, the son-in-law of his old friend Colonel House. Bernard Baruch, who rivaled House for the president's favor, explained Wilson's break with House:

> «[265]When Wilson returned briefly to the United States at the end of February, major responsibility for pushing ahead with the Treaty fell on House. Upon the President's return to Paris, although there was no public evidence of a rupture, we know now that the President was deeply disturbed and disappointed at the compromises House had made in his absence. In his zeal and self-confidence House had gone too far on his own, making commitments which Wilson felt had undercut his position»

A convalescent Wilson ended his mandate practically incapacitated to perform any simple task, much less the presidency. After his death, the cases of presidential incapacity in the White House were regulated. The Federal Reserve, the income tax, and the American entry into the

---

[264] Japan proposed for the League of Nation a clause of racial equiality that was dismissed. The British legation threatened to withdraw his support to Wilson's project if the proposal was included, because it would became a substantial threat to British colonialism.

[265] Bernard M. Baruch, *The Public Years*, p. 138.

First World War ended the economic prosperity of their country and laid the foundations of its future ruin. His role in Paris was the cause of innumerable conflicts throughout the world, including the Second World War.

The war was not related that much to the old quarrels between the French and Prussian empires as one might think, but rather to the ambitions of the Anglo-Saxon world, the benefits of a powerful international economic elite, the centralization of power and the political aspirations of the Zionism. The First War, as we know by the testimonies of its protagonists, was only an excuse to forward a new international order.

THE RUSSIAN REVOLUTION: COMMUNISM (1905-1917)

«Ultimately, from whatever point of view we look at this question, we come always to the same sad conclusion, the rule of the great masses of the people by a privileged minority. The Marxists say that this minority will consist of workers. Yes, possibly of former workers, who, as soon as they become the rulers of the representatives of the people, will cease to be workers and will look down at the plain working masses from the governing heights of the State; they will no longer represent the people, but only themselves and their claims to rulership over the people. Those who doubt this know very little about human nature.

These elected representatives, say the Marxists, will be dedicated and learned socialists. The expressions "learned socialist," "scientific socialism," etc., which continuously appear in the speeches and writings of the followers of Lassalle and Marx, prove that the pseudo-People's State will be nothing but a despotic control of the populace by a new and not at all numerous aristocracy of real and pseudo-scientists. The "uneducated" people will be totally relieved of the cares of administration, and will be treated as a regimented herd. A beautiful liberation, indeed!...

According to Mr. Marx, the people not only should not abolish the State, but, on the contrary, they must strengthen and enlarge it. And turn it over to the full disposition of their benefactors, guardians, and teachers – the leaders of the Communist party, meaning Mr. Marx and his friends – who will then liberate them in their own way. They will concentrate all administrative power in their own strong hands, because the ignorant people are in need of a strong guardianship; and they will create a central state bank, which will also control all the commerce, industry, agriculture, and even science. »

Mikhail Bakunin, *Statism and Anarchy*, 1873.

Khazaria

At the beginning of the 20th century, the majority of the world's Jewish population was concentrated in Central and Eastern Europe and the Western part of Russia. Since the nineteenth century the migratory flows of Jewish population went from East to West, fleeing the repression in the Russian Empire to Austria, Germany and then the United States.

The first colony in Palestine, Rishon LeZion, was founded in 1882 with the financial support of Baron Edmond de Rothschild, a member of the French house. After the First World War they began the foundation of Jewish colonies in Palestine and continued with greater intensity after the Second World War. During those years there were also relevant movements of the Jewish population to other parts of the world, many of them towards the United States.

The origin of the Jews of Central and Western Europe, the so called "Ashkenazi" [266], is still under study today. In 1976 the Jewish writer of Hungarian origin, Arthur Koestler, published in his controversial work *The Thirteenth Tribe* that the Ashkenazi Jews, currently the most widespread in the world, did not come from Semitic tribes emigrated from the easternmost part of the Mediterranean Sea, a place that today occupy Israel and Palestine, but were native inhabitants of the Caucasus and nearby areas, converted into a later time to the Jewish religion.

Koestler suggested that the origin of Ashkenazi Jews dated back to the time of the Khazar Empire, which was born in the seventh century and lasted until the eleventh century. Apparently forgotten by history, the size of this superb empire at its peak ranged from Kiev in the east to the Aral Sea in the east. To the south it was bordering with two other conflicting empires, the Byzantine Empire to the southwest and the Sassanid (Persian) Empire to the southeast.

---

[266] The name comes from Ashkenaz, the great-grandson of Noah named in the Genesis 10:3. Ashkenaz is a descendant of Jafet, son of Noah and brother of Sem.

Khazaria was located in the Caucasus, at the center of the conflict between the Christian and Muslim empires, a factor which led King Bulan to the conversion of his empire to Judaism in the middle of the 8th century. After the death of Muhammad in the year 632 in Europe there were several waves of Islamic invasions. Pushed by the invasions of Islam to the east, and by their Christian neighbors to the west, the Khazars embraced the religion of Moses as an identity to preserve their own survival as a nation. Koestler explains that in the eighth century Khazaria sealed an alliance with Byzantium[267]:

> «It is perhaps not surprising, given these circumstances that in 732 – after a resounding Khazar victory over the Arabs – the future Emperor Constantine V married a Khazar princess. In due

[267] Arthur Koestler, *The 13th Tribe*, electronic version, chapter 1, p. 3.

time their son became the Emperor Leo IV, known as Leo the Khazar…

A few years later, probably AD 740, the King, his court and the military ruling class embraced the Jewish faith, and Judaism became the state religion of the Khazars.»

Koestler's work is based on Encyclopedia Judaica, composed of text of the most relevant Jewish scholars of the time. He explain in his entry "Khazars" [268] that it is: *"A people of Turkish origin whose life and history are interwoven with the very beginnings of the history of the Jews of Russia."* The Khazars, originally a pagan people, embraced the Jewish faith sometime between the seventh and eighth centuries, and the article goes on to say that *"the conversion took place in 620. According to others, in 740."*

The most important source for the story of Khazaria is the correspondence between King Khazar and Joseph Hasdai ibn Shaprut, a Jewish physician who held the position of Ambassador of the Caliphate of Cordoba in the year 960. In one of the so-called "Khazarian letters" King Joseph explained how the conversion of his empire happened. Centuries before, there was a king named Bulan who called three sages in order to choose what their religion would he adopt; one sage was Muslim, another was Christian and the last one a Jewish. The Jewish sage asked the other two sages, Christian and Muslim, what religion they would choose if they were to abjure their own. Both the wise Christian and the Muslim recognized that their second alternative would be the Jewish religion. The wise Jew prevailed and Bulan embraced Judaism along with all his people. Other Arab sources corroborate this fact, although they only speak of the conversion of the king and the nobility, but do not mention the conversion of his people. One of Bulan's successors, Obadiah, invited several Jewish scholars to

---

[268] Professor D.M. Dunlop of the University of Columbia, an authority in Khazar studies, Dr. Antal Bartha, J.B. Bury, M.I. Artamonov o A.N. Poliak, professor of Jewish Medieval History in the University of Tel Aviv. Cyrus Adler, *Jewish Encyclopedia, vol. IV,* p.p. 1-2.

the country and founded synagogues and schools throughout the country.

The history of the Khazars could explain why in the early twentieth century most of the world's Jewish population was concentrated in the center and eastern part of Europe, a geographically distant area of the *Promised Land* of Israel. Koestler's work would also explain the historical gap for the Jewish people before the eleventh century, and would clarify an essential anthropological aspect: Why most of the world's Jewish population has a phenotype much closer to the Turkish people and Caucasians -close to the homeland of the Khazar Empire- which today is inhabited by the inhabitants of the Palestine area.

The entry "Statistics" of the Encyclopedia Judaica[269] corroborates the information known about the Khazars, and indicates that in the year of its writing (1901) there was more than 11,087,000 Jews in the world. According to that entry about 10,475,000 Jews or 94.48% of the total, were of Ashkenazi origin. Only 314,000 or 2.83% were Sephardic or Levantine, coming from Spain and Portugal, while 150, 0.001% were natives of Nablus, in the zone of the Middle East where modern Israel is located today.

If we combine the demographic and historical data contained in the Encyclopedia Judaica, which supports Koestler's thesis, we reach the conclusion that Ashkenazi Jews -and by extension practically all Jews today- would be Jewish because of their faith, but not ethnically Jewish: People of Caucasian descent converted to Judaism in the middle of the 8th century. The Khazars, according to Koestler, would be the thirteenth tribe of Israel, appearing long after the twelve biblical tribes. Koestler concludes that, in reference to European Jews, that *"Genetically they are more closely related to the Hun, Uigur and Magyar tribes than to the seed of Abraham, Isaac and Jacob. Should this turn out to be the case, then the term "anti-Semitism" would become void of meaning, based on a misapprehension shared by both the killers and their victims."*

---

[269] Cyrus Adler, *Jewish Encyclopedia, vol. XI*, p. 533.

The theory of Koestler clears many doubts but opens new questions. What happened to the Israelite Jews is a question that Koestler does not address in detail. Without a nation of their own, and persecuted throughout Europe, possibly most of the Jews in the world ended up integrating in the places where they dwelled, due to the several forced conversions and expulsions suffered in the Middle Ages.

This historical aspect of the Jewish people has become taboo because of its connotations for the legitimacy of the State of Israel founded in 1948. If the current Jewish inhabitants of Israel were not descendants of peoples born in the geographical area then occupied by Palestine, but Europeans and Caucasians instead, their "historical right" to populate a territory already inhabited by the Palestinians would be seriously compromised.

This information comes from the Encyclopedia Judaica, composed by some of the greatest Jewish scholars of his time, and the work Arthur Koestler, one of its great intellectuals. He was imprisoned by the fascist regimes in Spain and France, so no one should find anti-Semitic motives just because a century after being written those highlight some inconvenient facts.

The Russia of the Tsars

In the eighteenth century an important portion of the Jewish population in Europe lived in the regions of Hungary and Poland. In 1722, under the reign of Emperor Peter I the Great, Poland suffered the first of several partitions, which caused a huge amount of Jewish population to be incorporated into the Russian Empire. The Tsars decided that the entire Jewish population within the boundaries of the Russian Empire would be confined to the newly conquered lands in Turkey, with two objectives; The first was to repopulate the new occupied areas, and the second was an attempt to avoid any kind of ethnic or religious conflicts, given that Russia was a predominantly Slavic empire of an orthodox Christian religion.

Peter I was followed by Catherine the Great, who signed several decrees further reducing the rights of the Jewish population. These decrees included the "Pale of Settlement" or *chertá osedlosti* of 1791, which restricted the places of permanent residence for Jewish citizens to an area between the Baltic Sea and the Black Sea. This made Poland a huge Jewish ghetto within the Russian Empire.

In 1812, after the Russian victory against Napoleon's army, the country had to make a considerable effort to carry out its reconstruction. The French emperor had reached the heart of Moscow, and only embers remained from that city. Tsar Alexander I relaxed the Pale of Settlement established in 1772 by Catherine the Great, making concessions to artisans, doctors and other Jewish professionals to integrate them into the country. Freemasonry and all kinds of secret societies were banned in 1822. This was one of the most progressive czars and put in place policies to improve the situation of the Jewish people, although it is true that the reforms were late, since most European ghettos they had disappeared by the end of the 18th century. The Judaica Encyclopedia affirms:

> «[270]During his reign (1801-25) more measures for internal reform were inaugurated than under any other of his predecessors, from the days of Peter the Great (died in 1725). He prepared the way for the emancipation of the serfs, and promoted education, agriculture, commerce and manufacturers, literature and fine arts. »

The Encyclopedia Judaica also narrates that Alexander I, a Czar with a liberal spirit, favored the Jews and tried to improve the conditions of all Jewish affairs in many aspects:

> «[271]A special commission was summoned, by a ukase [decree] issued Oct. 9, 1802, to draft a set of regulations, which resulted in

[270] Cyrus Adler, *Jewish Encyclopedia, vol. I*, p. 345.
[271] Cyrus Adler, *Jewish Encyclopedia, vol. I*, p.p. 345-346.

the "Enactment concerning the Jews" or Dec. 9, 1804. Under this enactment the Russian Jews obtained the right to buy and rent land in all the western and southern provinces (this led to the foundation of the first Jewish agricultural colonies in Russia); to enter all the elementary and high schools and universities: to establish factories in all the provinces in which they were permitted to dwell; and to visit all other provinces of Russia on business, upon the condition that they and their families adopted the German style of dress in order that they might not differ from the natives in outward appearance. They were promised all the rights of citizens as soon as they should have shown diligence and skill in agriculture and handicrafts. Alexander even offered the Jews land in the neighborhood of St. Petersburg and Moscow, provided they were willing to confine themselves to agricultural pursuits. »

Alexander I built hospitals for Jews and strengthened their efforts to integrate them into the Russian economy.

« [272]That Alexander was at this time much in earnest in his endeavors to ameliorate the position of the Jews is shown by his remark: "If, through my efforts to improve their condition, I should succeed in bringing forth only one Mendelssohn from among the Russian Jews, I shall be abundantly rewarded."...

In 1815 a census of the Jews was taken, and surnames were given to all Jewish families. Alexander issued a ukase (1818) directing the election of three deputies from among the Jews, who should reside in St. Petersburg, and be empowered to bring all Jewish affairs before the government. »

Despite the privileges enjoyed by some segments of the Jewish population, for the most part they did not have the same rights as other Russian citizens, being unable to rent properties, run taverns or live

[272] Cyrus Adler, *Jewish Encyclopedia, vol. I*, p. 346.

outside the western area of the Russian Empire. At some point, and for reasons not developed in the Encyclopedia, Tsar Alexander I took a turn in his policy of openness towards the Jews:

> «[273]At the Congress of Aix-la-Chapelle (1818) Alexander brought forward the question of the condition of the Jews […]
>
> After the Congress Alexander altogether abandoned his former liberal ideas and adopted a reactionary policy. Owing to this, the following restrictive measures characterized the closing years of the czar's reign: The rescript of May 4, 1820, forbidding Jews to keep Christian servants; that of Aug. 10, 1824, prohibiting foreign Jews from settling permanently in Russia; and the edict of Jan. 13, 1825, removing the Jews from villages to towns and cities in the governments of Mohilev and Vitebsk. »

Tsar Nicholas I, who followed Alexander I in 1825, was more hostile to the Jews than his father:

> «[274]Nicholas I had tried in his own harsh, autocratic way to Russianize the Jews. Among other austere measures he introduced the canonists' school for the military education of Jewish minors, who were forcibly torn from their parents. They had to pass through a rough discipline and were often compelled to join the Greek Orthodox Church. »

His reign was known by a distrust of the Jewish people greater than that of any of his predecessors. Nicholas I was obsessed with the forced conversion of the Jews to Christianity, and in his reign innumerable laws were established aimed at reducing their rights of citizenship, mobility, establishing special taxes, and others related even to their clothes. New restrictions were imposed on Jews' access to

---

[273] Cyrus Adler, *Jewish Encyclopedia, vol. I*, p. 346.
[274] Cyrus Adler, *Jewish Encyclopedia, vol. I*, p. 346.

universities and political life, and by June 14, 1892, some 14,000 Jewish artisans had been expelled from Moscow. In the last decade of the nineteenth century pogroms or "ethnic cleansing" and other anti-Jewish manifestations intensified in the country. The repressive measures were also extended to Catholics, Lutherans and Armenians, always in favor of the Orthodox Church. The Jews began to embrace Zionism, an emerging Jewish nationalist movement that sought the emancipation of the people of Israel[275].

Alexander II, who ascended the throne in 1855, was known as "the liberator" because in 1861 he released tens of thousands of serfs throughout the Empire, who until then had been literally vassals in a feudal regime of agrarian servitude. The Tsar changed their legal status and gave them land on property, which expropriated the large landowners in exchange for a fair price. The peasants or "kulaks" were only required in return to pay a small annual fee. This Tsar also abolished capital punishment.

Alexander II contributed to maintain the balance of powers in the world, playing a decisive role in the American Civil War, in a little-known historical episode. In the year 1862 the British Prime Minister Gladstone and the French Emperor Napoleon III threatened to intervene in the course of the Civil War, which faced the North and the South of the United States. England and France intended to support the southern side in order to provoke the division of the United States into two weaker countries, as the emerging nation began to overshadow the European powers. Contrary to this idea, Alexander II declared that Russia would not maintain its neutrality and would support the United States in case European powers intervened against Lincoln's army. In the autumn of 1963, the army of the Union was under the imminent threat of an attack or blockade of the powerful Franco-British fleet. But Alexander II, the liberator of the Russian serfs, came to the aid of Abraham Lincoln, the emancipator of African-American slaves. Russia deployed its Baltic Sea fleet in the port of New York on September 24,

[275] Cyrus Adler, *Jewish Encyclopedia, vol. X,* p.p. 523-526.

and on October 12 its fleet in the Pacific stopped at the port of San Francisco, ensuring with this maneuver the European neutrality in the American conflict. Probably this was not to the liking of European financiers like the Rothschilds, who had bet heavily on the secessionist victory, investing a fortune in southern bonds.

Alexander II devoted his reign to improve the conditions of the unprivileged, and among them of the Jews, although they were not granted rights more similar to those that already enjoyed in other countries:

> «[276]Aware of the mistakes his father had made in his despotic policy toward the Jews, Alexander endeavored to correct them, and early manifested a friendly disposition toward his Jewish subjects. He abolished the cantonists' school, admitted Jews to the high schools and universities, and by the laws of March 16, 1859, and of Nov. 27, 1861, he granted to Jewish scholars, university graduates, wholesale merchants, manufacturers, and (1865) artisans the privilege of settling, under certain conditions, outside of the Pale, in the interior provinces of Russia…
>
> It should not be overlooked, however, that the emancipation of the Jews had at that time been completed in most of the countries of western Europe; and that these privileges were granted only to certain classes of Jews in Russia for political and economic reasons, the object of the government being to promote the commercial and industrial interests of the interior provinces. For the masses of the Jewish population these reform laws accomplished little, since the 2,500,000 Jews within the Pale, not belonging to the privileged class, were still debarred from the right of settlement and could not emigrate from the overcrowded provinces of Poland and Lithuania. »

---

[276] Cyrus Adler, *Jewish Encyclopedia, vol. I*, p. 346.

Jewish newspapers were authorized such as *Sion*, *Den*, *Yevreiskaya Biblioteka* and *Voskhod* and some published in Hebrew as *Ha-Meliz*, *Ha-Karmel* or *Ha-Zefirah*. New exceptions to the "Settlement Limits" were introduced and qualified Jews or those of certain social levels were allowed to settle outside the limits to which they had been confined; merchants first, doctors later, artisans and those who complete military service[277].

A great reformer and modernizer of the Russian Empire, in his reign the first outbreaks and revolutionary revolts took place, and the attacks against his life were incessant. In 1866 Alexander II suffered his first assassination attempt while he was in his garden, but when he was about to be shot by Dimitri Karakozov a man removed the aggressor's weapon and the tsar escaped unharmed. Again in 1879, when he was walking in the street he was attacked by a student, Alexander Soloviev. When he saw a weapon in his hands, the Tsar run away and left unharmed although Soloviev shot him in five occasions. In 1879 another revolutionary group *Narodnaya Volia* "The Will of the People" blew up the train in which he was traveling, but much to his luck his car was not reached. In 1980, the same group tried it again at the Winter Palace, and the Tsar once again escaped unharmed, although another 67 people were injured or killed.

On March 13, 1881, the Tsar was going in his carriage to review the troops, when the young revolutionary Nikolai Rysakov threw a bomb under his carriage. The Tsar was unharmed because he traveled in an armored carriage, a present of Napoleon III. The explosion killed a Cossack and seriously injured several but the Tsar was only shaken by the explosion. He was warned that there might be other assassins, and he agreed to leave the place quickly, but firstly he wanted to inspect the hole left by the explosion. Then a second man named Ignacy Hryniewiecki threw another artifact at the Tsar's feet that exploded and eventually ended his life. The chief of police Dvorzhitsky would write:

---

[277] Cyrus Adler, *Jewish Encyclopedia, vol. X,* p. 518.

«[278]I was deafened by the new explosion, burned, wounded and thrown to the ground. Suddenly, amid the smoke and snowy fog, I heard His Majesty's weak voice cry, 'Help!' Gathering what strength I had, I jumped up and rushed to the emperor. His Majesty was half-lying, half-sitting, leaning on his right arm. Thinking he was merely wounded heavily, I tried to lift him but the czar's legs were shattered, and the blood poured out of them. Twenty people, with wounds of varying degree, lay on the sidewalk and on the street. Some managed to stand, others to crawl, still others tried to get out from beneath bodies that had fallen on them. Through the snow, debris, and blood you could see fragments of clothing, epaulets, sabres, and bloody chunks of human flesh. »

A third man, Ivan Emelyanov, was also identified among the crowd. He carried a briefcase with explosives in case the second attempt also failed. The tsar was evacuated to the Winter Palace, leaving behind a trail of blood. There he received Extreme Unction and died in terrible agony. One of the last projects on which Alexander II worked was the creation of the Duma, a parliament for Russia. He was one of the few monarchs in history who on his own initiative set out to give a parliament to his people. Alexander II suffered a fate similar to that of his friend Abraham Lincoln.

Encyclopedia Judaica also mentions that some of the Alexander II measures were incomplete and left some legal gaps that led to the abuse of the Jews: "Nevertheless, the Russian Jews fully appreciated the good intentions of the czar and have always regarded him as their liberator." And concluded: "[279]When the assassination of Alexander by nihilist conspirators became known, the Jews of Russia deeply mourned the loss of the benevolent czar and liberator."

---

[278] Edward Radzinsky, *Alexander II, The Last Great Tsar*, 2005, p. 415.

[279] Cyrus Adler, *Jewish Encyclopedia, vol. I*, p. 347.

In the decade following the assassination of Alexander II, the Tsars allowed or encouraged anti-Semitism, based on the circumstance that a significant number of members of the *Narodnaya Volya* executive committee were of Jewish ethnicity[280]. The Judaica Encyclopedia denied any cause-effect relationship: "[281]It was certainly not the fault of the Jewish masses that some of the quickly Russianized Jewish students and other youths took an active part in the revolutionary movement of the seventies." And added: "The participation of some Jewish youths in the revolutionary movement of the Nihilists was made use of to lead the Russian people to believe that the Jews were connected with the conspiracy which had resulted in the murder of Alexander II. Hostility against the Jews was fostered in order to divert the attention of the discontented elements, and if possible to suppress the revolutionary movement."

His heir, Alexander III, succeeded him, and distinguished himself by an absolutist rule, paying special attention to the Slavic population and trying to russify the rest of the country's ethnic groups. Shortly after Alexander III ascended to the throne, anti-Jewish riots or pogroms took place in the country, in Elizabethgrad (April 27 and 28), Kiev (May 8 to 11), Shpola (May 9), Ananiev (9) May), Wasilikov (May 10) and Konotop (May 10), which continued in very different parts of the country during the following six months. "[282]In these riots thousands of Jewish homes were destroyed, many families reduced to extremes of poverty; women outraged and large numbers of men, women, and children killed or injured."

The Encyclopedia states that the abuses were carried out in the face of the passivity of the Tsar's government and even suggests that

---

280 Jews like Aaron Gobet, Solomon Wittenberg, Meir Mlodetsky and Grigori Goldenberg were members of the Executive Committee of the Organization. Also were members Aaron Zundelevich and Saveli Zlatopolsky. Nancy Synkoff, *Socialism*, Jewish Virtual Library. Website revised in 2013.

281 Cyrus Adler, *Jewish Encyclopedia, vol. I,* this and next quotation, p.p. 346-347.

282 Cyrus Adler, *Jewish Encyclopedia, vol. I,* p. 347.

with his consent. In a circular issued by order of the Tsars, General Ignatiev attributed the riots to the alleged exploitation that the Jewish had exerted over the Slavic population. In Warsaw, in 1881, twelve Jews were killed and many women were assaulted. In Nyezhin the soldiers murdered and looted the property of a Jewish family, and in Lubny three soldiers murdered a family of six Jews. In Balta in 1882, another eight Jews were killed and two hundred people were wounded. Thousands of their houses were demolished and their property looted throughout the empire. The "Temporary Laws" of May 15, 1882 drastically diminished the rights of the Jews, confining them back to the Pale of Settlement. More than thirty thousand Jewish homes were reduced to ashes and hundreds of thousands immigrated to the United States. In 1890 the British minister Gladstone declared that he had "read with pain and horror the various statements respecting the sufferings of the Jews in Russia, and that the thing to do, if the facts could be established, was to rouse the conscience of Russia and Europe in regard to them. [283]"

The last of the Tsars, Nicholas II, had an ambiguous behavior towards the Jews. According to the Encyclopedia Judaica, he softened some of the measures imposed by his predecessor, but they were deprived of their main sources of income by nationalizing the alcohol trade, prohibiting their participation in the construction of the Siberian railway or forbidding their language in their businesses, in addition to other commercial limitations. Violence and expulsions of Jews in the country resumed, and an ordinance was issued prohibiting Zionist meetings. The Jewish Encyclopedia affirms that "All these measures of oppression were carried out by the government (as was admitted by Von Plehve to the Zionist leader, Dr. Herzl) because of the participation of Jewish youth in the socialistic movement[284]."

---

[283] Cyrus Adler, *Jewish Encyclopedia, vol. I*, p. 348.
[284] Cyrus Adler, *Jewish Encyclopedia, vol. X*, p. 527.

TSAR NICHOLAS ROMANOV AND HIS FAMILY, 1911

Tsar Nicholas II in the center. Left to Right Tatiana, Maria, Tsarina Alexandra, Anastasia, the heir Alexis Nicolaievich and Olga.

The Revolution of 1905

The history of Judaism is closely intertwined with that of Socialism. Socialism was considered an extension of their emancipation movement and it was also a symbol of his struggle against the oppression of the tsars, starting with Karl Marx himself, father of communism and a leader of Jewish origin. The Jewish Encyclopedia points out that "Jews have been prominently identified with the modern Socialist movement from its very inception[285]". In 1897 the Federation of Jewish Workers was founded for Lithuania, Poland and Russia, better known as the "Bund", which would have an enormous relevance in the advent of Socialism in Russia.

Demonstrations, strikes, riots and assassinations took place all over Russia after the arrival of Alexander III. Bogolepov, Minister of Education, was assassinated in 1901 by the Social Revolutionary Party, in retaliation for the May Laws, which limited access to the university to Jews. In 1902 the Minister of the Interior Sipyagin was assassinated, for the discontent with the laws that relegated the Jews to the "Pale of Settlement". In 1903 Bogdanovich, governor of Ufa followed and in 1904 the prime minister Von Plehve. Grand Duke Sergius, uncle of the Tsar was assassinated in 1905 and in 1906 General Dubrassov.

Important families of Jewish financiers such as the Rothschilds or the Schiffs refused to have deals with Russia, and refused to participate in the country's finances until the fall of the tsars. On the powerful Rothschild family, indicates the 1905 Encyclopedia of Judaica[286]:

> «Of recent years the Rothschilds have consistently refused to have anything to do with loans to Russia, owing to the anti-Jewish legislation of that empire, though on one occasion the members of the Paris house joined in a loan to demonstrate their patriotism as Frenchmen. »

---

285 Cyrus Adler, *Encyclopedia Judaica, vol. XI*, p. 418.
286 Cyrus Adler, *Encyclopedia Judaica, vol. X*, p. 497.

Jacob Schiff, his agent in the United States, would do the same until the fall of the tsars[287]:

> «Mr. Schiff on numerous occasions refused to participate in Russian loans, and used his great influence to prevent the entry of Russia into the money markets of America, solely because of the ill-treatment of the Jews by the Russian Government. »

Schiff, in charge of the most important investment house in the United States, *Kuhn & Loeb*, not only denied credit to Russia but he also financed massively the Tsar's enemy Japan, in the 1905 Japanese-Russian War. Japanese Finance Minister Bakatani stated that[288]:

> «When Japan was undertaking, in London in the spring of 1904, to negotiate a loan of ten million pounds and was finding difficulty in securing the amount "Mr. Schiff in a single conversation with Mr. Takahashi offered to underwrite single-handed a half of what we wanted." He concluded with the statement: "The amount of our loan subscribed by Mr. Schiff from the first to the fifth issue arrives at a grand total of £39,250,000." »

Schiff financed pre-war Japan with almost forty million pounds out of his own pocket, and instrumentalized the issuance in the United States of 200 million dollars of Japanese war bonds, a real fortune of the time. This loan was well know at the time and it is confirmed by several sources[289].

On February 8, 1904 Japan made a declaration of war against Russia and only three hours later they attacked the Russian fleet berthed

---

[287] Cyrus Adler, *Jacob Henry Schiff, A Biographical Sketch*, The New York American Jewish Committee, 1921, New York, p. 16.

[288] Cyrus Adler, *Jacob Henry Schiff, A Biographical Sketch*, p. 15.

[289] Seymour Brody, *Jewish Heroes and Heroines in America: 150 True Histories of American Jewish Heroism*, 1996, Lifetime Books Inc., Hollywood.

in Port Arthur. Tsar Nicholas II was so perplexed by the attack that he did not declare war on Japan until eight days later. The dispute arose around Manchuria, the northeastern region of China. In spite of being an industrialized country and extremely rich in natural resources, Russia's finances were not in the best possible condition, and among the great powers only France contributed with loans. Despite this, Russia proved incapable of winning a single battle.

The case astonished the entire Western world, since it was the first time that an Asian power, of a tiny geographical extension like Japan, inflicted such a humiliating defeat on a Western power of the size of the Russian Empire. The American Army General Smedley Butler attributed the Japanese victory to the change of loyalties of the American government, influenced by the participation of some American financiers in dealings with Japan.

> «[290]Back in 1904, when Russia and Japan fought, we kicked out our old friends the Russians and backed Japan. Then our very generous international bankers were financing Japan.»

On September 5, 1905, Russia signed peace with Japan in the Treaty of Portsmouth. Tsar Nicholas II had no interest in continuing the war, especially when his domestic affairs became more and more complicated. The year that the war with Japan began, Russia was crumbling, torn inside with strikes and conflicts promoted by various socialist groups.

Nicholas II pointed directly to the Jewish people as the cause of economic ruin and unrest in the Empire. The government of the tsars published the *Protocols of the Elders of Zion*, the alleged minutes of a group of international Jewish leaders whose aim was the world domination of the *goym* or non-Jews through corruption and deception. The documents were taken as reference for other later anti-Semitic works like *The International Jew* of Henry Ford or the *Mein Kampf* of Adolf

[290] Smedley Butler, *War is a Racket*.

Hitler[291]. Many Jews in Europe worried about the rise of anti-Semitism, and years later in Germany, their worst fears would be confirmed.

The mistreatment of the tsars to the Jewish people was inexcusable from any point of view, but destabilizing economically a country like Russia and waging a war with Japan, Jacob Schiff and the Rothschilds might not realize the bad service they were doing to their people in Russia, and in Europe, generally speaking. The Jewish population in 1897 represented a 4.13 per cent of the 126 million inhabitants of the Russian Empire[292].

If there was a before and an after in the relationship between the people and the Tsars, that turning point occurred on January 22, 1905, the so called "Bloody Sunday". That day, a peaceful and orderly march was called in St. Petersburg to deliver a request to the Tsar at the Winter Palace, calling for improvements in the conditions of the country's workers. The Tsar saw his image worsening after the military defeat against Japan, but he was still a figure appreciated by the people. Inexplicably and without a warning, the guard detached at the Winter Palace opened fire against the unarmed civilians who had gathered to protest peacefully. The exact number of victims is not known, but these could reach a few hundreds. It is known that the Tsar was not in the Winter Palace that day, not even in the city, but the Bolsheviks already had the spark they needed to start the first revolution of 1905. The workers of Russia joined en masse to the Revolutionary Socialist Party. The Tsar then opened a commission of inquiry to clarify what had happened, and Alexander II's parliamentary project, the Duma, was set in motion again. The amnesty offered to political prisoners in 1905 was an opportunity for many exiled Bolshevik revolutionaries to return to

---

[291] Some time later it was determined by experts that the Protocols, published in 1905 by a Russian officer named Serguei Nilus were a plagiarism or rewriting or a former work, the *Dialogue in Hell Between Machiavelli and Montesquieu* published in Brussels in 1865. The original text was a pamphlet of an author named Maurice Joly against Napoleon III.

[292] Encyclopedia Judaica, Vol X, p. 529.

the country in a fateful year for the country. The revolutionaries inspired by the ideas of Marx and Engels took control of St. Petersburg from October to December 1905 and formed the Soviet in St. Petersburg, with the revolutionary Leon Trotsky heading it. Strikes spread throughout the country, most factories closed and railroads were paralyzed. After the "Bloody Sunday" the strikes and riots spread throughout the country and the political position of the Tsar became very precarious.

On December 16, Trotsky and a large part of the members of the Soviet were arrested. On December 20 Alexander Parvus - Hebrew name Israel Helphand - took control of the Soviet, and called a massive strike that paralyzed the entire country. The insurrection broke out in the big cities, but on December 30 the troops loyal to the Tsar regained control of the country. Nicholas II kept his promise to form the Duma and to limit the powers of the monarchy. Trotsky was deported to Siberia in 1907, but managed to escape to the United States, where he was very active until his return in 1917. Lenin also escaped that year and returned in time for the Second Russian Revolution of 1917. Lenin and Trotsky spent their exile years in the financial capitals of the Western world.

LEON TROTSKY

Revolutionary Bolshevik, first leader of the Soviet of Petrograd.

Trotsky

Born by the Hebrew name Leiba Davidovich Bronstein, the life of Leon Trotsky is an open book, and one can read it in his autobiography. The son of a Ukrainian landowner, Trotsky spent his first years in his native village of Kherson, until in 1898 and only 19 years old was arrested in relation to his Marxist militancy. After a tour by various prisons, Trotsky was sent to his first exile in Siberia in 1900 for four years, which he avoided by fleeing to Russia in 1902 without serving his sentence. He confessed in his memoirs that that year he began his strange journey in a bourgeois institution such as Freemasonry, and then understood its special revolutionary significance[293]:

> «It was during that period that I became interested in freemasonry. For several months, I avidly studied books on its history, books given to me by relatives and friends in the town. Why had the merchants, artists, bankers, officials, and lawyers, from the first quarter of the seventeenth century on, begun to call themselves masons and tried to recreate the ritual of the medieval guilds? What was all this strange masquerade about? Gradually the picture grew clearer… In certain branches of freemasonry, elements of an obvious reactionary feudalism were prominent, as in the Scottish system. In the eighteenth century, freemasonry became expressive of a militant policy of enlightenment, as in the case of the Illuminati, who were the forerunners of revolution;-on its left, it culminated in the Carbonari. »

Trotsky accurately points out that Masonic lodges in Europe, since the time of the Enlightenment and due to its peculiar characteristics -it was a secret and international association of influential intellectuals and bourgeois- acted as centers of propagation of a mixture of emerging

[293] Leon Trotsky, *My Life, An Attempt at Autobiography*, Charles Scribner's Sons, 1930, New York, chapter 8 (ebook).

revolutionary ideas, generally contrary to the existing authority of the time, to the so-called "old regime". Among all these ideas that could be called progressive, revolutionary, anti-monarchical, secular and socialist, the Zionist influence stood out, being the same Masonic institution inspired by personalities, myths and symbols of Judaism.

In his flight Trotsky escaped by train to Vienna, where he met Victor Adler[294], a Marxist Jew and father of the Austrian Social Democracy, which helped him to hide. Then Zurich, Paris, London, Liege, Brussels, Heidelberg and Munich, where he stayed at the home of his friend Alexander Parvus (born Israel Helphand). From there he returned to St. Petersburg, where he lived under a false identity between Russia and Finland, until the revolution began. Trotsky returned in time for the great strike of October 1905, which paralyzed the country's factories.

Trotsky, along with Alexander Parvus and Lev Kamenev (born Rosenfeld), organized the 1905 revolution. Kamenev, another revolutionary leader, was married to Trotsky's sister. Leon Trotsky became the leader of the short-lived Soviet of St. Petersburg (a city later known as Petrograd) until the end of 1905. But the strike began to die out and the government regained control. In 1906 the first elections to the Duma were held and that year a Constitution was promulgated. Trotsky was sentenced to a second exile in perpetuity in Siberia but in 1907 he escaped again. That year he got in contact with Rosa Luxemburg (Róza Luksemburg), another Jewish Marxist of Polish origin who led the Spartacist uprising in Germany in the year 1919[295].

---

[294] His son, Friedrich Adler, assassinated in 1916 the Austrian Chief of Ministers count Karl von Stürgkh, with three shots. Friedrich was sentenced to death but a court decision reduced it to 18 years of prison, and finally he was liberated after two years.

[295] Rosa Luxemburg and Karl Liebknetch founded in 1916 the Spartacist League, the seed of the German Communist Party (KPD) in 1918. The Spartacist Uprising was a Marxist movement that tried to overthrow the Social Democrat government of Friedrich Ebert, the first President of the Weimar Republic. With

Trotsky did more than anyone to spread the communist revolution all over the world: Berlin, Jena, Copenhagen, Vienna, the Balkans and Zurich again, where he met Karl Radek (born Karól Sobelsohn), another of the leaders of the Workers Party.

Leon Trotsky was well connected with all the factions of the Party, with the Mensheviks -the moderate revolutionaries, the minority faction- and with the Bolsheviks -radical revolutionaries, the majority faction-. In 1914 Trotsky met in Paris with Yuli Martov (born Zederbaum)[296], one of the leaders of the Mensheviks, and Trotsky also maintained a close correspondence with the Bolshevik leader Pavel Axelrod (born Borisovich).

In my first work I spoke about Freemasonry and the Illuminati, whom Trotsky calls "the forerunners of revolution" and its influence on the French Revolution and others. There is a remarkable parallel in the development of the French Revolution and the Russian Revolution, as if the same forces guided the development of both movements. The two revolutions were of an essentially anti-monarchical and anti-clerical nature. In both the revolutionaries splintered into a moderate faction -the Girondists and the Mensheviks- and the radical wing -Jacobins and Bolsheviks-. During a brief interlude the revolutionary regime coexisted with a democratic system –the Duma in Russia, the National Assembly in France- until the radical faction devoured the moderate ones and the Parliament, establishing a reign of terror. French socialists like Babeuf, Marechal and others were, after all, the ideological precursors of Communism.

In September 1915 the most prominent members of socialism in Europe attended the Zimmerwald Conference: for the Russian Mensheviks were Axelrod and Martov; by the Bolsheviks Lenin and Zinoviev (real name Hirsch Apfelbaum); by the Socialist Federation of

---

the support of Marshall Hindenburg, the new communist revolution was suffocated and all his leaders, including Luxemburg, were executed.

[296] He was co-founder with Lenin of the revolutionary journal Iskra and eventually he was leader of the Menshevik faction.

the Balkans, Christian Rakovsky; by Poland Karl Radek and Adolf Warski (born Jerzy Adolf Warszawski). Trotsky was also present as representative and a founder of the revolutionary newspaper *Nashe Slovo* "our word" of Paris. The conference concluded with a manifesto in which they called for the international proletarian union. In 1916 Trotsky was expelled from France, officially for his presence in the Zimmerwald Congress, although his incendiary articles in *Nashe Slovo* made him a very uncomfortable guest for the French government. He was escorted to the Spanish border, where he was arrested in Madrid, and then he moved first to Cadiz and then to Barcelona, where his European journey ended. From there he left with his family on the transatlantic *Montserrat* to New York, where he arrived on January 13, 1917.

Regarding the time he resided in United States Trotsky claimed that "his only profession in New York was revolutionary socialist", but as Professor Sutton pointed out there were some inconsistencies in his autobiography; How did he paid rent for his apartment on Vyse Avenue, a well-off neighborhood that nobody would expect for a jobless proletarian? The apartment had all the luxuries of the time, such as a telephone and a refrigerator, and occasionally used a limousine with a driver, according to his own memories[297]. Trotsky claimed that his only income in America came from his sporadic collaborations with a small Marxist newspaper called *Novy Mir*, but he had an uncommon standard of living for a socialist revolutionary with no known trade. Who were his American benefactors? Where did his income come from?

After his visit to the United States, Trotsky soon took advantage of the amnesty granted by the Kerensky government to the revolutionaries, and on March 27, 1917, he embarked with his family on the ship *S.S. Kristianiafjord*, leaving New York for Russia. He was about to complete a revolutionary course that had begun in 1905. In the strange passage of the ship there were a large number of Russian

---

[297] Leon Trotsky, *My Life, An Attempt at Autobiography*, chapter 22.

citizens with an American passport, as well as some prominent American industrialists. On April 3, 1917, the ship called at Nova Scotia, Canada, where Leon Trotsky was arrested by the police along with his family and five other Russian socialists, on suspicion of being agents of Germany.

Trotsky carried an American passport and $ 10,000 in cash, a fortune for the time which he claimed it was given by some German citizens in the United States[298]. Trotsky also had the support of his cousin Abraham Zhivotovsky, a Kiev banker who in 1918 was already acting on behalf of the Bolsheviks[299].

Anthony Sutton linked the release of Trotsky to a diplomatic cable of the British government advocating for his release, and a month after being imprisoned, on May 4, Trotsky was set free. It is even stranger that Trotsky, a well-known socialist revolutionary, managed to obtain an American passport from the administration of Woodrow Wilson. The American government not only did not stop Trotsky's return to Russia with $ 10,000 but also provided the documents for his trip. It seems equally absurd to think that the British, American and Canadian intelligence services were unaware of who Trotsky was and the repercussions that his trip to Russia would have for the three Allied countries in the Cordial Entente, United States, Canada and Great Britain. The Russian Revolution collapsed their main ally in the fight against Germany, causing its withdrawal of Russia from the World War I. The fall of the Tsars unnecessarily extended the war, and costed the lives of many American, British and Canadian soldiers at the battlefront.

When the revolution triumphed in Russia in 1917 it was not Trotsky but Lenin, who seized power. Trotsky was the expected

[298] Sutton, *Wall Street and the Bolshevik Revolution*, p. 28.

[299] Mentioned by different sources as Givotovsky, Jivotovsky or Givatovzo. For some authors he was the father of his wife Natalia Sedova, for others, the "uncle Abram" which Trotsky mentions in his memories. Probably Sutton's affirmation that he was his cousin is correct (*Wall Street and the Bolshevik Revolution*, p. 122).

candidate to succeed him, but a long convalescence allowed Josef Stalin to take the lead. Trotsky still played an important role as a diplomat, negotiating the withdrawal of Russia from the First World War with the Treaty of Brest-Litovsk, but he was gradually removed from the power and finally expelled from the USSR in 1929. After wandering out of his fatherland for several years, in 1937 Mexican President Lazaro Cardenas granted him political asylum in his country. In 1940 he suffered an attempt of assassination when a group of men shot repeatedly his bed, but he and his wife heard the attackers and had time to save their lives by hiding behind a wall. A few months later Ramón Mercader, a Spanish agent of Stalin's secret police, the NKVD, managed to get close to him pretending to be an admirer and when he had the chance he stuck an ice ax in his head. Trotsky died in agony the following day. Many Marxist romantics still think that if Trotsky, and not Lenin or Stalin had prevailed the revolution would have been different: the communist utopia would have flourished in Russia and Marx's socioeconomic system would have been accepted all over the world.

In June 1907 Russia regained control of the country, which had been in the hands of Trotsky and Parvus. The Prime Minister of Nicholas II, Peter Stolypin, declared martial law and tens of thousands of Russian revolutionaries fled to the United States, which became a sanctuary for terrorists. Stolypin was a great reformer in all areas: he gave a constitution to the country, granted freedom of the press and legalized all political parties. The army and the navy were modernized. The small farmers took three quarters of the land and an industrial explosion occurred. Russia started producing more grain than the United States, Canada and Argentina combined. Moreover, Russia was beginning to become a great oil power thanks to its wells in the Caucasus, which in 1901 produced more than half of the world's oil[300].

Stolypin had the same tragic luck of Alexander II. The Marxist revolutionaries dynamited the house of Prime Minister, resulting in the

---

[300] Anthony Cyril Sutton, *Western Technology and Soviet Economic Development, 1917 to 1930*, Stanford University, 1970, California, p.p. 4, 16.

explosion 28 dead and 33 injured. Among the victims were Stolypin's children: His fifteen-year-old daughter was thrown out of the window was split in two by the explosion, and his three-year-old son was also injured[301]. The last assassination attempt against Stolypin took place on September 14, 1911. He was shot dead in cold blood by policeman Dimitri Bogrov (Mordecai Gershkovich) in the presence of the Tsar and his family. The murder took place in the opera, repeating Lincoln's assassination. And like Lincoln, Stolypin died after several days agonizing. In September, he planned to inaugurate a monument in Kiev in honor of Tsar Alexander II. Stolypin survived ten attacks, even more attempts to end his life than Alexander II.

[301] The New York Times, 26 August, 1906, *Bomb Kills 28, Hurts Stolypin*.

VLADIMIR ILICH ULIANOV, LENIN

Revoutionary Bolshevik, first leader of the Soviet Russia.

Lenin

Soon a man named Alexander Ulyanov would join the Russian revolutionary movement. He was the son of a high school inspector and the eldest of six brothers. Before becoming a member of the party, he was required to prove his courage by assassinating Tsar Alexander III. His attempt failed, and after being put on trial he was executed. His younger brother Vladimir Lenin (born Ilich Ulyanov) also joined the cause, and he eventually became the leader of the Bolsheviks and first dictator of the newly born Union of Soviet Socialist Republics.

Lenin began law studies but was expelled from the university. In 1895 for his participation in various riots Lenin, Martov and other revolutionaries were arrested and sent into exile in Siberia from 1897 to 1900. On his return Lenin moved to Switzerland, and it was then when he and Martov decided to publish a revolutionary newspaper called *Iskra* or "The spark", whose name was quite a declaration of intentions. Lenin's wife, Nadezhda Krupskaya, was the secretary of the publishing house and Trotsky joined two years later. The newspaper *Isrka* was printed in Germany and the editorial board met in London and later in Genoa. The copies were smuggled into Russia. Few of the initiators of the communist movement in Russia were really proletarians and almost all of them were rather educated intellectuals, just as Lenin was.

In February 1900 Lenin concluded his exile and was allowed to return to Switzerland. In the summer of 1903 the Congress of the Workers' Party took place in Brussels, and its chief aim was to coordinate all the Marxist groups under a single party. The meeting was attended by the foremost Marxist leaders, although they soon had to move the congress to London due to the intervention of the Belgian police. Lenin represented the most radical faction, which had the most popular support, in contrast with the moderate faction led by Martov. After this split, both factions were called Bolshevik (majority) and Menchevik (minority).

After the failure of the revolution of 1905, Lenin left Petrograd with Zinoviev, and despite the arrest warrant hanging over him, no one got in his way. The 5th International Congress of the Workers Party which took place in London in 1907 became a war of accusations between various socialist factions, due to the failure of the revolution of 1905. Lenin came to the conclusion that the only formula of success for Communism was to implement the system on an international scale, and in 1919 the First Communist International or *Komintern* took place, bringing together leaders from all over the world. His goal was to extend the socialist revolution outside the borders of Russia. During the twentieth century the entire world felt the tentacles of Communism.

In 1917 Lenin began his own financing campaign that included robbery, blackmail, extortion and all kinds of illegal practices. Any new member had to pass his initiation robbing a bank, killing a traitor or a spy or blowing up a police station. Just as his deceased brother did. The Bolsheviks gradually gained power until Tsar Nicholas II abdicated on March 2, and the following day his brother Grand Duke Michael Aleksandrovich renounced to succeed him.

The Revolution of 1917

In July 1914 Russia entered the First World War in support of the Entente and against Germany. Its economic situation only worsened after its war with Japan first, and with Germany later. Afterwards, a number of strikes in all sectors followed in the country. The country was still immersed in the war when a second revolution in 1917 broke out, precipitating the exit of the conflict in 1918.

Lenin returned on April 3, 1917 and presented his April Theses, giving a breath of fresh air to the revolution. The provisional government of Kerensky called for a general amnesty that included not only political prisoners but also common prisoners, and thousands of criminals were released only in St. Petersburg. The most absolute anarchy extended throughout the Russian Empire. Upon leaving prison, the revolutionaries returned with more force than ever to complete the revolution begun years before.

From March to November 1917, a provisional coalition of parties was established, being briefly led by conservative Georgy Lvov of the Constitutional Party, and then by the socialist Alexander Kerensky of the Social Revolutionary Party. For a brief period of time three different forces claimed to legitimately hold power over the country. Firstly, the Petrograd Soviet with a radical revolutionary fashion, secondly the Kerensky parliamentary government, of a more moderate and democratic style, and finally the disempowered government of the Tsar.

The helplessness of Nicholas II became evident after the troops mutinied when they were asked to quell the increasingly frequent street riots. In a wrong decision the Tsar temporarily suspended the Duma, but on March 12 the deputies refused to dissolve it and formed a provisional government led by Kerensky. This government began to coexist in parallel with the establishment of a new Soviet. On September 1 the commander-in-chief of the Russian army Lavr Kornilov, loyal to the Tsar, ordered the Cossacks to attack Petrograd. During Kornilov's uprising the interim government of Kerensky and the Bolsheviks united against the Tsarist troops.

In October 1917 the Bolsheviks decided that it was time to conclude with the duality of power in Russia and formed a revolutionary military committee in the Petrograd Soviet. On the night of October 24 to 25 the Winter Palace, the former residence of the Tsars which at that time served as the center of the provisional government of Kerensky, was seized. The coup to the Kerensky democratic government was known by him in advance and had even appeared in the press. If the plans of the Bolsheviks to give a coup were well known and public so well in advance, why did Kerensky did nothing to stop it, why didn't he send troops? The truth is that both Kerensky and Lenin were revolutionary socialists with slight ideological nuances. Fyodor Kerensky, father of Alexander Kerensky, was the director of the school in Simbirsk where Lenin studied, and probably Lenin and Kerensky were already old acquaintances. The taking of the Winter Palace was not a *coup d'état* but the staging needed to transfer power from one hand to another. There was no bloodshed: the cadets and the Cossacks were ordered to leave their garrison. The Red Army only had to wait to march on the Palace. The democratic government did not exert any resistance to be replaced by the Council of People's Commissars or *Sovnarkom,* established by the Russian revolutionaries.

On November 8 Lenin was ahead of Trotsky in the race to lead the Revolution and he was elected as President of the Council of People's Commissars by the Congress of Russian Soviets. But Trotsky still remained at the forefront for some time as he was sent to negotiate peace with Germany.

In the winter of 1917 the Bolsheviks controlled Moscow and St. Petersburg. The Tsar, his wife and daughters were shot along with several servants. According to the most recent investigations the royal family was executed in Ekaterinburg on July 18, 1918. The last remains of the Russian royal family were found in a mass grave in 2007, and regarding the speculations about the luck of their daughter Anastasia, it seems that none of the children of the tsars survived. Lenin's leadership was brief, because in August 1918 he received three shots from the revolutionary socialist Fanya Kaplan, and his health only worsened since then. He suffered several brain strokes that left him prostrate and speechless by 1923 and died in early 1924. Josef Stalin seized power several years before Lenin's death in 1922. Trotsky went to exile in 1929.

JOSEPH STALIN

General Secretary of the Communist Party of the Soviet Union.
Together with his Vice President Vyacheslav Molotov.

Stalin

Josef Vissarionovich Dzhugashvili, better known by his nickname Joseph Stalin -meaning "man of steel"- was born in Gori, Georgia, in 1878. His family moved to the city of Tbilisi when he was very young. His alcoholic father mistreated him and his mother, which possibly helped to forge his cold character and lacking any empathy. He was educated in a seminar of the Orthodox Church but he did not finish his studies and joined the socialist movement very young.

In 1900 Stalin came into contact with revolutionaries of the newspaper *Iskra.* In Baku he led several strikes and from 1902 to 1917 he suffered several arrests, including being exiled to Siberia. He went underground and his merits made him rise in the hierarchies of the socialist movement as one of its most important members. After the revolution of 1917 he took over the most important newspaper in the country, *Pravda.*

At the beginning of the revolution, Stalin was one of Lenin's trusted men, in charge of doing the dirty work. Stalin participated in assassinations, terrorism and propaganda and in the collection of money for the Bolshevik cause, through extortion and robbery. One of his most well-known works was the robbery to a bank in Tbilisi. In 1907 Stalin heard of a large transfer from the *Imperial Bank* and organized an ambush with his comrades in which they used homemade weapons and explosives. About 40 people died in the robbery, and the loot included 250,000 rubles, a considerable fortune.

After the death of Lenin, in 1924 Stalin allied with Kamenev and Zinoviev to form the *troika*, a faction of power within the party opposed to Trotsky. Stalin was an ambitious, calculating and tenacious man, and his power within the party increased until in 1929 he overtook his three rivals, Trotsky, Kamenev and Zinoviev.

Stalin represents a good example of what a Communism in practice means to a country. A recent attempt to express in figures the rigors of communism in Russia has been *The Black Book of Communism*, written by a team of university professors headed by Stéphane Courtois, director of the National Center for Scientific Research in France. This work accounted for 20 million victims of the reign of terror of the Soviet Union[302]. These are extremely prudent estimates, based on the scanty data rescued from the hermetic communist system, which hid the traces of its atrocities to the West and its own population.

Among the mass brutalities committed in the Soviet Union we can mention the *decossackization* or murder and deportation of the Cossacks of 1920 and the *deculackization* of 1930 to 1932, the persecution of the kulaks or humble farmers to whom Alexander II gave small parcels of land for the agricultural development. The best known act of cruelty of the Soviet regime were the between seven and ten million Ukrainians killed the great genocide of *Holodomor* (which means "death by starvation"). In 1932 Ukraine was still reluctant to join the Soviet collectivist system and Stalin decided to take exemplary measures. He deprived the country of its crops, its livestock and all food sources for two years and left its population to die slowly and agonizingly. Due to the famine created artificially in Ukraine the streets of the cities were filled with corpses that nobody was picking up and the population gave themselves to cannibalism to survive, even though the food was abundant in the country. Ukraine was one of the main grain producers of the Russian Empire.

The climax of the Stalin's terror regime was the "Great Purge" carried out between 1936 and 1938. On December 1, 1934 a young Leonid Nikolayev assassinated Sergei Kirov, the Communist Party secretary. Immediately the former Bolshevik leader issued the Law of the first of December, which allowed summary trials with a maximum of 10 days of proceedings, without the presence of the accused and with death sentences of immediate and unappealable application. The result was at least 690,000 victims according to Courtois. Stalin seemed to emulate the "Great terror" unleashed in the French Revolution by

[302] Stéphane Courtois *et al.*, *The Black Book of Communism*, Harvard University Press, 1999, Cambridge, p. 4-10.

the Jacobin leader Robespierre, after the assassination of the revolutionary Jean Paul-Marat in 1793.

The numbers can not in any case depict the extreme cruelty of the medieval tortures, murders and brutalities committed by the Soviet regime on any citizen who was considered, with or without a reason, a "counterrevolutionary". The best of possible luck of a traitor to the revolution was a death or exile to the *gulags*, concentration camps where the most violent common criminals coexisted with political dissidents. The worst scenario for a convict was torture followed by a summary execution of the traitor and his family. Its instruments of political repression were the *NKVD* and the *Cheka*, Stalin's political police.

The book *Gulag Archipelago* by Russian Nobel Prize winner Alexander Solzhenitsyn describes in detail the different stages of terror in the communist regime. In a first phase the Bolsheviks promptly dispatched the bourgeois oppressors and the clergy. Later, when the burden of the taxes of the Bolsheviks sunk all the small shopkeepers, the "gold rush" came and ravaged the country in 1929[303]. It meant any citizen suspected of possessing and hiding gold, solely because of his social status or if he had been denounced by another citizen, was immediately arrested and locked up. Neither the proletarian origins nor the services rendered to the revolution would save him from being prosecuted. For days the prisoner would be given only salty foods without water. Only if he *spit* his gold would he have some water, a cup of fresh water for every gold coin. If any citizen found himself in such a disgraceful situation his future would be very dark: he would be *beaten, burned, tortured and boiled*, according to Solzhenitsyn until death or until his captors were convinced that he was not hiding any gold. The process to get out of those "autos-da-fe" was somewhat complicated; if he surrendered all his gold at first chance this would be a mistake. The interrogators might think that some gold was still kept hidden and therefore they would continue with their inquiries. Nor was it

[303] Alexander Solzhenitsyn, *Archipiélago Gulag, vol. I*, Harper & Row, 1973, New York, p.p. 52-54.

appropriate to hold too much without confessing, as the obstinacy of the accused could be interpreted as rebellious attitude and this would have disastrous consequences. If the detainee did not have an ounce of gold, he should abandon up all hope.

Brutality, torture and arbitrariness at the time of applying the law were established in Russia. Any dissident or traitor, guilty of the charges attributed to him or victim of an interested fabrication –the majority of the convicted were innocent- would have an unpleasant encounter with Stalin's secret police. His methods, although primitive, were extremely effective. Solzhenitsyn described in detail the techniques applied to the suspects, which almost always ended with a signed confession in which the prisoner incriminated himself in everything that his Bolshevik captors wanted[304]:

> «As early as 1921 interrogations usually took place at night. At that time, too, they shone automobile lights in the prisoner's face (the Ryazan Cheka - Stelmakh). And at the Lubyanka in 1926 (according to the testimony of Berta Gandal) they made use of the hot-air heating system to fill the cell first with icy-cold and then with stinking hot air. And there was an airtight cork-lined cell in which there was no ventilation and they cooked the prisoners. The poet Klyuyev was apparently confined in such a cell and Berta Gandal also. A participant in the Yaroslavl uprising of 1918, Vasily Aleksandrovich Kasyanov, described how the heat in such a cell was turned up until your blood began to ooze through your pores. When they saw this happening through the peephole, they would put the prisoner on a stretcher and take him off to sign his confession. »

Death was in many cases better than banishment to a *gulag*. There prisoners were subjected to hunger, extreme cold, forced labor and all kinds of ill-treatment. The prisoner would die after going through a

---

304 Alexander Solzhenitsyn, *Archipiélago Gulag, vol. I*, p. 98.

longer and more painful process. Article 58 of Stalin's criminal code implied that any action -or inaction, according to Article 6- aimed at undermining the power of the state would be considered counterrevolutionary. In practice he assumed that an exhausted, malnourished or sick prisoner who could not continue his work would be undermining the power of the state and could be executed[305]. Despite the barbaric cruelty of the Communism exceeded any other ideology in qualitative and quantitative terms, history treated its regimes with extreme condescendence. The communist military support rendered to the Allies during the two World wars made them soften the image of brutality of the Soviet dictator.

Communism was an aseptic ideology that rejected religion and the identity symbols of any country, central elements in nationalisms. Communism was also different from American imperialism, British colonialism or fascist expansionism in another aspect: It would not be satisfied just with being a political doctrine limited to a territory or group of territories, it aspired to be universal. From Russia, the *class struggle* spread to other countries in western and northern Europe, stealthily infiltrating in politics through communist parties which functioned as puppet satellites of the Soviet Union. In 1919 the failed Munich Soviet was formed, which lasted a month. In 1919 the brief Hungarian Soviet Republic led by Bela Kuhn was formed. Romania followed in 1921. In Spain the formation of the Asturias Soviet in 1934 was one of the immediate causes of the civil war. And in 1939, Russia occupied the Baltic republics of Lithuania, Latvia, Estonia and a part of Finland, with whom it went to war. It is impossible to impose the totalitarian views of Marxism in a country without the upheaval of an important part of the population, so the final stage of any Marxist movement usually is a violent revolution.

The terror of the communist regime, as it happened in the French Revolution, ended the lives of all its leaders in the internal struggles for absolute power. The first great leader in exile was the Menshevik

---

305 Alexander Solzhenitsyn, *Archipiélago Gulag, vol. I*, p. 61.

Martov, who in 1920 left Russia and went to Germany after being arrested several times. He died of tuberculosis in exile in 1923. At the end of the 1930s Josef Stalin organized a purge within the party and the military which ended with most of the former leaders of the revolution shot for treason. Many men loyal to Trotsky, who was then in exile, were accused of serving a crypto-fascist conspiracy in the Soviet Union. Several of them recognized their collaboration with the intelligence services of foreign powers. His confessions were obtained after weeks of torture and under threat of executing the entire family of the suspect, although these promises of leniency were not fulfilled.

During the purge, Stalin particularly attacked the leaders of Jewish origin close to Trotsky. The first of the great trials took place in August of 1936 took the life of Zinoviev[306] and Kamenev[307]. Karl Radek[308] and Yakov Ganetsky[309] were convicted in the January trials of 1937. In the trial of March 1938 Genrikh Yagoda[310] and Bela Kun followed[311]. That year Christian Rakovsky, the right hand of Trotsky, was sentenced to 21 years in prison. He never served his full sentence because he was shot in 1941 with Olga Kameneva, the sister of Trotsky and wife of Kamenev. Stalin even jailed the wife of his closest man, Vyacheslav Molotov, probably due to her Jewish ancestry, and she was one of the main reasons why Molotov fell into misfortune inside the party. The bitter end of Lenin and Trotsky is also known, and probably behind the death of Lenin was also the hand of the brutal dictator Stalin.

---

[306] President of the Soviet of Petrograd and the Komintern.

[307] President of the Soviet of Moscow and the Executive Committee of the All-Russian Congress of the Soviets.

[308] He negotiated the Peace of Brest-Litovsk, co-founded the Communist Party in Germany and was Secretary of the Komintern.

[309] He was entrusted the financing of the Bolshevik movement.

[310] Yagoda was the Commissar for Internal Affairs, the NKVD.

[311] He was the leader of the revolution in Hungary, where a Soviet Republic briefly came to life, from March 21 until Augist 1 of 1919.

The Red Cross Mission of 1917

In August 1917, a delegation of the American Red Cross marked the beginning of commercial relations between the United States and the Bolsheviks. The mission was funded entirely by William Boyce Thompson, a mining developer and one of the Federal Reserve directors close to Morgan. Professor Anthony Sutton made it clear that although the objectives of the mission to Russia were apparently humanitarian, but the truth was quite different[312]:

> «The majority of the mission, as seen from the table, was made up of lawyers, financiers, and their assistants, from the New York financial district. The mission was financed by William B. Thompson, described in the official Red Cross circular as "Commissioner and Business Manager; Director United States Federal Bank of New York."»

The members of the mission, whose list includes Sutton in his book, were largely assistants to Boyce Thompson; mining promoters, consultants, contractors and lawyers. The members of the delegation also included Allen Wardwell, a Director at *Greenwich Savings Bank*, *Bank of New York & Trust Co.* and later co-director of the *Georgian Manganese Company* with Averell Harriman. Wardwell was a founding partner in one of the most prestigious banking law firms in *New York Davis, Polk & Wardwell.* His father, Thomas William Wardwell, worked for the Rockefellers as treasurer of the *Standard Oil of New Jersey* and the *Standard Oil of New York*, and was also director of the *Greenwich Savings Bank*. Other members of the humanitarian mission were Robert I. Burr, vice president of *Chase Securities*, and Frederick M. Corse, representative of the *National City Bank* in Petrograd. Ultimately, the Red Cross mission to Petrograd was led by Morgan and Rockefeller company directors.

---

312 Anthony Sutton, *Wall Street and the Bolshevik Revolution*, p. 74.

In addition to sponsoring the Red Cross mission, Thompson gave a million dollars out of his pocket to the Bolshevik cause. Sutton cites an article in the *Washington Post* of February 2, 1918[313]:

> «William B. Thompson, who was in Petrograd from July until November last, has made a personal contribution of $1,000,000 to the Bolsheviki for the purpose of spreading their doctrine in Germany and Austria.
>
> Mr. Thompson had an opportunity to study Russian conditions as head of the American Red Cross Mission, expenses of which also were largely defrayed by his personal contributions. »

Sutton also quotes a cable from *J.P. Morgan & Co.* in New York to Thompson in Petrograd broadcast on December 8, 1917[314]:

> «New York Y757/5 24W5 Nil — Your cable second received. We have paid National City Bank one million dollars as instructed — Morgan. »

Davison's biography, written by his partner Lamont[315], cites the Red Cross's mission to Petrograd, and of course Colonel House was also aware of its true purpose, which was to consolidate the Bolshevik government and to take advantage of Russia's civil war economically:

> «[316]January 2, 1918... Lamont come to tell of Russia and of Thompson's work there. He found I was in partial agreement with Thompson and therefore in disagreement with the English,

---

313 Sutton, *Wall Street & the Bolshevik Revolution*, p. 83.

314 Sutton, *Wall Street & the Bolshevik Revolution*, p. 83. quoting Hermann Hagedorn *The Magnate: William Boyce Thompson and His Time (1869-1930).*

315 Thomas W. Lamont, *Henry P. Davison The Record Of A Useful Life*, Harper & Brothers, 1933, London, p. 288.

316 *The Intimate Papers of Col. House,* vol. III, p. 389.

French, and American Governments regarding the policy that should be adopted towards Russia at this time. God only knows who is right, but, at least, I feel that I am on the safe side when I advise that literally nothing be done further than that an expression of sympathy be offered for Russia's efforts to weld herself into a virile democracy, and to proffer our financial, industrial, and moral support in every way possible.»

House and the brotherhood of international bankers had been supporting the Bolsheviks even before they came to power. The communist rule in Russia was far from being a democracy.

Capitalists in the Bolshevik Russia

After the revolution of 1917 a civil war followed and lasted until 1923. The Bolsheviks gradually took over the power of Russia, but after the revolution and the subsequent war, the economy stopped entirely. The factories were in perfect condition of technical preservation but only a few of them were operational: A large number of engineers and qualified workers died or fled the country. It was necessary for capitalist managers and technicians to come and reactivate all sectors of the Soviet economy, through private and public-private concessions to companies, which in some cases were complemented by agreements of technological assistance. This was done with foreign capital mainly of German, British and American sources[317].

In October of 1920, when the outlook of the Russian civil war was favorable to the Bolsheviks, the first great economic colonists appeared. The most important investor of the emerging Russia of the soviets was Washington B. Vanderlip. A complete stranger in the economic landscape, Vanderlip led an investment syndicate that was appointed as

[317] Anthony Sutton, *Western Technology and Soviet Development, 1917 to 1930*, p. 5. The technical and economic collaboration of the West with the Soviet Union, since it's inception, is widel described by Sutton in this academical work.

a fiscal agent of the Soviet government to arrange purchases in the United States of 3,000 million dollars. He also provided Lenin's Russia with huge amounts of material of all kinds, from industrial supplies to basic products:

> «[318]Vanderlip's syndicate is also to act as fiscal agents for the Russian Government in the purchase of an enormous quantity of American goods -5,000 locomotives, 50,000 box cars, 25,000 pairs of footwear are a few of the items he [Vanderlip] mentions.»

It was not long before links with Wall Street were established: Washington admitted that he was a cousin of Frank Vanderlip, the Rockefeller's banker. Although he denied that the powerful family took part in the agreement, few believed him[319]. Commissar Litvinov said that the same Frank A. Vanderlip, president of the *National City Bank* had visited Moscow a month earlier to negotiate with the Economic Council of the Soviets, something that the Vice President of the Russian-American Chamber of Commerce hastened to disprove[320]. A year after forming the Vanderlip union, *Standard Oil* joined the group, taking a quarter of its stock[321].

And while the Communists confiscated from the Russian bourgeois all their industries, and executed the small peasants to whom Tsar Alexander had granted reduced parcels of land, they awarded to American investors concessions such as Washington Vanderlip's in the Kamchatka Peninsula, with an extension of 400 square miles. The Vanderlip union was granted the exploitation of oil, coal and fisheries in the gigantic and rich region[322].

---

[318] New York Times, November 21, 1920, *W.D. Vanderlip Says Soviet Has an Army of 4.000.000.*

[319] New York Times, December 13, 1920, *Vanderlip Tells What Russia Wants; Gives Detail Of $3,000,000,000 Order, Open to American Business Men.*

[320] New York Times, October 27, 1920, *Taken for F.A. Vanderlip.*

[321] New York Times, January 11, 1922, *Standard Oil Joins Vanderlip Project.*

Of course the Russians expected something in return: Vanderlip had introduced himself as an emissary of Warren G. Harding, leader of the Republicans and future President of the United States, promising in his name that the United States would recognize the new regime. Harding, however, came out to deny any relation to the matter, possibly annoyed by the inadequate publicity for the future statesman[323].

Vanderlip was not the only American to do great business in Russia. Manganese, for example, is an element used in the manufacture of steel. In 1913 Russia produced 52% of manganese worldwide, three quarters of it was extracted from the Chitauri mines in the Caucasus[324]. The exploitation of Chitauri manganese had been granted to a holding company of German companies called *Tschemo A-G*, but was later nationalized by the Soviets. On July 12, 1925, a private concession was granted to the *W.A. Harriman Company of New York*, in a deal that also featured the German banks *Deutsche Bank* and *Disconto-Gesellschaft*. Shortly after the arrival of the American capitalists, the business got in serious financial trouble after the manganese prices collapsed, but Averell Harriman did not leave empty handed. Between July and August 1928 he agreed with the soviets to rescind his concession in exchange for compensation worth three and a half million dollars[325]. The money was reimbursed to the Harriman through a loan provided by Averell Harriman himself, breaking thus the current trade restrictions with the Soviet Union. In 1929 the U.S. Morgan's *Steel Corporation* replaced the Harrimans with a five-year concession for the exploitation of the Russian manganese. Averell Harriman would be appointed Ambassador in the Soviet Union a few years later, and he knew how to properly compensate Stalin for his advantageous deal in Chitauri.

---

322 New York Times, October 26, 1920, *American Contract With Soviet Russia.*

323 New York Times, October 27, 1920, *W.D. Vanderlip's Deal With Lenin.*

324 *Western Technology and Soviet Development, 1917 to 1930*, p. 86.

325 *Western Technology and Soviet Development, 1917 to 1930*, p. 91.

The oil sector, one of the main industries of the Russian economy was another example of the devastating effect of the victory of the Bolsheviks on the country. Drillings carried out before the Russian Revolution in the Baku fields reached about 15 kilometers per month. Since the socialist revolutionaries took control of the Caucasus, from 1921 to 1923, no new drilling was carried out, nor was the existing ones deepened, and the crude oil was lost as it got mixed with the water. The paralysis of rich oil fields in Russia increased world oil prices, much to the Rockefeller's rejoicing.

The motor industry was very backward in Russia and there were no vehicle factories in Soviet Russia until *Fiat* and *Ford* signed agreements with the Soviet Union in 1928 and 1929[326]. Ford established between 1921 and 1938 a cooperation agreement with the communists[327] and created the Gorki automobile manufacturing plant, the most important in the country. In 1933 it produced 100,000 trucks a year in Russia. In the 1950s and 1960s American soldiers found that Vietnamese guerrillas led trucks surprisingly similar to their old *Ford* models. Those trucks, with few modifications, came from the *Ford* plant in Gorki[328].

The agricultural industry also suffered a great delay and it was barely motorized. Thanks to the American capital, *International Harvester* opened the most important plant in the country in Lyubersty, located next to Moscow[329]. In 1926 a *Ford* report noted that "International Harvester, which lost large amounts of money in Russia for the nationalization of its property and equipment, is now extending a two-year loan to the Soviet government[330]."

Finally, *Radio Corporation of America* and its parent company *General Electric* helped to create the Russian radio stations, the main one in Moscow[331]. The electrification of the country was carried out by

---

[326] *Western Technology and Soviet Development, 1917 to 1930*, p. 44.

[327] *Western Technology and Soviet Development, 1917 to 1930*, p. 246.

[328] *Wall Street and The Rise of Hitler*, p. 90.

[329] *Western Technology and Soviet Development, 1917 to 1930*, p. 131.

[330] *Western Technology and Soviet Development, 1917 to 1930*, p. 143.

International General Electric, mainly through its German subsidiaries *A.E.G.* and Swedish *A.S.E.A.*[332]

There are countless examples of American capitalists building Stalin's Russia. The centralized Soviet economy became the dream of the great American capitalists, the perfect economic colony, a captive market that generated monopolies protected by the State in all sectors. The first great paradox of the Bolshevik triumph is that the ill-fated Russians thought they had led a popular revolution, but what they did was to hand over the keys to their country to a handful of international capitalists. The second great paradox is that the United States invested a large amount of resources, private capital but also money from the American taxpayer, to keep the revolution alive. Years later the country would waste thousands of lives in Vietnam and other proxy wars, fighting Communism.

[331] *Western Technology and Soviet Development, 1917 to 1930*, p. 250.

[332] *Western Technology and Soviet Development, 1917 to 1930*, p. 185-187. Companies of American capital behind Communist Russia were also crucial for the later development of Nazi Germany. *International Harvester, Ford, A.E.G.* or *I.G. Farben* are some good examples.

KARL MARX

Father of Scientific Socialism and author of the Communist Manifesto.

DERUTRA

The Warburg brothers, masters of political intrigue, conspired against Russia from *Kuhn & Loeb* and then lead their reconstruction. Much of the development of the chemical industry in the country was carried out by the German company *I.G. Farben*[333]. Max Warburg was a director in Germany, and Paul was in its North American branch.

Another visible case of American capitalists in Bolshevik Russia was that of *DERUTRA*, or "*Deutsche-Russian Transport*", a Harriman-Warburg capital joint venture that was awarded the monopoly of maritime and rail transport infrastructures in Russia[334]. The new public-private group would combine the experience of the Harrimans and the Warburgs, each contributing a quarter of the capital, and the remaining half would be held by the Soviets. The group developed and operated all the railway and maritime lines and infrastructures of Bolshevik Russia. In 1923 the Warburg made some startling statements in the *New York Times*, requesting international recognition for the new government of Russia:

> «A leading member of the Warburg banking house told the Associated Press today that the German commercial interests purposed to take the Moscow régime as it was and as a government in fact. He said he did not look for the early downfall of Lenin and Trotzky and that he believed their forced disappearance from the Government would result in unspeakable chaos. »

---

333 *Western Technology and Soviet Development, 1917 to 1930*, p.p. 209-210.

334 *Western Technology and Soviet Development, 1917 to 1930*, p. 274. The quote is from New York Times, June 27, 1921, *Big German Plans to Exploit Russia*. See also New York Times, July 25 1923, *Big Shipping Deal Made With Russia; Group, Including Harriman Lines and White Star, Gets Passenger Traffic Monopoly*.

The prominent member of the Warburg house was probably Max Warburg or his right-hand, Carl Melchior. That voice complained about the lack of attention from the United States to Bolshevik Russia and pointed to Lenin and Trotsky as the best political assets for the country. Warburgs unhesitatingly called for a recognition of Russia's new government because the contrary "deprived them of practical advantages, which should be seized immediately." Russia was still immersed in a bloody civil war, but international bankers rushed to recognize the coup. The American capitalists were so demanding that even Lenin, in a letter to his assistant Lezhava[335], complained about the conditions they wanted to impose: They claimed two thirds of the voting rights in DERUTRA in exchange for half the capital invested:

«Jan 23, 1922

> About the project for Harriman's entry, let me tell you the following: unless I am mistaken, the main provision of the Derutra contract was that we and the Germans have an equal number of votes on the board. If Harriman joined up with the Germans, i.e., as part of the German half, that would, of course, be acceptable, but if the Germans plus Harriman have two-thirds of the votes, and we—one-third, that is, of course, unacceptable. In that case, a second society should be set up alongside Derutra, in which we and Harriman would have an equal number of votes. In these circumstances, the combined operations of the two societies would fully ensure our interests and those of Harriman.
>
> Lenin»

Bolsheviks should not be so unhappy with the deal, as some years later they awarded Harriman the mines of Chitauri.

---

[335] Letter of Lenin to A.M. Lezhava, January 23, 1922, *Lenin Collected Works, vol. 54*, 1965, Progress Publishers, Moscow, p. 448.

JACOB HENRY SCHIFF

Banker leading *Kuhn & Loeb & Co.*

Zionism and Marxism

On March 24, 1917 the *New York Times*[336] published news about a meeting of socialists in Carnegie Hall on the occasion of the public celebration of the triumph of the Russian Revolution over the regime of the tsars. The auditorium, built by the steel tycoon Andrew Carnegie, in whose factories workers died by the dozens, was a curious meeting point to celebrate the victory of international socialism.

During the event several well-known personalities expressed their satisfaction and some even acknowledged their contribution to the Bolshevik cause. The most interesting speakers was the rabbi and maximum representative of world Zionism, Stephen S. Wise. Messages from President Woodrow Wilson and banker Jacob Schiff were also read, congratulating themselves on the fall of the Tsar, their ally in war.

> «An authority on Russian affairs, George Kennan[337], told of how a movement by the Society of the Friends of Russian Freedom, financed by Jacob H. Schiff, had at the time of the Russo-Japanese war spread among 50,000 Russian officers and men in Japanese prison camps the gospel of the Russian revolutionists. 'And,' said Mr. Kennan, 'we know how the army helped the Duma in the bloodless revolution that made the new Russia last week.'
>
> The galleries were largely filled with Socialists…
>
> Mayor Mitchel was introduced by Herbert Parsons, President of the Society of Friends of Russian Freedom...

---

[336] New York Times, March 24, 1917, *Pacifists Pester till Mayor Tells Them Traitors*.

[337] Georg Kennan was a russologist who spoke in favor of the Bolsheviks in several articles published in the *New York Times* and other newspapers. Not to be confused with is distant cousin George F. Kennan, American diplomat who analyzed the authenticity of the Edgar Sisson documents.

'America, the great democracy, is proud tonight because democracy in Russia has supplanted the greatest oligarchy that remained on the face of the earth.' Then the Mayor stepped back and said:

'But I submit we have another reason to be proud. It is now inevitable, so far as human foresight can make a prediction, that the United States is to be projected into this world war...'

Rabbi S. S. Wise, a worker for world peace but not an extreme pacifist, was introduced...

'I am a member and a teacher of a race of which half has lived in the domain of the Czar and as a Jew, I believe that of all the achievements of my people, none has been nobler than that part the sons and daughters of Israel have taken in the great movement which has culminated in the free Russia.'...

It was after a review of the struggle of the Russian revolutionists, of whom he has been the leading American writer, that Mr. Kennan told of the work of the Friends of Russian Freedom in the revolution.

He said that during the Japanese-Russian war he was in Tokyo, and that he was permitted to make visits among the 12,000 Russian prisoners in Japanese hands at the end of the first year of the war. He told how they had asked him to give them something to read, and he had conceived the idea of putting revolutionary propaganda into the Russian Army.

The Japanese authorities favored it and gave him permission...

'The movement was financed by a New York banker you all know and love,' he said, referring to Mr. Schiff, 'and soon we received a ton and a half of Russian revolutionary propaganda. At the end of the war 50,000 Russian officers and men went back to their country ardent revolutionists. The Friends of Russian Freedom had sowed 50,000 seeds of liberty in 100 Russian regiments. I do not know how many of those officers and men were in the Petrograd fortress last week, but we do know what part the army took in the revolution.'

Mr. Parsons then arose and said:

'I will now read a message from White Sulphur Springs sent by the gentleman to whom Mr. Kennan referred.' This was the message:

'Will you say for me to those present at tonight's meeting how deeply I regret my inability to celebrate with the Friends of Russian Freedom the actual reward of what we had hoped and striven for those long years! I do not for a moment feel that if the Russian people have under their present leaders shown such commendable moderation in this moment of crisis they will fail to give Russia proper government and a constitution which shall permanently assure to the Russian people the happiness and prosperity of which a financial autocracy has so long deprived them[338].

'JACOB H. SCHIFF'»

This message from President Wilson was read:

'The American Ambassador in Petrograd, acting under instructions from this Government, formally recognized the new Government of Russia. By this act the United States has expressed its confidence in the success of and its natural sympathy with popular government.

"WOODROW WILSON."»

The great American protagonists of the Russian Revolution made a series of unusual statements, explaining their participation in such event better than this author could do.

---

[338] By "financial autocracy" he probably meant the tzars' government.

First, George Kennan spoke; a Russologist who had published countless articles critical of the tsars regime. In his speech he explained that the "Society of Friends of Russian Freedom", despite its altruistic name, was in fact an instrumental society devised by Jacob Schiff and the Russian socialists to infiltrate the Marxist ideology among the Russian prisoners during the Russian-Japanese war, in order to turn them against their country. A war, it should be emphasized, that was possible in the first instance thanks to Schiff himself, who financed Japan massively and suffocated the economy of Russia. The indoctrination of Russian soldiers in Marxism during their captivity made possible the reign of terror of the Bolsheviks.

After Kennan, the mayor of New York, John Mitchel, spoke. He seemed to anticipate in several months the entry of the United States in the First World War. Subsequently, the message of Jacob Schiff was read, where he congratulated himself on the success of his "struggle", and then the message of Wilson, who also endorsed the Bolshevik's cause.

The most remarkable intervention was that of an old acquaintance, Stephen S. Wise, that "pacifist, although not a radical one". The omnipresent leader of Zionism made an express recognition of the role that world Jewry played in the fall of the tsars, and of the subversive activities of Zionism against the government of Russia.

There is a matter here that has been a taboo but that is one of undoubted historical interest to understand the Russian Revolution and communism as a political movement; the role of Zionism. I have provided quite a few different sources, and the protagonists have spoken themselves. The Rothschilds and Jacob Schiff strangled the Russian economy while arming Japan before the Russo-Japanese war. They then created large amounts of Marxist literature and anti-Czarist propaganda and spread it among Russian prisoners of war. Even the ideological father of communism, Karl Marx, was of Jewish origin, heir to a long rabbinical tradition.

Within the group of leaders of Russian revolutionaries we also find an important number of men hiding their Jewish origin after an adopted name: Leiba Bronstein, real name Leon Trotsky, was one of the top Bolshevik leaders and headed the Petrograd Soviet in 1917; Yuli Martov (Zederbaum) was the leader of the Mensheviks; Lev Kamenev (Rosenfeld) was the brother-in-law of Trotsky, head of the Moscow Soviet, second in command of Lenin and member of the *Troika*; Grigori Zinoviev (Hirsch Apfelbaum) was the third member of the *Troika* with Kamenev and Stalin; Pavel Axelrod (Borisovich) was another prominent Bolshevik leader; those responsible for the economic area of the movement were Alexander Parvus (Israel Helphand), Jacob Ganetsky (Fürstenberg) and Karl Radek (Karol Sobelsohn); Genrikh Yagoda was responsible for the NKVD, the fearsome political police; And finally Vladimir Lenin (Ulyanov), the author of the "April Theses" and President of the Council of People's Commissars of the Soviet Union, Jewish only by maternal descent. Stalin was in fact the only great non-Jewish leader.

It is likely that hiding his name with an alias they simply tried to deceive the tsarist police, although statistically. It is, however, a very striking number of Jewish leaders, taking into account that the Encyclopedia Judaica recognizes that in the time of the tsars the Jewish population just it represented 5% of the Russian Empire. The cascade of admissions made in the Carnegie Hall auditorium and the innumerable sources cited show that the Zionist participation in the Russian Revolution goes beyond mere conjecture.

In 1920 Winston Churchill published a series of articles in the *Sunday Illustrated Herald*, being the most controversial one entitled "Zionism versus Bolshevism. A struggle for the soul of the Jewish people." In the text Churchill differentiated the Jewish people in general, of whom he spoke with admiration and what he called the "national Jews", of the "international Jews", whom he characterized as a "sinister confederacy":

> «This movement among the Jews is not new. From the days of Spartacus-Weishaupt[339] to those of Karl Marx, and down to

[339] Adam Weishaupt was a Jew, founder of the Illuminati of Bavaria, known by his

Trotsky (Russia), Bela Kun (Hungary), Rosa Luxembourg (Germany), and Emma Goldman (United States), this world-wide conspiracy for the overthrow of civilization and for the reconstitution of society on the basis of arrested development, of envious malevolence, and impossible equality, has been steadily growing. It played, as a modern writer, Mrs. Webster, has so ably shown, a definitely recognizable part in the tragedy of the French Revolution. It has been the mainspring of every subversive movement during the Nineteenth Century; and now at last this band of extraordinary personalities from the underworld of the great cities of Europe and America have gripped the Russian people by the hair of their heads and have become practically the undisputed masters of that enormous empire. »

Churchill linked the Russian Revolution to the Bavarian Illuminati, a Masonic movement of the late eighteenth century that tried to initiate a revolution in Germany, and which was linked by several authors of the time also with the French Revolution. Trotsky already referred to the Illuminati as "the forerunners of revolution." Churchill pointed out the quite obvious fact that the leading world leaders of communism were of Jewish origin. The later British Prime Minister and Nobel Laureate in literature emphasized the prominence of some Jewish personalities in the revolutions that began in the late eighteenth century and lasted until the twentieth, suggesting a line of continuity between these two revolutions.

During the Paris Peace Conference of 1919, the British delegation treated with great generosity the interests of Stephen Wise and the international Zionists, especially with regard to the creation of the State of Israel in Palestine. Winston Churchill developed the provisions of the Balfour Declaration of 1917 in a document known as "White

'nom de guerre' Spartacus. The fact that Rosa Luxemburg named his Spartacist revolution inspired by the gladiator who led a rebellion against the Roman Empire is not a coincidence. My first book dealt with Freemasonry and Illuminism.

Paper" in 1922, which established that the Jews should live with the Arabs in Palestine, much to the dismay of the Zionists. Some years later, during the Second World War, he gave the blood, sweat and tears of the Englishmen for the Jewish people. Accusing Churchill of anti-Semitism means completely ignoring the history and motivations of this British statesman.

It does not seem fair either, to judge all the Jewish people for the acts of a radical political faction. Large numbers of Jews in Russia put themselves at the head of the communist revolution, persuaded by the international bankers and Zionists that Marxism was the only way for their people to emancipate, and so it was for a time. Nor is it possible to affirm that the triumph of Communism is only attributable to the Jewish world, since important Protestant and Anglo-Saxon banking houses also participated. The Jewish people ended up being one more victim of Stalin's horror, and only some international bankers took advantage of the new regime.

In 1918 the Council of People's Commissaries or Sovnarkom issued a decree condemning all forms of anti-Semitism, and Stalin maintained this positive attitude toward the Jews until the Great Purge. The relationship of Judaism with the soviets was preferential until Stalin took a radical shift towards the end of his regime of terror. After Stalin lost his confidence in Trotsky in 1929, he deported him out of the Soviet Union. Trotsky was Lenin's natural successor, but Stalin, a cunning and ruthless character, gained the advantage to lead the party. Trotsky and his followers did not resign themselves to failure and in later years he tried to get rid of Stalin by all means.

During the purges Stalin got rid of the old guard; He shot Kamenev and his wife Olga, Trotsky's sister. The rest of the leaders ended up dead or disappeared. Stalin, one of the few Slavic leaders, showed a particular cruelty with the Jews in this stage. Men of his trust such as Zinoviev and Yagoda were also sentenced, and he even removed from his side the Vice-President Molotov, mostly because he married to a Jewess.

The Scandinavian Connection

Almost all the protagonists of the Russian Revolution are well known. In the nineteenth century Marx and Engels picked up the baton of the French enlightened philosophers and established the ideological foundations of the new revolution. Lenin and Trotsky, with their charming oratory and sharp pen contributed in Russia as did Mirabeau or Marat in France. Stalin, the man of gunpowder and bullets that emerged from the lower strata of the party, reached supreme power and exercised it for thirty years in the old empire. He prevailed much to the surprise of his rivals, all of them more educated and intelligent than he was. His violent means made him prevail in a political movement fundamentally governed by violence. But all revolutions, including the communist, needed capital. Israel Helphand, known in the movement by his alias "Parvus", was the ideal man. His name is barely mentioned among the protagonists of regime change in Russia, and yet its importance surpasses all the leaders described above.

Helphand was born in 1867 to a wealthy Jewish family residing in Minsk, although he immigrated during his youth to Odessa. In 1886, at the age of only nineteen, he left the Russian Empire for the first time to study in Switzerland, first in Basel and then in Zurich, where he received his doctorate in Philosophy.

Helphand embraced the socialist doctrine during his stay in Switzerland and in the following years his promotion of this ideology caused him to be expelled from several cities. In 1900 he changed his place of residence to Munich, where he met Lenin for the first time. His apartment in Schwabing, the bohemian district of Munich, became a meeting point for revolutionaries in exile. Trotsky and his wife were lodged there, and in his apartment Rosa Luxemburg met Lenin[340]. Helphand actually persuaded him and the other *Iskra* editors to work from Munich. Christian Rakovsky, a prominent Bulgarian socialist and

---

[340] Zbyněk Zeman & Winfried Scharlau, *The Merchant of Revolution. The Life of Alexander Israel Helphand*, Oxford University Press, 1965, London, p. 57.

later a business partner of Helphand gave them false passports to reside there[341].

Helphand returned to Russia after the establishment of the Petrograd Soviet in 1905 and published the "Financial Manifesto" where he fostered the population to start an economic and fiscal insurrection. He demanded the Russian people to stop paying taxes and to withdraw all their deposits from the banks. Shortly after he was arrested with Trotsky and the other Soviet leaders, and he was deported to Siberia, but like many of his comrades he had no trouble escaping across the German border while on his way to exile. He never saw his country again[342].

After a long experience collaborating in socialist publications, in 1910 Helphand arrived in Constantinople, where he began to amass an important fortune. Little is known about the origin of the money, although the most common speculations related to the arms trade for the interests of the German Krupp and the British Vickers, who did great business in the Balkan War. Christian Rakovsky, an educated man well used to the area, became his right hand and his chief agent there. The network of contacts and the experience of Helphand allowed him to offer supplies, financing, contacts and intelligence to the Young Turks political movement[343]. His influence in this political movement grew and he became the editor of his newspaper *Turk Yurdu* in 1912.

The existing nationalisms in the Balkans clashed with the territorial ambitions of the European powers and the internal tensions in Turkey. The Balkan War from 1912 to 1913, anticipated a much greater conflict. After the assassination of the Habsburg heir in Sarajevo in 1914, the stance of the Socialist International was favorable to peace. Marxism denounced –to some extent, quite accurately- that the war was a struggle of capitalists sustained thanks to the blood of the proletarians.

---

[341] The son of a Bulgarian landowner, President of the Soviet of Ukraine between 1918 and 1923. Rakovsky was one of Trotsky's closest allies.

[342] Zeman & Scharlau, *The Merchant of Revolution,* p.p. 81-100.

[343] Zeman & Scharlau, *Merchant of Revolution*, p.p. 126-136.

Helphand, however, publicly demanded Turkey's support for Germany, explaining the advantages this would bring for the country. He also published articles in Bulgarian and Romanian media, neutral powers at the beginning of the First World War, calling on the Socialists to unite against Russia, and therefore in favor of Germany. Rakovsky also promoted the German cause in both countries with some degree of success: Bulgaria entered the war on the side of Germany, and Romanian support to the Entente was delayed. Rakovsky was arrested in Romania at the end of 1916 for exercising anti-war propaganda and after the rapid defeat of that country he reappeared in Stockholm in 1917[344]. The German intelligence facilitated its transit to Stockholm and later stated that "Christo Rakovsky, a Rumanian Socialist born in Bulgaria, runs a Russian socialist paper in Stockholm. Formerly, he was connected with us and he was working for us in Rumania" [345].

Neither Helphand nor Rakovsky owed any allegiance to the German cause; they despised the Kaiser as much as his cousin the Tsar, but the Germans were necessary travel companions for the Bolsheviks. For Bolsheviks, the triumph of the Entente would mean the triumph of Tsarism, and for the Germans a total military defeat. The chances of a German victory vanished with the entry of Russia into the war, and their only hope was to establish a peace on the eastern front. That

---

[344] Zeman & Scharlau, *Merchant of Revolution*, p. 139.

[345] Zbyněk Zeman, *Germany and the Revolution in Russia 1915-1918, Documents from the Archives of the German Foreign Ministry,* Oxford University Press, 1958, London, p. 85. During the Great Purge of 1938 Rakovsky was judged for conspiring against the revolution, helped by foreign powers. Rakovsky acknowledged having worked for the British secret services since 1924, and the Japanese since 1934. He explained that years before he was blackmailed with an allegedly forged letter that related him to the German intelligence since 1915. Rakovsky rejected the authorship of such a letter and having collaborated also with the Germans, but we know Rakovsky lied. It wouldn't be smart for him to make a completely truthful confession if that questioned the very foundations of the revolution. See *Report of Court Proceedings in the case of the Anti-Soviet "Block of Rights and Trotskyites"*, 1938, Moscow, p.p. 289, 300-301.

would only be possible if they were able to drive Russia into a total internal crisis. Bolsheviks used the crisis of capitalism as a tool to carry out their own social revolution. The Kaiser little cared about the fate of his cousin Nicholas II, as the Duke of Orleans did not care about the fate of his cousin Louis XVI.

* * *

The documents contained in the archives of the German Ministry of Foreign Affairs reveal that in January 1915 Helphand managed to attract the attention of high German officials. He met in Constantinople with the German Ambassador, Baron Hans von Wangenheim, and Helphand expressed the identification of the Bolshevik cause with the German cause[346]:

> «"The interests of the German government", Helphand stated bluntly, "are identical with those of the Russian revolutionaries." Helphand said that the "Russian Democrats could only achieve their aim by the total destruction of Tsarism and the division of Russia into smaller states. On the other hand, Germany would not be completely successful if it were not possible to kindle a major revolution in Russia."»

In February 1915 Jagow, the German Secretary of State, invited Helphand to the Ministry of Foreign Affairs in Berlin, where he held a meeting with several diplomats. Helphand promised Brockdorff-Rantzau a strike in Russia for January 1916, coinciding with the anniversary of the great strike of 1905 that paralyzed Russia during the war with Japan[347]. Helphand delivered a memorandum to the German Ministry with a detailed plan to establish anarchy in Russian country thanks to the Bolsheviks, who promised to carry out a campaign of

---

[346] Zeman & Scharlau, *Merchant of Revolution*, p.p. 136-137.
[347] Zeman and Scharlau, *Merchant of Revolution*, p.p. 179-180, 183.

revolution, sabotage and strikes. It contained precise instructions for each region of the Russian Empire, for the adjacent countries and even for the United States. It also contained recommendations to handle the matter in press. This is an extract of the "technical preparations for a rising in Russia", the document in which Israel Helphand exposed to the Germans his plan to send Russia into chaos[348]:

« (a) Provision of accurate maps of the Russian railways, showing the most important bridges which must be destroyed if traffic is to be crippled, and also showing the main administrative buildings, depots and workshops to which most attention should be devoted.

(b) Exact figures for the amount of explosives required to achieve the aim in every case. Here, consideration must be given to the shortage of materials and to the difficult circumstances in which the tasks will be carried out.

(c) Clear and simple instructions for the handling of explosives in blowing up bridges, blowing up large buildings, etc.

(d) Simple formulas for the preparation of explosives.

(e) Preparation of a plan for resistance to armed forces by the rebel population in Petrograd, including special consideration of the workers' quarters, the defence of houses and streets, the construction of barricades, and defence against cavalry and infiltrating infantry.»

---

348 Memorandum of Dr. Helphand, "Preparations for a Political Mass Strike in Russia", March 9, 1915. Ministry of Foregin Affairs of Germany, Zbyněk Zeman, *Germany and the Revolution in Russia*, p.p. 151-152.

The Germans immediately understood the military advantages that Helphand's plan would provide and soon provided all the economic and logistical support necessary to carry it out.

«*Herr Fröhlich to Minister Bergen at the Foreign Ministry*[349]
Berlin, 26 March 1915.
Subject: Dr. Alexander Helphand-Parvus

The Deutsche Bank has sent me the transfer note for a further 500.000 marks, which I enclose herewith.

I should like to draw your attention to my letter of 20 March[350], in which I observed that Dr. Helphand requires a total of one million marks, 1 exclusive of losses incurred in exchange, and that any such losses incurred in Copenhagen, Bucharest, and Zurich, together with any other expenses, will thus have to be borne by us.

I would therefore ask you to make the necessary transfer to the Deutsche Bank so that I may be able to pay Dr. Helphand this difference also.

Yours,

FRÖHLICH.»

Some months later the sum sent to the Bolsheviks increased by another five million marks:

«*The State Secretary of the Foreign Ministry to the State*
Secretary of the Treasury.
Berlin, 6 July, 1915

---

[349] *Germany and the Revolution in Russia*, p. 3. Diego von Bergen was the German Ambassador to the Holy See, Fröhilch was probably a public or military officer.
[350] Those expenses allude to the aforementioned memorandum of Helphand.

Five million marks are required here for the promotion of revolutionary propaganda in Russia. As this sum cannot be covered out of the funds at our disposal, I would like to request your Excellency to put it at my disposal by charging it to include it in Article VI, Section II of the extraordinary budget. I should be extremely grateful to Your Excellency if you would inform me on what action is.

JAGOW»

This request was granted on July 9. In addition, another two million were required[351], and later another 15 million marks:

[352]« *The State Secretary of the Foreign Ministry to the State* Secretary of the Treasury
Berlin, 9 November 1917.

On the basis of the discussions between Minister von Bergen and Ministerial Director Schroder, I have the honour to request Your Excellency [the Secretary of the Treasury] to put the sum of 15 million marks at the disposal of the Foreign Ministry, for use on political propaganda in Russia, charging it to Paragraph 6, Section II of the extraordinary budget. Depending on how events develop, I should like to reserve the possibility of approaching Your Excellency again in the near future with the request that you agree further sums.

KÜHLMANN»

---

351 Zeman, *Germany and the Revolution in Russia*, p. 73
352 Zeman, *Germany and the Revolution in Russia*, p. 75

The request for additional funds was confirmed and the door remained open for future sums of money.

«[353]*The Under State Secretary to the Minister in Stockholm*
[Brockdorff-Rantzau].
Berlin, 10 November 1917.

For Riezler,

Half of desired sum will be taken on Sunday by Feldjager. Remainder on Tuesday. Further sums available if necessary…

BUSSCHE»

Helphand estimated that 20 million rubles would be necessary to carry out the revolution[354]. Zeman gives account in his work of more than twenty million marks, and considers the most accurate number would be close to the 30 million[355]. The German weekly *Der Spiegel* quantified German support for the Bolsheviks by at least 26 million marks[356].

The Germans were very disappointed with Helphand when no major strike occurred in 1916, and they ceased their economic support. They even suspected that part of the money sent could go directly into Helphand's pocket[357]. However, the Bolsheviks were successful and the strike came a year later than promised. The German-Russian business operations of Helphand continued during that time.

* * *

---

[353] Zeman, *Germany and the Revolution in Russia*, p. 79.
[354] Zeman, *Germany and the Revolution in Russia*, p. 9.
[355] Zeman & Scharlau, *Merchant of Revolution*, p. 231.
[356] Der Spiegel, December 10, 2007, *Revolutionär Seiner Majestät*.
[357] Zeman & Scharlau, *Merchant of Revolution*, p.p. 189-190.

Helphand was already a full-fledged bourgeois, a very successful one. He combined its commercial operations with the acquisition, financing or controlling a wide network of socialist publications throughout the world. The list of newspapers that he came to control include *Turk Yurdu* (Turkish Homeland) in Turkey, *Internationale Korrespondenz* (International Correspondence), *Verlag für Sozialwissenschaft* (Social Science Studies), *Die Glocke* (The Bell) and *Wiederaufbau* (Reconstruction) in Germany. He also subsidized and provided support for other publications of Russian socialists in exile, such as Trotsky's newspaper *Nashe Slovo*, or Lenin's, *Isrka.*

Helphand settled in Copenhagen in June 1915, where he founded the "Institute for the Study of the Social Consequences of War" [358]. Far from being a historical research center, the Institute acted as a center for publications related to the interests of the revolution, a front for managing the money obtained from Germany and a recruiting center for young socialists in the Nordic countries. Helphand attracted to his institute the Ukrainian socialist Moisei Uritsky, the man who years ago was in charge of transporting the newspaper *Pravda* (Truth) to Russia, a journal that Trotsky edited in Vienna.

At that time he also counted on the help of a Polish socialist named Jakob Fürstenberg, whose adopted name was Hanecki. Fürstenberg was his correspondent in Russia when Helphand founded in Germany an import-export company called *Handels og-Eksportkompagniet*[359]. He traded mostly with Russia, and the protection of the German government ensured Helphand excellent and profit.

> «It dealt in a variety of goods, from stockings and contraceptives to raw materials and machinery: Helphand procured copper, rubber, tin, and corn for Germany's war economy, while exporting chemicals and machinery to Russia.

[358] Zeman & Scharlau, *Merchant of Revolution*, p. 160-161.

[359] "Trading and Export Company". *Merchant of Revolution*, p.p. 196-198.

Some of the goods were covered by export licenses, others were smuggled…»

The experience of Fürstenberg with Helphand was very useful to him and when the revolution triumphed the Bolsheviks put him at the head of the *Soviet National Bank*[360].

Helphand developed in Copenhagen a close relationship with Brockdorff-Rantzau, who was then the German ambassador in Denmark, and the German officer became his greatest supporter in the Ministry of Foreign Affairs. As we know later on, in 1919, he was the man in charge of negotiating peace in Paris. In fact, all relevant men in the postwar German period knew the unspeakable pact between Germans and Bolsheviks, but none of them mentioned it in their memoirs; Foreign Minister Brockdorff-Rantzau, Kaiser Wilhelm, President Ebert, General Ludendorff, Finance Minister Matthias Erzberger, who signed the armistice of 1918, and future Chancellor Scheidemann were well aware. Of course the banker Max Warburg was also part of the plan[361]. The reasons for such a silence is evident; the socialist agitation that they created in Russia turned against Germany, which in 1918 was about to fall into the clutches of Marxism.

The Ministry of Foreign Affairs gave clear instructions to suppress any news concerning his collaboration with the Bolsheviks, in the local or foreign press. If the people of Entente countries or Russia knew that the Bolsheviks were agents in the pay of the Kaiser, their plan would be in jeopardy:

---

[360] Zeman & Scharlau, *Merchant of Revolution*, p. 165.

[361] Zeman quotes Max Warburg several times. A German officer, for instance, affirms as regards of the support lent to the Bolsheviks, that Max "only considers matters from the commercial angle." (*Germany and the Revolution in Russia*, p. 63). And when in 1916 the Germans had the idea of founding an editorial company to disseminate pro-German propaganda (*op. cit.*, p. 92) Max espressed his opinion that "the project [was] not only plausible, but profitable".

«[362]The Russian newspaper *Riech* for 20 July announced that two German General Staff officers called Schidicki and Luebers had told a Russian lieutenant, by the name of Jermolenko, that Lenin was a German agent. It also said that Jacob Furstenberg and Dr. Helphand (Parvus) were German agents acting as intermediaries between the Bolsheviks and the Imperial government.

I consider it essential, first of all to discover whether these German General Staff officers, Schidicki and Luebers, in fact exist, and then, if at all possible, categorically to deny the report in Riech.

BROCKDORFF-RANTZAU»

The response to the publications that linked the Kaiser government with the Bolsheviks did not take long:

«[363]The suspicion that Lenin is a German agent has been energetically countered in Switzerland and Sweden at our instigation.

Thus the impact of the reports on this subject supposedly made by German officers has also been destroyed...

BUSSCHE»

* * *

Despite the Bolsheviks and the Germans tried to avoid any light on the subject their success was only partial. In addition to the quoted records kept in the Ministry of Foreign Affairs, in 1917 the Kerensky government, which was extremely docile to the revolutionaries,

---

362 Zeman, *Germany and the Revolution in Russia*, p. 68.
363 Zeman, *Germany and the Revolution in Russia*, p. 68.

published a series of documents linking important Bolsheviks such as Lenin and Fürstenberg with the German government. The accusations of the Kerensky government against the Bolsheviks were as follows:

> «[364]The investigation established that Yakov (cover-name 'Kuba') Hanecki-Fürstenberg, while residing in Copenhagen during the war, had close financial connections with Parvus, an agent of the German government.
>
> Moreover the activity of Parvus as a German and Austrian agent was directed towards the defeat of Russia and the separation of the Ukraine. »

And keeps on explaining:

> «[365]For this purpose and with the money received . . . they organized propaganda among the civilian population and in the army, appealing to them to refuse immediately to continue military operations against the enemy; also, towards the same end, to organize in Petrograd, from 16 to 18 July 1917, an armed insurrection against the existing order...»

Trotsky himself, in his *History of the Russian Revolution*, also picked up the version of the provisional government of Kerensky, although of course he denied it[366]

> «The leaders of a revolutionary party, whose lives for decades had been passed in a struggle against rulers, both crowned and uncrowned, found themselves portrayed before the country and

---

[364] Zeman & Scharlau, *Merchant of Revolution*, p. 226. His source was Alexander Kerensky, head of the provisional government; R. P. Browder and A. F. Kerensky, *The Provisional Government of 1917*, Stanford, 1962, vol. III, p.p. 1464-5.
[365] Zeman and Scharlau, *Merchant of Revolution*, p. 226.
[366] Leon Trotsky, *History of the Russian Revolution, vol. II*, p. 62. Electronic version.

the whole world as hired agents of the Hohenzollern [the dynasty of the German Kaiser]. »

The event that definitively silenced Germany's participation in the Russian Revolution were counterfeited documents that gained notoriety in the United States in 1918. That year Edgar Sisson, a member of the Committee on Public Information of the United States was sent to Petrograd and acquired a series of documents, mostly correspondence between the Bolsheviks and the German General Staff. These documents allegedly proved the collaboration of Germans with the Russian revolutionaries. Convinced of the authenticity of the documents, Sisson exerted strong pressures on the State Department until it was published. Edgar Sisson's documents suggested that the German General Staff financed the Russian Revolution through banks such as *Imperial Bank, Deutsche Bank, Disconto-Gesellschaft* and those of course mentioned Max Warburg and his bank *M.M. Warburg & Co.* According to these documents, the German military intended to end the war on the Eastern Front, and after financing the coup to the Tsar they hoped to obtain from the Bolsheviks commercial advantages for Germany and military information of the Entente countries.

The American diplomat George F. Kennan enumerated in the 1956 *Journal of Modern History* the various elements that contradicted the authenticity of Edgar Sisson's documents (graphological, linguistic, stylistic, formal, etc.) The fact that such documents were deliberate falsifications is a matter out of dispute now, but who created them and for what reason? Even if those were false, the information contained is confirmed in solid sources like the documents of the Ministry of Foreign Affairs. Professor Sutton concluded that if those documents ended up in Sisson's hands it was probably with the sole interest of diverting attention from a series of verifiable historical facts. These were a fabrication, yes, but possibly were inspired by original documents; when the Commissar for Public Order Weismann referred to them, he claimed that they were *partially* falsified[367]. Sutton did not mention in his books the archives of the German Ministry of Foreign Affairs, probably because he did not know the work published by Zeman in 1958, but his suspicions were right.

* * *

Helphand became a very important figure in Germany, and was an adviser to President Friedrich Ebert on Russian affairs and other matters. His actions in support of the revolution paradoxically made him an outcast among his comrades. Helphand was seen as an amoral, traitor, millionaire and a true merchant of the revolution, who represented the opposite of what international socialists pretended to be. Rosa Luxemburg, Trotsky, Lenin and the others turned their backs on him, and their dispute with the socialist writer Maxim Gorki contributed to this[368].

Helphand was an uncomfortable element for the revolutionaries but he was necessary -critical- for the revolution. When the German Foreign Ministry put at his disposal one million German marks, he urged his agent Rakovsky to distribute the money obtained among the revolutionaries emigrated in Paris. When living in New York, Trotsky claimed to have received most of his funds for the revolutionary newspaper *Nashe Slovo* from Rakovsky, although from his tribune Trotsky openly attacked Helphand[369]. Lenin also received a priceless support from him in Munich. It is doubtful whether Trotsky or Lenin

---

[367] Zeman, *Germany and the Revolution in Russia*, p. 10.

[368] In 1902 Maxim Gorki, the first great "writer of the proletariat" shared with him the copyright of his literary works in the West. They agreed to share 1/5 for Gorki, 1/5 for Helphand and 3/5 for the party. His work was a worldwide success, but by 1905 neither Gorki nor the party had received any money. The party estimated that Helphand owed them some 130,000 German marks (*Merchant of Revolution*, p. 69-70, 123.) The issue was settled with Helphand within the party, but his reputation would remain tarnished forever.

[369] Zeman and Scharlau, *Merchant of Revolution*, p. 155.

ignored the origin of the two or three tens of millions of German marks that paid for the revolution. Stalin probably discovered some years later, and this was the cause of the purge linked to the trial of Trotsky's supporters.

* * *

The Germans not only provided important sums of money to the Bolsheviks, but they also organized their return transit to Russia. The Swiss Socialist Fritz Platten[370] coordinated with the Germans the return of the exiles to Russia in a sealed wagon, so that no one could establish a relationship between the Kaiser and the Bolsheviks. Seven years before, a group of bankers embarked on a similar trip in a sealed car to Jekyll Island.

The trip began on April 9, 1917 in Gottmadingen, a small town on the border between Switzerland and Germany. From South to North, the revolutionaries moved across Germany until they reached the port of Sassnitz, and continued by boat to Malmö, in Sweden. They resumed their trip to Stockholm, and from there they left for their final destination, Petrograd.

The official documents in the archives of the Ministry of Foreign Affairs offer an exceptional chronology to understand the Russian Revolution from a new perspective; Germany's[371]:

> Document nº 15. March 23. "Leading Russian revolutionaries here wish to return to Russia via Germany as they are afraid to travel via France because of the danger from submarines… Since it is in our interests that the influence of the radical wing of the Russian revolutionaries should prevail, it would seem to me

---

[370] Platten was one of the founders of the Communist International. He was exiled in the Soviet Union, deported during the Stalinist purges and executed in 1942.

[371] Zeman, *Germany and the Revolution in Russia*. I have decided to name the number of document rather than the pages.

advisable to allow transit to the revolutionaries there. ZIMMERMANN."

Document n° 16. March 25 "High Command of the Army instructs me to telegraph as follows: 'No objections to transit of Russian revolutionaries if effected in special train with reliable escort...' LERSNER"

Document n ° 24. April 2 "According to information received here, it is desirable that transit of Russian revolutionaries through Germany take place as soon as possible, as the Entente has already begun to work against this move in Switzerland. I therefore recommend all possible speed in your discussions with representatives of the committee. BUSSCHE"

Document n ° 27. April 4 "Platten, the secretary of the Social Democratic party, came to see me on behalf of a group of Russian Socialists and, more particularly, of their leaders, Lenin and Zinoviev, to voice a request that a number of the most important *emigres*, twenty to sixty at the most, be allowed to travel through Germany immediately. ROMBERG. [372]"

Document n° 35. April 8 "It is absolutely essential also that the German press ignore the affair as long as it is not discussed abroad. If discussion becomes unavoidable, it should not add any commentary and, above all, should not pin any hopes on the affair such as might compromise the *emigres.* On no account should Swiss role of mediation be mentioned. ROMBERG."

Document n° 36. April 9 "Dr. Helphand has requested to be informed immediately of the arrival in Malmo or Sassnitz of the Russian refugees travelling from Switzerland through Germany. Helphand wishes to meet them in Malmo.

BROCKDORFF-RANTZAU.[373]"

---

[372] This telegram is particularly interesting because it bring to light the fact that the heads of the movement like Lenin or Zinoviev were perfectly well informed of the support of Germany to their cause, and even about it's economic assistance.

[373] Helphand was in Copenhagen at the time Lenin and the other *emigres* arrived.

Document nº 37. April 9 "I wish to emphasize again that *emigres* have taken no steps to procure permission to travel in Sweden and therefore rely absolutely on the action requested by us. ROMBERG."

Document nº 39. April 10 "Minister in Stockholm has been instructed to approach Swedish Government on the subject of journey of Russian *emigres* through Sweden.

BUSSCHE."

Document nº 40. April 10 "Scheidemann and Ebert have travelled to Scandinavia with my approval… I therefore recommend that you do not, for the moment, take any steps ZIMMERMANN.[374]"

Document nº 42. April 11 "According to report of Imperial Minister in Stockholm, Swedish government permits transit of Russian emigres. ZIMMERMANN."

Document nº 45. April 13 "Thirty-three Russian *emigres* arrived at Malmo yesterday, were welcomed at Trelleborg by the Mayor of Stockholm, and immediately travelled on to Stockholm. They told their comrades that there were still a considerable number of Russian *emigres* in Switzerland who had not been able to travel as their passport formalities had not been completed. Whether reason for this lies on German or Swiss side is not known. BROCKDORFF-RANTZAU."

Document nº 51. April 17 "Lenin's entry into Russia successful. He is working exactly as we would wish.… Platten was turned back by the English at frontier, a fact which has aroused considerable attention here.[375] GRÜNAU."

It is not known if both leaders met, but it is more possible, as Zeman points out, that Lenin used as emissary a common friend: Fürstenberg. (*Merchant of Revolution*, page 216).

[374] Respectively they were the future chancellor and the future President of Germany.

[375] At this point it becomes evident that the governments of Switzerland, Sweden

Document nº 59. May 10 "Please draw the attention of the emigres returning to Russia, through suitable agents, to the idea that they should demand from their government the publication of agreements made by the old Russian regime with England and France. STUMM.[376]"

Document nº 61. June 3 "Lenin's peace propaganda is growing steadily stronger, and his newspaper Pravda already prints 300,000 copies. Work in the armament factories is either at a standstill, or has sunk to very low production figures. The transport crisis continues to grow more acute and, as a result, the supply of food to the towns and the army is suffering. ZIMMERMANN."

Document nº 66. July 17 "Dr. Helphand, who has returned from Stockholm, had a favourable impression of his various discussions with the Russian revolutionaries. He said that the influence of Lenin, and of the other groups working for a general peace, was continuing to grow, in spite of all the claims to the contrary made in the press of the Entente countries. (Memorandum, unsigned)."

Document nº 73. November 8 "I urgently recommend that all public announcements of amicable agreement with Russia be avoided in the German and Austrian press. Amicable agreement with imperial states cannot possibly be accepted as a watchword by the Bolsheviks. They can only justify peace with Germany by citing the will of the people and Russia's desperate position. LUCIUS."

Document nº 77. November 10 "The revolution in Petrograd, which has at least temporarily placed the power into the hands of Lenin and his followers, has come sooner than we had thought

---

and England were well informed of the return of the Bolsheviks to Russia, and they did few or no efforts to stop the return of the revolutionaries to Russia, an Allied country.

[376] This is another verifiable fact. In November the Bolsheviks published the secret agreements of the Treaty of London of 1915, between Italy and the Entente.

possible… If Lenin and the Bolsheviks should succeed in maintaining their power, then they will be forced to carry out with the utmost vigour the governmental programme which they have formulated. In this context, their promise to bring Russia a 'democratic peace' will occupy first place, and we therefore seem to have reached a decisive turning-point in the peace question. CZERNIN."

The great strike of Helphand was a total success for Bolsheviks and Germans. Kühlmann, an official of the German Ministry of Foreign Affairs, reported on the critical situation in Russia:

«[377]*The State Secretary to the Foreign Ministry Liaison Officer* at General Headquarters.
Berlin, 29 September 19.

For the information of the High Command of the Army.

The military operations on the Eastern front, which were prepared on a large scale and have been carried out with great success, were seconded by intensive undermining activities inside Russia on the part of the Foreign Ministry. Our first interest, in these activities, was to further nationalist and separatist endeavours as far as possible and to give strong support to the revolutionary elements. We have now been engaged in these activities for some time, and in complete agreement with the Political Section of the General Staff in Berlin (Capt. von Hülsen). Our work together has shown tangible results. The Bolshevik movement could never have attained the scale or the influence which it has today without our continual support…

According to the most recent reports received here, the situation in Russia is that the country, whose economic life has been shattered, and

[377] Zeman, *Germany and the Revolution in Russia*, p. 70.

which is only just being held together by English agents, could be expected to collapse as a result of any further, fairly powerful shock.

KÜLMANN»

The rest of the story is widely known. In December 1917, peace negotiations between Russia and Germany officially began, and Trotsky signed the Brest-Litovsk peace treaty in March 1918.

Although the success was mainly attributable to Helphand, Lenin informed him through Radek that he would not be allowed to return to Russia, since "the cause of the revolution should not be touched by dirty hands"[378]. This was a terrible blow to Helphand, who also lost his distinguished position in the German government after the Spartacist uprising of 1918. He died of a heart attack in 1924, repudiated by Russians and Germans. After his death, his luxurious 32-room mansion on the island of Schwanenwerder was occupied by Goebbels, Hitler's Minister.

The papers of the Ministry of Foreign Affairs of Germany end with the romantic image that cultural Marxism has granted to the Russian Revolution. Trotsky and Lenin were not the liberators of the proletariat but twice traitors to Russia. In 1905 they allied with Japan to weaken the position of the tsars, and in 1917 they conspired with Germany to establish their own autocracy.

* * *

The second part of the Scandinavian operation took place in Stockholm and its protagonists were not Germans but Americans. The Nordic countries, because of their neutrality and proximity to Russia, were well suited to channel money to the Bolsheviks. Sutton told the story of a banker named Olof Aschberg, representative of the banking house in Sweden called *Nya Banken*. He was the financial liaison of the

---

[378] Zeman and Scharlau, *Merchant of Revolution*, p. 246.

American bankers in Russia. In 1915 Aschberg met with representatives of Morgan in New York, and again in Petrograd in 1916 with members of the Morgan and Rockefeller houses, *Guaranty Trust* and *National City Bank* respectively[379].

In August 1916 Olof Aschberg announced in the *New York Tim*es a loan of 50 million to Russia, a money that could only be used in purchases from the United States, mainly ammunition. Aschberg's *Nya Banken* instrumentalized the loan of 7.5% interest for a banking syndicate led by the *National City Bank*, with *J.P. Morgan & Co.*, *Kidder, Peabody & Co.* and *Lee Higginson & Co.* He also obtained a credit of 150 million rubles as a remuneration from the Russian government[380].

In 1922 Olof Aschberg (*Nya Banken*) met in Stockholm with German banker Emil Wittenberg (Director of *Nationalbank fur Deutschland*), Russian banker Aaron Scheinnman (the future head of the Soviet Union Central Bank, the *Gosbank*) and the American Max May (Vice President of *Guaranty Trust*). The Bolsheviks gratified the Morgan group that year, when the Bolsheviks founded the *Ruskombank*, the Russian Bank of Foreign Trade. They put Olof Aschberg in charge. Max May was appointed director of the foreign branch of the first international bank of the Soviets[381].

---

379 Anthony Sutton, *Wall Street & the Bolshevik Revolution*, ver p.p. 53-63.

380 New York Times, August 4, 1916, *Olof Aschberg Predicts Many Openings for American Capital. Says War Aids Russia*. See also New York Times, June 14, 1916, *Rusia Gets Loan of 50.000.000 Here. Group of Bankers Close Deal to Cover Munition Purchases for the Zar.*

381 Anthony Sutton, *Wall Street & the Bolshevik Revolution*, p.p. 60-61.

THE ROOSEVELT REVOLUTIONS: THE NEW DEAL AND THE WORLD WAR II (1933-1945)

"For more than twenty years… I preached the lessons I learnt in WIB [War Industries Board] the importance of centralized authority…; the need to regulate not only prices, but money, manpower, production –all the elements of economy; the importance of a tax programme to put the cost of war, as nearly as possible, on a pay-as-you-go basis; the necessity of preventing inflation and profiteering; and above all, the need to preserve the health of economy so as not to run the risk of losing the peace after winning the war. These were some of the lessons I learned from my War Industries Board experience and which I tried to impart, unfortunately not very successfully.

But the lessons to be learned from WIB were not confined to questions of war. The WIB experience had a great influence upon the thinking of business and government. WIB had demonstrated the effectiveness and the advantage of industrial co-operation and government planning and direction. We helped inter the obsolete dogmas of laissez-faire, which had for so long moulded American and political thought. Our experience taught that government direction of economy need not to be inefficient or undemocratic, and suggested that in the time of danger it was imperative. This lesson was applied fifteen years later when the New Deal drew upon the experience of the WIB to mobilize the economic resources of the nation to meet the emergency of the great depression."

Bernard M. Baruch, *The Public Years*, p.p. 76-77.

FRANKLIN DELANO ROOSEVELT

32th President of the United States, the only one reelected for four terms.

The Great Depression

When World War I began, and based on previous conflicts, none of the countries involved thought it would be a military campaign that would extend over time for years. This opinion was sustained on the belief that the powers would remain within a system based on a gold standard, a condition that was not fulfilled:

> «[382]The magnitude of the war and the fact that it might last for more than six months were quite unexpected for both sides and were impressed upon them only gradually. It first became clear in regard to consumption of supplies, especially ammunition, and in the problem of how to pay for these supplies. In July 1914, the military men were confident that a decision would be reached in six months because their military plans and the examples of 1866 and 1870 indicated an immediate decision. This belief was supported by the financial experts who, while greatly underestimating the cost of fighting, were confident that the financial resources of all states would be exhausted in six months. By "financial resources" they meant the gold reserves of the various nations. These were clearly limited; all the Great Powers were on the gold standard under which bank notes and paper money could be converted into gold on demand. However, each country suspended the gold standard at the outbreak of war. This removed the automatic limitation on the supply of paper money. Then each country proceeded to pay for the war by borrowing from the banks. The banks created the money which they lent by merely giving the government a deposit of any size against which the government could draw checks. The banks were no longer limited in the amount of credit they could create because they no longer had to pay out gold for checks on demand. »

---

[382] Caroll Quigley, *Tragedy & Hope*, p. 256.

During 1914, in the earliest months of the war, gold reserves were quickly depleted. The powers at war left the gold standard and kept on printing money without being backed by precious metals -called fiduciary money- and thus they were able to extend indefinitely their capacity to get indebted. This was part of the plan of the international bankers, who accepted the fiduciary money only temporarily.

> «[383]the bankers secretly devised a scheme by which their obligations could be met by fiat money (so called Treasury Notes), but, as soon as that crisis was over, they then insisted that the government must pay for the war without recourse to fiat money (which was always damned by bankers as immoral), but by taxation and by borrowing at high interest rates from bankers. »

The countries in conflict financed the World War I by means of a combination of taxes, debt, devaluation and fiat money. Fiat money and devaluation generated inflation, and inflation eroded the results of the creditor banks, which saw their debts repaid in paper money with a diminishing value. In many countries prices rose up to 200-300% and public debt rose to 1,000%[384]. For this reason from 1919 onwards international bankers did everything in their power to return to the gold standard and thus restore the value of the money they borrowed.

International bankers, who ruled the boards of directors of major central banks, allowed the nations to abandon the gold standard in conflict during the First World War, reaching levels of money issuance, indebtedness and inflation never imagined before. They had taken the genius of the fiat money out of the lamp to wage war, and when it finished they requested everything to return to the original *status quo.*

> «[385]The bankers' point of view was clearly expressed in a series of government reports and international conferences from 1918 to

[383] Caroll Quigley, *Tragedy & Hope*, p. 316.
[384] Caroll Quigley, *Tragedy & Hope*, p. 318.

1933… Accordingly, the financial efforts of the period after 1918 became concentrated on a very simple (and superficial) goal — to get back to the gold standard — not "a" gold standard but "the" gold standard, by which was meant the identical exchange ratios and gold contents that monetary units had had in 1914.»

The two largest central banks in the world, the Federal Reserve and the Bank of England, agreed to this and led the return to the gold standard:

«[386]In the 1920's, they were determined to use the financial power of Britain and of the United States to force all the major countries of the world to go on the gold standard and to operate it through central banks free from all political control, with all questions of international finance to be settled by agreements by such central banks without interference from governments. »

Bernard Baruch, who described himself as a market speculator, agreed that the crash was the result of the monetary policies implemented by the Federal Reserve, at the request of the Bank of England:

«[387]Nothing did more to spur the boom in the stocks than the decision made by the New York Federal Reserve Bank, in the spring of 1927, to cut the rediscount rate. Benjamin Strong, governor of the bank, was chief advocate of this unwise measure, which was taken largely at the behest of Montagu Norman of the Bank of England. Ostensibly this easy money policy was designed to stop the flow of gold out of England. »

---

[385] Caroll Quigley, *Tragedy & Hope*, p. 328.
[386] Caroll Quigley, *Tragedy & Hope*, p. 326.
[387] Bernard M. Baruch, *The Public Years*, p. 208.

The return to the gold standard required a huge contraction of the money supply and this was exactly what the central banks did. They continued with the process of monetary contraction even after achieving the return to the gold standard, a dangerous process that detonated with the Crash of 1929. The League of Nations, through its financial committee, also exerted great pressure in all member countries in the same way.

Monetary stabilization was uneven among the powers, and created large economic imbalances. The deflationary strategies to reduce prices and cancel the debt were mostly increasing taxes, contracting the money and credit, or increasing the number of goods produced. The last of the great countries to return to the gold standard was France in 1928[388], but the result was ephemeral, because the Crash of 29 returned most of the powers to the fiat money. England left the gold standard again in 1931 and other great powers followed.

* * *

Ironically, one of the main reasons alleged to establish the Federal Reserve System in the United States was to eliminate the previous shortages of liquidity. The basic premise since its inception was therefore that the supply of money would automatically increase based on the needs of commerce and industry. The year 1920 marked the time of the Federal Reserve's largest credit expansion to the banking system before the Second World War. There was no predefined mechanism to reduce the money supply, so some of the most important member banks of the Federal Reserve were asked to refuse to extend new loans and cancel existing ones, something that caused or at least aggravated the crisis of 1920-1921 Then, from 1921 to 1926, the Federal Reserve allowed a general expansion of the money supply with somewhat high interest rates. From mid-1927 until August 1929 the supply remained virtually unchanged, and from then on, until 1933, the

---

[388] Caroll Quigley, *Tragedy & Hope*, p.p. 329-335.

money supply contracted by a third[389]. Between January and July of 1928 the Federal Reserve raised the discount rates from 3.5% to 5%. And again in August 1929 the rates rose to 6%[390].

Some authors affirmed that there was an excess of credit at the end of the 1920s, but it is not accurate to say that there was a mismatch between the real needs of the economy and the amount of credit. The only certain thing is that an important part of the money necessary for the productive economy had been diverted towards the financial economy, making an excessive number of loans to brokers. During the stock market boom, loans to stockbrokers increased from 2,000 million dollars to 8,000 million dollars and this led to an era of wild speculation in the stock markets.

The abrupt end of easy money monetary policies destroyed the American economy. In the four months following the crash of 1929, loans to brokers for 4,000 million were canceled, and another 4,000 million in the following three years were withdrawn. The reduction of the money supply by 8,000 million between 1929 and 1933 -a third part of the money in circulation-, caused the number of commercial banks to decrease from 26,401 to 14,771[391].

Curtis B. Dall, the son-in-law of Franklin Delano Roosevelt, was a well-known financier on Wall Street, who later married to the President's daughter Anna Eleanor Roosevelt, from 1926 to 1934. He was a Colonel in the air force and worked as a manager at *Lehman Brothers* with Roosevelt's right hand, Herbert Lehman, and with Frederick M. Warburg, Felix Warburg's son[392]. Dall was in the New York Stock Exchange the infamous "Black Thursday" of 1929, the day

---

389 Wright Patman, *A Primer on Money*, p.p. 99-100.

390 Timothy Cogley, Federal Reserve Bank of San Francisco, *Monetary Policy and the Great Crash of 1929: A Bursting Bubble or Collapsing Fundamentals?,* March 26, 1999.

391 Wright Patman, *A Primer on Money*, p. 83.

392 Curtis B. Dall, *FDR. My Exploited-Father-in-Law,* p.p. 26, 27.

when many investors jumped into the void from the New York skyscrapers:

> «[393]The 24th day of October, 1929! It was not as financial writers often comment "a sharp technical reaction, resulting from an over-bought position." It was the long-in-coming, housecleaning. Actually, it was the calculated "shearing" of the public by the World-Money powers, triggered by the planned sudden shortage of the supply of call money in the New York money market. »

The Nobel Prize of Economics, Milton Friedman, in *A Monetary History of the United States, 1867-1960*[394], supported the thesis that the main cause of the crash was the monetary and credit contraction that culminated with the rate hike of August 1929. Even the Federal Reserve does not deny its responsibility in the crash today.

After the Crash of the 29, the governments of Hoover and Roosevelt resorted to government interventionism to solve a problem that was not related to the productive economy but with the erratic monetary policy of the Federal Reserve. The arrival of Franklin Delano Roosevelt to the White House in 1933 furthered the tendency to increase the government size. His political program, the *New Deal*, meant greater public expense, more economic coercion and growing taxes. It literally a meant to be a "new way of doing things" and it was based on the ideas of British economist Lord Keynes. The public deficit undertaken by the New Deal was sustained with a mixture of taxes and debt, a formula that always cheered the banking industry up. Prices and wages were fixed by politicians and competition was restricted, which greatly pleased the big monopolists. As it has been proven many times,

---

393 Curtis B. Dall, *FDR. My Exploited-Father-in-Law,* p.p. 48-49.

394 Milton Friedman & Anna Schwartz, *A Monetary History of the United States,* Princeton University Press, 1963, Princeton.

most socialists have actually been crony capitalists hidden under a disguise of moral superiority.

The *National Recovery Administration* or *NRA* was founded a public institution to centralize the American economy in times of peace with an iron fist, just as the Board of Military Industries of Bernard Baruch did during World War I. In order to reduce rampant unemployment Roosevelt put the civilian population to work on dams, roads and other public works, as Stalin, Hitler or Mussolini did. Some charity measures helped to alleviate the situation in the short term, but the big picture proves that the New Deal only produced the longest and deepest period of misery in the twentieth century, the Great Depression.

Murray Rothbard, another prominent economist, stated that the crash was triggered by the policies of the Federal Reserve -even a speculator like Baruch agreed to that-. And Rothbard also shared with Friedman the opinion that Roosevelt's New Deal -a mere extension of Hoover's last months in the oval office- did not bring any stability to the world economy, but caused instead the depression to extend for a decade:

> «[395]Historians have regarded Herbert Clark Hoover as the last of the laissez-faire presidents. Instead, he was the first New Dealer.
>
> The massive Hoover program was, indeed, a characteristically New Deal one: vigorous action to keep up wage rates and prices, to expand public works and government deficits, to lend money to failing businesses to try to keep them afloat, and to inflate the supply of money and credit to try to stimulate purchasing power and recovery. Herbert Hoover during the 1920s had pioneered the proto-Keynesian idea that high wages are necessary to assure sufficient purchasing power and a healthy economy. The notion led him to artificially raising wages — and consequently to

---

[395] Murray N. Rothbard, *Relieving the Crash of '29*, Inquiry magazine, November 12, 1979. Retrieved from Mises Institute website in 2016.

aggravating the unemployment problem — during the depression…

After Hoover's term, Franklin D. Roosevelt simply continued and expanded Hoover's policies across the board, adding considerably more [economic] coercion along the way. Between them, the two New Deal presidents managed the unprecedented feat of making the depression last a decade, until we were lifted out of it by our entry into World War II. »

In 1933 Roosevelt removed the United States from the gold standard and signed Executive Order 6102, which prohibited American citizens from possessing gold, establishing an obligation to exchange it at a fixed price. The objective of the gold confiscation decree was to increase the country's ability to expand the supply of money again. By depriving Americans of gold he destroyed their only refuge against inflation. The gold ban was a frequent measure in communist and fascist regimes of the twentieth century. Until the 70s an Americans did not fully recover their right to own or acquire gold without restrictions. The metal obtained went to the Treasury and was kept at Fort Knox. The case of Fort Knox is a greater mystery even than the Federal Reserve, since its gold reserves never have been audited nor inspected by the Congress. Only under the presidency of Ronald Reagan a minimum fraction of the reserves could be inspected, and nowadays such a reserves of gold could not even exist.

An Italoamerican Story

A year before the Crash of 29 the Morgan group met a tough rival in Wall Street, the successful banker Amadeo Pietro Giannini. This genius of banking built his empire by offering financial services to immigrants and middle-lower class Americans, instead of focusing on big fortunes, as the banking industry usually did. He soon realized that the American banking system was not as democratic as his own.

Giannini, the son of Italian immigrants of humble origins, founded the Bank of Italy in San Francisco in 1904. Before acquiring *Bank of America* in 1928, he decided to request the consent of "The Corner", this was the name of the office that occupied *J.P. Morgan* at 23 Wall Street. According to his biographer Julian Dana[396], a meeting between the Morgans and the Italo-American banker was organized. The Morgans assured him that he would be welcome in New York: "I'll see Seward Prosser and the Federal Reserve officials at once" he said "you will certainly be welcomed into the banking picture here".

At his next meeting, Seward Prosser, Chairman of the Board of the Clearing House of Payments of New York[397] and President of *Bankers Trust*, explained to Giannini his conditions: "We don't favor ownership of banks by holding corporations. However we'll be glad to welcome you to the Street if you will agree to do away with all but twenty percent of your holdings of this consolidated bank [Banker's Trust?]"

Giannini reluctantly agreed, and when he was already distributing his shares in the market a spokesman for the Federal Reserve announced that he would not allow Giannini the creation new trusts if he didn't get rid of his shares in the *Bank of America.* Giannini went to Washington to meet with Roy Young, the then Governor of the

[396] Ferdinand Lundberg, *The Rich and the Super-Rich*, Bantam Books, 1969, New York, p.p. 382-384, quoting Julian Dana, *A.P. Giannini, Giant in the West*, p. 162.

[397] The *New York Clearing House* is the most important and the oldest in the country. The institution guarantees the settlement of payment obligations contracted in stocks, bonds, currency exchange and derivatives markets.

Federal Reserve, who explained that the decision was not in his hands and he could do nothing. Giannini felt cheated and went back to the market to buy back the shares he had sold.

He met Francis D. Bartow, a *J.P. Morgan* partner who instructed him: "Right or wrong, do as you are told down here". Giannini replied raging: "The hell I will". The next day he met with Jackson Reynolds, president of the *First National City Bank*, who warned him: "You have made such a tremendous success that I'm not trying to give you advice on what you should do, A.P… you may have been badly treated –have all the law on your side. But if I were you I'd take my orders and say nothing. If you don't – well, they'll knock you down and walk all over you". Giannini replied defiantly: "If they try it they'll have the biggest damn scrap on their hands they ever tackled."

Amadeo Giannini emerged unscathed from this battle, unlike what happened to Heinze and Morse in 1907. A few years later, the Morgan group sought to control his holding *Transamerica Corporation*, but Giannini was again able to defend his position. His concept of a bank serving society at the time of the Great Depression caused the *Bank of America* to grow at a dizzying pace and eventually to become the country's first bank.

This story proves that twenty-five years after the death of the founder of *J.P. Morgan & Co.* its banking group continued to run Wall Street. During the years of the New Deal Thomas Lamont, a very capable man, remained at the head of that economic empire, but he was not the old titan, and the power of the Morgan group diminished during the Great Depression and the New Deal. Bank of America today is one of the four largest banks in the United States along with *J.P. Morgan*, *Citigroup* and *Wells Fargo.*

FDR: International Banker, 1910-1928.[398]

Just like Woodrow Wilson, President Franklin D. Roosevelt (also known by the acronym FDR) publicly denounced the existence of an industrial and financial plutocracy that ruled the destinies of America. In his speech in Columbus, in 1932, he referred to President Hoover's membership of a small economic elite:

> «[399]Appraising the situation in the bitter dawn of a cold morning after, what do we find? We find two thirds of American industry concentrated in a few hundred corporations and actually managed by not more than five human individuals. We find more than half of the savings of the country invested in corporate stocks and bonds, and made the sport of the American stock market. We find fewer than three dozen private banking houses, and stock selling adjuncts of commercial banks, directing the flow of American capital. In other words, we find concentrated economic power in a few hands, the precise opposite of the individualism of which the President [Herbert Hoover] speak. »

Strangely enough, the life and fortune of Franklin Roosevelt were closely linked to the invisible plutocracy he denounced, possibly more than any other president. Roosevelt was never the President of the people or the protector of the dispossessed, as he wanted his electorate to believe, and as many historians have glorified him. Just like Wilson, his greatness was perpetuated and increased by his leading biographers, who idealized his figure in uncritical works. Franklin was an international speculator, related to all the pieces of the Anglo-Germanic

---

[398] This section is based mainly on the works *Wall Street & FDR* by Sutton, *The Roosevelt Genealogy* by Charles B. Whittelsey and *America's Secret Aristocracy* by Stephen Birmingham.

[399] Anthony Sutton, *Wall Street & FDR,* p. 14.

financial establishment, member of two of the most powerful families in the American industry and politics. In a letter to Colonel House, Franklin Roosevelt made a statement similar to that of Woodrow Wilson years before:

> «[400]The real truth of the matter is, as you and I know, that a financial element in the larger centers has owned the Government ever since the days of Andrew Jackson — and I am not wholly excepting the Administration of W.W. [Woodrow Wilson] The country is going through a repetition of Jackson's fight with the Bank of the United States — only on a far bigger and broader basis. »

There was a fundamental difference between Wilson and Roosevelt: Wilson was never part of the Anglo-German establishment but its instrument, while Franklin was a banker with several generations of bankers behind him, going back no less than the *First Bank* era by Alexander Hamilton. The economic powers that lent their support to the campaign of Herbert Hoover in the elections of 1928 turned their backs on him and lent their support to their rival Roosevelt in the elections of 1933. What was the great affront of Hoover? He rejected the 1931 Swope Plan, a project that proposed establishing a centralized economic system in the United States. The Swope Plan came to life during Roosevelt's term under a new guise, the New Deal.

In 1933 Franklin Delano Roosevelt won the presidential election against then President Herbert Hoover, who was running for re-election. After the presidency of Wilson, Roosevelt became the second socialist president of the United States. His economic plan, the New Deal, was a Marxist system that gave all the economic protagonism to the State. Paradoxically FDR was also a successful financier and

[400] President Franklin Delano Roosevelt to Col. Edward Mandel House, November 21, 1933, *F.D.R.: His Personal Letters* (New York: Duell, Sloan and Pearce 1950), p. 373. As quoted by Sutton *Wall Street & FDR*, p. 13.

industrialist, and was on the boards of directors of major American trust and international investment firms. Anthony Sutton in his work *Wall Street & FDR* picked up the extensive business affiliations of the president that all his biographers seemed to agree to omit[401]:

> «To be specific, Franklin D. Roosevelt was, at one time or another during the 1920s, a vice president of the Fidelity & Deposit Company (120 Broadway); the president of an industry trade association, the American Construction Council (28 West 44th Street); a partner in Roosevelt & O'Connor (120 Broadway); a partner in Marvin, Hooker & Roosevelt (52 Wall Street); the president of United European Investors, Ltd. (7 Pine Street); a director of International Germanic Trust, Inc. (in the Standard Oil Building at 26 Broadway); a director of Consolidated Automatic Merchandising Corporation, a paper organization; a trustee of Georgia Warm Springs Foundation (120 Broadway); a director of American Investigation Corporation (37-39 Pine Street); a director of Sanitary Postage Service Corporation (285 Madison Avenue); the chairman of the General Trust Company (15 Broad Street); a director of Photomaton (551 Fifth Avenue); a director of Mantacal Oil Corporation (Rock Springs, Wyoming); and an incorporator of the Federal International Investment Trust.»

Eustace Mullins was more explicit than Sutton in speaking FDR's banking career [402]:

> «Franklin D. Roosevelt himself was an international banker of ill repute, having floated large issues of foreign bonds in this country in the 1920s. These bonds defaulted, and our citizens lost millions of dollars, but they still wanted Mr. Roosevelt as President. The New York Directory of Directors lists Mr. Roosevelt as

---

[401] *Wall Street & FDR*, p.p. 17-18.

[402] Eustace Mullins, *Secrets of the Federal Reserve*, p.p. 155-156.

President and Director of United European Investors, Ltd., in 1923 and 1924, which floated many millions of German marks in this country, all of which defaulted. Poor's Directory of Directors lists him as a director of The International Germanic Trust Company in 1928. Franklin D. Roosevelt was also an advisor to the Federal International Banking Corporation, an Anglo-American outfit dealing in foreign securities in the United States. »

Franklin attended the law school of the University of Columbia but he never graduated. His first job was at *Carter, Ledyard & Milburn*, a law firm specialized in banking whose most remarkable client was *J.P. Morgan*. In 1916, when Roosevelt went to Washington D.C. as Deputy Secretary of the Navy, Thomas Lamont -a Morgan's partner- lodged him at his home in New York[403].

FDR had a political career before his arrival at the oval office. During World War I he was a senator of the Democratic Party for the State of New York (1910-1914 and Deputy Secretary of the Navy (1912-1918). His life as a public officer allowed him to jump into the world of finance in 1921 as Vice President of *Fidelity & Deposit Co.*, a company that sold and purchased public bonds, an area where public and private interests converged. Roosevelt lacked experience in the sale of bonds but his past in the Democratic Party and his connections with the Republican Party provided by his uncle Theodore Roosevelt gave him qualifications for a managerial position in a company of this sort. He only had to secure public contracts thanks to his political contacts.

In 1922 Roosevelt took the leap to international business by speculating on the German hyperinflation of 1922-1923 through *United European Investors, Ltd.*, a company dedicated to investment in assets in Europe. The draconian reparations set by Morgan bankers to repay the Allies during the First World War forced Germany into a massive devaluation, unprecedented in recent European history. That situation made it easy for any foreign speculator with a handful of hard currency

403 Anthony Sutton, *Wall Street & FDR*, p. 13.

-dollars or pounds- to acquire properties and other assets in Germany, provided its currency was worthless paper. Roosevelt was the president of *United European Investors, Ltd.* and its board of directors also included John von Berenberg Gessler[404] and Wilhelm Cuno, both co-directors with Max Warburg of *HAPAG* in Hamburg. Cuno and his policies in the German chancellorship had been the first cause of German hyperinflation, and thanks to *United European Investors*, he also became one of the leading speculators who benefited from the economic dismantling of his country. Roosevelt remained until 1926 in *United European Investors.*

Then, in 1927, FDR also participated in *International Germanic Trust Co.*, a company whose founders included Herman A. Metz, director of *I.G. Farben*, E. Roland Harriman of *W.A. Harriman & Co* and himself. The meetings of its board of directors were held at the headquarters of the *International Germanic Trust* located in the Standard Oil Building, and sometimes also in the *Bankers Club*, the exclusive bankers' meeting point that occupied the three last floors of the Equitable Life Insurance Building in 120 Broadway. *Equitable Life* was one of the companies close to the Morgan group, where Roosevelt's private offices were also located[405]. FDR was on the board of directors of this corporation until 1928, the year in which he resigned from his position[406]. That same year the *International Germanic Trust* was included in the select and hermetic club of the member banks of the Federal Reserve[407]. Franklin was already a full-fledged member of the fraternity of international bankers.

---

[404] The Berenberg-Glossler family owned the oldest investment bank still active today, the *John Berenberg, Gossler & Co.* o *Berenberg Bank* founded in 1590.

[405] J.P. Morgan and E.H. Harriman had an important stock in the insurance firm *Equitable Life*, the biggest of the country.

[406] Sutton, *Wall Street & FDR*, p.p. 42-50. Roosevelt's economic affiliations are also available in news published in the *New York Times* between 1922 and 1929.

[407] New York Times, January 31, 1928, *Now in Federal Reserve; International Germanic Trust Admitted to Membership.*

The Roosevelts

The Roosevelt surname has its origin in Holland, being originally Van Rosenvelt. The Roosevelts have possibly been the most prolific familiar saga in politics in the United States, followed at close range by the Bush family. Franklin was the only President in the history of the United States who did not respect the unwritten rule of not remaining in power for more than two terms, and so he enjoyed the presidential powers for four terms, until his death. The four mandates of Franklin, together with the two of Theodore Roosevelt, gave them 21 years of presidency during the first fifty years of the 20th century.

In 1903 Franklin Delano Roosevelt married Eleanor Roosevelt, a surname she did not inherit when she married, but she was a niece of his uncle Theodore Roosevelt. The marriage between cousins was officiated Samuel Endicott Peabody, director of Groton, the most exclusive school in the United States. Samuel Endicott was a distant cousin of George Peabody, the Morgan's first partner in England. This does not have a great historical value but it helps to illustrate how small the circles of the American elite were.

The Roosevelts had a large number of active members in politics, Republicans and Democrats alike, in the shadow of the two presidents. Several Roosevelts were in high positions, such as Robert Barnwell Roosevelt, Clinton Roosevelt, Nicholas Roosevelt or Theodore Roosevelt Jr., creating a small hereditary regime in the United States. The involvement of the Roosevelt family in the early history of banking and railways in the country have remained as almost unknown aspects of this presidential family. These were some of the most prominent Roosevelts:

* <u>*Isaac Roosevelt II (1726-1794)*</u>: Isaac was a politician and co-founder in 1784 of the *Bank of New York* and its second President. He was, along with Alexander Hamilton, one of the ten representatives of New York who voted in 1788 to adopt the Constitution of the United States.

* *James (Jacobus) Roosevelt (1760-1847)*: FDR's great-grandfather, was a politician and banker at *Bank of New York,* like his father Isaac. James sold to John Jacob Astor, the founder of the Astor fortune, the land that comprises the exclusive New York area that includes the streets 110 to 125 with Fifth Avenue and East River, at a price of $ 25,000. He also founded the family investment bank *Roosevelt & Sons of New York* in 1797, which was run by Roosevelts for at least five generations. The main business of *Roosevelt & Sons* has historically been the sale of municipal bonds, which we assume would be very profitable for this family of politicians.

* *Cornelius Roosevelt (1794-1871)*: The son of James Jacobus and one of the founders of *Roosevelt & Sons*. He also participated in the creation of the *Chemical Bank*, which later became part of the *Chase Manhattan Bank*.

* *James Alfred Roosevelt (1825-1898)*: An outstanding banker, Vice President of the *Bank of Savings of New York* and the *Chemical Bank of New York*. One of the directors of the *New York Life Insurance Trust.*

* *Theodore Roosevelt (1858-1919)*: The first American president of the Roosevelt saga, belonging to the Republican Party. Grandson of Cornelius Roosevelt.

* *James Roosevelt I (1828-1900)*: The father of Franklin Delano Roosevelt and his brother James Roosevelt Roosevelt. James was born of the marriage of Isaac Daniel Roosevelt (1790-1863) and Mary Rebecca Aspinwall (1809-1886). James married his second cousin Rebecca Brien Howland, with whom she had her first child James Roosevelt "Rosey" Roosevelt. When his wife died, James I married his second cousin Sarah Ann Delano, with whom he had his second son, Franklin Delano Roosevelt. Cases of family intermarriages were not uncommon in the Roosevelt family.

FDR's father was a railway and transport tycoon; General Manager of *Cumberland & Pennsylvania Railroad*, president of Louisville, *New Albany & Chicago Railroad*, *Susquehanna Railroad Co.*, *Champlain Transportation Co.*, *Lake George Steamboat Co.*, *New York & Canada Railroad Co.*, *Delaware and Hudson Canal Co.*, President of the *Maritime*

Canal Company of Nicaragua, Vice President of the *Delaware and Hudson Railway*, President of the *Southern Railway Security Company*, and Director of the *Consolidated Coal Company of Maryland*, a coal company that was the ideal complement to its transportation business.

* *James Roosevelt "Rosey" Roosevelt (1854-1927)*: James was a stepbrother of Franklin Delano. His second wife was Helen Schermerhorn Astor, a member of one of the largest American family fortunes, the Astor, founders of the Waldorf-Astoria hotels. Rosey served in several positions in American diplomacy.

* *William Emile Roosevelt (1857-1930)*: The son of James Alfred and cousin of Theodore Roosevelt. This banker succeeded his father in leading *Roosevelt & Son*. A Director of the *Chemical Bank of New York*, of the *Gallatin National Bank*, and of the *Astor National Bank*, the bank of the Astor family.

* *George Emlen Roosevelt (1887-1963)*: The cousin of Franklin and Theodore. George Emlen was heavily involved in business reorganizations, at least 14 of those were related to railroads. He was also Director at the boards of several banking institutions such as *Guaranty Trust Company*, the *Chemical Bank*, and the *Bank of Savings of New York*. He later directed the family firm *Roosevelt & Son.*

* *Franklin Delano Roosevelt Jr. (1914-1988)*: The fifth son of FDR, a politician and businessman. He married Ethel du Pont, a member of the chemical and weapon empire Du Pont in first nuptials, and with Felicia Schiff-Warburg in fifth nuptials. His father FDR could hardly have taken any decision contrary to the interests of the directors of *Kuhn & Loeb*, his political family.

The Delanos[408]

The Delano family has historically been even more influential than the Roosevelt family. The first to arrive in the United States was Philip Delano in 1621 (a surname known with different spellings, "Delano", "de la Noye" or "de Lannoy"). Those de Lannoy are related to the high European aristocracy, being one of the oldest lineages in the nobility that still exists. The genealogy developed by the Delano family states that the origins of this saga are found in the Actii, a powerful patrician family that lived in Rome in the year 600 AD. [409] In Sutton's words:

> «[410]According to the Delano family history, "Franklin shared common ancestry with one third of his predecessors in the White House." The Presidents linked to FDR on the Delano side are John Adams, James Madison, John Quincy Adams, William Henry Harrison, Zachary Taylor, Andrew Johnson, Ulysses S. Grant, Benjamin Harrison, and William Howard Taft. On the Roosevelt side of the family, FDR was related to Theodore Roosevelt and Martin Van Buren, who married Mary Aspinwall Roosevelt. The wife of George Washington, Martha Dandridge, was among FDR's ancestors, and it is claimed by Daniel Delano that Winston Churchill and Franklin D. Roosevelt were "eighth cousins, once removed." This almost makes the United States a nation ruled by a royal family, a mini monarchy. »

The Delanos were also closely related to the Brown banking family, and several of them were *Brown Brothers* partners. It is convenient to mention again that several partners of the British branch of the Brown

---

[408] Anthony Sutton, *Wall Street & FDR*, p.p. 19-22.

[409] Joel Andrew Delano and Mortimer Delano Lannoy, *The Genealogy, History, and Alliances of the American House of Delano, 1621 to 1899,* 1899, New York, p.p. 92-93.

[410] Anthony Sutton, *Wall Street & FDR*, p. 19.

bank, *Brown & Shipley,* held seats in the management of the Bank of England, and one of them even became Prime Minister of Great Britain. In the North American branch, *Brown Brothers Harriman*, their success was equally remarkable. They had members in the Federal Reserve as Frederick Adrian Delano. The American investment house *Brown Brothers Harriman*, in which at least four Delanos worked, was the nexus of union with another great presidential dynasty, the Bushes. Prescott Bush, the patriarch of the Bush family, became a partner of the firm by marrying the daughter of George Herbert Walker, the President of *BBH*. Some years later FDR appointed Averell Harriman, founding partner of *Brown Brothers Harriman*, as American Ambassador to the Soviet Union, at a crucial period in relations between the two super powers. The bankers have always taken good care of the people loyal to their interests. These were some of the prominent American Delanos:

* *Columbus Delano (1809-1896)*: An American Congressman for the Republican Party (1864-1869), Commissioner of Internal Revenue Service (1869-1870) and Secretary of the Interior under the presidency of Ulysses S. Grant (1870-1875), position that had to leave because his son John Delano was involved in a fraud related to land grants, while he held public office.

* *Frederick Adrian Delano II (1863-1953)*: Sara Ann Delano's brother and FDR's uncle was a relevant railway magnate, president of *Wheeling & Lake Eerie Railroad*, *Wabash Railroad* and *Chicago, Indianapolis & Louiseville Railway*. In 1914 Wilson appointed him Vice Chairman of the Federal Reserve and in 1934 Roosevelt appointed him Chairman of the National Resources Planning Board, another central planning governmental institution from which Uncle Fred could allocate public resources in whatever way he considered most convenient.

* *Eugene Delano (1844-1920)*[411]: The father of Moreau Delano and a partner of *Brown Brothers & Co.*, Eugene was related by family lines with

---

[411] New York Historical Society Museum & Library, *Guide to the Records of Brown Brothers Harriman 1696 -1973*, 1995, website revised in 2015.

the founders of *Brown Brothers*. It has been impossible for me to connect him with other Delano lines, as I ignore his paternal filiations.

* *Moreau Delano (1877-1936):* Moreau was a partner of *Brown Brothers & Co.*, the investment bank that later would be *Brown Brothers Harriman*. In 1914 Wilson appointed him a member of the Federal Reserve. Like other Delanos he was related to the Brown bankers' family; their maternal cousins, William Adams Brown and Thatcher M. Brown were grandsons of James Brown, one of the original founders of *Brown Brothers*, and were married respectively to the sisters Helen Gilman Noyes and Caro Lord Noyes[412].

* *Lyman Delano (1883-1944):* The cousin FDR was also a railway executive, president of the *Atlantic Coast Line Railroad*, and director with Averell Harriman on several boards of transport companies such as *Aviation Corporation*, *Pan American Airways*, *P & O Steamship Lines*, and in another half a dozen railroad companies[413].

* *Warren Delano Robbins (1885-1935):* First cousin of FDR, American Ambassador in Portugal and Chief of Protocol of the USA.

* *Preston Delano (1886-1961):* Appointed by Henry Morgenthau as Comptroller of the United States Currency from 1938 to 1953, the longest period someone has held the position. The Office of the Comptroller of the Currency of the United States, under the Secretary of the Treasury, is in charge of authorizing the creation of banks, as well as their regulation and supervision.

* *Moreau Delano Brown (1905-1974)*: The son of Thatcher M. Brown and Lord Caro Noyes and nephew of Moreau Delano. He was also a member of the Brown investment firm, *Brown Brothers.*

---

412 As explained, Delano, de Lannoy and de la Noyes are the same surname with a different graphy.

413 Acording to Sutton, *Wall Street & FDR*, p. 20.

Bernard Baruch

Herbert H. Lehman

John J. Raskob

Edward Mandel House

Henry Morgenthau Jr.

Henry Morgenthau Sr.

THE DONORS OF THE DEMOCRAT PARTY

Frankfurt and the Elections for the state of New York in 1928.

The Roosevelt's relations with the Frankfurt Syndicate were very close since the time of his uncle Theodore Roosevelt. The biography of Otto Kahn, partner of *Kuhn & Loeb*[414] states that "Roosevelt often sought Kahn's opinions on various problems". We know by Kahn's biography that Jacob Schiff had angrily complained to the first president of the Roosevelt saga about the anti-trust prosecution of his friend Edward Harriman, and probably his plea made some effect in Teddy Roosevelt, because the Harriman issue came to nothing.

Franklin was part of a political party theoretically opposed to his uncle Theodore, but the young Roosevelt knew how to maintain good rapport with Frankfurt. According to the memoirs of James Paul Warburg, son of the legendary banker Paul Warburg and Roosevelt knew each other long before he made the leap to the presidency[415]:

> «It so happened that I had known the President elect's eldest son, James Roosevelt, for some years, because he had been living in one of the cottages on my Uncle Felix's estate in White Plains. »

So cordial were the relations of FDR with the partners *Kuhn & Loeb* that upon his arrival at the White House he appointed James Paul Warburg as budget director[416]. He also married his son, Franklin Delano Roosevelt Jr. to Felicia Schiff-Warburg, the sister of James Paul Warburg and granddaughter of Jacob Schiff. The United States was officially a family business, a branch office of the Frankfurt syndicate.

We know the 26th President, Theodore Roosevelt, was guided in economic matters by Jacob Schiff and Otto Kahn of *Kuhn & Loeb.* And his nephew and 32nd President, Franklin Delano Roosevelt, faithfully

---

414 *The Many Lives of Otto Kahn*, p.151.

415 Anthony Sutton, *Wall Street & FDR*, p. 96.

416 Eustace Mullins, *Secrets of the Federal Reserve*, p. 156.

followed the dictates of Herbert H. Lehman, a New York senator and partner of the family banking firm *Lehman Brothers.* Frank Freidel, Roosevelt's principal biographer -he devoted six large volumes to his life and political work- explained some of the connections of FDR with the banking industry of New York:

> «[417]Mrs. Roosevelt remembers that at the time of a banking crisis when FDR was Governor that he sent for Lieutenant Governor Herbert Lehman, himself a banker, to give him advice. Lehman made the necessary decisions, and FDR accepted them, but Lehman then paced the floor. FDR could not pace because he could not walk. He sat in his chair and remarked that if Lehman, once he had made up his mind, would stop worrying, he would be much more useful the next day. »

Freidel also points out that when Roosevelt ran as a candidate for Governor of the State of New York, he did not hesitate to take Herbert H. Lehman as Lieutenant Governor. And when Roosevelt won the presidency of the United States, Herbert H. Lehman replaced as Governor of New York[418]:

> «In talking to the press, he referred to his physical condition in joking terms like these[419].When he was asked if he would go South after each session of the legislature, he made a laughing reference to the fact that the acting governor would be a banker: "I can leave the combination of my safe to Colonel Lehman, knowing that it will be in safe hands."»

---

[417] Frank Freidel, *Franklin D. Roosevelt. The Ordeal,* Little, Brown & Company, 1954, Boston, p. 121.

[418] Frank Freidel, *Franklin D. Roosevelt. The Ordeal*, p. 260.

[419] In 1921 Roosevelt suffered a viral infection of polio that paralyzed his legs, and he could only recover in part some years later. He frequently visited the thermal waters of Warm Springs, which were said to be beneficial to treat his illness.

To be more precise, Roosevelt could leave the combination of his safe to Herbert Lehman because Herbert Lehman was the one who filled it with money. Before he became Governor of the State of New York, his financial situation was far from excellent. FDR had a good social position, but not as to allow a campaign for Governor of the State of New York in 1929. Freidel gives an image of the figures collected for the elections that year[420]:

> «Finances, always a headache for Democrats, were doubly so in a depression year. […] It would take three to four hundred thousand dollars to finance a successful campaign.
>
> Surprisingly, campaign contributions came in much better than… expected. In the end he had collected more money for the gubernatorial campaign than he had in any other year except 1928. Since it came into various committees, it was difficult to estimate the total. The Democratic Party officially reported expenditures of $128,000 and a deficit of $27,000 compared with an official Republican report of $276,000 in expenditures and a $103,000 deficit. However, through other committees, the Democrats gathered more money. »

Crises generate great opportunities and that was the case. The 29 Crash made it possible for the Frankfurt Syndicate to win the New York governor's election for FDR and the Democratic Party. On the origin of the funds, Freidel adds:

> «Herbert Lehman and his family were again the heaviest contributors, followed by the Morgenthaus. Other notable contributors were: Alfred E. Smith, Gordon Rentschler, President, National City Bank, Vincent Astor, John Raskob, Cleveland Dodge, Mrs. Caspar Whitney, August Heckscher, and Nathan S. Jonas of Manufacturers' Trust Company, William H. Woodin,

[420] Frank Freidel, *Franklin D. Roosevelt. The Triumph*, p. 159.

Ralph Pulitzer, Felix and Paul Warburg, Samuel Seabury ($250), and Archibald B. Roosevelt, son of Theodore Roosevelt ($100). »

The biography elaborated by Freidel is certainly complimentary towards FDR. It follows that the main contributors to his political takeoff as Governor of New York were two Jewish families, the Lehmans and the Morgenthaus. Both families received a generous compensation for their contributions to the Democratic Party in the Roosevelt candidacy: the banker Herbert H. Lehman was awarded the position of Lieutenant Governor of the State of New York, and later was the successor of Roosevelt in the post of Governor. Some years before, Woodrow Wilson had named his father Henry Morgenthau Mr. American ambassador to the Ottoman Empire (Turkey). Morgenthau Sr. lent considerable financial support to Wilson's campaign in 1912, and was elected chief financial officer of the Democratic Party in 1912 and again in 1916.

Henry Morgenthau Sr. had already poured a remarkable amount of money in Wilson's campaign in 1912, and the President rewarded him with the position of American Ambassador to the Ottoman Empire (the modern Turkey). He was elected Chief Financial Officer of the Democratic Party in 1912 and again in 1916. Some years later the fortune of Henry Morgenthau also contributed to FDR's campaign. This undoubtedly led to the election of his son Henry Morgenthau Jr. as Secretary of the Treasury and also he became a key element in several of the most notable policies of the Roosevelt administration such as the New Deal, the Morgenthau Plan to dismember Germany after World War II and the creation of the World Jewish Congress with American public funds. Morgenthau also had a leading role in devising a global banking architecture in Bretton Woods, and in fact most of the Roosevelt administration's policies were not attributable to the President but to Morgenthau himself.

Roosevelt filled his government with some of the most radical Zionists in the country. One of them was Felix Frankfurter, a well-known lawyer and law professor who was appointed by Roosevelt to the Supreme Court in 1939. In a letter to FDR in 1928 Frankfurter congratulated himself for his election as Democratic candidate for Governor of the New York State[421]:

> «My dear Franklin Roosevelt
>
> Your nomination is, of course, occasion for National rejoicing. But I am still a New Yorker in spirit and so find special reasons for self-satisfaction. It gives one new strength when such pure-mindedness and real public zeal find popular acclaim. As a Jew I am particularly happy that your nomination prevented the New York contest from degenerating into an unworthy competition for the "Jewish vote." Now all good and wise citizens ought to be drawn to your standard. »

After the Lehmans and Morgenthaus we also find as key supporters to Roosevelt's campaign the Astor and Warburg families, banks such as *City Bank* (Rockefeller) or *Manufacturer's Trust* (Morgan), and John Raskob (the man of *Du Pont* and *General Motors*). This was how bankers got political influence in the United States, that's how banking Zionism made its way into the public offices of the following American governments, both Democrats and Republicans.

Bernard Baruch and the Presidential Election of 1933

In 1933 the presidential campaign of FDR began. Professor Sutton quoted Pulitzer Arthur M. Schlesinger Jr. in *The Age of Roosevelt*[422] to explain the origin of the funds raised:

---

[421] Max Freedman, *Roosevelt and Frankfurter. Their correspondence 1928-1945*, The Bodleian Head, 1967, London. p. 38.

[422] Sutton. *Wall Street & FDR*, p. 16, quoting Schlesinger, *The Age of Roosevelt. The Crisis of the Old Order 1913-1933*, Houghton Mifflin Co., 1957, Boston, p. 275.

«Schlesinger notes that after the 1928 election the Democratic Party had a debt of $1.6 million and "Two of the leading creditors, John J. Raskob and Bernard Baruch, were philanthropic Democratic millionaires, prepared to help carry the party along until 1932". John J. Raskob was vice president of Du Pont and also of General Motors, the largest corporation in the United States. Bernard Baruch was by his own admissions at the very heart of Wall Street speculation. Schlesinger adds that, in return for Wall Street's benevolence, "they naturally expected influence in shaping the party's organization and policy."»

Who were they? John J. Raskob was the accountant and personal secretary of Pierre S. du Pont since 1901, and the President of the family business *E.I DuPont de Nemours & Co.* and *General Motors*, both companies' stock being held mainly by du Pont. He climbed positions until in 1918 he became the vice president of both companies. John J. Raskob was therefore working in the interest of the du Pont family and on his behalf. From 1928 to 1932 Raskob was Chairman of the Democratic National Committee, the principal governing body of the Democratic Party. Strangely enough, John J. Raskob, who was one of the main economic supporters of Roosevelt, also participated very actively in associations opposed to his policies such as the American Liberty League, contrary to the policies of the New Deal[423]. It was certainly unlikely that the du Pont could launch a real campaign against

[423] This organization lasted from 1934 until 1936, the year in which Roosevelt renewed his term. Some of its members were Raskob, Pierre and Ireneé du Pont, Al Smith (ex Governor of New York and rival of Roosevelt to head the Democrat Party) and John W. Davis (Morgan's attorney). His treasurer was Grayson M-P Murphy (Morgan) and Robert S. Clark was one of his main economic supporters. These names appear in the following section. Keep them for future reference. See New York Times, August 23, 1934, *League is Formed to Scan New Deal, "Protect Rights"* and *Facts About the American Liberty League*, National Press Building, 1936, Washington D.C.

FDR, especially if we consider his son Franklin Delano Roosevelt Jr. married Ethel du Pont in 1937. The du Ponts financed Roosevelt and those who were against him, endorsing the saying of "keep your friends close, and your enemies closer". Perhaps for this reason Roosevelt never had a real opposition and could maintain himself in power for four terms.

Regarding Bernard Baruch, thanks to his support for the Democratic Party, Wilson granted him full powers over American industry during the First World War, which he exerted from his position in the War Industries Board. During the Second World War Roosevelt offered him the direction of the War Production Board, although due to his advanced age, he finally decided to place him in an annex public department, the Office of War Mobilization. His role in American military development did not end there, and the next president, Harry S. Truman, appointed him American representative to the United Nations for the Atomic Energy Commission. The United States paid a high price for Baruch's support of the Democrats, holding him for almost twenty years as head of the American military industry, and participating in a Zionist cause that had nothing to do with the interests of the American people.

GEN. SMEDLEY DARLINGTON BUTLER

One of the most decorated soldiers of the United States.

The White House Coup, 1934

> "You will have a revolution, a terrible revolution. What course it takes will depend much on what Mr. Rockefeller tells Mr. Hague to do. Mr. Rockefeller is a symbol of the American ruling class and Mr. Hague is a symbol of its political tools. "
>
> Leon Trotsky, *New York Times*, December 13, 1938.[424]

At the beginning of Roosevelt's term there was an event that foreshadowed a revolution in the United States. In November of 1934 Smedley Darlington Butler, a retired General of the American Army, requested to declare before a special committee of the Congress of the United States that investigated Nazi propaganda and other subversive activities on America. Butler was the most decorated military man in the history of the United States: he was one of the two Marines in history to receive two Medals of Honor from Congress, and he subsequently received the Medal of Valor.

Smedley Butler testified before the Special Committee led by congressmen John W. McCormack and Samuel Dickstein that elements close to the Morgan group had offered him to lead a fascist coup in the United States. In first place, the objective was to replace Roosevelt with General Hugh Johnson, the director of the *National Recovery Administration*[425], although in a strange twist they informed Butler that Roosevelt's position had changed and the new plan would be to

---

[424] Frank Hague was mayor of Jersey, the fiefdom of Standard Oil for 30 years, and Vice President of the Democratic National Convention. New York Times, 13 December, 1938, *Trotsky Predicts Revolution in U.S.; He Expects Rockefeller to Tell Hague How to Run It.*

[425] The NRA or National Recovery Administration was an administrative institution created by New Deal. It was authorized to fix prices and minimum wages, promote industrial alliances and monopolies, and suspend anti-trust laws by means of "codes of fair competence".

support him. The transcript of Butler's statements before the committee of the United States Congress left a testimony that I summarized here[426]:

On July 1, 1933, retired General Smedley Butler answered a phone call from Washington inviting him to meet with veterans of the American Legion. That same day he received the visit of two maimed soldiers, Gerald C. MacGuire of Massachusetts and William Doyle of Connecticut, in a black limousine. The soldiers tried to persuade him to give a speech before other soldiers of the American Legion at their next convention in Chicago. Butler asked how could he go without being invited, and MacGuire and Doyle offered him the chance to attend as a delegate for Hawaii. The General drew the conclusion that one of the objectives of both men seemed to be to expose the administrators of the American Legion. He replied that he did not live in Hawaii, closing conversation with MacGuire and Doyle with a denial.

A few days later the veterans reappeared in their limousine. They insisted that Butler should appear at the Legion convention in Chicago. They promised to bring two or three hundred legionaries from all over the country in a train to take them to the convention. The veterans would demand that Butler speak for them and give a speech on their behalf. "Make a speech about what?" Butler replied. The speech was a proposal to change the American monetary system for the gold standard. Butler answered flatly "I do not know about a thing about gold." He explained that no legionary he knew would be interested in paying for a trip to Chicago. MacGuire and Doyle promised to pay the attending legionaries one hundred or one hundred and fifty dollars for a five days trip to Chicago and back.

Butler was amazed that two simple retired and handicapped soldiers came to the meeting in a chauffeured limousine and could

---

426 Investigation of Nazi Propaganda Activities and Investigation of Certain Other Propaganda Activities, Special Committee of Un-American Activities, 37º Congress, Second Session. November 24, 1934. U.S. Government Printing Office. Parts I, II and III.

afford such expenses. "How can you pay it? You are disabled soldiers. How do you get the money to do that?" To which they replied "Oh, we have friends. We will get the money." They exhibited a bank statement of what Butler recalled to be a total of $ 42,000, to show that they had contributions of considerable size. Again they said goodbye to the General with a negative response.

In August, Butler met MacGuire and once again he asked him about the origin of his funds: "Where did you get all this money? It cannot be yours." MacGuire said they received funds from nine men, donations between 2,500 and 9,000 dollars and his goal was to take better care of the soldiers. He explained Butler that he worked for Colonel Grayson M-P Murphy, a New York broker who had an office at 52nd Broadway[427]. He explained that Grayson Murphy himself had put the initial $ 125,000 to found the American Legion and was not happy because he had not received anything in exchange for his money. Then he showed him another deposit for $ 64,000 in one of his accounts.

On September 1, 1933, Butler went to a military convention of the 29th Division in Newark, and much to his surprise MacGuire appeared again knocking on the door of his hotel room. During the conversation he left a wad of bills on his bed worth $ 18,000, coming from some contributions made by his mysterious benefactors. Butler replied suspiciously: "If I try to cash one of those thousand-dollar bills, you would have me by the neck." MacGuire allegedly answered. "We can change them into smaller denominations." It was a large sum and Butler, suspecting that there might be some murky business behind the offer, he played along with MacGuire and asked him to introduce him to your superiors to know more.

---

[427] Liutenant Col. Grayson Mallet-Prevost Murphy happened to be a director in the *Anaconda Copper Mining Company*, one of the biggest trusts of the 20th century (Rothschild, Rockefeller). He was also a Director in *Guaranty Trust Co.* (Morgan), *Bethlehem Steel* (Schwab and Morgan) *New York Trust Co., Goodyear Tyre & Rubber* and Chief Commisssioner of the American Red Cross.

A few days later Butler received at his home MacGuire's superior, Robert Sterling Clark[428], a military officer who served General Butler's command years ago. Clark insisted on persuading him and explained vaguely that the speech proposing the return of the United States to the gold standard was just for the veterans to collect part of their pay in gold and not in paper. He said that he had thirty million to invest and told him that his main interest was to fight for democracy. Given Butler's reluctance, Clark asked, "Why do you want to be so stubborn? Why do you want to be different from other people? We can take care of you. You have got a mortgage on this house." Butler, somewhat surprised that he was aware of the state of his finances, refused once more and took him to the room where he kept all the medals and honors of his military career. Clark apparently understood the message and gave up. Butler later learned that the matter of the gold standard appeared at the American Legion convention in Chicago, which he had decided not to attend.

Far from desisting, in August of 1934 Butler received a call from MacGuire, who wanted to organize a meal in Boston in honor of Butler, and offered him $ 100,000 for a speech. MacGuire finally revealed his true interests and explained that he had been in Italy, Spain, Germany and France studying the role of veterans in the rise of Mussolini's fascism, Hitler's Nazism and a French organization whose name Butler could not remember in a first moment, but that turned out to be a fascist group of French veterans called "Crux du Feu".

MacGuire explained that Roosevelt *was with his group*, but that they were running out of money to finance his government and the President would not want to change the mode of financing. Butler, puzzled, asked; "The idea of this great group of soldiers, then, is to sort of frighten him, is it?" MacGuire responded that the objective was to stage a false attack on Roosevelt: "No, no, no; not to frighten him. This is to sustain him when others assault him." MacGuire assured Butler

[428] Sterling Clark served under Gen. Butler in the Boxer War. He was a well known art collector, horse breeder and heir of the empire of the sewing machines Singer.

that he could raise an army of 500,000 men and three million dollars to begin with, and up to three hundred million if necessary. "You know the American people will swallow that. We have got the newspaper. We will start a campaign that the President's health is failing. Everybody can tell that by looking at him, and the dumb American people will fall for it in a second." Butler probably knew that a private army was not recruited to support a democracy and he suspected that there might be something real behind the proposal of MacGuire, Doyle and Clark.

MacGuire continued: "When I was in Paris, my headquarters were Morgan & Hodges. We had a meeting over there. I might as well tell you that our group is for you, for the head of this organization. Morgan & Hodges are against you. The Morgan interests say that you cannot be trusted, that you will be too radical, and so forth" Butler pretended to be interested in the proposal: "No; I was interested in it, but I would not head it."

Butler, suspecting that nobody would believe only one testimony, sent to the offices where MacGuire worked, *Grayson M.P. Murphy & Co.* at 52 Broadway, a man of his trust named Paul Comely French, a reporter for the *Philadelphia Record* and the *New York Evening Post.* MacGuire repeated to French the same story about analysis of fascism he did in the Germany, France and Italy cases and explained to him that a fascist system was necessary to save America from communism[429]. MacGuire spoke to French mentioning on several occasions the need for a leader like Butler, "the need of a man on a white horse", adding that "We might go along with Roosevelt and then do with him what Mussolini did with the King of Italy[430]."

---

[429] This was one of the main reasons for Hitler's rise to power, he was proposed as the sole alternative to Communism in Germany.

[430] The plan, in short, consisted in using Butler to implement a Fascist state. His charisma would be enough to attract half of the American Legion and the veterans of war. Probably at some point they would get rid of Roosevelt, as Mussolinli got rid of King Victor Emmanuel III in Italy. Roosevelt was part of the group but he was disposable. And probably Butler was disposable too.

This was what Smedley Butler and Paul Comely French stated under a sworn statement in a special committee of Congress on November 24, 1934, the so-called McCormack-Dickstein Committee.

During the committee hearings he quoted a third witness with no relation to Butler, Captain Samuel Glazier, who gave a version that fit perfectly with the events described by the General, and implied that some elements of Wall Street were preparing to establish a fascist government. Glazier was the commanding officer of a Civilian Conservation Camp[431] in Elkridge, Maryland. Glazier claimed he had received a letter sent on behalf of General Malone to receive Jackson Martindell, a Wall Street banker. During his visit Martindell asked him several questions about the operation of his field because he was interested in building other similar work fields for industrial purposes. Martindell gave a very specific figure "500,000 young men", and according to Glazier's statement, his tone was anti-Semitic and came to suggest a coup in the United States.

It's not irrelevant to mention that during one of the conversations with Butler MacGuire offered the general to lead an army of specifically 500,000 veterans[432]:

> «He [MacGuire] said. "I went abroad to study the part that the veteran plays in the various set-ups of the governments that they have abroad. I went to Italy for 2 or 3 months and studied the position that the veterans of Italy occupy in the Fascist set-up of government, and I discovered that they are the background of Mussolini. They keep them on the pay rolls in various ways and

---

[431] The Civilian Conservation Camps (CCC) worked from 1933 until 1942 to create jobs for young unemployed American. The camps offered a subsistence wage in exchange for public works in the country. This is another example of how closely the Roosevelt's New Deal resembled other central planned economies like those of Stalin, Hitler or Mussolini. The camps lasted until enlistments for the Second World War started. (See points 7º, 8º and 9º of the Communist Manifesto.)

[432] Investigation of Nazi and Other Propaganda, p.p. 17-18.

keep them contented and happy; and they are his real backbone, the force on which he may depend, in case of trouble, to sustain him. But that set-up would not suit us at all. The soldiers of America would not like that. I then went to Germany to see what Hitler was doing, and his whole strength lies in organizations of soldiers, too. But that would not do. I looked into the Russian business. I found that the use of the Soldiers over there would never appeal to our men. Then I went to France, and I found just exactly the organization we are going to have. [Crux de Feu]"…

He [MacGuire] told me that they, had about 500,000, and that each one was a leader of 10 others, so that it gave them 5,000,000 votes. And he said, "Now, that is our idea here in America— to get up an organization of that kind". »

When MacGuire was called to testify, he accepted most of the history of Butler and French, he acknowledged his trips to Europe and his participation in a committee for the return to the gold standard. However, he denied the conspiracy denounced by Butler, alleging that he had always supported Roosevelt and the current leaders of the American Legion. In his statement MacGuire fell into several contradictions and was not able to explain or justify by means of receipts the movements in his bank accounts worth tens of thousands of dollars. These records corroborated the dates and amounts indicated by General Butler, both the $ 42,000 and $ 64,000 receipts, and the $ 18,000 offered in cash. MacGuire's military pension was only $ 37 per year but he had movements in his accounts of tens of thousands of dollars. The banks involved in such transactions were *Manufacturer's Trust Co.* [433], *Central Hanover Bank, First National Bank, Seamen's Bank for Savings, Chase Bank, Irving Trust Co.*, and *Grayson M.P. Murphy & Co*[434]. These were the hidden benefactors of MacGuire, who also confessed to

433 $13,000 were delivered to MacGuire by J.K Olyphant, the Vice President of *Manufacturer's Trust.*

434 All mentioned banks were aquired by J.P. Morgan.

having received $ 10,000 from the *Bankers Club*. He finally admitted that during his travel to France he received his mail at the offices of *Morgan & Hodges*.

On November 21, 1934 in the *New York Times*[435] appeared on the cover the "Coup to the White House", with the following headline: "Gen. Butler Bares 'Fascist Plot' To Seize Government by Force; Says Bond Salesman, as Representative of Wall St. Group, Asked Him to Lead Army of 500,000 in March on Capital". It followed: "Hugh S. Johnson, former administrator of the NRA, was scheduled for the role of dictator, and that J.P. Morgan & Co. were behind the plot."

On November 22, literally overnight, many of the newspapers that picked up the news with great interest completely changed their treatment of the matter, showing their skepticism and relegating this information to inside pages, before Butler could present any evidence. The following *New York Times* headline read "Credulity Unlimited"[436] and summarized Butler's testimony: "Details are lacking to lend verisimilitude to an otherwise bald and unconvincing narrative." The matter was buried a few days later and hardly received more interest from the press, giving authenticity to the statement of MacGuire: "You know the American people will swallow that. We have got the newspaper."

The shareholding of the main media of the country was under the control of the same bankers that Butler denounced, and for no apparent reason happened to insult the general who years before had won. Going into detail on the question of who controls the media in the United States would be an excessively extensive task, but it is enough to take, for example, the two most influential newspapers in the country; *The Washington Post* today belongs to the descendants of Eugene Isaac Meyer, a Germanic Jew who bought it in bankruptcy in 1933. He was not only the owner, but also the president and editor.

---

[435] New York Times, November 21, 1934, *Gen. Butler Bares "Fascist Plot" To Seize Government by Force.*

[436] New York Times, November 22, 1934, *Credulity Unlimited.*

And who was Meyer? He was a banker with *Lazard Frères* -a banking institution in which his father had been a partner- in 1918 the first Executive Director of the *War Finance Corporation*, in 1930 Chairman of the Board of Governors of the Federal Reserve, and in 1946 the first President of the *World Bank*. The Meyer family eventually changed their Jewish surname to a more Anglo-Saxon one, Graham. It was virtually impossible for the *Post* to maintain an editorial line contrary to the great banking fraternity.

Something similar happened with the *New York Times*. In 1896 the German ascent Jew Adolph Simon Ochs acquired a newspaper in a financial situation as ruinous as the *Post*. Morgan secured funding for Ochs to get hold of the newspaper. The Ochs-Sulzberger family has remained in control of the chief New York journal until today. This is actually the story of almost all newspapers today, operating in a sector with a large number of competitors, low profitability and where their survival depends on combining their editorial line with the economic interests of their shareholders, various political groups and its advertisers[437].

---

[437] Democrat Congressman for Texas, Oscar Callaway, requested in 1917 an investigation in the Congress on the dominance of the main American journals by Morgan and other economic interests close to his group. A report stated in Congress; «In March, 1915, the J.P. Morgan interests, the steel, ship building and powder interests and their subsidiary organizations, got together 12 men high up in the newspaper world and employed them to select the most influential newspapers in the United States and sufficient number of them to control generally the policy of the daily press in the United States. These 12 men worked the problems out by selecting 179 newspapers... They found it was only necessary to purchase the control of 25 of the greatest papers...; an agreement was reached; the policy of the papers was bought, to be paid for by the month; an editor was furnished for each paper to properly supervise and edit information regarding the questions of preparedness, militarism, financial policies and other things of national and international nature considered vital to the interests of the purchasers.» New York Times, February 14, 1917, *For Press Investigation.; Moore Asks Inquiry into Charges on Preparedness Campaign*.

The McCormack-Dickstein Commission, like the American press, seemed to take a hard braking, and the next day they determined that there was no reason to call to testify to personalities involved like Thomas W. Lamont, Grayson M-P Murphy or General Hugh Johnson. The testimony of a war hero and American army general with 33 years of active service seemed insufficient to be taken into account by the media and by the investigation committee. Objectively, what did a military officer, of an irreproachable character, had to gain, already retired and without any political ambition?

Not enough attention has been paid to Butler's testimony, and when it has been mentioned, it has been posed as a failed coup attempt "against" Roosevelt, although this is entirely incorrect. As explained to Butler, Roosevelt was *with* the group of bankers, and although at first they thought to do without him to implement his fascist government, then they reconsidered his position[438]:

> -I said, "What do you want to do with it when you get it up?"
>
> -"Well," he said, "we want to support the President."
>
> -I said, "The President does not need the support of that kind of an organization. Since when did you become a supporter of the President? The last time I talked to you were against him."
>
> -He said. "Well, he is going to go along with us now."
>
> -"Is he?"
>
> -"Well, what are you going to do with these men, suppose you get these 500,000 men in America? What are you going to do with them?"
>
> -"Well," he said, "they will be the support of the President."
>
> -I said, "The President has got the whole American people. Why does he want them?"
>
> -He said. "Don't you understand the set-up has got to be changed a bit? Now, we have got him— we have got the President. He has got to have more money. There is not any more money to

[438] Investigation of Nazi and Other Propaganda, p.p. 17-18.

give him. Eighty percent of the money now is in Government bonds, and he cannot keep this racket up much longer. He has got to do something about it. He has either got to get more money out of us or he has got to change the method of financing the Government, and we are going to see to it that he does not change that method. He will not change it."

When MacGuire spoke of "we" he was referring to Grayson Murphy and the financial interests that he represented. Did certain American financial interests related to Morgan supported the establishment of a totalitarian regime on America? It does not seem unreasonable at all, particularly if we take in consideration that these were the same bankers who supported Fascism and Communism.

In reading between the lines Butler's statement we can fathom what are the missing pieces in the story, which seems to be somehow convoluted. The triumph of Roosevelt was the result of the support of that financial element that in his own words "dominated the government since the days of Andrew Jackson." Shortly after becoming President, in 1933, Roosevelt tried to turn his back on the Anglo Germanic banking system that rose him to the presidency, and he tried to go on his own. Determined to recover the money invested in Roosevelt, the international bankers considered forming a group of veterans across the country, led by Butler, to put a little fear of Roosevelt and make him reconsider his position. If this plan didn't work, perhaps plan B would establish in the United States a fascist dictatorship led by someone more docile like General Hugh S. Johnson, the administrator of the NIRA, the economic program set by Roosevelt that in itself was already a proto-fascist system.

Roosevelt therefore was not the victim of the bankers, but a vassal who at some point tried to bite the hand that fed him. He finally reconsidered his position and decided to go along with the bankers again. Or maybe the bankers simply ran out of money and thought that it would be more profitable for them to put an end to the New Deal's democratic fiction and establish a dictatorship in the United States.

When the issue was publically known Roosevelt did not take any reprisals against the bankers, possibly because doing so would be against their own interests.

In January 1935 a journalist of the socialist newspaper *The New Masses*[439], John L. Spivak, denounced that a substantial part of French and Butler's testimony was removed from the final text of the McCormack-Dickstein Committee. In essence, they removed parts that directly involved a) President Roosevelt in tune with the coup group b) General Hugh S. Johnson, responsible for the NRA and c) Various business interests, including:

- James H. Perkins, President of the *National City Bank*.
- John W. Davis, lawyer at the law firm specialized in banking *Davis, Polk & Wardwell*, and General Counsel of the United States, Ambassador to the United Kingdom, Democratic candidate for president in 1924 and Director of the *Council of Foreign Relations*.
- *Remington & Co.*, a firearms company owned by the Du Ponts, which was expected to provide the Army with the necessary credit, weapons and military equipment.

Congressman John W. McCormack acknowledged in a letter to Spivak that a part of the testimonies were deleted from the final committee text. Spivak's articles in *The New Masses* continued to theorize about the Morgan bankers', Rockefeller's and Kuhn & Loeb's relationship, albeit in a somewhat substantiated manner and apart from Butler's testimony.

It is possible that Butler would have confused, exaggerated or even fabricated a part of the story, but his action could also have aborted the establishment of a fascist government in the United States by making

---

[439] John L. Spivak, The New Masses, *Wall Street's Fascist Conspiracy. Testimony that the McCormick-Dickstein Comitee Supressed*, January 29, 1935.

public his conversations with those involved. A coup sponsored by international bankers, working hand in hand once again.

Paying the Debts of the Democrat Party, 1945-1948

As it happened in the Russian Revolution and the First World War, international financiers used their privileged position in American banking and industry to perpetuate their economic influence and extend it beyond the United States. In particular, the Frankfurt group pressured the American administration to promote a political agenda that fit the interests of Zionism, a Jewish nationalism whose aspirations were far beyond founding a State for its people. It was a subtle form of imperialism, more financial than military, but it made use of the American war machine when it was deemed necessary. The beginning of the era of Zionist influence can be traced back to the Democratic governments of Wilson and Roosevelt, but it remained intact and even grew in later Republican governments. The United States progressively became an economic protectorate of the Frankfurt Syndicate, to the point that the interests of the Zionist world began to precede those of the American people.

In September 1947 the United Nations General Assembly adopted resolution 181 which recommended the establishment of a partition in Palestine, enabling the birth of the State of Israel on May 14, 1948. James Forrestal[440], the first defense minister in the history of the United States United, was one of the few members within the Democratic Party to warn of the growing Zionist influence on American politics.

---

[440] Forrestal was Liutenant in the Air Force during WWI. He worked in investment banking in *Dillon & Read & Co.* de 1916 a 1940 replacing its founder, Clarence Dillon, as its President in 1937. He was Secretary of the Navy (1944-1947) and first Secretary of Defense of the United States (1947-1949), in the Roosevelt and Truman terms. In March 1949 President Harry S. Truman dismissed him as Secretary of Defense of the United States and two days after he was confined in the Bethesda Naval Hospital, allegedly due to psychiatric problems, against his will and practically incommunicated. On May 22 he appeared dead, after falling from the 16th floor while in hospital. He was found with a piece of bathrobe sash cloth tied around his neck. The official version named suicide as the cause of the death, but the circumstances were very controversial.

Forrestal noted in his diaries that even before arriving at some kind of international consensus on the Palestinian issue, the United States was decided to carry out the partition unilaterally and by arms if necessary. On the death of James Forrestal his personal papers were expurgated by the Department of Defense before being allowed to be published. Despite any possible deletion or amendment, it is an essential material to understand the unconditional support of the United States to the State of Israel. Forrestal, for example, refers to a conversation that took place on October 6, 1947 with Robert Emmet Hannegan, President of the National Committee of the Democratic Party from 1944 to 1947[441]:

> «Hannegan brought up the question of Palestine. He said many people who had contributed to the democratic campaign fund in 1944 were pressing hard for assurances from the administration of definitive support for the Jewish position in Palestine. »

Hannegan, the person in charge of funding the Democratic Party, was very concerned to some important contributors. These taxpayers who pushed for the creation of the State of Israel were undoubtedly characters such as Lehman, Morgenthau, Baruch or Frankfurter, those Jews who pushed up the party in times of economic tribulation.

Sometime later, Forrestal held a meeting with Senator McGrath, Hannegan's successor at the head of the National Committee of the Democratic Party. His position on the Zionist cause was the same as his predecessor's. Forrestal concluded in his conversation on November 26, 1947 that American support for the creation of the State of Israel was based solely on the generous contributions of the Zionists to his party[442]:

---

441 The management committee of the Democrat Party. *The Forrestal Diaries*, The Viking Press, New York, 1951, p. 323.

442 James Forrestal, *The Forrestal Diaries*, p.p. 344-345.

«Forrestal derived several points from McGrath's conversation. In the first place, Jewish sources were responsible for a substantial part of the contributions to the Democratic National Committee, and many of these contributions were made "with a distinct idea on the part of the givers that they will have an opportunity to express their views and have them seriously considered on such questions as the present Palestine question."»

On February 3, 1948, Franklin Delano Roosevelt Jr., the son of the late President, tried to persuade Forrestal to change his position on the partition of Palestine. The United Nations had issued resolution 181 in favor of the creation of the State of Israel, but such a resolution was not binding[443]:

«Visit today from Franklin D. Roosevelt, Jr., who came in with a strong advocacy of the Jewish State in Palestine, that we should support the United Nations "decision," and in general a broad, across-the-board statement of the Zionist position. I pointed out that the United Nations had as yet taken no "decision," that it was only a recommendation of the General Assembly, that any implementation of this "decision" by the United States would probably result in the need for a partial mobilization[444], and that I thought the methods that had been used by people outside of the Executive branch of the government to bring coercion and duress on other nations in the General Assembly bordered closely onto scandal. He professed ignorance on this latter point and returned to his general exposition of the case of the Zionists.

He made no threats but made it very clear that the zealous in this cause had the conviction of trying to upset the government policy on Palestine. I replied that I had no power to make policy

[443] James Forrestal, *The Forrestal Diaries*, this and next quote, p.p. 362-364.

[444] Forrestal thought that for this purpose it was necessary to mobilize a division, a military unit made of 10,000 to 15,000 men (p. 365).

but that I would be derelict in my duty if I did not point out what I thought would be the consequences of any particular policy which would endanger the security of this country. I said that I was merely directing my efforts to lifting the question out of politics, that is, to have the two parties agree they would not compete for votes on this issue. He said this was impossible, that the nation was too far committed and that, furthermore, the Democratic Party would be bound to lose and the Republicans gain by such an agreement. I said I was forced to repeat to him what I had said to Senator McGrath in response to the latter's observation that our failure to go along with the Zionists might lose the states of New York, Pennsylvania and California–that I thought it was about time that somebody should pay some consideration to whether we might not lose the United States. »

That same day Forrestal held a meeting with Bernard Baruch, who warned him with a certain degree of threat about his disagreements regarding the Palestinian question:

«Had lunch with B[ernard] M. Baruch. After lunch, raised the same question with him. He took the line of advising me not to be active in this particular matter and that I was already identified, to a degree that was not in my own interests, with opposition to the United Nations policy on Palestine. He said he himself did not approve of the Zionists' actions, but in the next breath said that the Democratic Party could only lose by trying to get our government's policy reversed, and said that it was a most inequitable thing to let the British arm the Arabs and for us not to furnish similar equipment to the Jews.»

The czar of the War Industries Board, Bernard Baruch, said that if the Democrats gave up on the State of Israel it would mean a certain electoral defeat, and implicitly acknowledged that the United States was already providing arms to the future State of Israel. Baruch seemed to forget that the Arabs had been allies not only of the British, but also of the Americans in the last war.

That day the alarm bells of the international bankers rang and Forrestal received a phone call from Winthrop Aldrich[445], the President of *Chase Manhattan* Bank of New York, who was also concerned about Forrestal's position on Palestine. To some degree it is not surprising that the Zionists bankers pressured the government to achieve their political objectives, but it is rather strange that Anglo-Saxon banks, of non-Jewish origin, supported this agenda too with such a vigor. Perhaps this was further evidence of the unconditional alliance between the small group of international bankers, an mutual agreement on all aspects: social, political, geostrategic, and others which went beyond economic policies.

[445] Winthrop Williams Aldrich was one of the three sons of Senator Nelson Aldrich, one of the celebrated members of the trip Jekyl Island in 1910, and President of the *Chase Manhattan Bank*. His sister, Abigail Aldrich was married to John D. Rockefeller Jr. The son of Abigail (Abby), Nelson Aldrich Rockefeller, made his political career in the Republican Party as Governor of New York (1959-1973) during the two terms of Eisenhower, and he was also a candidate to lead the Republican Party in 1960, 1964 and 1968, but he had to resign himself with the vice presidency of the United States (1974-1977) during the term of Ford. Nelson occupied several chairs in the public service for Democrats like Roosevelt and Truman, proving the capital was able to dialogue with any ideology. The second brother of Winthrop, Richard S. Aldrich, was a congressman from 1923 to 1933.

THE GERMAN REVOLUTION: NATIONAL SOCIALISM (1933-1945)

"Whatever you call the collectivist system — Soviet socialism, New Deal socialism, corporate socialism, or National socialism — it is the average citizen, the guy in the street, that ultimately loses out to the boys running the operation at the top."

Anthony Sutton, *Wall Street and the Rise of Hitler*, 1976.

HERBERT CLARK HOOVER

Mining Engineer, Chairman of the Commission for Relief in Belgium and 31° President of the United States.

The Commission for Relief in Belgium.

We go back in time to tell the story of the world wars from a different angle, the angle of Germany. When World War I began, one of the first victims was Belgium. It was an objective of high military value for Germany since it offered the best access to attack the north of France. On August 2, 1914, German diplomacy summoned the Belgian Minister of Foreign Affairs to allow the passage of the German army to France. If Belgium became a neutral power and eased the transit of the German troops, they, in exchange, promised to respect Belgium's sovereignty and territorial integrity, and they would repair any possible damage caused. Belgium refused German proposal, as this would "sacrifice the honor of the nation and at the same time betray its duty toward Europe."[446] Given this refusal to his ultimatum, Germany declared war on Belgium on 4 August and took control of the country in just two weeks.

In 1914 Belgium was a highly industrialized nation with a population of seven million inhabitants, and contrary to what was published then, it had an important agricultural and livestock production, necessary to sustain a long military campaign. Their food, like the rest of the goods produced by their labor force, could be requisitioned by the German occupying army to sustain its war effort.

Neither Germany nor Belgium were allowed to import food, so to alleviate the expected Belgian great famine, in September, three of Belgium's most powerful men had the idea of forming a humanitarian committee in avoid a humanitarian crisis. The body that would channel humanitarian aid was the *National Committee for Relief and Food*, or *N.C.R.F.* and the men behind its foundation were the powerful chemical industrialist Ernest Solvay and the bankers Emile Francqui and Leon Lambert de Rothschild. Francqui was its President and Solvay was the executive director[447].

---

[446] George I. Gay, *Public Relations of the Commission for Relief in Belgium, vol. I*, Stanford University Press, 1929, California, p.1.

In October, several Americans appeared to support the idea of forming a larger committee led by the United States, a country still neutral. The American ambassadors in Britain, Walter Hines Page, and in Belgium, Brand Whitlock, together with two mining promoters called Millard Shaler and Herbert Hoover, used various diplomatic channels from Allied and neutral countries to form a new committee of international scope. On October 22, the Commission for Relief in Belgium was born under the direction of Herbert Hoover, an American resident in London, who years later would be the 31st president of the United States. The Commission for Relief in Belgium, with headquarters in London and New York, had the *N.C.R.F.* as a correspondent in Belgium.

The American Rockefellers were the first to contribute to the newly created Humanitarian Committee for Belgium, and in 2014 John D. Rockefeller Jr. made a first shipment of essential goods through the *Rockefeller Foundation*, worth $ 275,000[448]. The Rockefellers allocated one and a half million dollars from October 1914, until they withdrew from the humanitarian operation in January 1915[449]. The American banks, members of the Belgian Humanitarian Committee were, as one might expect, the *National City Bank* of the Rockefellers, together with *Guaranty Trust*[450] of the Morgan group. The aid came through the port of Rotterdam in the Netherlands, a neutral country, and then by train to the Belgian border.

When a virtually unknown mining promoter named Herbert Hoover took over the Committee without charging a penny for it, the

---

[447] The first institution formed was the *Comité National de Secours et d'Alimentation, CNSA or "National Committee for Relief and Food"*. Web of the Belgian American Educational Foundation, reviewed in 2015.

[448] New York Times, November 2, 1914, *The Millions of Rockefeller for War Relief.*

[449] New York Times, January 31, 1915, *Rockefeller out of Belgian Relief, Foundation Turns Work Over to Comission and Closes Its Bureau.*

[450] *Food for Belgium. Bulletin of the Commission for Relief in Belgium*, February 13, 1915, New York, p. 8.

news reached the United States of a man who finally worried about building something amidst such a destruction. But was this really the case, or as with the International Red Cross, born a few years later, there interests were not entirely humanitarian? The choice of Hoover, as it will be seen later, was not casual.

William Jennings Bryan, then secretary of state of Woodrow Wilson, informed about the formation of the Commission for Relief in Belgium to his Ambassador in Germany:

> «[451]*The Secretary of State to Ambassador Gerard.*
> [Telegram.]
> DEPARTMENT OF STATE,
> Washington, October 7, 1914.
>
> Department has received following from London, which you may communicate to Imperial Foreign Office: Belgian committee has been formed at Brussels under the patronage of the American and Spanish ministers for the purpose of importing foodstuffs for the poor of Belgium. The German authorities in occupation have consented and the Belgian Minister here informs me that under instructions from his Government he has obtained permission of the British authorities for the export of supplies on condition that they be despatched by this Embassy and consigned to our Legation at Brussels. I believe it would be well to obtain a definite assurance from the German Government of their approval of this humanitarian project the execution of which is in charge of an American citizen, Mr. Shaler, who is now in London purchasing supplies.

[451] *Belgian Relief*, The American Journal of International Law, Vol. 9, No. 3, Supplement: Diplomatic Correspondence Between the United States and Belligerent Governments Relating to Neutral Rights and Commerce (June 1915), American Society of International Law, p. 314.

Please take up informally with Foreign Office and cable reply.

BRYAN. »

Officially, the commission appeared as an initiative of the American ambassador in Belgium, Brand Whitlock and the Spanish ambassador in London, Alfonso Merry del Val and Zulueta. But we can glimpse the hand of the true architects of the commission, Baron Leon Lambert de Rothschild and his business partner Emile Francqui. The noble object of this committee was to create a supply of food for Belgium that the German soldiers could not requisition, only to maintain the Belgian civilian population. The German government soon favored the idea, since in this way it would be freed from the burden of feeding the population of an occupied country, and there would be greater availability of food for Germany.

«[452]*Minister Whitlock to the Secretary of State.*
[Telegram.]
AMERICAN LEGATION,
Brussels, October 16th, 1914.

As I have already reported to the Department, a committee of not- able citizens of Brussels was appointed several weeks ago under patron- age of the Spanish Minister and myself to give food to the poor of this city. This work, which had the approval of the Belgian Government and of the German military authorities, has been carried on with excellent results. But now a grave situation confronts the land. In normal times Belgium produces only one-sixth of the foodstuffs she consumes. Within two weeks there will be no more food in Belgium.

Winter is coming on and there are thousands who are without home and without hope, therefore it is necessary to extend this

[452] *Belgian Relief*, The American Journal of International Law, p.p. 314-315.

relief work to the whole of Belgium. My Spanish colleague and I have been requested by the local Belgian authorities and by the German military authorities to permit the organization, under our patronage, of a committee that will undertake to revictual all of Belgium and we have secured from the German military authorities formal official assurance that all food- stuffs shipped into Belgium in the care of the committee and intended for the feeding of the impoverished civil population will be respected by the soldiery and not made the object of military requisition. It is now necessary to obtain permission from the English Government that foodstuffs may be shipped into Belgium. In view of this fact Gibson goes to London to-morrow with messages from the Spanish Minister and me to the respective ambassadors of our countries to lay the subject before them. Baron Lambert and Mr. Franqui, representing the Belgian Relief Committee, will accompany him to acquaint the Belgian Minister in London with the situation[453] and ask him to present the matter to the British Government. Our hope is that the Belgian Minister can arrange, and if there be no impropriety in their so doing, that the American and Spanish ambassadors may assist him in arranging for the passage of the provisions which the Committee is ready to buy. I trust the Department will approve this course and further it by instructions to London. It is not money but food that is needed. If some appropriate means can be found to call the attention of our generous people at home to the plight of the poor in Belgium, I am sure that they will send succor and relief for the winter that is drawing near. It seems to me to be a work of mercy that will touch the hearts of those who are brought to understand it and give our people in America an opportunity to serve nobly in a high cause.

[453] Could it be possible that the Belgian ambassador in London was not aware of the dramatic situation his country was going through, where seven million of his citizens were starving to death?

WHITLOCK.]

An appeal to the good feelings of politicians and citizens would be enough to make the public funds and private donations to flow. Once the committee was formed, there were three big points to cover; to obtain the agreement between Allies and Central Powers, to organize the logistics of such an operation, and obviously the biggest problem; to know who would pay the invoices for the thousands of tons of food and basic necessities sent to Belgium.

Unlike countries at war such as Russia or France, Belgium was a country occupied by Germany, and therefore the Germans should honor their responsibility to feed the occupied countries. This was reflected in the international treaties on war. Hoover's first approach to the German finance minister made it clear that it was the Frankfurt bankers who were managing the German finances.

[[454]*Memorandum, by HOOVER, of a conversation with DR. KARL HELFFERICH, Imperial Finance Minister, 4 February 1915, concerning the indemnities and the financial proposals of the Minister*

Berlin, 6 February 1915

At 6 o'clock I had a meeting, accompanied by Mr. Heineman, with the Finance Minister, Mr. Helfferich. Mr. Heineman having seen him previously, he was well informed as to our proposals. He stated at once, however, that the proposed abandonment of the contribution from Belgium was wholly and absolutely impossible. He stated that Herr Zimmermann could not have understood what we meant. He stated that some other way would have to be found to assist the Commission, and suggested that we go to Brussels and place our requirements before the Local Government, and that he

[454] George I. Gay, *Public Relations of the Commission for Relief in Belgium*, p. 245-247.

would ask them to assist us in every way possible. I told him that this was a matter which concerned the Imperial Government itself, that the questions of feeding seven millions in Belgium, three millions in France, and ten millions in Poland 19 were all wrapped up in one question, and that was the question as to the control of imported foodstuffs through neutral committees, and that I presumed these committees would have to be, from the nature of things, American, and that it was due to anybody who undertook such a labor that his requests should receive attention from the highest.

I explained the voluntary character of our effort, the philanthropic origin of our funds, the additions which we had had to these funds from Belgian sources, and the absolute vital importance to the German Government from a military point of view that we should continue our action, and stated that unless we could be properly recognized by the Government and helped in our work by them, it would ultimately dwindle down to a service totally inadequate to the millions of people.

The Minister then made a series of suggestions as to other methods. He proposed that the contribution on Belgium should be increased and that we should be handed the increased contribution.

To this I replied that this would be nothing but paper and that we must have gold. He then suggested that we might have bills drawn by the people from whom we purchased foodstuffs, and have these bills accepted by the Belgian banks, and that through the friends of the German Government in New York they could arrange to have these bills discounted and even renewed, lie explained to me that Mr. Warburg,- 0 the head of the banking firm of Warburg and Company of Hamburg, was a brother of Mr. Warburg of Messrs. Kuhn, Loeb and Company of New York, head of the American Government National Reserve Board, and that the National Reserve Board [the Federal Reserve[455]] was anxious to

[455] German Minister of Finance, Helfferich, talks about Paul Warburg's Federal

set up a large business in bills, diverting especially South American bills from the London to the New York market, and that Mr. Warburg in New York would be in a position to induce the various banks to discount these bills, and he stated that no doubt they would be renewed from time to time until the war was over.

I explained to him that there were two weaknesses in his proposal: The first was that I saw no reason why any Belgian bank should accept these bills, as we had no money to pay any Belgian bank; that although we sold a portion of the foodstuffs the money which we received was dissipated in caring for the destitute and in paying communal officials; and that I could set' no more reason why a Belgian bank should accept such bills than any other bank in the world; the other difficulty was that the amount of such bills would run into ten millions of dollars per month and that it would go on for nine months at least. We had some argument on the question and he stuck to his point tenaciously and said we should see Mr. Warburg, with whom we had already discussed the matter. He again repeated that the idea of abandoning the contribution from Belgium was wholly impossible for three reasons: (1) The technical arrangements under which the contributions had been set up requiring the abandonment of the rights of local generals, and other inter departmental arrangements which could not be broken down; (2) it would be equivalent to the German Government paying for the food of the Belgians; and (3) the English Government could say that it compelled the Germans to do it.

I replied that this was not my view; that the possession of the contribution placed in the hands of the Germans a club which they could use to force the English and French to pay out two million pounds per month in gold to feed the Belgians; and that all it meant to the Germans was the abandonment of forty million

---

Reserve as "National Reserve". His confusion in choosing the name is easy to understand, because in 1915 the majority of the Ameircan people didn't even know of the existence of their own central bank, much less its name.

francs worth of doubtful paper. He suggested that we might expand the contribution, the Societe Generale to discount the provincial bonds as in the old case, and to print similar currency against them, and that the Imperial Government might entertain some method of guaranteeing their exchange value and interesting their friends, Messrs. Warburg and the German agents in New York, to raise money against such guaranteed exchange.

I pointed out that sooner or later this would mean the export of gold from Germany, that in any case it means the inflation of the Societe Generale currency to a disastrous point. I informed him that in any event his method was one which required the Americans to loan the money, the Belgians to repay the loan, the Germans hanging on to their indemnity from Belgium; that if I went back to England and replied to question of the English Government that the Germans had refused to relax the pressure on Belgium, the English must at once give publicity to their offer, and that I did not think any American banker would care to loan money to the Belgians under such circumstances.

We parted in order to see Mr. Warburg at the Adlon Hotel.]

The Warburgs were leading the German war economy, and some years later they also led the German intelligence operations through *HAPAG*. Hoover had a meeting with Max Warburg that day, and the next day he met with Carl Melchior, financial advisor of the bank *M.M. Warburg & Co.* in Hamburg.

The financing of the Belgian operation, according to the memorandums of Hoover, was directed by the brothers Warburg and *Kuhn & Loeb.* It is impossible to know to what extent they benefited from the humanitarian operation in Belgium, since such data did not appear in any official statistics, but it is undeniable that there must have been a significant profit derived from the management of a fund of almost one billion dollars[456].

[456] We could include as beneficiary the personal aide of Hoover in Belgium, Lewis

[457]*Memorandum, by HOOVER, of a conversation with MAX M. WARBURG, the German banker, 4 February 1915, concerning methods of financing Belgian relief.*

BERLIN, 6 February 1915

At 7:30 1 had a meeting with Mr. Warburg, accompanied by Mr. Heineman, at the Adlon. He informed us generally of the position as he understood it from the Minister of Finance, and we discussed the matter at some length. He agreed with us that there was no banking operation in it unless we secured a similar amount of money to the accepted bills and deposited this money somewhere. He also agreed that the amount of money involved was very much larger than he had been led to believe. He informed me of the success he had had with discounting the bills for the cotton shipments from the United States to Germany and that he believed through Kuhn, Loeb and Company in New York and the influence which they maintain he could secure the discount of a considerable amount of grain bills for our purpose, but that as there was a break in our financial chain due to the fact that we distributed all the money, it was therefore obvious that this could not be done. We discussed the project of increasing the Société Générale's currency issue placed on an increased contribution, and in response to a remark of mine that if I were the manager of the Société Générale I would commit suicide before I would create a paper currency of what would apparently amount to nine hundred

Lichtenstein Strauss. When he finished with his duties there, Paul Warburg included him in the staff of *Kuhn & Loeb,* where he became partner in 1929. Strauss married the daughter of a partner, Jerome Hanauer. In 1944 he worked in naval intelligence under Vincent Forrestal, who was then Secretary of the Navy.

457 George I. Gay, *Public Relations of the Commission for Relief in Belgium,* p.p. 247-248.

million francs secured on the assets of that bank and of the so-called provincial guarantees, Mr. Warburg remarked that he would have committed suicide some time ago if he had been the manager of the Société Générale. Mr. Warburg was very affable and sympathized with the humanitarian aspects of this matter, offering his services in any way which we would command. We asked him to see the Finance Minister [Helfferich] and explain that the projects which he laid down were infeasible and that the short straight method was to adopt our proposal. He promised to see the Minister that evening.]

Hoover faced some disagreements in the way of financing of the operations; Germans wanted to pay for food shipments with Belgian currency, while the Americans did not trust the value of Belgian paper, a country militarily occupied and economically exhausted. For that reason they demanded to Germany the payment of the food in gold. To solve this setback Hoover held talks with German Finance Minister Karl Helfferich, with bankers Max Warburg and Carl Melchior of *M.M. Warburg & Co.*, and with the German Chancellor Theobald von Bethmann Hollweg[458].

The German banker Hjalmar Schacht had an idea that unraveled the situation, proposing that Belgian government issued what he called "humanitarian bonds". The idea was accepted by all parts, but there was still a stumbling block; the United States could not issue loans to a conflicting power such as Germany, and the Belgian economy was not credible enough to be the guarantor of the loan. Without a solid source of funding, the Commission for Relief in Belgium plan would never be carried out. Hoover solved the problem of the American blockade with a legal chicanery, issuing a loan to Belgium, a neutral power, with the backing of the Imperial German Government.

---

[458] The Bethmanns were the most powerful bankers of Frankfurt until the arrival of the Rothschild, and for years they were rivals. Bethmanns were Christian.

[[459] *Memorandum by HOOVER, of a conversation with DR. SCHACHT and HERR VON LUMM, Chairman and Vice-Chairman of the Reichsbank, 9 February 1915, concerning methods of financing relief by means of a Belgian loan, guaranteed by Germany*

BERLIN, 9 February 1915

I had a meeting at the Reichsbank at twelve o'clock and there were present Dr. Schacht, Mr. von Lumm, the Chairman and the Vice-Chairman of the Reichsbank, and Mr. Heineman.

The meeting was called to consider the financial proposals put forward by the Finance Minister, those put forward by Dr. Schacht and others…

as they expected to borrow the money from American agencies, I would be glad enough to inform them of such conditions as must necessarily surround any attempt on the part of the Belgians to borrow money in America, either with or without German assistance; that they must bear in mind that the American Government had practically prohibited the making of loans to any of the belligerent governments, and that therefore this loan would have to be neutral. It could only be made neutral by virtue of being guaranteed on both sides [Belgium and Germany].

The conversation lasted a long time, chiefly in German, and the Chairman of the Reichsbank seemed initially much opposed to the idea; but after infinite discourse they seemed all agreed on the proposals as above laid down, that is, that if the Belgians wished to borrow fifty million dollars in America, the German Government would unqualifiedly guarantee the loan.]

---

[459] George I. Gay, *Public Relations of the Commission for Relief in Belgium*, p.p. 257-258.

The final result was far from what it was initially agreed, and the humanitarian operation, which lasted until 1917, would be paid by several means: For the most part, the funds came in this order from the government of the United States, a neutral power, to a lesser extent from the governments of England and France, and finally through the Belgian "humanitarian bonds". Only a small part came from donations. It might be a bit shocking for the reader to discover that the Allied countries took over for three years the maintenance of Belgium during World War I, actually a responsibility under the scope of their enemy, Germany[460]. It is certain that Germany contributed little or nothing to the humanitarian operation.

Public donations were collected in cash, food and other basic consumer goods, and once the financial side was settled, the logistical aspect had to be considered as well. The project included the supply of 80,000 tons of food per month and the use of 40 vessels dedicated to this purpose[461]. This meant opening a secure trade route for the merchant ships of the Commission for Relief in Belgium, which had secured a tradelane free from attacks from the belligerent powers[462]. Only the supply of those provisions channeled by the commission, which exclusively enjoyed the trade of essential goods with Belgium - not only food- could be guaranteed. In practice, the committee had a monopoly on trade with Belgium, and the finances were organized by the Warburg through *Kuhn & Loeb* in New York, and Emile Francqui in Belgium.

With no hesitation Hoover offered the exclusive of the transport of the goods to the German shipping company of the Warburgs, *Hamburg-America Line*, instead of having companies from a neutral country. It is true that the espionage operations of *Hamburg-America Line* in the United States were not known until a couple of years later, but granting both the financing and the logistics of the operation to

[460] Obligation included in the Hague Convention of 1907.

[461] George I. Gay, *Public Relations of the Commission for Relief in Belgium*, p. 305.

[462] *Belgian Relief*, The American Journal of International Law, p. 323.

companies dependent on the Warburgs was at least conspicuous, due to the arbitrariness, the exclusivity and the Germanic origin of the companies and their owners. As soon as the humanitarian committee tasks began, Hoover had a meeting with the director of *Hamburg-America Line* in Germany, a Jewish shipowner named Albert Ballin, to discuss the matter of transporting the goods.

> [[463]*Memorandum, by HOOVER, of a conversation with HERR BALLIN, 11 5 February 1915, concerning the attitude of the German Government toward the financial proposals of the C.R.D.*
>
> Berlin. 6 February 1915
>
> At 10:30, accompanied by Mr. Heineman, I called on Herr Ballin at the Esplanade Hotel and spent about an hour and a half with him. I explained that I had originally made the appointment with him some two or three weeks ago with a view to discussing the transfer to our service of some of the Hamburg-American freight ships.- but that while the negotiation for government permission was going well, things had constantly taken a change and a great difficulty had arisen before us which had prevented any further progress in the shipping matter.
>
> I then sketched to him briefly our history and present position, and how necessary it was that we should find some point of accommodation between the belligerent governments…
>
> After a considerable discussion of various points I shook hands on leaving, and as a parting word he stated: "You can depend on me to help with all my might."]

There remained a third and important aspect to be solved, and it consisted in obtaining the cooperation of all the powers in conflict.

---

[463] George I. Gay, *Public Relations of the Commission for Relief in Belgium*, p.p. 218-219.

Germany agreed without any reservation from the moment the plan was proposed, since in any case it would have to feed the Belgian population and the operations of the committee involved avoiding a considerable headache. As a result of the commercial blockade of the Allies on their ports the Germans already had serious problems to feed their own civilian and military population, and even more to the Belgians.

England also did not put too many objections to the American initiative, and only formulated some minimum conditions, among which included a maximum price of transport and the obligatory nature of the company and the crew that chartered the ships were from neutral countries.

France, however, did not accept the idea of sending provisions to Germany, and even less to use boats from a German company. France saw things differently than Britain, since French soldiers were the ones who died at the battlefront. The Great War was one of the most dramatic war conflicts to be remembered; the soldiers spent months huddled together, suffering from hunger and cold in the narrow trenches, which could come down and bury them at any moment. They fought for small areas of land with little progress and the bodies were piled up in no man's land for weeks without any side dared to remove them. This situation of almost permanent tables was maintained until the first tanks and the fearsome chemical weapons appeared.

Hoover urged France to accept the actions of the committee, which had already been approved by the English and Germans, and which would also benefit a part of its population in the area of occupied France. This is how Louis Chevrillon, an agent of the Humanitarian Committee for Belgium, described the position of the French government.

> [[464]*Letter, CHEVRILLON to HOOVER, outlining the objections of the French Government to the use of German interned ships by the C.R.B.*

---

[464] George I. Gay, *Public Relations of the Commission for Relief in Belgium*, p.p.

PARIS, 6 October 1915
H. C. Hoover, Esq., President
The Commission for Relief in Belgium, London

Dear Hoover:

I have had several long conversations yesterday at the French Foreign Office with the outcome that the ship question is decidedly hiking a bad turn. There was a note in the handwriting of Mr. Delcasse himself giving his opinion as inclined to be adverse, and, curiously enough, a very long letter from Mr. Klobukowski, the French Minister to Belgium, very strongly giving his arguments against the proposed combination...

> "In the first place it is a known fact that the Hamburg-America
>
> Company is on the verge of failure and the proposed combination might just save it. The upkeep of the boats in New York is a very considerable expense, of which that Company would be relieved.
>
> "The boats having a neutral crew, many German sympathizers might be employed in the service, which might lead later to deplorable consequences...
>
> "Finally, the proposed combination is nothing else but 'dealing with the enemy.' The Allied Governments still consider that the work of the Commission is only tolerated under the plea of humanitarianism. The duty of provisioning and victualing the populations in a territory occupied by German troops is incumbent upon the German Government; the work is performed at the expense of the Allied nations under protest, and the idea of chartering a German fleet, of

---

328-329.

paying a German company, of relieving it from an enormous expense, of guaranteeing its ships from any attack, of putting them in perfect train for immediate action after the war is over, all this for a service which Germany should perform, cannot for a moment be entertained. No Allied Government could accept such a paradoxical position as that of a German fleet of steamers circulating freely, the only steamers of any of the belligerent governments immune from war risks or capture."

Such will be the reasons presented by the French Government in answer to the English suggestion, and I am afraid that the Foreign Office here will refuse to budge from its position unless some profound modification of the proposed arrangements is agreed upon…

Yours sincerely

(Signed) L. Chevrillon»

The French put on the table the tremendous incongruity that the Allies had to allocate their own economic resources for the indirect support of their German enemy. Moreover, the operation seemed to be tailored to the interests of the German fleet of the Warburgs, whose ships were then losing a fortune in dry dock due to the blockade of the Allies. The approval of the French government had to wait until March 1916, but by then Ballin already had other plans for the *Hamburg-America Line* fleet.

[[465]Letter, *WILMINK* to *HOOVER*, reporting the refusal of the German Government to permit the use of the interned ships

[465] George I. Gay, *Public Relations of the Commission for Relief in Belgium*, p.p. 330-331.

AMSTERDAM, 1 July 1916

Herbert Hoover, Esq.
Chairman of the Commission for
Relief in Belgium, London

Dear Sir:

I have received today a letter from Mr. Ballin asking me to inform you that a favorable decision in the question of tonnage for your Commission is not to be expected for the moment. According to Mr. Ballin the opinion in Berlin seems to be that with the Belgian ships at your disposal you can provide sufficiently for the feeding of the Belgian population, and for this reason apparently they will not allow — at least not for the moment — the use of German tonnage for this purpose.

For your guidance, I expect to be in London some time during the latter half of July and will not fail to make an appointment, in case you might wish to see me.

I am, dear Mr. Hoover,

Yours sincerely

(Signed) Wilmink]

By 1916 the idea of using German ships was no longer an optimal plan for the *Hamburg-America Line.* The conditions and the price imposed by the English were not favorable for the shipping company, and the risks had to be considered, since the Belgian Commission had lost six ships by mines or torpedoes in the North Sea. Germany put in place a well-known plan to use the resources of *Hamburg-America Line* in smuggling, espionage and sabotage operations in the United States.

The First World War is a conflict whose course has always been studied from the military point of view, but its most decisive aspect was the commercial war between the powers. At the beginning of the war Germany chose to respect commercial vessels transiting waters in conflict in compliance with international laws, but after seeing its economy asphyxiated by the trade blockade of the Allies, in 1916 the position of many German politicians and military went through to establish underwater war without restrictions, which in practice involved the destruction of any allied or neutral ship, civil or military, that traded with their enemies. The detractors of the strategy pointed out, not without reason, that this contravened the international conventions on the laws of war and free navigation. They feared the negative impact it would have on Germany in diplomatic relations with neutral powers such as the United States. It is no less true that the British were the first to breach these agreements, establishing a commercial blockade on Germany.

In December 1916 the German Chancellor von Bethmann-Hollweg proposed peace to the Allies. It is difficult to determine whether the proposal was made with sincere aims, or as some historians point out, Germany hoped that if the Allies rejected their outstretched hand, this could give them a status of moral superiority that would soften the adverse diplomatic effects of unrestricted underwater warfare.

The Belgian humanitarian operation, as initially proposed, only offered advantages for Germany; it passed on the burden of feeding Belgium to Allied and neutral countries, while at the same time providing a useful outlet for German ships, permanently anchored in neutral ports and with high maintenance costs. The final result was not so satisfactory for *Hamburg-America Line*, and all its ships were finally seized by the Allies as part of the reparations established in the Peace of Versailles. At the end of the war Albert Ballin ended his life with a shot, he was said, desperate for the collapse of his company.

It is not surprising that Germany relied blindly on the men of Frankfurt, Warburgs, Rothschilds, Schiff and *Kuhn & Loeb,* during the

First World War. Since 1914 they had had a vital role in the Commission for Relief in Belgium and in 1917 their bank caused the collapse of Russia, one of the most powerful enemies of the Kaiser.

The humanitarian project was not free of controversy in the United States. The Belgian director of the project, Emil Francqui, had to respond in the New York Times to the request of Senator William M. Calder to investigate the shipment of food shipments in poor condition, which produced intoxications in the Belgian population[466]. There were also complaints about the arbitrariness when making purchases, and the inflation that produced in the United States the export of food for ten million people in Europe. Hoover was accused of manipulating the food market thanks to the hundreds of millions of funds he had under his control. Senator Reed of Missouri called Hoover "the foremost war gambler in the wheat market" and claimed that he had taken advantage of humanitarian funds to manipulate the market and rig the price of food in the Chicago market[467].

According to a book published by John Hamill, one of Hoover's biographers, all goods were distributed on the ground through the Belgian branch, the *C.N.S.A.* directed by Francqui, which was organized into committees and subcommittees in the various Belgian provinces. The entire financial part in Belgium was carried out through its bank *Société Générale de Belgique.* It is doubtful that the American Congress had a real notion of what was happening on the other side of the Atlantic Ocean, and it is more doubtful that Francqui, who had absolute control over the distribution of food, would find any opposition to his decisions in Belgium. Of course, the German occupiers would avoid any interference in the operations of Francqui, and so would do the Belgians, fearing that the latter could interrupt the supply of basic consumer goods[468]. The Germans could not confiscate

[466] New York Times, March 6, 1919, *Belgian Rebukes Senator Calder; Statement that Spoiled Food Was Sent for a Relief a Detestabe Slander, Says Francqui.*

[467] New York Times, January 17, 1917, *Attacks Hoover as Arch Gambler; Rigged American Food Markets for Benefits of Belgians, Senator Reed Asserts.*

the supplies sent, but as long as Francqui imported the food through the Humanitarian Committee, the Germans could continue to requisition the Belgian harvests. Francqui became the master of Belgium in controlling the distribution of food. His bank not only coordinated the entire operation in Belgium, but also capitalized the issuance of "humanitarian bonds" and developed the functions of a central bank during the war[469]. This was a great success for the main agent of the Rothschilds in Belgium.

Hamill's book also denounced that the food and the rest of the goods were not given *charitably* but were sold, and not only those provided by the American government, but also those that came from the selfless donation of American citizens. Another author, Walter Liggett corroborates it:

> «[470]Most Americans have the idea the Commission for Relief in Belgium was a charitable enterprise; that the money was privately subscribed; and that the Belgians gratuitously received the food. Nothing could be further from the truth. Donations from Great Britain amounted to $17,000,000 and the people of the United States despite wide-spread publicity gave only $11,000,000. Belgium itself gave about $90,000,000[471], and the remainder of the $809,227,097,000 total was appropriated by the British, French and United States treasuries. »

The book written by Gay, a member of the Belgian Humanitarian Committee, was the main official document made available to the

---

[468] John Hamill, *The Strange Career of Mr. Hoover Under Two Flags*, William Faro Inc., 1931, New York, p.p. 314-324.

[469] George I. Gay, *Public Relations*, p. 248. Gay's book suggests Francqui's bank issued at least the equivalent to 900 million francs.

[470] Walter Liggett, *The Rise of Herbert Hoover*, p. 230.

[471] By means of relief bonds, mostly, nothing really came out of the Belgians's pocket.

public about the committee's activities. It was generous in data on the amount of food distributed by the commission, the tonnage used and other statistics, but did not go into detail the most important issues. These gaps mainly affected the distribution procedure and the committee's accounting, the financing, the origin of the income, the data of purchases or sales. And of course Gay's book did not mention the "sale" of basic "humanitarian" goods. Liggett and Hamill's claims about the sale of the relief goods may seem ridiculous, but it may be more ridiculous to think that Americans would give Belgians their daily food ration only by presenting a coupon. No American in 1914 would receive a free meal in his country just because he needed it.

The website of the *Belgian American Educational Foundation*, the heir organization of the Commission for Relief in Belgium, acknowledges that the commission obtained a benefit of one hundred million dollars, although it states that "most of it was used for the care of the destitute", and the rest of the funds, 33,766,000 dollars, were used to form the new foundation[472].

Even the *New York Times* pointed out in a 1917 editorial the hypocrisy of American "humanitarian" operations in Belgium:

> «[473]The hand that allots is American, not the hand that gives. Of $250,000,000 spent, the United States, so innocently proud of its Belgian largesse, has given $9,000,000. The people of Belgium and Northern France are kept alive by the Allied Governments. These, with a thousand burdens, give them $14,000,000 a month. The lavish United States, heaping fat profits from the sale of supplies for Belgium and Northern France, has poured out in two years $9,000,000! »

The *New York Times* is clear when it talks about *sales* and *gross profits*, and its figures are very similar to those provided by the other two

---

[472] The Belgian American Educational Foundation, web revised in April 2014.
[473] New York Times, January 31, 1917, *Why Mr. Hoover was Ashamed*.

sources. Combining the information obtained from these three sources, Liggett, the heir foundation of the Commission for Relief and the American newspaper, we can extrapolate some approximate figures of the five years of humanitarian operations in Belgium:

THE COMMISSION FOR RELIEF IN NUMBERS, 1914-1919.

Total approximate funds of the Belgian Commission: from 800 to 900 million dollars. Benefits obtained by the committee: 100 million dollars.

* American government: from 250,000,000 and 380,866,077 $[474]
* French government: $ 202,529,511
* British government: $ 107,831,412
* Belgium, through Hoover's "humanitarian bonds": $ 90,000,000
* Donations from British citizens: $ 17,000,000
* Donations from American citizens: between $ 9,000,000 and $ 11,000,000

Approx. funds of the Commission: from 800 to 900 million dollars.
Profits reaped by the commission: 100 million dollars.

The profit of the "humanitarian" committee was 100 million dollars or 11%, a profitability that would seduce any investor, specially if you don't have to put a dollar of own capital at risk. We don't know in detail what was the use of the funds collected, the benefits obtained, if the purchase and sale prices of the products were adjusted to the real market price, or what was the salary or indirect pecuniary benefit perceived by the associates of Hoover and Francqui. In short, it is impossible to determine the good or bad use of the funds because the

[474] The discrepancy close to 130 millions between different sources probably refers to the 100 millions in profits. In some cases these profits might be recorded as profit re invested, and in others excluded.

statistical section of Gay's book, the main official document to justify the spending of 1,000 million dollars of donations and public funds, does not contain the necessary data.

* * *

It is not an easy task to understand the diverse motivations that pushed the belligerent countries to agree in this unnatural humanitarian scheme, and each author contributes with a different version. It has already been pointed out that the Germans were more than happy that the occupied Belgium received food paid for by their enemies. This would also make it possible for them to confiscate a larger quantity of the goods and food produced in Belgium. We also know that the United States did not organize the operation for altruistic purposes and that the country benefited directly and indirectly from the monopoly of the trade with Belgium. Some private interests possibly reaped extraordinary profits, such as the Warburg, their partners of *Kuhn & Loeb*, Emil Francqui or Baron Leon Lambert de Rothschild. Even selling at a market price, the committee obtained its goods and services for a very low sum of money, in some cases even at zero cost.

> «[475]A large proportion of the provided by the for Belgian Relief were purchased in on chartered steamships, passed through Holland payment of duties or railroad rates, and then by volunteer workers in rent-free stores to a population which no except to purchase the goods, regardless of quality, at prices asked. Naturally, under these conditions, the Commission profited tremendously. »

There is a perfectly plausible explanation from the economic point of view; the Belgian Commission offered a perfect captive market in Belgium to be able to sell products of first necessity. Herbert Hoover might not earn a penny for his work, and maybe he did not benefit in

[475] Walter Liggett, *The Rise of Herbert Hoover*, p. 231.

any way from the Belgian operation, but when he presented his candidacy for the presidency, his old bankers friends, who made huge profits, were able to keep up[476].

The most baffling question is, why would France and Britain agree to such an unusual scheme that forced them to feed the Belgians at their own expense? The most usual explanation is that if the Allies fed the Belgians, the Germans could not force the population to work in exchange for food. Liggett points out the incongruity of the situation:

> «[477]The British and French, well aware from the beginning that their only chance of winning the war depended upon starving Germany, would raise objections to sending food to Belgium on the theory that if the Allies and neutrals didn't feed the Belgian people, the Germans would have to, This, of course, would decrease the supplies available for the Germans themselves.»

The answer, according to the author, is that possibly they did it only to please the Americans. France and England, like Germany, played the card of American sympathy and they were eager to please Wilson's wishes, knowing that US support for one side or another would change the course of the war. According to Liggett, the plan came from the American Ambassador to the United Kingdom, Walter Hines Page, an avowed Anglophile who had from the beginning the intention that the United States declared war on Germany. Hoover at

---

[476] Take for instance the case of two of Hoover's aides. Prentiss N. Gray was one of the directors of the Committee in Brussels, and Julius Barnes was part of the council in New York. None of both did anything noteworthy before their work in Belgium, where they earn a bit more than their daily allowances and some dolar-a-year symbolic fees. When they finished their work in the Committee, Hoover set them to work in the "public service". Some years after, in 1930, Gray simultaneously held chairs in 14 corporations simultaneously, including the presidence of *J. Henry Schroder Banking Co.* Barnes was director of the same bank and held a chair in 12 corporations, presiding over four companies and being the chairman of five. Hamill, p. 361-363.

[477] Walter Liggett, *The Rise of Herbert Hoover*, p. 228.

first was reluctant due to his German descent, but he did what was expected of him. And it is clear that the main motivation of the committee was not humanitarian, but economic, according to this author:

«[478]The first three active In Brussels were Millard Shaler and two other American engineers connected with Emil Francqui's African copper interests.

I do not wish to imply that Solvay, Francqui, Baron Lambert, Ambassador Page, Millard Shaler, Hoover, and scores of others were not actuated by sincerely decent impulses to aid suffering humanity. I feel sure they were. It was simply unthinkable that 7,000,000 men, women and children should be allowed to starve and no one doubts that there would have been acute distress had not relief been forthcoming. But the point I am trying to make is, that while these men realized the humanitarian side of the situation, they also had in mind their own pecuniary or political interests...

His political reasons behind Hoover's selection are probably much simpler. Ambassador Walter Page endorsed Hoover to Washington, and from the very start of the war Page was as pro-British as any peer in England… I think Page realized that an American in this position could be a tremendous influence in dragging the United States into the wax on the Allied side and that admittedly was Page's purpose from the very first… Hoover doubtless intended to be wholly neutral, and his German financial connections and partly German ancestry probably convinced Berlin that he would be perfectly fair as, indeed, I think he was almost to the end of 1916. Then, apparently realizing the inevitable, Hoover fulfilled Page's expectations by coming to the United States and helping persuade Wilson to break relations with Germany.

---

[478] Walter Liggett, *The Rise of Herbert Hoover*, p.p. 224-227.

The difficulties of the actual relief undertaking itself probably were exaggerated at the time by overly-enthusiastic newspaper-men or paid publicists. Germany, Great Britain, France and Belgium were all anxious to co-operate. Germany agreed to the proposal for a neutral relief commission with little delay, and Great Britain and France were ready with substantial donations the day that Germany agreed. Later, the United States Treasury paid the bills…

The facts in this connection are rather interesting: The hostilities between Germany Belgium started on August 5; Brussels surrendered on August 26; Louvain was sacked August 29; and the people of Namur were cut off and virtually starving by September 5. »

In other words: Belgium went from normality to a generalized famine thirty days after Germany declared war on it. The country had an important food production of its own and was not as dependent on imports, as international public opinion was led to believe. The "great famine" was so unexpected that, as we saw earlier, the Belgian Ambassador was not even aware of the "situation" of his own country.

The spirit of the Belgian Commission were indeed very similar to that of the War Industries Board. It was a centralized purchasing system managed by businessmen that had their own private economic interests in the conflict. The Germans themselves also set up a centralized purchasing system for the basic goods at the beginning of the war, and only one banker in Germany was able to undertake such a patriotic-and lucrative-effort:

«[479]As the Allied blockade drove up food prices and provoked riots, secure Food supplies became a top priority. Early on, Max suggested that food purveyors be placed under state supervision to prevent profiteering. Max, Ballin and Melchior helped to organize the Imperial Purchasing Company, to import food under

479 Ron Chernow, *The Warburgs*, p. 173.

government auspices. The Warburg bank [M.M. Warburg & Co.] advanced payment and provided foreign exchange for such imports. »

John Hamill noted that the Germans not only benefited from the activities of the Belgian Commission indirectly, but also obtained part of the food, diverted through unofficial channels, through resale and military requisitions. He states that Germany would never have surpassed the bad harvests of 1916 without the existence of this humanitarian plan. Hamill's conclusion about the committee was therefore much simpler than Liggett's:

«[480]The whole aim and object of the Belgian Relief was to provide Germany with food… thus cruelly and unnecessarily prolonging the terrible war which, without the slightest shadow of a doubt, would otherwise have come to an end in 1916 through the breakdown of Germany from hunger. »

It seem to be a daring opinion but it is worth remembering that the economic interests promoted by the Belgian Commission were the same ones that unnecessarily prolonged the war by supporting the Bolshevik Revolution. The international bankers did not know about a homeland or borders and the war was a valid instrument to produce the most profitable business; debt on a massive scale.

Ludendorff, the head of the German General Staff on the Eastern Front, acknowledged that in 1917 the issue of food had become the most troublesome issue in sustaining the war[481]:

«The question of food-supplies was of equal importance to the people and the army, to man and beast. The work of the army in

[480] John Hamill, *The Strange Career of Mr. Hoover Under Two Flags*, p.p. 329-330.

[481] Erich Ludendorff, *My Own Story. August 1914-1918, vol. I*, Harper, 1919, Londres, p.p. 414.

the field depended in a high degree upon their rations. That and leave are the two decisive matters in morale. I thus had to give to the question of food my full attention. The reduction in morale at home was equally due to the food situation. The human body did not receive, especially in albumen and fats, the necessary nourishment for the maintenance of physical and mental vigor... The individual did not even receive his official ration, which of itself was fixed too low to maintain his full strength. »

The "altruistic" humanitarian aid of the Belgian Commission ceased abruptly when the United States entered into war with Germany. The Belgian Commission was also a success for the United States, as a country, and the war simply ended when the Americans decided so. After the German surrender, the English commissioned a report on the state of the German population to the physiologist Ernest Henry Starling, who published it in 1919 under the name of *Report on Food Conditions in Germany*. The work on the ground revealed that already in 1916 the Germans were in their last breath. An average male required the intake of about 3,000 calories a day and women needed 2,200. In the case of workers in heavy industry, the caloric intake needed could rise to 4,000 or 5,000 calories. In April 1916 the German rationing plan meant for an average German, male or female, a contribution of only 1,985 calories. In autumn of that year the ration was reduced to 1,344 calories, and by the winter of that year an average German had already lost between 15% and 25% of his weight, and if they survived it was thanks to his dwindling reserves of body fat[482]. The Hindenburg Plan redoubled the industrial efforts of Germany, which was forced to withdraw men from the country's agrarian force. Only the poor quality of the food, and the epidemics derived from the famine caused the death of more than 900,000 Germans, according to British sources[483]. It

---

[482] John Hamill, *The Strange Career of Mr. Hoover Under Two Flags*, p.p. 343-344.
[483] *The Blockade of Germany*, National Archives of UK Government, website revised in April 2012.

is undeniable that only the food imported by Hoover and Francqui kept the Germans fighting. Without this food the war would have ended one or two years before: Germany would have been unable to sustain its military campaign due to the lack of food.

The Commission began as a modest project to help evacuating American citizens from Belgium and alleviate the starvation of the civilian population, but it gradually expanded its functions and economic resources, as Hoover's plea to raise more funds regularly appeared in the major American newspapers. Hoover did not receive a penny, that's probably true, but from 1914 to 1919 he was handed over control of one billion dollars from American, British, French and Belgian donations. And in the postwar years, he even got more money.

There was no "humanity" for the vanquished, who remained under the effects of the blockade, and they were deprived of sustenance for a few more months, until after the peace in Paris had been signed. And afterwards, as in the case of Belgium, Germany was only allowed to import the food approved by Herbert Hoover, to whom the American newspapers already called the "dictator of food". Once unleashed, Hoover's humanitarian fever seemed to have no end, and in the post-war period Woodrow Wilson put him in charge of an institution created to his measure, the *American Relief Administration.* From that position he continued distributing food throughout Europe, this time with the authority conferred directly by the American government.

In 1921 Hoover allocated 20 million in aid for the Bolsheviks, and even Lev Kamenev, the President of the Moscow Soviet, thanked the United States for being"the first to provide humanitarian aid in a formal and large-scale manner[484]." Again the distribution of humanitarian aid would be decisive to favor a side in an armed conflict.

* * *

---

[484] New York Times, October 7, 1921, *18 Nations Meet to Help Russia. Impressed by Hoover plan but May Again Ask Soviet to Permit Investigation.*

The Commission for Relief in Belgium gave visibility to Herbert Hoover in Europe and America, and was his springboard to the presidency, although little was known of him in politics before his work in Belgium. As in the case of Roosevelt, most of his biographers made uncritical hagiophies and explained nothing about his professional experience before the Belgian Commission. But there were two notable exceptions.

John Hamill wrote in 1931 *The Strange Career of Mr. Hoover under Two Flags*, a biography certainly critical, and sometimes bordering on sensationalism. In 1933, and possibly caused by the legal harassment of Hoover's lawyers, Hamill was forced to sign an affidavit stating that all the information contained in his book was false. For this reason, almost no allusions have been made to his work. However, in 1932 the editor of a Minnesota newspaper called Walter Liggett published *The Rise of Herbert Hoover*, a book that corroborated Hamill's claims in many ways. Liggett was an accredited journalist who worked in the most important New York newspapers such as the *New York Times*, the *Sun*, the *New York Post* or *Daily News*[485]. Possibly the works of both authors heavily contributed to Hoover losing the re-election in 1933.

Herbert Hoover was the son of Quaker peasants, was born in 1874 in a town of Iowa. His parents died when he was a child and he came under the tutelage of his uncle. He started working when he was very young and managed to afford his university engineering studies at Stanford. Hoover began his mining career in San Francisco as an assistant to the Janin brothers, a well-known mining consultants in the eastern United States who worked frequently for the Rothschilds and the Guggenheims[486]. His first big solo job was at an Arizona mine

---

[485] *Guide to the Ligget Family Papers*, University of New York, website revised in March 2015. This author has been able to verify some of the facts quoted by Ligget, the main source of this section. Unlike Hamill, Liggett never withdrew the statements published in his book, but his muckracking costed his life. He was shot in 1935 in front of his family, for an issue not related to his Hoover biography.

[486] Walter Liggett, *The Rise of Herbert Hoover*, p.p. 48-49.

owned by the Rothschild's *Exploration Company of London*. The Janin brothers and the employees of the company were soon impressed by their work. Louis Janin hired him for other assignments, and in 1896 he was sent to Australia to work for a mining company of London, *Bewick, Moreing & Company*. This company managed more than twelve gold mines in Eastern Australia and offered him a salary of $ 5,000 a year and expenses included[487], a real fortune for a 23 year old boy. The mine obtained excellent results, although Hoover created himself a reputation of ruthless manager and he ended up being expelled from the company due to constant acts of defiance to his superior.

The director of *Bewick, Moreing & Company*, Charles Moreing, who was happy with the work of Hoover in Eastern Australia, decided to give him in 1898 a new opportunity for his company to be done with Kaiping coal mines in China. In order to acquire properties in the Asian continent, in 1899 Charles Moreing established a company in China called *The Oriental Syndicate*. On this occasion the young Hoover would charge $ 15,000 a year plus expenses for his services in the country.

The Kaiping mines were owned by the Chinese government and the company included stock in most nearby infrastructures such as ports, railways and even a small fleet of steamships. When Hoover arrived in the country it employed about 20,000 men, although indirectly five times that amount depended on the company. The company that operated the mine though a concession was the *Chinese Engineering & Mining Co*[488]. In 1900 it was the largest company of China and being quite conservative its value was around $ 50,000,000. It paid 12% on its profits in dividends to its shareholders that were mostly wealthy mandarins and merchants from China[489]. The Chinese

---

[487] Walter Liggett, *The Rise of Herbert Hoover*. p.p. 51-53.

[488] The Chinese company founded by *Bewick, Moreing & Company* was named *The Oriental Syndicate*, and the name of the company that managed the Kaiping mines was more specifically called the *Chinese Engineering & Mining Co.* To keep the story simple I will refer to the parts as *Bewick, Moreing & Company* and the Kaiping mines.

shareholders had already rejected several offers from foreign investors, including previous offers from Charles Moreing, but the old Asian empire was full of wealthy western men with more colonial pretensions than business over China. Liggett points out that the Rothschilds had their own agents on the ground looking for concessions, and it is possible that Charles Moreing himself was one of them.

The decline of the Chinese imperial regime was more than evident, and the instability of the country was one of the reasons why Chinese shareholders considered allowing foreign capital. In the middle of the century, from 1839 to 1842, the First Opium War of China took place with Great Britain, and from 1856 to 1860 the Second Opium War against France, Great Britain and the United States. The reason for both wars was the refusal of the Chinese emperors to let the Western powers sell opium to their country. The wars were settled with defeats of China, who had to accept the so-called "Unequal Treaties" of Nanking (1842) and Tientsin (1858), which forced the country to accept the import of opium, and open its ports to trade with the West in very unfavorable conditions. In 1865 the British Empire founded in Hong Kong the *Hong Kong and Shanghai Banking Corporation*[490] or *HSBC* by its abbreviations, a bank with the purpose of financing trade between China and the United Kingdom. A trade based mainly on opium trafficking, it is worth remembering.

Between 1899 and 1901, as a result of these and other outrages of the Western powers to China, there was the Boxer rebellion, a group of Chinese nationalist militiamen tired of seeing how the foreigners plundered the country's riches. The anti-Western movement was quickly stifled by the joint effort of China and the great Western nations with interests in the country, and their leaders were executed. The uprising also gave Russia an excuse to occupy a part of China with its army, including the precious Kaiping mines. The Russian invasion convinced shareholders that the safest way to prevent Russia from

---

[489] Walter Liggett, *The Rise of Herbert Hoover*, p.p. 72-73.

[490] Hong Kong became a British colony after the Treaty of Nanking.

claiming the mine was to accommodate foreign capital, and in 1901 the Chinese director of the mine acceded to the entrance of the group of Herbert Hoover and Charles Moreing.

In 1900 the agreement was ready for *Bewick, Moreing & Company* to enter the shareholding of the Kaiping mines, but there was a problem; In order to fulfill the contract he needed the 100,000 pounds pledged in the agreement with the Chinese owners. Liggett explains that certain Belgian capitalists facilitated a credit from the *Banque d'outre-mer* for that amount and in return they obtained a considerable stock in the Kaiping mines[491]. Those "Belgian capitalists" who are never named by the author were almost certainly Emil Francqui and Baron Leon Lambert de Rothschild, and it is possible that money never came out of the account of the *Banque d'outre-mer*. Liggett doubted the transaction would have taken place, while Hamill claimed that *Banque d'outre-mer* made a mere account entry, making a transaction to the *Bank of Tientsin* for the value agreed and wiring the money back to Belgium the next day[492].

The contract presented by Hoover and the Anglo-American capitalists to Chang Yen Mao, the director of the mine, imposed leonine conditions on the Chinese shareholders. Prior to the signing of the contract, Hoover and his partners at *Bewick, Moreing & Company* presented Chang Yen Mao a memorandum setting out fair and reasonable conditions, in which he would continue to be general manager of the mine, and where decisions would be taken by the vote of the board of shareholders, Chinese and British alike. The final contract was completely different and it excluded the other shareholders in any decision making, so the Mandarin insisted that he would not sign the main document if the supplementary memorandum was not signed too. Much to their dismay, Hoover and his associates agreed to sign of the attached memorandum, although its statements were never put into practice.

---

[491] Walter Liggett, *The Rise of Herbert Hoover*, p. 98.

[492] Liggett, p. 99. Hamill, p.p. 79, 80.

Immediately after the signing of the contract the new Anglo-American management of *Bewick, Moreing & Company* reorganized the capital of the mine without asking the original Chinese shareholders - who still had the majority of the stock-, valuing their properties in 1,000,000 pounds, and issuing the same number of shares worth one pound each[493]. That is how the shareholding distribution of the mine remained after the new distribution made by Hoover and its partners[494].

$ 1.000.000	Full stock of the *Chinese Engineering & Mining Co.*
$ 375.000	Remained in hands of the original shareholders.
$ 150.000	*Oriental Syndicate*, as payment for its services.
$ 424.993	Delivered among diplomats and influential man.
$ 50.007	For Charles Moreing.

Chinese shareholders received only 375,000 shares, 150,000 shares went to the Eastern Union of Hoover, and 50,007 directly to the pocket of his boss, Charles Moreing. Hoover greased the operation by distributing for free the 423,993 remaining shares between private citizens, public officers and diplomats, with the intention, as expressed in a letter, to persuade[495] *"a sufficient number of people of prominence and influence in such a manner that the governments of these countries could not continue their diplomatic intentions without injuring their own citizens."* Hoover could have distributed almost half of the company's shares for free, just to bribe officials, politicians and influential people in China, probably most were Westerners, or simply to fill the pocket of his friends.

The 100,000 pound contribution from the *Bewick, Moreing & Company* investors represented only 10% of the book value of the mine and much less than 1% in terms of its real value. But with such a tiny

---

[493] Walter Liggett, *The Rise of Herbert Hoover*, p. 99.
[494] Walter Liggett, *The Rise of Herbert Hoover*, p. 87.
[495] Walter Liggett, *The Rise of Herbert Hoover*, p. 100.

participation Hoover granted himself and his associates 62.5% of the stock. Meanwhile, the Chinese shareholders that contributed 90% of the book capital saw their participation diluted to 37.5% of the company's ownership. The profitability obtained by Hoover for Moreing was monstrous, even more so considering that the Kaiping mines was already a company that produced large dividends before the entry of foreign capital.

Once the agreement was signed, the Chinese investors were completely separated from the management of the Company and excluded from all meetings. In July 1901 Emile Francqui, formerly Belgian consul in China, and one of the directors of the mine interceded to appease the interests of some Belgian investors. But as a partner and friend of Hoover it is doubtful that he had the slightest intention of solving the problem. It is very likely that Francqui, the Belgian consul in China and one of the mine directors[496], was one of the "people of influence" to whom Hoover had "gratified" with a good handful of shares. Hoover's success in China was total and he was made a partner of *Bewick, Moreing & Company* of London in 1902.

It was evident that his ultimate goal was not to exploit the resources of the mine but to fleece the shareholders. A parallel board of directors was established in London. No meetings were held in China and Chines shareholders were not allowed to participate. No accounts were submitted until well past one year. And when they finally did it nobody took them seriously[497]. The modus operandi of Hoover's *Oriental Syndicate* to fleece its shareholders brings to mind the "Morgan method" described by Gustavus Myers for the *U.S. Steel*; Sinking the value of the stock by diluting capital, distributing extraordinary dividends and bonuses to its board of directors, speculating on the value, and finally leaving the stock before the foreseeable crash. Hoover was not the nominal director of the *Oriental Syndicate*, but he was the

[496] Liggett, p. 99, Hamill, p.p. 75, 312.
[497] Walter Liggett, *The Rise of Herbert Hoover*, p. 102.

chief responsible for carrying out the tasks entrusted to him by Charles Moreing.

The lack of honesty of the Hoover's *Oriental Syndicate* became notorious among all Western investors in China, and made the Chinese more reluctant to make deals with foreigners. At the time of the old Chinese shareholders meeting, the mine was much more profitable than when it was managed by the Hoover team. China protested by very different diplomatic channels to the English Foreign Office, but Hoover had covered that contingency by amicably distributing a large number of shares of the mine. That did not prevent the Chinese government from taking the case to British justice in early 1905. The case was seen in London by Judge Joyce, and most of the accusations by the Chinese government proved true. In the trial Hoover confessed the repeated threats to the director of the mine, Chang Yen Mao, and a letter from him was presented as an evidence that management took over control by force[498]. A report by Hoover was also submitted stating that only coal stocks from the Kaiping mines were valued at 8,125,000 pounds, so he was forced to acknowledge that its value was at least 10,000,000 pounds, ten times the amount in which he himself had valued in books[499].

In his ruling, Judge Joyce stated that the memorandum signed by Hoover and his associates was binding and its terms had to be enforced. He expressed his opinion that the distribution of 424,993 shares had been carried out fraudulently and without the consent of Chinese shareholders, and he opened the door to new legal claims for that concept[500]. The control should be restored to Chang Yen Mao and the Chinese shareholders, and Moreing and his associates paid the costs of the trial, which in the judge's opinion, they had unnecessarily extended[501]. The Anglo-American investors went to an appeals court,

---

498 Walter Liggett, *The Rise of Herbert Hoover,* p.p. 91, 95.

499 Walter Liggett, *The Rise of Herbert Hoover,* p. 117.

500 Walter Liggett, *The Rise of Herbert Hoover,* p.p. 100-101.

501 Walter Liggett, *The Rise of Herbert Hoover,* p.p. 118-119.

which in 1907 handed down the verdict of Judge Joyce. *Bewick, Moreing & Company* had to compensate the Chinese shareholders and restore their rights[502], but Hoover and the board of directors, confident that a British judge could do little or nothing to enforce this ruling in China, never carried out such terms. Hoover remained one of the directors of the mine until 1911.

When he put on the hat of the Belgian humanitarian committee, Hoover took with him his former partners in the Kaiping mines; his right hand was Millard Shaler and he also led Emmanuel De Wouters[503]. Upon his arrival in Belgium in 1914 he already had a considerable fortune, thanks to his experience as a mining promoter and speculator, but he had a limited experience in philanthropic tasks before managing hundreds of millions of dollars of public money and donations. He was another case of a speculator "with a vocation for public service" very similar to that of Bernard Baruch. The story of the Kaiping mines was the most notorious example of inappropriate behavior by Hoover, but it was not the only case in his career as a mining developer, of course. What is reflected in these pages is only a fraction of what is told in the biographies of Liggett and Hamill, which place Hoover in the midst of such amount of fraud, speculation and corporate irresponsibility, that if half of what is narrated by these authors is true, never a rogue like Hoover would have ruled the destinies of the United States until today.

* * *

Hoover was known in many places of the world for his mining activities, but he was a complete stranger in American politics until the First World War. When the mandate of Woodrow Wilson came to an end, Herbert Hoover seemed to be the ideal candidate for the Democrats, and as Liggett points out:

---

502 Walter Liggett, *The Rise of Herbert Hoover,* p 122.

503 Ligget p. 224, Hamill p. 312. Both men appear in other oficial documents of the Commission.

«[504]Hoover was favored by Wilson who expected him to carry on the fight to put the United States into the League of Nations and he also was on intimate terms with Col. Edward House…»

But Hoover had also served for the Republican Party as Secretary of Commerce under Presidents Harding and Coolidge, so he could perfectly run in a presidential campaign under the sign of either of the two major American parties, the Democrats or the Republicans. The fraternity of international bankers did not care under what political sign would Hoover or any other candidate run, as long as he followed his instructions to the letter. Surely the bankers considered that after eight years of government by the Democrats, the prospects would be more favorable if they presented him as a Republican.

The launch of his presidential career had an exceptional sponsor. On January 22, 1920 the *Philadelphia North American* published the news of a lunch organized by Colonel Edward Mandell House in honor of Herbert Hoover, which was attended by many media magnates of the country. The meal arranged by House marked the beginning of the political career of Hoover, who finally ran as a Republican candidate.

«[505]COL. HOUSE DINNER WAS BIRTHPLACE OF HOOVER BOOM. –TEXAN'S TACTICS SEEN IN SUDDEN CALL FOR CANDIDATE.

"Washington, January 22,

"The sudden effulgence of the Hoover star in the firmament of presidential possibilities is not a cosmic accident. It is the result of well and carefully laid plans, under the direction of that practiced President maker, Col. E. M. House.

[504] Walter Liggett, *The Rise of Herbert Hoover,* p. 298.
[505] Walter Liggett, *The Rise of Herbert Hoover,* p.p. 299-300, 303.

"The chronology of the Hoover boom begins with the return from Europe of Col. House, sick in body and sore at heart over the heartless treatment he had suffered at the hands of President Wilson. Having had the luxury of private ownership of a presidential administration for more than six years, Col. House refused to be thrown in the discard without ceremony.

"What was done prior to December 3 in the way of getting a new President for the quiet little Texas Colonel does not yet appear. The first fact of record is that on December 4 the New York World, whose chief recent claim to fame had been its unfaltering devotion to President Wilson, editorially announced that it would not stand for a third term for him.

"The very next day, December 5, Col. House gave a dinner at his apartments. Among the Colonel's guests were Ralph Pulitzer and Frank Cobb, respectively owner and editor of the World; Cleveland H. Dodge, a very rich man, hitherto a friend of the President and Col. House; and Cyrus H. K. Curtis, publisher of the Public Ledger, of Philadelphia.

"On the following Monday, December 8, the World published a story in which its veteran political reporter, Louis Seibold, occupied several columns telling that Col. House and the President were on the outs. A great deal of the several columns was taken up with a recapitulation of the Colonel's value as a counselor and his shrewdness as a political manager.

"Soon Hoover talk began to spring up with apparent spontaneity in various quarters. There was mysterious discussion as to his availability as a candidate for either party. Hoover headquarters were opened here and there, frequently under the management of a former member of Mr. Hoover's food administration[506].

---

[506] Today it's the *Food & Drug Administration*. These campaign members were former Hoover employees whose incomes skyrocketed by his public work.

"About the middle of December the Public Ledger devoted nearly two columns of space to exalting Mr. Hoover, without declaring for him for President; but, as the Ledger did not retract or mitigate its praise next day, it was considered very showy for the Ledger.

"About that time came the announcement that a group of capitalists had purchased the Washington Herald.

"Among these were Charles R. Crane[507] and Julius Barnes. Crane is a rich Chicago manufacturer, who had been a big contributor to the Wilson campaign and had since that time been on intimate terms with Col, House. Barnes is the Federal wheat dictator and a close friend of Hoover. The other capitalist in the group was Hoover himself.

"Within four days, the New York World made its declaration for Hoover. Explaining its position, the World said it would be glad to support him as a candidate on a platform that 'represented the historical principles of the Democratic Party;' it would 'be glad to support him as an independent candidate on a platform of progressive liberalism;' and it would 'not hesitate to support him as the Republican candidate on a platform representing the kind of government which Mr. Hoover exemplified in his public career.'

"The World's declaration set the old Democratic organization by the ears. The Senators who meekly have taken orders from Wilson for seven years in the hope of inheriting his mantle couldn't see Hoover with a telescope, and they used a megaphone in telling it to the world.

"But the widespread Hoover uprising left little doubt that the able noiseless Col House had done a good job. The New Republic, a periodical devoted to spreading Col. House's kind of internationalism and operated by Col House's personal friends, comes out this week for Hoover. The Devoted "E.S.M." editorial

---

[507] Charles R. Crane is mentioned by Professor Sutton in relation with the Bolshevik Revolution. See *Wall Street & the Bolshevik Revolution*, chap. II.

writer of Life also picks Hoover as the successor of Wilson in its adoration of the White House.

"In the meantime the other Democratic aspirants are living in dread that the little Texas Colonel will give another dinner. From present appearances that would make Hoover -unanimous in the Democratic convention…" »

Hoover's candidacy is another great example of the existence of that "financial element" that, as Roosevelt acknowledged in a letter to Colonel House, "had taken over the government of the United States." An element which for Wilson was "so organized, so subtle, so vigilant, so intertwined, so complete and so omnipresent that it is better not to speak, more than in whispers, when one speaks to condemn it." That was exactly element that House represented.

Theodore Roosevelt, Woodrow Wilson, Herbert Hoover or Franklin Delano Roosevelt responded -consciously or not- to the interests of international financiers. All of them were accountable to the same economic elite composed of no more than ten or twelve bankers whom they publicly disavowed, but who privately courted. The alternation between two parties fed the belief in American people to be governed by a democratic system, but this was only a delusion. The question for international bankers was not to determine whether a candidate was favorable or contrary to their interests, but which of the two candidates would be more favorable to them. Regardless of his Democratic or Republican affiliation, few presidents after Wilson, including himself, were alien to this influence. Teddy Roosevelt was also a President in the hands of the bankers, whom they timely rescued in the elections of 1912 to divide the Republicans and deliver the victory to Wilson. The last played his part until he realized that he had been an instrument in the service of international financiers at the end of the war, and turned his back on House, the representative of the bankers within the Democratic Party. By then it was late and there was little he could do to remedy his past mistakes. After a brief interlude of time the banking fraternity opted for Hoover, a candidate already tested in various scenarios such as China and Belgium.

Like many other residents of the White House, Hoover made the mistake of thinking that he was in charge or maybe he just tried to do the right thing for the first time. Opposing the so-called "Swope Plan" cost him his reelection in favor of Roosevelt. During the Great Depression the president of *General Electric*, Gerard Swope, proposed in 1931 a plan that integrated a system of pensions, health and social security within the companies of more than fifty employees[508]. Swope's corporate socialism was evidently not a manifestation of the altruistic wishes of the president of *General Electric* to share the profits of his company with society and thus contribute to the development of humanity. It was instead a monopolistic plan to integrate within the large corporations the functions normally performed by an elected government. His plan also included a pricing system and the incorporation of unions within the corporate structure. The coordination of the whole system would be in charge of the Federal Trade Association, a non-democratically elected body. Hoover denounced in his memoirs that Roosevelt's policies were a fascist system, a copy of the failed Swope Plan he had rejected.

> «[509]Among the early Roosevelt fascist measures was the National Industrial Recovery Act (NRA) of June 16, 1933. The origins of this scheme are worth repeating. These ideas were first suggested by Gerard Swope (of the General Electric Company) at a meeting of the electrical industry in the winter of 1932. Following this, they were adopted by the United States Chamber of Commerce. During the campaign of 1932, Henry I. Harriman, president of that body, urged that I agree to support these proposals, informing me that Mr. Roosevelt had agreed to do so. I

---

[508] The Swope Plan is included for analysis in *Wall Street & FDR* by Sutton.

[509] Herbert Hoover, *The Memoirs of Herbert Hoover. The Great Depression, 1929-1941*, The McMillan Company, 1952, New York, p. 420.

tried to show him that this stuff was sheer fascism; that it was merely a remaking of Mussolini's "corporate state" and refused to agree to any of it. He informed me that in view of my attitude, the business world would support Roosevelt with money and influence. That, for the most part, proved true. »

His refusal to Plan Swope, caused the bankers to reject Hoover, and they opted for Roosevelt. FDR launched the *National Recovery Act*, as a central part of its economic program the "New Deal", which reflected the same principles of corporate socialism contained in the Swope Plan. When General Smedley Butler denounced some years later the plot of some elements related to the Morgan group to establish the government of an industrial oligarchy in the United States. He pointed exactly to the same elements that were behind Plan Swope and the New Deal.

* * *

ÉMILE FRANCQUI

President of the *Comité National de Secours et d'Alimentation* in Belgium, Director of *Société Générale de Belgique*, Executive Director of *Banque d'Outremer*, Executive Director of *Union Minière du Haut Katanga*, Minister of State of Belgium.

The cause of the success in the business world of Herbert Hoover, and as the propeller that caused his rise to the presidency was the pervasive influence of the Frankfurt Syndicate. Hoover worked for them in his first mining activities, then led the Belgian Commission surrounded by Warburgs and Rothschilds, and finally he received the political backing of the American kingmaker, Colonel House.

Hoover was also the protégé of Emile Francqui, the chief agent of Baron Leon Lambert de Rothschild in Belgium, and before that, he was the representative of their mining interests in the Belgian Congo. Hoover and Francqui had met each other at least since 1901. That year Francqui was in charge of "mediating" between the Chinese shareholders and the Hoover investor group, and that same year the two coincided in a concession in China of the Hankow-Canton railway[510].

Probably they were acquaintances even before that, since Emil Francqui was a Belgian consul in China from 1897 to 1902, and Hoover worked in the Kaiping mines between 1899 and 1901[511].

There is a considerable number of interests common to Hoover, Francqui and Lambert. For example, the *Banque d'Outremer*, which provided the 100,000 pound loan to Hoover and his associates to take over the Kaiping mines, was one of the Rothschild banks in Belgium[512]. Leon Lambert and other associates were owners of a significant number of shares in it. Francqui was appointed director of the *Banque d'Outremer* in 1902.

---

[510] John Hamill, *The Strange Career of Mr. Hoover Under Two Flags*, p. 75.

[511] Walter Ligett, *The Rise of Herbert Hoover*, p. 69.

[512] In regards the Rothschild influence *Société Générale de Belgique* you can check Emma Rothschild et Al, *The Rotschild Archive, Review of the Year April 2004 to March 2005*, The Rostschild Archive Trust, p. 14. Website revised in 2015.

Regarding stock of *Banque d'Outremer*, almost half the 65.000 shares were in hands of the Rothschilds and their partners: *Banque de Paris et des Pays-Bas* (12.000), *Société Générale de Belgique* (9.420), *Banque León Lambert* (4.800), *Banque de Bruxelles* (2.600), Franz Philippson (2.600). According to R. Brion en J.-L. Moreau, *Banque d'Outremer*, *Inventaire des archives de la Banque d'Outremer S.A. et de la Société Agefi S.A.*, 1899-1957, BE-A0510 / I 301. Web revised in 2015.

The second connection was *Société Générale de Belgique*, the bank that financed the humanitarian operation of Hoover in Belgium. It was also an institution of the Rothschild sphere, where Leon Lambert held a considerable stock. Francqui was appointed its director in 1912.

Francqui's relationship with the Rothschilds can be traced at least until 1891, the year in which he worked in the service of Baron Leon Lambert in the Belgian Congo. The *Union Minière du Haut Katanga* was founded in 1906 as an important copper extraction mine, and in the 1950s its mines also extracted in the Belgian Congo an important part of the world cobalt production. Subsequently the company exploited huge amounts of uranium and radium. The company was owned by the Congolese government and several shareholders, but the effective control was of the *Société Générale de Belgique* bank. By owning to the mine, the Belgian bank controlled more than half of the economy of the African country until 1960, the year in which the Congo gained its independence. Over the years, the enormous mining wealth of the Belgian Congo did not leave any sort of prosperity to the country, although it was extremely profitable for its shareholders.

One of the six shareholders who founded in 1891 *Union Minière du Haut Katanga* was precisely Baron Leon Lambert de Rothschild[513]. The instrumental company to control it was named *Compagnie du Congo pour le Commerce et l'Industrie.* The company was founded with a capital of three million francs divided into 24,000 shares, of which the Congolese government only obtained 10% of the stock.

---

[513] S. Rosenthal, *Le Développement Economique du Katanga*, 2a Ed., Societé Belge de Librairie, 1911, Brussels, p.p. 8-13.

STOCK OF THE *COMPAGNIE DU CONGO* OR *UNION MINIÈRE DU HAUT KATANGA*, 1891.

A total of 18.000 ordinary shares and 6.000 preferred shares, totaling 24.000. Formed with a capital of tree million francs.

* Congolese government: 600 preferred shares and 1.800 ordinary shares, a total of 2.400.

* *Compagnie du Congo pour le Commerce et l'Industrie* 1.080 ordinary shares and 250.000 francs in kind, (the equivalent to another 500 shares) as a payment for the Alexandre Delcommune expedition of prospection.

* Other shareholders (15.120 ordinary shares), of which the chief were:

-*Compagnie du Congo pour le Commerce et l'Industrie* (1.000 ordinary shares)

-Baron Leon Lambert de Rothschild (225)

-*Société Générale de Belgique* (225)

-*Banque de Bruxelles*[514] (200)

-*Banque de Paris et des Pays-Bas (PARIBAS)* (200)

-Bunau-Varilla[515] (200)

-Philippson[516] (175)

-*Seligman Frères*, Paris (125)

-An English group whose main shareholder is the *Ochs* group of London (1.565).

-*Murchison Crown Exploration and Mining Company* (200)

-*Colonial Foreign Corporation* (200)

-Rest of small investors (10.805)

---

[514] *Banque de Bruxelles* and *Banque Leon Lambert* merged in 1974. New York Times, June 1, 1987, *Leon Lambert; Banker Collected Art.*

[515] Philippe-Jean Bunau-Varilla was the French developer of the Panama Canal. The fifty million dollars which United States used for the Purchase of the Canal to France were wired by the French bank of Anthony J. Drexel and J.P. Morgan.

[516] Probably Franz Moses Philippson, a German Jewish banker, shareholder of *Banque d'Outremer*. He replaced Leon Lambert as President of the "Israelite Council of Belgique". His father Ludwig and his grandfather Moses fostered the Haskala or "Jewish Enlightment" movement with Moses Mendelssohn. In 1864 Ludwig Philippson founded with Max Arnhold *Gebrüder Arnhold* bank.

Among the main investors of the Congolese mining monopoly we can easily identify Baron Leon Lambert as the largest individual shareholder with 225 shares, being one of the six founding partners of the *Compagnie du Congo*, which in turn had another 2,080 shares. Additionally he held an important degree of control in the mining company through various French-Belgian banks of the Rothschild sphere, worth more than a thousand shares. It is possible to conclude that a relevant part of the capital of the mine was within the scope of influence of the Rothschild family.

* * *

Emile Francqui, one of the greatest fortunes in the history of Belgium, was an orphan who was sent in 1884 by King Leopold II of Belgium, to the Belgian Congo, at the age of twenty-one. The young Francqui was part of the occupation army of about seventeen thousand men called *Force Publique*. The *Force Publique* was composed mainly of black natives, although its officers and non-commissioned officers were all Belgians. It operated at the same time as a police squad and occupation army, which forced the Congolese population to work in conditions of slavery, suppressing any riot in a bloody and summary manner. The *Force Publique* used force under any excuse, and the *chicotte*, a whip made of rhinoceros skin, was used regularly by the Belgian settlers in the Congo until the year of its independence in 1960. It was not uncommon to see a native whipped to his death. Limb amputation was also a habitual punishment of the natives by the Belgian occupiers, and the Congo became one of the African countries that suffered the worst atrocities in the colonial era. Francqui left the country with the rank of Captain.

In 1891, the year that the Compagnie du Katanga was founded, the company organized two expeditions to carry out new prospections on the ground. One departed from the east coast under the direction of M. Stairs, and the other from the west side, was directed by Emile Francqui. Years later, in 1896, Francqui became Consul of Belgium in

China until 1902, the year in which he established contact with Hoover. The Belgian monarch Leopold II thanked him for his services, and also did the Rothschilds, who made him director of *Société Générale de Belgique* and the *Banque d'Outremer*, two of the most important banks in Belgium. Francqui was appointed Minister of State by King Leopold III and acted as the representative of Belgium in the Dawes Plan of 1924.

As for Baron Lambert and the Belgian branch Rothschild, it is worth mentioning some interesting banking landmarks.

THE ROTHSCHILD BANKS OF BELGIUM

1928 *Société Générale de Belgique* acquired the *Banque d'Outremer*.
1940 Some old Drexel partners working in the Morgan group rescued the original name of *Drexel & Co.* in the creation of a new firm.
1965 *Drexel & Co.* merged with *Brown Brothers Harriman* to form *Drexel, Harriman & Ripley*.
1974 *Banque de Bruxelles* and *Banque León Lambert*, merged to form the *Banque Bruxelles Lambert*.
1976 *Banque Bruxelles Lambert* and *Drexel, Harriman & Ripley* formed a new investment bank named *Drexel, Burnham & Lambert* that failed in 1994. Today *Groupe Bruxelles Lambert* is a highly diversified group and one of the top 10 companies of Belgium. *Société Générale de Belgique*, that for years was the most important Company of Belgium, was absorbed in 2003 by a French industrial group.

The Weimar Republic, 1918-1933

We return to Versailles in 1919, where the "big four" of the Entente met, surrounded by a cohort of international financiers empowered to decide not only the fate of the vanquished Germany, but also the borders of many other nations across the planet.

After the arrival of the German delegation to Versailles, headed by the Minister of Foreign Affairs, the count Ulrich von Brockdorff-Rantzau found a Paris completely hostile. The Germans soon realized that they would not have a voice or a vote, and that all the decisions had already been taken at the preliminary meetings of the Peace Conference, to which Germany had not been invited.

In May 1919, Brockdorff-Rantzau gave a speech protesting the terms imposed by the Entente, that he considered a breach of agreements reached for the Armistice of November 1918, and the principles contained in Wilson's fourteen points. Brockdorff-Rantzau did not evade the responsibility of Germany although he considered that his country was not the only one to blame. The German Minister gave his speech sitting, as a deliberate insult to his audience[517]. In June, when it was clear that the Allies had no intention of negotiating any of the essential aspects of the treaty, Brockdorff-Rantzau resigned his position as German representative, along with other members of the delegation, refusing to sign what he considered a dictum contrary to the agreements reached before and after the armistice.

* * *

Meanwhile, in November 1919 Germany sanctioned a new Constitution in the German town of Weimar. For this reason, the interwar period that lasted until the rise of the Nazis to power was called the Weimar Republic. The new Constitution gave Germany a

[517] Caroll Quigley, *Tragedy & Hope*, p. 272.

constitutional republic in which the President, a moderator and head of state, coexisted with the Chancellor, who performed the executive functions.

After the violent revolts that shook the country after the war, and fearing a fate similar to that of his cousin Tsar Nicholas II, Kaiser Wilhelm II abdicated in November 1918 and went into exile. This revolutionary movement was promoted from the Russia of the Soviets and culminated with the Spartacist uprising, which was stifled by the Social Democratic President Friedrich Ebert. It finished when its main promoters, Rosa Luxemburg and Karl Liebknecht, were captured and executed. The president of the Reichsbank, Hjalmar Schacht, stated that "in March 1919 the revolution was responsible for the loss of 1,200 lives in Berlin alone" and Chernow pointed out that the number of deaths throughout Germany were ten times that amount[518].

After the capitulation of Germany in World War I, the reparations set by the victors were set at around 132,000 million gold marks, although 82,000 million were set aside and finally forgotten. It was established that the payment of the remaining 50,000 million would be effective when Germany had a surplus, and its trade balance was positive.

In order to pay this debt, the German government did nothing but issuing more and more money and borrowing large amounts from its central bank, the Reichsbank, and consequently the German frame collapsed at a dizzying pace after 1921. Under normal circumstances 20 marks per sterling pound were exchanged, and at the end of Chancellor Wilhelm Cuno's term in 1923, the rate was 20,000,000,000 marks per pound. The hyperinflation affected especially the lower social strata, causing unemployment, strikes, great social discontent and a political instability that eventually gave rise to separatist movements in the area of the Ruhr and a *coup d'état.*

---

518 Hjalmar Schacht, *My First Seventy Six Years*, p.p. 157-158 & Chernow, *The Warburgs*, p. 210.

In 1923 the first alarm signal came with the Putsch of Munich, a failed coup led by Adolf Hitler and other prominent Nazis such as Rudolf Hess, Ernst Röhm, Hermann Goering or Heinrich Himmler. Erich Ludendorff, one of the members of the German General Staff and hero of World War I, also joined. Years later Ludendorff turned his back to Nazism and recriminated Hindenburg his decision to appoint Hitler as Chancellor in 1932.

The inability of the Weimar Republic to fulfill its payments resulted in reprisals by its French and Belgian creditors, who militarily occupied the German industrial region of the Ruhr between 1923 and 1925, a rich mining area in Western Germany. The occupation produced strikes, resistance to the invaders and riots among the German population. In 1923, the United States promoted a commission to stabilize the German economy and restructure its debt in such a way that the Weimar Republic would be able to pay the heavy economic reparations, and a banking union led by *Guaranty Trust* extended a loan to Germany. In the first years the German government fulfilled its commitments, but soon it was evident that in such debt levels it would not be able to maintain payments over time. The result of the commission was the 1924 Dawes Plan, named after commission chairman Charles Gates Dawes, a wealthy banker and American politician. The Dawes project included the Franco-Belgian withdrawal from the Ruhr basin and the granting of a loan of 800 million dollars so that Germany could repay its debt. In other words, the plan was to organize a circular scheme of debt in which the United States would lend to Germany, so that in turn it would repay its debts to the United States and the rest of the Allied countries. The loan-repayment-loan system developed by Dawes favored Germany, which according to Carroll Quigley "allowed Germany to begin a career of wild financial extravagance"[519], enabling the country to borrow byond imagination thanks to the financial back of the Allies.

---

[519] Caroll Quigley, *Tragedy & Hope*, p. 309.

«Germany was able to borrow abroad beyond her ability to pay, without the normal slump in the value of the mark which would have stopped such loans under normal circumstances. It is worthy of note that this system was set up by the international bankers and that the subsequent lending of other people's money to Germany was very profitable to these bankers. »

The American banks reaped great benefits and Charles Dawes the Nobel Peace Prize in 1925. Dawes would be Vice President of the United States from 1925 to 1929 under the mandate of the Republican Calvin Coolidge and in 1932 he became President of the board of the *City National Bank & Trust.* Quigley continues rightly pointing out that the Dawes plan's loan system was a great pyramid scheme:

«The only things wrong with the system were (a) that it would collapse as soon as the United States ceased to lend, and (b) in the meantime debts were merely being shifted from one account to another and no one was really getting any nearer to solvency. In the period 1924-1931, Germany paid 10.5 billion marks in reparations but borrowed abroad a total of 18.6 billion marks. Nothing was settled by all this, but the international bankers sat in heaven, under a rain of fees and commissions. »

The Dawes plan was, as professor Quigley points out, "largely a J. P. Morgan production" [520], and he adds that a relevant part of the loans were used to form the great German industrial cartels "Using these American loans...Germany was able to rebuild her industrial system to make it the second best in the world by a wide margin."

There were no trusts to create in the United States, Morgan had created them all, but at his death his banking empire continued to form trusts beyond frontiers. The big German cartels were financed with money from the Americans, who years later would have to shed their

[520] Carroll Quigley, *Tragedy and Hope*, p. 308.

blood in Europe. These cartels were the main economic support of National Socialism and formed the armed wing of the Nazi military industry. Most of these big industrial groups had an American matrix company or were heavily invested by United States capital.

On the meantime, in Germany, the German Central Bank or *Reichsbank* was reorganized under the watchful eye of allied nations, and led by the expert hand of Hjalmar Schacht, a central figure to understand Hitler's rise to power and World War II. Germany paid part of the reparations of the Dawes Plan from 1924 to 1929, and at the end of that period the country owed its creditors more than at the beginning. Naturally, the Dawes Plan could not meet the needs of the European victims or the American creditors, and soon the need to establish new payment conditions became evident.

The Young Plan of 1929 was developed in honor of American industrialist and politician Owen D. Young who would chair the second commission of "experts." The participation of Morgan bankers was even more noticeable than in the previous plan. Young, Vice Chairman of the board of the *Federal Reserve Bank of New York* and director of the United States International Chamber of Commerce was a well-known agent of the Morgans. Young was also chairman of the board of directors of *General Electric* between 1922 and 1945, responsible for its subsidiaries in Germany *A.E.G.* and *Osram*[521] and administrator of the *Rockefeller Foundation* and the *Council of Foreign Relations*[522] since 1928.

---

[521] Young was also a founder of the media giant *Radio Corporation of America*, a subsidiary of *General Electric*, and was on the direction of other media as the *National Broadcasting Company* (*NBC)* and *RKO Pictures*. Young was chairman of the board of *General Electric* in 1922, the year that Gerard Swope, author of the Swope Plan, was named President of the company.

Swope held director seats in the German subsidiaries like *A.E.G.* & *Osram*, and American like *N.B.C.* and *R.C.A.* Finally, Swope was Director in *National City Bank of New York* of the Morgan group, one of the most active banks in the loans of the Dawes Plan. (*Wall Street and the Rise of Hitler*, p.p. 51-52.) Young did not represent, therefore, the interests of the Entente countries, or even those of his

The Young Plan meetings in Paris took place in 1929 at the luxurious hotel George V. On the American side was Young himself with bankers John Pierpont Morgan Jr. (Jack), Thomas W. Lamont, Thomas Nelson Perkins[523] and Seymour Parker Gilbert II, all of them were bankers related to the Morgans[524].

Hjalmar Schacht led the German delegation as President of the German central bank[525]. At his right side he took Carl Melchior, representative of *M.M. Warburg & Co.* Max Warburg's personal emissary had been a delegate of Germany in the Paris Peace negotiations of 1919, and later he became a member of the *Bank for International Settlements*. Representing the German industry there were

---

own country, but rather the needs of an enterprise conglomerate.

[522] In parallel to the Paris Conference of 1919 House promoted a study group to establish the basis of the post-war world. The *Council of Foreign Relations* appeared as a consecuence of several meetings in the Majestic Hotel. The guiding principles of *CFR,* which self-defines as "a non partisan group of ideas", has influenced deeply the course of the foreign and domestic policy of the United States during the twentieth century. The fact that it is a non partisan group does not mean that it has not a political agenda. *CFR* could better be defined as a banking lobby; Founded by House, the saint patron of the American bankers, some directors known to us were Otto Kahn and Paul Warburg (*Kuhn & Loeb*) or Averell Harriman, in addition to Frank Altschul (*Lazard Freres*), Leon Fraser (President of the *First National Bank,* member of *BIS,* Director in the Federal Reserve). The Presidents of *CFR* until 1985 were in this order Russel C. Leffingwell (President of *J.P. Morgan*), John J. McCloy (President of *Chase Manhattan Bank* and the *World Bank*) and David Rockefeller (President in *Chase Manhattan Bank,* Director of the Federal Reserve).

[523] Perkins was an old partner of Owen D. Young. He came from a family linked to the railroads, being himself President of *Boston & Maine Railroad* and director in the *Southern Pacific Railroad*. Director in *AT&T* with other partners of Morgan like George F. Baker and his son. During WWI he was chief counsellor of the WIB with Bernard Baruch, and Purchasing Assistant for the Secretary of Defense.

[524] His participation in Schacht op. cit., p. 239. His son Seymour Parker Gilbert III in the 1980's was Director of the investment bank *Morgan Stanley*.

[525] Hjalmar Schacht, *My First Seventy Six Years,* p. 236.

Albert Vögler, president of *Vereinigte Stahlwerke* (United Steelworks) and Ludwig Kastl, of the National Association of German Industrialists. On the French side there was Emil Moreau, Governor of the *Bank of France.* Hjalmar Schacht, President of the *Reichsbank* recalled the Young Plan:

> «[526]The Young Conference opened in Paris in February 1929, at the Hotel George V…
>
> Now we all sat at the same table, the Germans among the rest — Americans, British, French, Belgians, Japanese.
>
> The President of the Reichsbank (myself) led the German delegation which, in addition, consisted of Vogler, General Manager of the United Steel Works and his deputy, Privy Councillor Kastl, of the National Association of German Industrialists, and my own deputy Melchior, of the Hamburg banking establishment of Warburg & Co. In my immediate entourage were Director Blessing and my secretary, Fraulein Steffeck, of the Reichsbank.
>
> America was represented by Owen Young and Jack Morgan, the great son of the even greater Pierpont Morgan. On the French side was M. Moreau, President of the Central Bank.»

Hjalmar Schacht, the son of an accountant at the *Equitable Trust Company* in Berlin felt like a fish in the water surrounded by other Morgan's fellows. The Young committee, if one is able to understand the relationships among its participants, was an informal meeting between Morgan bankers. The role of France, as the main stakeholder, was anecdotal, and that of Belgium and the rest of the victims was nonexistent. Emile Francqui was the Belgian delegate in the Dawes and Young Plans. The Young Plan lasted only a few months; the crisis of the 29 spread from the United States to Europe and the credits to Germany ceased in 1930[527].

---

[526] Hjalmar Schacht, *My First Seventy Six Years*, p.p. 236-237.
[527] Carroll Quigley, *Tragedy and Hope*, p.p. 309-310.

In 1931 Germany again violated the Versailles agreements by forming a customs union with Austria, and France in retaliation withdrew its funds from both countries. This precipitated that on May 8 *Credit-Anstalt*, Austria's largest bank, announced losses of 140 million Schillings (about 20 million dollars). More than half of the Austrian economy depended on that bank, owned by Baron Louis Nathaniel de Rothschild. Its situation was already unviable years before, and although the Rothschilds and the Austrian government contributed 160 million schillings to cover the losses, the crisis inevitably spread to Germany.

The American President Herbert Hoover requested a one-year moratorium on the payment of the debt, and in 1931 and 1932 there were attempts to reduce or cancel the remaining debt. In 1933 Hitler refused to continue paying for reparations[528], much to the dismay of the New York banking union, led by *Lee, Higginson & Co*[529].

The Bank of International Settlements, 1930

In order to manage the payment of German reparations in 1930, the *Bank for International Settlements* was created with headquarters in Basel, Switzerland, as a banking superstructure owned by the central banks of countries throughout the world. Its creation was suggested in the Young Plan and approved in the 1930 Hague Agreements. The *Bank for International Settlements* (*BIS*)[530] facilitated international transactions between governments: Each central bank-there were seven countries originally had an account in the BIS, and operations between countries were closed with mere accounting entries, avoiding gold shipments, as it had been done until then. The *BIS* was "the bank of the

---

528 Carroll Quigley, *Tragedy and Hope*, p.p. 310-312.

529 Hjalmar Schacht, *My First Seventy Six Years*, p. 273. *Lee, Higginson & Co.* was the second bank funding the creation of the *General Electric* conglomerate in 1893. The first was *Drexel & Morgan*.

530 *Bank of International Settlements* or BIS.

central Banks" and it was the germ of the international banking system as we know it today.

The Governor of the *Bank of England*, Montagu Norman, known in the economic press as "the monetary dictator of Europe", and the *Reichsbank*'s, Hjalmar Schacht, were the promoters of the idea, which was incorporated into the Young Plan[531]. Emile Francqui, was one of the two Belgian directors and Carl Melchior of *M.M. Warburg*, was Vice President. The board of directors of the *BIS* in Switzerland included several representatives of Nazi Germany: the Minister of Economy Walther Funk, an SS officer named Oswald Pohl, the Executive Director of *I.G. Farben Hermann Schmitz*, and Baron Kurt von Schröder, owner of the bank *J.H. Stein Bank* where the funds of the Gestapo were deposited. The shareholders of the *Bank of International Settlements* were central banks. The *BIS* also worked as a meeting center for the most important central bankers in the West, to carry out informal, or rather secret meetings, for years. In the obituary of Benjamin Strong in the *New York Times* of 1928, it was noted: [532]

> «Mr. Norman, Bank of England, Strong of the New York Federal Reserve Bank, and Dr. Hjalmar Schacht of the Reichsbank, their meeting referred to at the time as a meeting of 'the world's most exclusive club'. No public reports were ever made of the foreign conferences, which were wholly informal, but which covered many important questions of gold movements, the stability of world trade, and world economy. »

The relationship between the Governor of the *Bank of England* and the Governor of the *Federal Reserve*, according to Carroll Quigley, was cordial too, even familiar:

---

[531] In 1929 Schacht proposed Owen Young the creation of a bank to manage the payment of the reparations. He answered "Dr. Schacht, you gave me a wonderful idea and I am going to sell it to the world" *My First Seventy Six Years,* p. 250.
[532] New York Times, October 27, 1928, *Benjamin Strong, Banker, dies at 56*.

«[533]Norman had a devoted colleague in Benjamin Strong, the first governor of the Federal Reserve Bank of New York. Strong owed his career to the favor of the Morgan Bank, especially of Henry P. Davison, who made him secretary of the Bankers Trust Company of New York (in succession to Thomas W. Lamont) in 1904, used him as Morgan's agent in the banking rearrangements following the crash of 1907, and made him vice-president of the Bankers Trust (still in succession to Lamont) in 1909. He became governor of the Federal Reserve Bank of New York as the joint nominee of Morgan and of Kuhn, Loeb, and Company in 1914. Two years later, Strong met Norman for the first time, and they at once made an agreement to work in cooperation for the financial practices they both revered.

These financial practices were explicitly stated many times in the voluminous correspondence between these two men and in many conversations they had, both in their work and at their leisure (they often spent their vacations together for weeks, usually in the south of France). »

Professor Quigley points out another function of the *Bank of International Settlements*, much more ambitious than a forum or an agency to facilitate transactions between central banks. International financiers intended to give birth to a global economic system ruled by themselves[534]:

«The powers of financial capitalism had another far-reaching aim, nothing less than to create a world system of financial control in private hands able to dominate the political system of each country and the economy of the world as a whole, this system was to be controlled in a feudalist fashion by the central banks of the world acting in concert by secret agreements arrived at in frequent

---

[533] Carroll Quigley, *Tragedy and Hope*, p.p. 326-327.
[534] Carroll Quigley, *Tragedy and Hope*, p.p. 324-325.

private meetings and conferences. The apex of the system was to be the Bank for International Settlements in Basle, Switzerland, a private bank owned and controlled by the world's central banks which were themselves private corporations.... Each central bank, in the hands of men like

Montagu Norman of the Bank of England, Benjamin Strong of the New York Federal Reserve Bank, Charles Rist of the Bank of France, and Hjalmar Schacht of the Reichsbank, sought to dominate its government by its ability to control Treasury loans, to manipulate foreign exchanges, to influence the level of economic activity in the country, and to influence cooperative politicians by subsequent economic rewards in the business world. »

Benjamin Strong of the *Federal Reserve*, Montagu Norman of the *Bank of England* and Hjalmar Schacht of the *Reichsbank*, were the most important members of the circle of central bankers. Charles Rist and Emile Francqui were their counterparts in France and Belgium. Although Quigley points out that in this system the central bankers were only the musicians, the orchestra directors were others:

«[535]It must not be felt that these heads of the world's chief central banks were themselves substantive powers in world finance. They were not. Rather, they were the technicians and agents of the dominant investment bankers of their own countries, who had raised them up and were perfectly capable of throwing them down. The substantive financial powers of the world were in the hands of these investment bankers (also called "international" or "merchant" bankers) who remained largely behind the scenes in their own unincorporated private banks. These formed a system of international cooperation and national dominance which was more private, more powerful, and more secret than that of their agents in the central banks. This dominance of investment bankers was

[535] Carroll Quigley, *Tragedy and Hope*, p.p. 327-328.

based on their control over the flows of credit and investment funds in their own countries and throughout the world. They could dominate the financial and industrial systems of their own countries by their influence over the flow of current funds through bank loans, the discount rate, and the re-discounting of commercial debts; they could dominate governments by their control over current government loans and the play of the international exchanges. Almost all of this power was exercised by the personal influence and prestige of men who had demonstrated their ability in the past to bring off successful financial coupe, to keep their word, to remain cool in a crisis, and to share their winning opportunities with their associates. In this system the Rothschilds had been preeminent during much of the nineteenth century, but, at the end of that century, they were being replaced by J. P. Morgan whose central office was in New York, although it was always operated as if it were in London (where it had, indeed, originated as George Peabody and Company in 1838)… »

Friedrich Ebert, President of the Weimar Republic (1919-1925)

Paul von Hindenburg, President of the Weimar Republic (1925-1934)

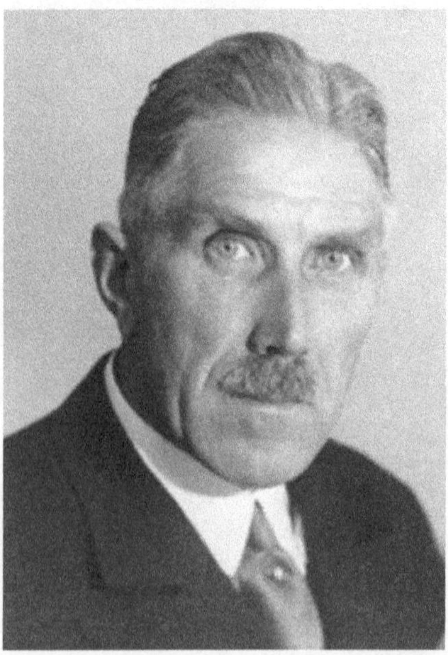

Franz von Papen, Chancellor of the Weimar Republic (1932)

Kurt von Schleicher, Chancellor of the Weimar Republic (1932-1933)

THE WEIMAR REPUBLIC

Von Papen and the Rise of Hitler

Friedrich Ebert was the first President of the Weimar Republic (1919-1925), and at his death he was succeeded by the military veteran Paul von Hindenburg (1925-1934). Von Hindenburg had been a Field Marshal and member of the German General Staff in the First World War together with Ludendorff and the Kaiser. When he became President of Germany in 1925, he was already 78 years old and he went into politics more moved by duty and at the request of some conservative politicians, more than by his own wish.

Seven years later, in March 1932, Paul von Hindenburg ran for re-election as President, again bound by the responsibility of restraining political extremism and knowing that his advanced age probably would not allow him to conclude his term. His rivals then were Adolf Hitler, of the Nazi Party and Ernst Thälmann, of the Communist Party. Von Hindenburg won again, and appointed the old spy Franz von Papen as chancellor in June[536]. The German political panorama was fragmented in many parties and the impossibility of obtaining significant majorities caused several foreign ministers to succeed each other, ruling on the basis of decrees, instead of a parliamentary majority. Shortly after Paul von Hindenburg's rise to the presidency, German Chancellor von Papen called for parliamentary elections, giving Nazism a second chance. This is one of the reasons why von Papen's chancellery has generally been considered the prelude to the Hitler government.

After the parliamentary elections of July 1932 Adolf Hitler and the National Socialist Party were the most voted force with 37% of the votes, taking 230 seats out of the 608, but not with an absolute majority. After knowing the results, von Papen declared to the press[537];

---

[536] In the German system the Chancellor exerercises the executive power, while the President is the Chief of state, exercising the role of moderator between political factions. In some countries President is also the supreme commander of the military forces of the country.

[537] Von Papen, *Memoirs*, p. 193.

«The result of the election shows that the time has come for the National Socialist movement to take an active part in the reconstruction work of the country»

Hitler had reached its peak of popularity by speaking to audiences of up to 100,000 people at the same time, creating a cult of his person similar to that of Mussolini in Italy. Von Papen made another extraordinary contribution to the Nazi victory by lifting the ban on the Brown Shirts, the National Socialist paramilitary army that imposed its own law and intimidated the civilian population on German streets. This is another admission drawn from his own memories[538].

Despite the election result, Paul von Hindenburg refused to appoint Hitler as the new Chancellor of Germany and opted again for von Papen. On August 12, von Papen personally conveyed to Hitler the President's decision:

«[539]'The President' I told him, 'is not prepared to offer you the post of Chancellor, as he feels that he does not yet know you well enough' I urged upon him the necessity of joining in a coalition government as proof that he and his party were willing to accept their share of responsibility for governing the country.»

Von Papen offered Hitler the vice-chancellorship or positions in the government for members of his party, but Hitler would never agree to form a government where he was not the leader, preferring instead to go to the opposition. Von Papen suggested Hitler to speak directly with President von Hindenburg and on August 13 both had an interview, but the President remained firm in his refusal to grant him the chancellorship. Von Hindenburg was aware of the dangers of Hitler, a corporal obsessed with the previous war, could represent for

---

[538] Von Papen, *Memoirs*, p. 193.
[539] Von Papen, *Memoirs*, p. 196.

Germany. Hitler again refused to support the investiture of another chancellor who was not himself.

Again Franz von Papen dissolved the German parliament, the Reichstag, calling for parliamentary elections on November 6, only a few months after the previous ones. In the parliamentary elections of November 1932 the Nazi party suffered a severe setback and fell to 33% of the votes and 196 seats. On November 19 von Hindenburg met with Hitler to offer him a coalition government with other center parties where he could occupy the chancellery, but he replied in a letter that he did not believe "that the crisis of government could be solved only in parliamentary terms, since that this would be contrary to their fundamental convictions[540]"

On that day, a group of prominent German businessmen headed by Hjalmar Schacht, the former President of the *Reichsbank*, sent a letter to President von Hindenburg, requesting the appointment of Hitler as chancellor. The letter, known as *Industrielleneingabe* or "letter of the industrialists" actually had only the signature of Fritz Thyssen as one of the great industrialists, and the rest of the signatories mostly stood out for their banking and institutional affiliations. There were also representatives of the agrarian world, whose landowners were worried about the possibility of being nationalized from their land, and some representatives of business associations and chambers of commerce[541].

In December, Paul von Hindenburg met with von Papen and with General Kurt von Schleicher, who was a friend of his son, Oskar Hindenburg[542]. Von Papen suggested that he gave the chancellery to him: he would try to govern by decrees, and with the help of the army and the police he would suppress the political parties to establish a new constitutional order. Kurt von Schleicher proposed von Hindenburg

---

[540] Von Papen, *Memoirs*, p. 215.

[541] A translation of the letter is included in the annexes.

[542] Von Papen, *Memoirs*, p.p. 123-124. Oskar Hindenburg and Kurt von Schleicher were old friends, they served together in the same regiment when they were younger.

that he hand over the chancellery to him: he would try to divide the Nazi party's strength, offering prominent members of the party a concentration government without Hitler. Hindenburg initially supported von Papen, but the next day changed his mind and opted for von Schleicher. The parliament was very fragmented and hardly von Schleicher could obtain the support to carry out the necessary reforms for Germany. The idea of a new government of von Papen was unthinkable, and the social fracture in the country was so pronounced that von Hindenburg feared a civil war. The exhausted German President, who would die two years later, collapsed before von Papen:

> «'My dear Papen,' he said, 'you will not think much of me if I change my mind. But I am too old and have been through too much to accept the responsibility for a civil war. Our only hope is to let Schleicher try his luck.' Two great tears were rolling down his cheeks as I shook his hand and turned to go. [543]»

Although von Papen had agreed to form a coalition government with Schleicher, in December 1932 he attended a dinner organized by a Cologne banker named Kurt von Schroeder, who invited him to a meeting with Adolf Hitler. Both held a meeting at Schroder's home, where Von Papen's parliamentary support for Hitler was created. They were also at the home of banker Wilhelm Keppler, then the economic head of the Nazi Party, and Heinrich Himmler. The old spy von Papen was still a master of intrigue. The meeting between von Papen and Hitler was made public and was understood as a betrayal of Schleicher. This meeting with Hitler was in fact one of the most recurrent questions to von Papen, years later, in the Nuremberg trials[544].

On January 22, 1933 von Papen took a more active role in favor of the Nazis and he asked the son of the President, Oskar von Hindenburg, to attend a secret meeting with Hitler in the house of the

---

543 Von Papen, *Memoirs*, p. 223

544 Von Papen, *Memoirs*, p. 226.

Nazi Joachim von Ribbentrop, to obtain his support. A man of an advanced age, Paul von Hindenburg was heavily influenced by his surroundings and his most trusted man was his son Oskar, who determined his agenda and many of his decisions. Hitler persuaded Oskar for one hour, and he left the meeting convinced of the need to appoint Hitler as chancellor. At the end of January the rumor spread that Schleicher intended to take a *coup d'état* to eliminate Paul von Hindenburg from the presidency[545]. Only under these premises did the president finally agree to depose Schleicher and appoint Hitler as the new chancellor. On January 30 Hitler came out jubilant from the Presidential Palace as the new Chancellor of Germany. Schleicher would be killed a year later on the night of the long knives.

The rest of the history of the rise of Nazism is well known; in 1933 the fire of the *Reichstag*, the German parliament, was attributed to the Communists but its authorship was unclear. Several laws were passed afterwards, aiming at increasing the power of Chancellor Adolf Hitler and reducing civil liberties. These laws were the Reichstag Fire Decree and Enabling Law.

In 1934 von Hindenburg died, and that year Hitler got rid of all his political rivals, inside and outside his party during the so-called "Night of the long knives." Von Hindenburg was the last president of the Weimar Republic, and at his death the office of the President and the chancellor converged into one, that of *Führer* or supreme dictator. The "Night of broken glasses" followed in 1938, and massacres of innocent Jews were carried out throughout the country.

---

[545] Von Papen, *Memoirs*, p.p. 235 and 243.

LORD MONTAGU NORMAN AND HJALMAR SCHACHT

The Govenor of the Bank of England and the President of the Reichsbank.

The Czech Gold

In 1938 Germany annexed Austria (a movement known as the *Anschluss*). Far from satisfying the territorial ambitions of Hitler, he targeted some Czechoslovak regions with a predominantly German population, known as the Sudeten. The insistence of Germany made that in 1939 the governments of France and Great Britain allowed Germany to annex the Sudetenland, following a policy of appeasement with the Nazis initialed in the Munich Pacts. Czechoslovakia, which maintained a reciprocal aid agreement with France, was not even allowed to be present at the trilateral conference in which its territory was dismembered.

After being granted the Sudetenland, Germany not only occupied the agreed territories, but also the entire Czechoslovakia, in breach of the covenants it had just signed. In September of that year the invasion of Poland took place that caused the beginning of the second war. When Hitler marched on Czechoslovakia, the first thing he did was taking control of his central bank and ordering the surrender of the country's gold reserves. The Czechs alleged that the gold had already been transferred via the *Bank of International Settlements* to the *Bank of England*, of which Montagu Norman was Governor. The BPI, however, immediately made the transfers requested by the Nazis, and Norman, as head of the Bank of England and one of the members of the *BIS* board, did nothing to prevent it. The Czech gold reserves held in the *Bank of England*'s account had an equivalent value of 5.6 million pounds. Czech gold was sold in Belgium, Holland and London and from there it went to Berlin. This is how the BIS explained the transfer of a document declassified recently by the *Bank of England*:

> «[546]On the 21st March 1939 the Chief Cashier received the request to transfer about £5.6 million gold from the B.I.S No.2

546 Unpublished War History (Part 3 Relations with Certain Overseas Countries) – Chapter 9, Web of the Bank of England, website revised in May 2015, p. 1293.

Account to their No.17 Account. The Bank (although it was no business of theirs) were fairly sure that the No.2 Account was a Czech National Bank Account and they believed, although they were not sure at the time, that No. 17 Account was a Reichsbank. The amount was transferred on the same day and a small further amount on the 22nd. Between the 21st and 31st March the gold received on the No.17 Account was disposed of, about £4 million going to the National Bank of Belgium and the Nederlandsdsche Bank and the remainder being sold in London.»

The *Bank of International Settlements* justified its neutrality in its supranational nature, and in the statutes signed by its member countries. In any case there would be several considerations. The first is that at the time that Germany claimed gold, at least formally, Czechoslovakia remained a sovereign country. The second is that the gold was in the custody of the *Bank of England* and not in Czechoslovakia, so the *Bank for International Settlements* had no authority to transfer the money. The third aspect to consider, and possibly the most important, is that the governor of the *Bank of England*, aware of the impending war between England and Germany, not only facilitated the transfer of Czech gold to the Nazis, but also refused to clarify the matter when asked by Parliament:

«On 26th May the Chancellor wrote to the Governor asking whether the Bank of England still held the Czech gold, as the information might help him to answer questions in the House. The Governor in his reply (30th May) did not answer the question, but pointed out that the Bank held gold from time to Time for the B.I.S. and had no knowledge whether it was their own property or that of their customers. Hence, they could not say whether the gold was held for the National Bank of Czechoslovakia. »

Despite the growing unrest of several *BIS* member countries, in June there were more money transfers from London to Germany:

«There was a further gold transaction on the 1st June when there were sales of gold (£440,000) and gold shipments to New York (£420,000) from the No.19 Account of the B.I.S. This represented gold which had been shipped to London by the Reichsbank. »

The Parliament demanded Montagu Norman to amend the *BIS* statutes in time of war, requiring the authorization of the British Treasury to carry out any transaction from the *Bank of England.* To the dissatisfaction of the British Parliament itself were added the complaints of the French directors of the *BIS* and the Americans. The same document published by the *Bank of England* indicated that some international gold transactions continued to be carried out during the war through the International Red Cross.

Hjalmar Schacht, Norman's friend and also a member of the Board of Directors of the *Bank for International Settlements* argued that "[547]Montagu Norman did more for peace than any party-political leader." Schacht was a friend of Norman's since at least 1923, the year they met during a trip to England[548], and this cordial friendship lasted until the end of his life, even in spite of the War. Norman even sponsored one of the grandchildren of the German banker, who was baptized as Norman Hjalmar.

Montagu Norman belonged to the most exclusive British financial aristocracy. Partner in *Brown, Shipley and Company* from 1900, his maternal grandfather Mark Collet was Governor of the *Bank of England* like him, and his paternal grandfather George Warde Norman was one of its directors. With these credentials Montagu Norman renewed his position as Governor of the *Bank of England* on an annual basis, for almost a quarter of a century, regardless of which party was in power.

In 1944 at the Bretton Woods Monetary and Financial Conference, the *Bank for International Settlements* became the source of disputes

---

[547] Hjalmar Schacht, *My First Seventy Six Years*, p. 233.

[548] Hjalmar Schacht, *My First Seventy Six Years*, p.199.

between the US delegation, consisting of Harry Dexter White and Henry Morgenthau, and the British delegation, led by the economist John Maynard Keynes:

> «Hostility to the B.I.S., first aroused over the question of the Czech gold, was still noticeable from time to time and the publication of the Twelfth Annual Report in the Summer of 1942 gave rise to a number of ill-informed questions in the House of Commons and to allegations in certain quarters that the B.I.S. was not observing neutrality, but was favouring the Axis powers...
>
> In November 1943 came the first official indication that the U.S.A. was likely to be hostile to the continuance of the B.I.S. after the war... Mr. Harry White of the U.S. Treasury stated that the B.I.S. had no significance in connection with his proposed Bank and that it was German-controlled.
>
> Perhaps even more typical of the consensus of opinion on the position of the B.I.S. in the post-war world was a recommendation by the United Nations Monetary and Financial Conference at Bretton Woods that the B.I.S. should be liquidated "at the earliest possible moment" (July 1944).»

The *World Bank*, created in 1944 on the proposal of the American Secretary of the Treasury Harry Dexter White and the *International Monetary Fund*, assumed in 1945 some of the functions that the *Bank of International Settlements* had played, and contributed to expand the political and economic dominance of the international banking. Regarding the *BIS*, despite the controversial role played in the Second World War was not liquidated and remains active today.

The Road to War, 1933-1937

Before the Second World War, in the spring of 1933, Roosevelt appointed US Ambassador to Nazi Germany to William E. Dodd, Professor of History at the University of Chicago, President of the

American Historical Association and Doctor for the University of Leipzig. His diaries are a fundamental document to understand the years prior to the outbreak of war.

On June 8, 1933, Dodd received a call from the president, who briefly informed him of his appointment to the embassy in Germany: "This is Franklin Roosevelt; I want to know if you will render the government a distinct service. I want you to go to Germany as Ambassador.[549]" Dodd accepted the offer and held two meetings with Roosevelt in June, before leaving for his assignment[550]. Roosevelt indicated his special interest in Dodd talking to Norman H. Davis, a banker of the Morgan group. Dodd did not record the content of his meeting with the banker but did make enough notes on his next meeting at the *National City Bank*[551]. He went to be informed about the affairs of the American banks in Germany and their problems to recover the money lent there. Although the *National City Bank* had no known affiliations with any Jewish bank, the meeting was almost exclusively attended by characters close to the Zionist environment, and much of the conversation was related to the suffering of Jews in Germany[552]:

> «July 3. Monday. We reached New York at about 9. I went at 10 to a conference at the National City Bank where State Department people had asked me to review the financial problems of German-American banks, involving payment of $1,200,000,000

---

[549] William E. Dodd, *Diaries of Ambassador Dodd*, p. 3.

[550] William E. Dodd, *Diaries of Ambassador Dodd*, p.p. 4-7.

[551] It's not pointless to mention again that Davis was Assistant Secretary of the Treasury and Under Secretary of State under Wilson's office. He and Thomas Lamont were the members appointed to calculate the German reparations in Paris. Davis was co founder of the *Council of Foreign Relations* and President of another exclusive discussion forum private to the bankers, the International Red Cross, from 1938 to 1944.

[552] William E. Dodd, *Diaries of Ambassador Dodd*, p. 9.

to American creditors who had been hoodwinked by bankers into making loans to German corporations. Vice-President Floyd Blair presided over the gathering. About ten other bankers attended.

All were concerned about the so-called "standstill" agreement with the Reichsbank president, Schacht, whereby American obligations were being paid in cheap marks rather than no marks at all and American bondholders were in the doubtful position of having to sell their securities at thirty cents on the dollar. There was much talk but no agreement other than that I should do all I possibly could to prevent Germany's defaulting openly, as that would upset financial interests in the United States. The National City Bank and the Chase National Bank hold more than a hundred millions of German bonds! If they could be sure of 4 per cent interest, instead of the original 7 per cent, they would be satisfied.

Then came a pre-arranged conference with Judge Julian W. Mack, Felix Warburg, Judge Irving Lehman, N. Y. Court of Appeals, brother of Governor Lehman, Rabbi Stephen S. Wise and Max Kohler, who is writing a biography of the Seligman family of New York. This conference had been arranged by George Gordon Battle, a liberal lawyer.

For an hour and a half the discussion went on: The Germans are killing Jews all the time; they are being persecuted to the point where suicide is common (the Warburg family is reported to have had cases of this kind); and all Jewish property is being confiscated. These were the subjects, in brief, of the conversation, and I was urged, as a liberal and humane person, to press for governmental intervention. I insisted that the government could not intervene officially but assured the members of the conference that I would exert all possible personal influence against unjust treatment of German Jews and of course protest against maltreatment of American Jews. We adjourned at lo o'clock and I took the train at 11 o'clock for Boston on a visit to Colonel House. »

There is no need to introduce some of the attendees such as the banker Felix Warburg, or Stephen S. Wise, rabbi and leader of world Zionism, that "pacifist but not a radical". Among those gathered at the *National City Bank* was also the Court of Appeals Judge Irving Lehman, of the powerful Lehman banking family. He was a cousin of the Governor of the State of New York and Roosevelt's political godfather, Herbert H. Lehman; Julian W. Mack was also present, he was a federal judge and pro-Jewish activist, Honorary President of the *World Jewish Congress*, President of the *American Jewish Congress* and of the *Zionist Organization of America*; Finally there was Max Kohler, official biographer of the Seligmans. Some people might wonder what a writer was doing at a meeting of international financiers; Kohler was one of those authors that bankers had on the payroll to make sure that future generations could correctly remember their greatness and not their darkest affairs.

The bankers shamelessly mixed two completely different topics, for their own benefit; the inhumane treatment of Nazi Germany to the Jews and the more than possible non-payment to the American banks. The bankers behind the Dawes Plan, who had allowed the financial orgy in Germany and its rearmament, felt a chill running down its back when in 1933 Hitler announced that he would not continue the payment of reparations to the Allies. The bankers appealed to the human side of the conflict to avoid the more than likely economic hole in their institutions, in the event that Germany failed to meet its financial obligations. President Roosevelt, however, had given clear instructions to Dodd[553]:

> «Last June Roosevelt said: "the bankers have gotten themselves into this. You must lend what personal, unofficial aid you can, but no more." Now the creditors, the New York bankers, have organized and pressed the government into fighting their

[553] William E. Dodd, *The Ambassador Dodd Diaries*, p. 74.

battles. I shall do what I can but agree with the Germans that rates of interest ought to be reduced to 4 per cent. »

It's not pointless to mention the fact that 1934 was the year of the failed coup to the White House denounced by General Butler. Roosevelt's relationship with international bankers might have cooled off that year, and they decided to show their protégé who really was in charge.

The next day came Dodd's last important meeting before leaving for Germany. On July 4, he met with old Colonel House, who was a man of greater confidence to President Wilson. Twenty years after he had Woodrow Wilson elected as President, he had not lost a bit of his influence in the Democratic Party. He informed Dodd that his nomination as Germany's Ambassador had been his suggestion to Roosevelt. And he gave a strange warning: "You should try to lessen the suffering of the Jews. They are clearly wrong and even terrible; but they should not be allowed to dominate economic or intellectual life in Berlin as they have done for a long time.[554]" It is surprising to hear these words from Colonel House, who since at least 1913 had done nothing but watching over the interests of the Zionist bankers, both in the Federal Reserve and in the Paris Peace Conference. Maybe again he was using his usual cynical style to probe his interlocutor.

On March 7, 1934, Dodd was in Germany and he had the opportunity to speak with the then Chancellor Adolf Hitler, in a meeting organized by Ernst "Putzi" Hanfstaengl, a common friend of Hitler and Roosevelt. During the meeting, Dodd pointed out that some of the main German spies of the First World War were in Hitler's cabinet, and no doubt he was referring to von Papen:

«[555]I then raised the subject of disagreeable and harmful propaganda, as suggested by Secretary Hull, saying that unwise

[554] William E. Dodd, *Diaries of Ambassador Dodd*, p.p. 9-10.
[555] William E. Dodd, *Diaries of Ambassador Dodd*, p.p. 88-89.

propaganda in 1915-16 had done a great deal to bring the United States into the World War. He pretended astonishment and asked for more details. I did not give names as two of the worst offenders are now officials of the Hitler regime: Von Papen, his second in command, and Dr. Fuehr of the Foreign Office. »

Hitler pretended his ignorance and asked for more details. Immediately after, Dodd brought up the negative perception that was had in New York about the painful Jewish situation in Germany. Hitler replied that he had saved Germany from Communism and that 59% of Russian officers were Jews.

Meanwhile, the Zionists in New York waged their own battle: On March 24, 1933 the *Daily Express* of London opened the edition with the headline "Judea Declares War on Germany - Jews of All the World Unite! - Boycott of German Goods" On August 7, the *New York Times* published a speech by Samuel Untermeyer, the Wall Street lawyer who conducted the Money Trust sessions, and a member of the Guggenheim family, summoned the Jews of the world to boycott Germany[556]. In September, Rabbi Stephen S. Wise did the same thing in a speech in Switzerland[557]. On March 7, 1934, a fictional trial was staged publicly in New York, the "Case of Civilization against Hitler" Attended by some of the most prominent leaders of the Wilson administration, including the mayor of New York, Fiorello LaGuardia. As defense attorney they appointed the German ambassador, who declined the invitation, and Stephen S. Wise came naturally as a witness for the Jewish people[558].

The history of Russia repeated again. Under the premise of the bad treatment of the Jewish people, the Zionist interests, represented by a

---

556 New York Times, August 7, 1933, *Untermeyer Back, Greeted in Harbor; Met by Jewish Groups, He Urges a United Front on Anti-Nazi Boycott.*

557 New York Times, September 6, 1933, *Boycott of Reich Demanded by Wise.*

558 Jewish Telegraphic Agency, March 6, 1934, *Expect Crowded Courtroom at Hitler 'trial' Tomorrow.*

handful of financiers with their own economic interests, used all their abilities for destabilization on Germany. An open "declaration of war" of the Jewish world against Germany -and not against Hitler- generated unnecessary tensions between the German population and the Jews who lived there. The role of Zionism in the outbreak of World War II was no lesser than in the Russian Revolution. In a private conversation British Prime Minister Neville Chamberlain confessed to Secretary of the Navy James Forrestal that "America and the world Jews had forced England into war.[559]" Chamberlain mistakenly mixed the role played by certain Zionist bankers -in cooperation with Anglo-Saxon, Protestant bankers- with the whole of the Jewish people, who knew nothing about their machinations.

The passivity of the German people in the face of the atrocities of the Third Reich is incomprehensible only from the point of view of their hypnotic devotion to Hitler. There was an anti-Semitic feeling in Europe prior to Nazism, precisely related to the activity of some Jewish financiers and their role in the fall of the Russian tsars. In France a great controversy arose in the late nineteenth century by the Dreyfus case, an Alsatian Jewish officer convicted of espionage, which was finally exonerated. Before the arrival of Hitler to the political scene, in 1922 a group of men assassinated in Germany to the Jewish politician and industrialist Walter Rathenau, the founder of the electrical cartel *A.E.G.* and a director in more than one hundred corporations. Rathenau was the Minister of Reparations of the German government, who some months earlier signed the Treaty of Rapallo to normalize relations with the Soviet Union. That same year in Genoa he gave a pro-Soviet speech that ignited the spirits of the most radical political groups in Germany. Executors strafed the car in which he was traveling and then they shot him with a machine gun and threw a grenade inside the vehicle. When Hitler came to power he erected a statue to his assassins. Even the Warburgs manifested their disagreement –sincere or not- over the issue of the Jewish boycott on Germany. Max Warburg

[559] James Forrestal, *The Forrestal Diaries*, p. 121-122.

still resided in fact in Germany. This is how Felix Warburg explained it to Dodd in 1934:

> «[560]At the request of Rabbi Lazaron of Baltimore, Max Warburg, eminent Hamburg banker and brother of Felix Warburg of New York, came to see me in the Embassy. He showed the effects of his troubled life the last year and now stands in danger of losing his life if he ever allows his opinions to become known to authorities here.
>
> He remained an hour. He thinks Rabbi Wise and Samuel Untermyer of New York have done the Jews of both the United States and Germany great harm by their craving for publicity. He said Felix Warburg was of the same opinion. Both these men are fully in sympathy with Colonel House in his efforts to ease off the Jewish boycott and reduce the number of Jews in high position in the United States. »

The default in the reparations was not the first breach of the terms signed by Germany in the Peace of Paris. Germany had already remilitarized the area of the Rhineland in the previous years, something prohibited in the Treaty of Versailles signed in 1919. A few months after Germany annexed Austria and Czechoslovakia, Hitler and Stalin documented the excellent relations between Fascism and Communism by signing the non-aggression pact Ribbentrop-Molotov of 1939[561]. The agreement included secret clauses like the invasion and partition of Poland between the Nazis and the Communists. In September 1939 Germany invaded Poland, and fifteen days later the Soviet Union invaded the other half. Poland had a special relevance for Germany, since after the First World War it was dispossessed of a good part of its eastern territory, and the country remained divided into two parts,

---

560 William E. Dodd, *Diaries of Ambassador Dodd*, p. 145.

561 The name refers to the German and Russian Ministers Joachim von Ribbentrop and Vyacheslav Molotov.

isolated by the so-called Danzig Corridor. Previously Poland had also been part of the Russian Empire.

Much to Hitler's surprise, who had seen the lukewarm response to his earlier acts of defiance, saw a few days later France and the United Kingdom declared war on him under a pact of mutual aid with Poland, but they did not declare war on Stalin. The Soviet Union was the great winner of the invasion of Poland and hardly suffered any casualties, since all the resistance had been broken two weeks earlier by Germany.

The General Staff and the Shadow Government

At the end of the Second World War, the United States undertook a thorough investigation into the causes of that new conflict, in order to eliminate the military potential of Germany and to avoid a possible third war. To this end, in 1945 the Senate formed a special committee - dependent of Bernard Baruch- and its conclusions were included in an extensive research in two volumes. It has rarely been quoted by academics, with the sole exception of Sutton, and it perfectly corroborates the information contained in the Nuremberg Trials. Some of its conclusions were surprising.

The American experts pointed out that the German General Staff, the high command of the American military, had been preparing the country for the second war before even signing the Peace of Paris in 1919, and more than a decade before the arrival of Adolf Hitler. The Weimar Republic worked tirelessly to rearm the country for a future conflict, correcting the strategic mistakes made in the First World War. With this idea in mind, and thanks to the consent and even the support of the successive chancellors, the German military leadership promoted a system of industrial cartels that manufactured the formidable German war machine for World War II. The General Staff, led by Kaiser Wilhelm II before the peace of 1919, remained unofficially active, hidden from the Allies. After the abdication and exile of the Kaiser, Marshal von Hindenburg and General Ludendorff remained in front of shadow government of the General Staff. The first man was President of the German Republic for almost a decade -more than a half of the Weimar Republic- and he was the one who appointed Adolf Hitler as Chancellor. The second man, Ludendorff, participated with Hitler in the 1923 Putsch. He was promptly forgiven, like Adolf Hitler himself. The leaders of that failed coup were treated with extreme mildness because they had only anticipated in a decade what the German General Staff had been planning for years.

During the Weimar Republic, countless chancellors passed through the office of Germany, but the shadow government of the General Staff of Hindenburg and Ludendorff remained unchanged until the arrival of the Hitler to power. Both men, of advanced age, lived long enough to see the horrors of Nazism, a creature they had helped to create. The document prepared by the American military experts explained their contribution to the war:

> «[562]Contrary to some general opinion to the effect that the Nazis were solely responsible for war preparations, there is a surprising record in the years immediately succeeding the end of the First World War during the tenure of the so-called Weimar regime of attempts not only private but official to evade the provisions of the Treaty of Versailles…
>
> One of the main features of this effort historically was, of course, the activities underground and apparent of the so-called General Staff group.
>
> Even before World War I was over, German military leaders wore analyzing the causes of their impending defeat and planning for the next war. They found few defects in German arms and military strategy. The main weakness that they discovered was in the field of war economics.
>
> The Treaty of Versailles abolished the German General Staff, but the German General Staff was able to circumvent that prohibition by continuing its work in various governmental

---

[562] *Elimination of German Resources*, p.p. 152-155.

> organizations such as the National Archives, where they purportedly worked on a historical study of the First World War.
>
> Not long after 1918, the German General Staff set up schools to train German officers in military economics and industrial organization. By the middle 1920's many German officers trained in those schools had been sent out to help and guide German industrialists to rearm Germany economically and industrially for World War II.
>
> When the Nazis came to power in 1933 they found that long strides had been made since 1918 in preparing Germany for war from an economic and industrial point of view. However, they also found that Germany was lacking in many basic raw materials and that her imports of those materials and her production of necessary synthetics would have to be increased. Working closely with the German General Staff, the Nazis achieved a high degree of success…
>
> Today, many people are inclined to give the Nazis credit and blame for Germany's accomplishments and policies from 1933 to 1935. In reality the German General Staff and the military German authorities wore equally responsible. During those years, Germany was in fact ruled by the Nazis in partnership with the German General Staff and the major industrialists. »

The whole of the German industry since 1918 was almost exclusively oriented to the formation of a militarized and completely self-sufficient economy, in the event of a great blockade like the one suffered in the First World War. Germany, a very deficient country in raw materials, solved its deficiencies by developing synthetic materials in all the industries of basic consumer goods, replacing cotton with synthetic textile fibers, creating gasoline from a process of enriched coal or manufacturing animal feed from wood to feed the cattle. In those cases in which their economy could not meet the needs of military production, they stockpiled raw materials acquired from other nations. Germany was preparing for war long before the arrival of the Nazis in power. They were just a necessary instrument to carry out the plans in which the General Staff and the German industry had worked for years.

In the 1920s the German government fostered a hyperinflation that the report describes as artificial, which surprisingly ceased almost instantaneously with loans in 1923 of the Dawes Plan. This artificial hyperinflation swept the wealth of the lower classes and broke much of the German industrial fabric, which was absorbed by the German cartels system, made up of conglomerates like *I.G. Farben*, *Vereinigte Stahlwerke*, *A.E.G.*, or *Thyssen*, companies that would later be the main economic support of the Nazis.

> «[563]All through the 1920's the German general staff and the industrialists continued their efforts to reorganize and prepare the German economic and industrial system for World War II. They instituted and managed inflation; they arranged for foreign loans to Germany; they were able to make arrangements with the Allies so that reparations actually were used to promote their plans rather than to impede them and they widened and strengthened the network of domestic and international cartel arrangements for the same purpose. »

Germany obtained more than 800 million from the Dawes Plan, and the financial backing of the Allies had also opened the doors to debt markets. With a blank check in the hand, the General Staff allocated a substantial amount of money to modernize the industrial capacity of the country, investing heavily in the development of machine tools[564], in order to automate the work and raise productivity. The stockpiling of machine tools and the technological superiority that Germany attained caused the perplexity even of the Americans, which was already the first economy in the world.

---

[563] *Elimination of German Resources*, p. 154.

[564] Machines capable of building another machines.

«[565]The possession by any nation of a large, installed stock of machine tools constitutes of itself a major element in defensive or offensive war-making capacity and outweighs the military potential of population numbers.

The capacity of any nation to produce machine tools in quantities is an even greater factor in war-making potential. Whereas machine-tool capacity installed may be said to add arithmetically to the military power of a given population, the possession of knowledge and capacity to build quantities of machine tools effectively multiplies that war potential in geometric progression.

In the light of this knowledge, Germany's war potential in machine
tools is a fact that is truly arresting. Recent studies and comparisons show that Germany not only has a very large number of machine tools but a capacity to produce them altogether disproportionate to any normal needs of the civilian economy. Germany, with a 1938 population of 70,000,000, had a machine-tool inventory and a machine-tool building capacity larger in 1939 than that of the United States, with more than 130,000,000 people and a more highly mechanized civilian economy. German over-all holdings compared to those of the United States on a 1939 peacetime basis are: 2 to 1 per capita of population; 3.2 to 1 per ton of steel capacity; 3.4 to 1 of production of civilian machinery; 16 to 1 per motorcar produced.
This disproportion in Germany's holdings of machine tools is even more striking in relation to other European countries. »

Overcapacity in Germany applied to any sector with potential military uses; steel, chemicals, automobiles, etc. The cooperation between industrialists and the General Staff developed an overwhelming industrial supremacy over their European neighbors, and

---

[565] *Elimination of German Resources*, p.p. 160-161.

made many surrounding countries, including several of the Allied countries, dependent on their technology, establishing an intricate system of trade agreements with other powers. The destruction of the German mark by hyperinflation led to a curious economic experiment, the return to bartering on an international scale. Germany would export to Europe part of its buoyant industrial production, in exchange for raw materials of primary necessity for the General Staff. The guidelines of the economic plans of the General Staff had two well-defined objectives; Maximize the military capability and obfuscate it from the sight of the Allies. Hiding its war potential Germany could quickly replenish its war capacity in case of suffering any setback, even in the event of a total defeat[566]. By devaluing its currency and masking the real size of its exports and revenues Germany could continue proclaiming its situation of national ruin and excuse the payment of reparations, while secretly violating the Paris peace agreements.

> «[567]The Dawes plan, adopted in August 1924, fitted perfectly into the plans of the German General Staff's military economists. A more than reasonable program of reparations payments was worked out... And the Allies undertook to float loans to enable German economic rehabilitation.
>
> With such guaranties, German business had little difficulty in floating private loans in other countries. German municipal and regional governments, as well as the Reich Government, shared the inflow. The result was a new construction boom whose stimulating effects on other industries caused many observers to write approvingly of the amazing recovery of Germany.
>
> There was surprisingly little intelligent analysis by foreign observers of the purposes for which the moneys were spent, or investigation of the soundness of the investments…

[566] Germany held relevant comercial agreements with Europe, but also did with Latin America, where it held important assets.
[567] *Elimination of German Resources*, p.p. 175-177

> Long before 1937 Germany had more than replaced the industrial capacity of the territories taken from her by the Treaty of Versailles…
>
> Not long ago President Roosevelt pointed out in a letter to Secretary of State Hull that "the history of the use of I. G. Farben by the .Nazis reads like a detective story." But the detective story had been running in serial form when Adolf Hitler had been a mere corporal on the Western Front. It had been running under the authorship of the German General Staff and the major German industrialists. »

The study of the American analysts indicates that the successive German chancellors were necessary accomplices, if not subalterns, of the German General Staff of Ludendorff and von Hindenburg. The military resurrection of Germany was supported by foreign ministers such as Wilhelm Cuno, the president of the company that organized German espionage during the First War, *HAPAG*. Cuno designed a hyperinflation tailored to the interests of the German State. The funds of the Dawes Plan, organized by bankers like Hjalmar Schacht, Morgan, Norman, Francqui and others made possible the German rearmament, creating a system of powerful industrial cartels that financed the electoral campaign of Adolf Hitler and formed his army.

Historians have often referred to the "economic miracle" that took place during the government of Adolf Hitler. The German miracle was actually related to the massive influx of credit from the United States, which, like a multiplication of loaves and fish, created an unusual situation of artificial abundance in a bankrupt Germany. The only economic contribution of Hitler was to repudiate the payment of the national debt. The Allied nations did not seem to understand the industrial transformation that was taking place in Germany, or they did not want to, because some economic elements benefited largely from trading with the enemy:

«[568]As a matter of fact, it is actually amazing that England, France, Russia, America, and all the other nations who have repeatedly suffered from German aggression stood by and allowed Germany to accumulate the raw materials she needed for the Second World War. With the exception of coal, and about one-third of her iron ore requirements, Germany possesses none or grossly inadequate amounts of strategic raw materials. Germany is dependent, wholly or in large part, on synthetic production or on imports from abroad for her petroleum, rubber, copper, manganese, nickel, lead, zinc, chrome, bauxite, industrial diamonds, opium, fats. She has solved the need for some of these materials by the production of synthetics within her own borders…

The so-called Weimar Republic—from shortly after the end of World War I to the ascendency to power of Hitler and the Nazis. During those years, the German military leaders and major industrialists helped to keep up the pretense of a democratic regime, but they were both restless under it and constantly seeking a means of replacing it…

Although Ludendorff took part in the National Socialist putsch in 1923, most people of importance were not yet ready to back the Nazis. The character of many of the Nazi leaders was too crude to appeal to the General Staff and the industrialists...

By 1929, however, the Nazis had enough of a popular following to make it seem possible that they might be able, with proper backing, to overthrow the existing regime. Some of the Nazi party leaders began to explain to the militarists and industrialists that the Socialist parts of the Nazi platform could safely be forgotten though its use must be continued in campaign oratory. A few of the Ruhr group began to send secret contributions to the party; but as a whole the Ruhr was not convinced until Hitler met with certain Ruhr bankers and other conservatives and convinced them that he could be trusted to set

---

[568] *Elimination of German Resources*, p.p. 178-182.

up a strong central government with a stable, aggressive, foreign policy.

During their first year in office, the Nazis were on probation so far as their monetary backers were concerned. The purge of 1934, which was publicized as a measure to rid the party of certain notoriously immoral and treasonable elements, was the blood price paid to reassure the doubters. Thereafter Germany was ruled by the party, in partnership with the major owners of combines and the German General Staff....

In effect, there was an unofficial super-governmental structure in Germany from 1934 to 1945 which included the Nazi government officials, the General Staff, and most of the important industrialists...The big German industrialists may claim that they took their orders from the Nazis—that they were sheep like the masses of the German people. But they were guilty of being more than sheep. They were full partners of the Nazi shepherds—just as were the members of the General Staff. »

The managed hyperinflation also served to consolidate the cartels system and uproot any hint of competition.

«[569]Mr. Schimmel. In regard to your exhibit 6, entitled "Unofficial Government," I gather that this partnership was not one between the Nazi state and the whole of German industry, but rather between the Nazi state and the major cartel groups. The partnership was used by members of the major cartel groups—corporations like Krupp and I. G. Farben and Vereinigte Stahlwerke—to dominate and to regulate very strictly the smaller and weaker German business groups. Is that not true?

Mr. Fowler. There was ample evidence shortly after the First World War to substantiate that. There developed an inflation which many observers, including General Morgan, of the British

[569] *Elimination of German Resources*, p. 148.

Control Commission, believed to be planned inflation. It wiped out a number of the smaller enterprises, and in the wake of that inflation the larger business organizations, such as I. G. Farben, were able to consolidate their positions.

The Chairman. The result of that period of inflation and deflation was that the major cartel groups, which cooperated closely with the German Government, were left at the end of the period with practically all Government business under its control; is that correct?

Mr. Fowler. Yes, sir. »

The report adds later on:

«[570]Various apologists for Germany have denied that inflation in Germany during the early 1920's was managed. But, General Morgan, who was in Germany through the period when it was in operation and in an exceptionally good position to discover the facts, stated the conviction that inflation had been "the instrument" of the underground General Staff to accomplish a large part of its program. Such a program could not have been carried out without the collaboration of the government of the Weimar Republic and of the major industrialists. The latter were in control of banking and, in addition, occupied many of the government offices concerned with public finance. They, furthermore, were the chief beneficiaries.

While small businessmen who did not understand the techniques of managed bankruptcy were ruined, and salaried workers and wage-earners were driven to desperate expedients in order to subsist with prices doubling overnight, a constantly narrowing group of the major industrialists were creating economic domains of-fantastic proportions. As company after company was forced to the wall, the successful manipulators bought them up.

---

570 *Elimination of German Resources*, p. 175.

The new empires built with the aid of inflation were not all within Germany. At the same time when Germany was pleading poverty and inability to pay reparations, German manufactured products were being sold abroad in large quantities, thanks to the low-production costs, and part of the proceeds from them were being used to acquire properties abroad—some of them German holdings that had been confiscated by the Allies.

The final triumph of inflation was its blackmail value. Germany's
ability to undersell other nations with goods produced under inflationary conditions began to cause trepidation among other trading nations in 1922. The speculation in the mark was also disturbing the money markets. The German Government insisted that it was powerless to handle the situation. Finally the Allies agreed to review the reparations question and to consider aiding Germany financially. The mark was abruptly stabilized. »

And further:

«[571]At the end of 1923 that Brig. Gen. John H. Morgan of the disarmament commission was able to state: Germany has now got. ingeniously camouflaged, that economic General Staff which was the dream of Rathenau… and the whole of the key industries of war—coal-tar products, sulfuric acid, nitric acid, aluminum, and all the rest— have been reorganized, subsidized, and controlled to this end. The whole of German industry and production have been reorganized by some astute and able brain with a view to making her independent of overseas supplies of material in the next war. »

Who were those "astute and brains" that the report alludes to? The main architect of the German hyperinflation was Wilhelm Cuno, the President of *HAPAG* who occupied the chancellery in this period.

---

[571] *Elimination of German Resources*, p. 412.

Roosevelt, who later led his country during the Second World War, benefited from hyperinflation through its societies in Germany. The servitude of the payment of its debt almost in perpetuity, together with its territorial dismemberment after the war inevitably pushed Germany to rearmament. This was the postwar period that international bankers planned. The successive chancellors folded to a greater or lesser extent to the plans of the General Staff's shadow government, so that Germany could recover its economic sovereignty and its frontiers prior to the first war. The reality is, as we have seen, that Germany remained in a war economy even after the armistice of 1918. After the aid of the Dawes Plan, the German economy, reanimated by the tricks of the financial conjuror Hjalmar Schacht, returned to normal:

> «[572]Late in 1923, after the Allies had been persuaded that review of the reparations question was to their advantage, the mark was abruptly stabilized. In addition to the gains listed by Morgan, inflation had furthered the long-range plans of the General Staff and their industrial collaborators in other ways. The Government, the great corporations, and the railways had emerged free of debt. Moreover, Germany had— used the proceeds of foreign speculation (in the mark) from 1919 to 1923 to meet the current deficit in her balance of trade, to make reparations transfers, and to build up a small volume of foreign holdings.»

In conclusion, hyperinflation allowed large German cartels to obtain a deficit that would allow them to avoid payment under the conditions imposed by the Allies, make their payments with a completely devalued currency and expatriate their profits to third powers in order to diversify risks and camouflage their balance sheets The Dawes Plan had other important positive effects for the German economy:

---

[572] *Elimination of German Resources*, p. 412.

«[573]The Dawes plan, which was adopted in August 1924, was even more useful in furthering the long-range plans of Germany. In addition to setting up a schedule of reparations payments that were to rise gradually (with about half the revenue to be derived from taxes on beer, alcohol, and other commodities that were state monopolies), the plan provided that Germany's obligations would end with payment in marks to the Allied representative in Germany; it was up to the creditors to find a way to transfer the moneys. As a result large sums were spent in Germany, thus stimulating German industrial production, especially in the machine and tool industry. Further, the Dawes plan arranged for the flotation of large governmental loans abroad.

With confidence in German economic stability thus confirmed, foreign agents of German big business had no difficulty in obtaining large loans in foreign markets. German states and municipalities also shared the inflow of investment funds. Certain foreign industrial corporations added to it by establishing branches in Germany. »

The Dawes Plan, perfectly suited for the international bankers, was the only element truly indispensable for executing the military plans of the German General Staff. Usually the Allies' ignorance of the German plans has been alluded to, but as early as 1923 the British general John H. Morgan denounced that the German machine was working at full capacity for a new war. If German rearmament, contrary to the Versailles agreements, was already known far in advance, it is difficult to understand why the Allies did nothing to prevent it. Strangely enough Germany managed to appease the Allies and was able to relax not only the financial pressure but also the controls that prevented its remilitarization. This happened thanks to the influence of the international bankers, that crowd of advisers who did the work of the great statesmen in the First war and later, in 1918, in Versailles.

---

[573] *Elimination of German Resources*, p. 412.

«[574]By 1928 Germany had lulled the Allies to the point where they agreed again to review the reparations question. The Paris Conference, which began in May 1929, drew up the Young plan; although this specified that Allied economic "supervision" should be ended, the Germans refused to sign unless French troops were withdrawn from the Rhineland. Under Allied pressure, Franco reluctantly agreed.

Before Germany could take advantage of the new terms, the international economic collapse occurred…

The trade policy, especially in the 1930's based solely on preparation for war, involved the curtailment of production of civilian goods, the export of goods that did not handicap the rearmament program, the forcing of such goods on customers without regard for their desires, and the sale at any price of goods that would aid in the accumulation of dollars, pounds, and Swiss francs…

While, the international economic collapse that began in 1929 must have caused various changes in the operational program of the underground General Staff, it did not in any way block it…

Even with the country an international bankrupt, public funds were still used to support research and build up production facilities for the synthetics essential if Germany was to enter a war. For example, the General Staff was especially concerned with the problem of animal foodstuffs, the lack of which had been a principal cause of the food shortage in 1918. In 1931 a representative of the Ministry of War visited the pioneer plant making a protein foodstuff from wood; subsequently the national treasury granted a considerable sum for further research and development on these lines. At intervals officers checked progress of the work.

In 1933 the economics section of the General Staff came above ground inconspicuously as the Wehrwirtschaftsstab (War

---

[574] *Elimination of German Resources*, p.p. 413-415.

Economics Staff)… The four-year plan, launched by the Hitler government as a National Socialist inspiration to make Germany self-sufficient, was actually the final phase of the General Staff's program of preparationfor war. »

The General Staff had the complicity of a large group of German industrialists headed by Max Warburg, who had no faith in the Weimar Republic. Max considered a number of possible reforms in the fragile constitutional system of Germany: Much to his own advantage, in 1919 he outlined a large-scale centralized system to limit the spending of the federal states, and in 1923 he worked with the industrialist Hugo Stinnes on the idea of a triumvirate with absolute powers in economic matters, which he called *Finanzdirektorium.* His opinion about the Weimar Republic was that "The parliamentary system in this form" in his own words "is not the right solution for difficult times."[575]

The German Cartels

When in 1924 the Dawes Plan loans were undertaken, two financial entities named *Dillon & Read & Co*[576] and *Harris, Forbes & Co.* led the New York banking syndicate. Both Banks issued more than half of the 826 million loan to Germany in the Dawes Plan. The whole of the Dawes Plan loans were divided among eight institutions[577]:

---

575 Niall Ferguson, *High Financier*, p. 34.

576 A Bank headed by Clarence Dillon, a Polish Jew born Lapowski. Appointed by Baruch Assistant Chairman of the War Industries Board.

577 Anthony Sutton, *Wall Street and the Rise of Hitler*, p. 29, quoting Robert R. Kuzcinski, *Bankers Profit from German Loans*, Hoover Institution, Washington D.C., 1932, p. 127.

Bank	Loan	Profits	% total
Dillon & Read & Co.	$ 241,325,000	2.7 millions	29,2%
Harris & Forbes & Co.	$ 186,500,000	1.4 millions	22,6 %
National City Co.	$ 173,000,000	5.0 millions	20,9 %
Speyer & Co.	$ 59,500,000	0.6 millions	7,2 %
Lee, Higginson & Co.	$ 53,000,000	n.a	6,4%
Guaranty Co. of N.Y.	$ 41,575,000	0.2 millions	5%
Kuhn & Loeb & Co.	$ 37,500,000	0.2 millions	4,5 %
Equitable Trust Co.	$ 34,000,000	0.3 millions	4,1 %
TOTAL	$ 826,400,000	10.4 millions	99,9%

A significant part of the loans were allocated to the development of German industry, and a sixth of the funds, 135 million, went to three industrial cartels[578]. The steelmaker *Vereinigte Stahlwerke* was the main beneficiary with a loan of 70 million dollars, followed by the company of Emil Rathenau, *Allgemeine Elektrizitats-Gesellschaft* or *A.E.G.* with 35 million, and the conglomerate of chemical industries *I.G. Farben* with 30 million. The three companies had a common denominator: Their corporate decisions were heavily influenced by American capital and participation on their boards of directors. These three companies, as it will be seen later, massively financed the rise of the National Socialist Party in Germany and formed the German military arsenal used against the Allies. The support of major German industrialists the Nazi cause such as the Thyssen, Krupp or Kirdoff is widely known but actually most of the support received by Adolf Hitler before the elections of 1932 came from companies with North American capital.

The Warburg biographer describes the consolidation of these new economic superstructures in Germany which resembled the American Money Trust. The apex of this system was the bank of Max Warburg[579]:

---

[578] Anthony Sutton, *Wall Street and the Rise of Hitler*, p. 29.

[579] Ron Chernow, *The Warburgs*, p. 275

«Awash with Foreign money, German industry embarked on a merger wave that produced huge trusts and cartels. Daimler and Benz merged. The new United Steelworks [Vereinigte Stahlwerke] arose, Second only in size to U.S. Steel. In 1925, six large chemical corporations formed the most massive trust, I.G. Farben, which ranked as Europe's largest Corporation. It would produce the bulk of dyes, pharmaceuticals, photographic film, nitrogen and magnesium made in Germany. Though a staunch free marketer, Max favoured industrial mergers and executed several of them, including that of two North Sea fishing concerns. Jewish financiers were catalysts of changes that embittered the losers… Max added a board seat on I.G. Farben to twenty-six other he now held. (By 1928, the Warburg partners collectively held eighty-seven director seats.) »

In 1938 *Vereinigte Stahlwerke* or the "United Steelworks" had a processing capacity of 50.8% of pig iron in Germany, more than all the other competitors together, in addition to 45.5% of the pipes and tubes, 36% of the heavy plates, 33.3% coal tar and 37.1% steel bars in Germany[580]. *Vereinigte Stahlwerke*, the steel and coal cartel, and *I.G. Farben*, the chemical cartel, were actually interdependent; these enterprises jointly controlled 95% of the production of explosives in prewar Germany, as well as other elements necessary for its manufactures.

I.G. Farben was in many regards the main tool of international aggression of the Nazi regime and it contributed directly to the cause of the Nazi Party with at least 400,000 German marks before the elections of 1932[581]. The giant *I.G. Farben* emerged from the aggregation of

---

[580] Anthony Sutton, *Wall Street and the Rise of Hitler*, p. 30.

[581] *Wall Street and the Rise of Hitler, p. 64.* See transcription of the original document in the Nuremberg Trials: *Trials of War Criminals before the Nuremberg Military Trials, vol. VII*: "The I.G. Farben Case", U.S. Government Printing Office, 1953, Washington, p. 565.

several companies in the chemical sector in what was called "Community of Interests of the Painting Industries" or *Internationale Gesellschaft Farbenindustrie A.G.* This business group came to dominate the entire German economy by forming a state within a state. The report of the Kilgore Committee of the United States Senate appraised the company in at least 6,000,000,000 reichsmarks:

> «[582]By 1939 I. G. acquired a participation and managerial influence in some 3 80 other German firms and over 500 foreign firms. The Farben empire owned its own coal mines, its own electric power plants, iron and steel units, banks, research units, and numerous commercial enterprises. There were over 2,000 cartel agreements between I. G. and foreign firms — including Standard Oil of New Jersey, DuPont, Alcoa, Dow Chemical, and others in the United States. »

In 1937 *I.G. Farben* had a monopoly over most of the elements necessary for a long military campaign in Germany. Twenty-eight of the forty-three products or groups of products manufactured by I.G. in 1943 they were essential goods for the *Wehrmacht*, Hitler's armed forces; essential components for making gunpowder, explosives, poisonous gases, gasoline or medical supplies. *I.G.* produced:

> «[583]Synthetic rubber, 100%; methanol, 100%; sera, 100%; lubricating oil, 100%; poisonous gases, 95%; nickel, 95%; plasticizers, 92%; organic intermediates, 90%; plastics, 90%; magnesium, 88%; explosives, 84; nitrogen, 75%; solvents, 75; gunpowder, 70%; calcium carbide, 61%; X-ray film, 50-60%; pharmaceuticals, 55%; insecticides and fungicides, 55%; synthetic resins, 53%; chlorine, 46%; high-octane gasoline, 46%; compressed gases, 45%; sulphuric acid, 35%; synthetic gasoline, 33%...

---

[582] *Wall Street and the Rise of Hitler*, p. 34, citando *Elimination,* p.p. 943-947.

[583] *Elimination of German Resources*, p.p. 986, 987.

although I. G. itself produced only 33 percent of Germany's synthetic gasoline, its processes were responsible for approximately 90 percent.»

The production numbers of *I.G. Farben* are surprising and possibly have no comparison in recent history. No company in the world except *Du Pont* in the United States, still at a great distance, was comparable to the *I.G. Farben* empire at that time. Among that 95% of poisonous gases of *I.G. Farben* was the Zyklon B gas, used in German concentration camps to gas millions of Jews. It is estimated that *I.G. Farben* made Zyklon B to kill 200 million people. And it was possible thanks to the loans of the Dawes Plan, a project entirely organized by the international bankers. In the interrogations of Nuremberg, of Doctor Von Schnitzler of *I.G. Farben* said that the board of directors was well aware of the use of Zyklon B gas in concentration camps[584]:

> «*Question.* During the last quarter, 1944, you said yesterday that a Mr. Müller-Cunradi alluded to you that the poisonous gases and the chemicals manufactured by I. G. were being used for the murder of human beings held in concentration camps?
> *Answer.* So I understood him.
> *Question.* Didn't you question those employees of yours further in regard to the use of these gases?
> *Answer.* They said they knew it was being used for this purpose.
> *Question.* What did you do when he told you that I. G. chemicals were being used to kill, to murder people held in concentration camps?
> *Answer.* I was horrified.
> *Question.* Did you do anything about it?
> *Answer.* I kept it for me because it was too terrible. I was always under the impression that these gases were not manufactured by us. I asked Müller-Cunradi, "Is it known to you and Ambros and

584 *Elimination of German Resources*, p. 988.

other directors in Auschwitz that the gases and chemicals are being used to murder people?"
Question. What did he say?
Answer. Yes; it is known to all I. G. directors in Auschwitz. »

In 1935 *I.G. Farben* not only worked tirelessly to re-arm Germany but also Japan, anticipating in several years his alliance in the Second War. Ambassador Dodd reported this to the State Department:

«[585]Illgner of I.G. Farben, the Chemical Trust, who has been in the Far East for a year, is said to have negotiated part of the pact and to have sold Japan vast supplies of war chemicals and gases. I have believed there was a secret pact of this kind for several months. While this story may not be true I am enough impressed to have telegraphed the State Department. »

During the 1920s, when the remilitarization plan of the German General Staff went full steam ahead, Max Warburg was one of the members of the board of supervisors[586] of *I.G. Farben.* In the Nuremberg trials prominent founders of the company like Carl Bosch, Fritz Teer Meer, George von Schnitzler and Kurt Oppenheim were charged of "war crimes". Max Warburg was the only founder of *I.G. Farben* who was not charged in the Nuremberg trials: In the 1930s he had been expelled from the board of directors of *I.G.* for the Nazis. The list of directors in the American board is even more surprising. Paul Warburg, Max's brother, was also of the *I.G. Farben* American branch, whose stock was controlled entirely by the German parent company. *I.G. Farben* thus played in the Second War the same role of

---

585 William Dodd, *Ambassador Dodd's Diaries,* p. 248.

586 The *Aufsichsrat* or supervisory board was a management organism parallel to the board of directors in some German companies. His belonging to that board is quoted by Sutton, Chernow and the Nurenberg Trials. Max remained in the board until 1932. See *Nuremberg Military Trials* vol. VII, p. 634.

subversion that *Hamburg America Line* had in the first. The protagonists were the same, the Warburg brothers, each occupying a seat on the board of directors on both sides of the Atlantic[587].

THE BOARD OF DIRECTORS OF AMERICAN I.G. FARBEN IN 1930[588]

Carl Bosch (German): Related also with *Ford Motor Co. A.G.* in Germany.
Edsel B. Ford (American): The son of Henry Ford and President of *Ford Motor Co. Detroit* from 1919 until 1943.
Max Ilgner (German): Nephew of Hermann Schmitz. Member of the Nazi military intelligence. Declared guilty in the trials of Nuremberg.
Fritz ter Meer (German): Chemist. Found guilty in the trials of Nuremberg.
H.A. Metz (American): Director of the parent company *I.G. Farben* in Germany and the *Bank of Manhattan* in the United States.
C.E. Mitchell (American): Director of the Federal Reserve Bank of New York and the *National City Bank*.
Hermann Schmitz (German): President of *I.G. Farben* from 1933 until 1945, member of the board of directors of *Deutsche Bank* and the *Bank of International Settlements*.
Walter Teagle (American): Director of the Federal Reserve Bank of New York and President of the *Standard Oil of New Jersey*.
Walter von Rath (German, naturalized American): Director of *A.E.G.*, linked also to *General Electric*.
Paul Warburg (American): First director of the Federal Reserve bank of New York and the *Bank of Manhattan*.
William E. Weiss (American): Director of *Sterling Products*.

---

587 Anthony Sutton, *Wall Street and The Rise of Hitler*, p.p. 33-34.
588 Anthony Sutton, *Wall Street and The Rise of Hitler*, p. 46.

Among the American directors of *I.G. Farben* we found that three of them were members of the boards of the Federal Reserve (Mitchell, Teagle, Warburg), two in the *Bank of Manhattan* led by Paul Warburg (Metz and Warburg himself), two in *Ford Motor Company* (Edsel Ford and Carl Bosch), one of the *Standard Oil of New Jersey* (Teagle) and one in the *Bank of International Settlements* (Schmidt).

In the Nuremberg trials only some of the German managers of the American subsidiary of I.G. Farben were convicted, while the Americans had no major setbacks.

* * *

It is not unusual to find *Ford Motor Company* members like Edsel Ford on the board of directors of a Nazi company like *I.G. Farben*. His father and the founder of the American company, Henry Ford, was one of the greatest businessmen in the history of the United States, and one of the first backers of Hitler since 1922. It is unknown whether he directly financed the rise of Nazism or not, however Ford repeatedly spoke out in favor of Hitler, who had in his office a picture of the American businessman[589]. In 1938 Ford was awarded with the highest decoration given by the Nazi government to a foreigner, the Great Cross of the German Eagle.

Ford was a man of contradictions. He proclaimed Jewish participation in the fall of the Tsars in his book *The International Jew*, but he built for the Bolsheviks the first modern car production plant in Gorky, Russia, in the 1930s. Years later Ford helped forming the mechanized arsenal of the Nazis in Germany thanks with the *Ford-Werke AG* plant in Cologne, subsidiary of the American company *Ford Motor Company of Detroit*. In 1928 most of the assets of *Ford A.G.* were transferred to *I.G. Farben*, and Edsel Ford became part of its board of directors in the United States[590]. Like the Harriman, Morgan,

---

[589] New York Times, December 20, 1922, *Berin Hears Ford is Backing Hitler*.
[590] *Wall Street and The Rise of Hitler*, p. 93.

Rockefeller, and Warburg, Ford collaborated equally with the Nazis and Bolsheviks, and thus obtained great economic benefits. The men of Wall Street were the best friends of European totalitarians.

I.G. Farben maintained a special collaboration with the *Standard Oil.* Walter Teagle, for example, one of its American directors, was the President of *Standard Oil of New Jersey*, Trustee of *Georgia Warm Springs,* Roosevelt's foundation, and Director at the Federal Reserve Bank of New York[591]. The cooperation between *Standard Oil* and *I.G. Farben* went beyond the economic realm, and included the transfer of technological patents, strategical for Germany to carry out a large-scale military campaign. *Standard Oil* made the most important contribution to the German military campaign by transferring *I.G. Farben* the carbon hydrogenation patent. This technology allowed the manufacture of synthetic gasoline through a process of enrichment (hydrogenation) of soft coal. In 1934 Germany produced only 300,000 tons of natural oil and less than 800,000 tons of synthetic gasoline. But coal was one of the few abundant raw materials there, so ten years later, using coal as a substitute for oil, the country produced six and a half million tons; 85% of the fuel was synthetic, made with the process of hydrogenation that *Standard Oil* transferred to *I.G. Farben*[592]. So critical was the fuel for Hitler's military plans that one of the chief reasons for launching the Operation Barbarossa of 1941 against Russia was its oil fields, which were the only solution to the desperate need for fuel that beckoned his army. Ambassador Dodd reflected his concern in 1935:

> «[593]At 11:30 we had all our experts, including the staff members, come to meet Mr. Phillips and give him up-to-date information about all phases of German activity. "Germany is one vast military camp," said Major Smith, Military Attaché. Our Commercial Attaché said, "In two years Germany will be

---

591 *Wall Street and The Rise of Hitler*, p.p. 68, 109.

592 Anthony Sutton, *Wall Street and the Rise of Hitler*, p.p. 21-22.

593 William Dodd, *Ambassador Dodd's Diaries*, p. 292.

manufacturing oil and gas enough out of soft coal for a long war, the Standard Oil Company of New York furnishing millions of dollars to help. »

The *Standard Oil* spent ten million marks seeking oil resources in Germany and building a large refinery in Hamburg[594], and more money later to develop oil substitutes[595]:

> «Why did the Standard Oil Company of New York send $1,000,000 over here in December, 1933, to aid the Germans in making gasoline from soft coal for war emergencies? Why do the International Harvester people continue to manufacture in Germany when their company gets nothing out of the country and when it has failed to collect its war losses? ».

In a letter sent on October 19, 1936[596], Ambassador Dodd expressed to President Roosevelt his concern at the dangerous American protagonism in German rearmament;

> «[597]The DuPonts have three allies in Germany that are aiding in the armament business. Their chief ally is the I. G. Farben Company, a part of the Government which gives 200,000 marks a year to one propaganda organization operating on American opinion. Standard Oil Company (New York sub-company) sent $2,000,000 here in December 1933 and has made $500,000 a year helping Germans make Ersatz gas for war purposes; but Standard Oil cannot take any of its earnings out of the country except in goods. They do little of this, report their earnings at home, but do not explain the facts. The International Harvester Company

---

[594] Anthony Sutton, *Wall Street and the Rise of Hitler*, p. 16.
[595] William Dodd, *Ambassador Dodd's Diaries,* p. 358.
[596] William Dodd, *Ambassador Dodd's Diaries, 1933-1938*, p.p. 303, 358.
[597] Anthony Sutton, *Wall Street and the Rise of Hitler*, p. 15.

president told me their business here rose 33% a year (arms manufacture, I believe), but they could take nothing out. Even our airplanes people have secret arrangement with Krupps[598]. General Motor Company and Ford do enormous businesses [sic] here through their subsidiaries and take no profits out. I mention these facts because they complicate things and add to war dangers. »

Rockefeller's *Standard Oil* also facilitated *I.G. Farben* the patent for tetra ethyl lead, developed jointly with *General Motors*. It was a compound that raised the octane rating of fuel by means of an enrichment process, a process critical for the operation of German aviation. In order to exploit the patent, *General Motors* and the *Standard Oil of New Jersey* formed a subsidiary, the *Ethyl Corporation*. This company sold *I.G. Farben* 20 million dollars in high octane fuel and aviation lubricants[599] and lent 500 tons of tetra ethyl lead to Germany in 1938, a few months before the foreseeable start of the war. This transaction was organized by the Ministry of Aviation of the III Reich and Mueller-Conradi, a director in *I.G.*, and it was carried out with the collateral guarantee of *Brown Brothers Harriman*, as usual acting as a proxy for the *Standard Oil* men.

«[600]*Letter from the Ethyl Gasoline Corporation to Brown Brothers Harriman & Co.*

Ethyl Gasoline Corporation
Nueva York, 21 September 1939.
Brown Brothers Harriman & Co.
New York, N.Y.

---

598 *Bendixx Aviation*, whose major shareholder was *General Motors*, provided Germany data about autopilots and aviation devices. *Wall Street and the Rise of Hitler*, p. 31.

599 *Elimination of German Resources*, p. 994.

600 *Nuremberg Military Trials* vol. VII, p. 1194.

Gentlemen:

We hereby confirm that on receipt of the amount of $835,200 plus $5,011.20 for accrued interest, all obligations of the party who received approximately 500 tons of fluid, as well as of Ed. Greutert & Cie., Basel, and the other guarantors, are fulfilled, and that all parties involved in this transactions are released from all liability in connection with it.

Very truly yours,

GRAHAM EDGARD (?)
Vice President
[Illegible signature]
Assistant Treasurer.»

The large presence of directors of *Standard Oil* in the *Ethyl Corporation* showed that its duty was to act as a firewall that would take the matrix away from any legal risk. Walter Teagle, President of *Standard Oil* and Director of *I.G. Farben* in the United States was a Director at the *Ethyl Corporation*, and so it was Alfred P. Sloan, President of *General Motors*[601]. A Germany without synthetic gasoline to mobilize its German tanks or without fuel to take off the fearsome *Luftwaffe* would have hardly survived more than one or two years at war.

Finally, the *Standard Oil* of the Rockefellers facilitated *I.G. Farben* the exclusive of the manufacturing process of synthetic rubber called "buna". This technology was not made available to the United States

---

601 *Elimination of German Resources*, p. 945, Sutton p. 74. *General Motors* was, by the way, a corporation very close to the Democrat Party. Pople of *Du Pont* and *General Motors* like John J. Raskob and Alfred Sloan contributed generously to it finances.

until well into the war, in 1940. The military advantage of synthetic rubber had been used for years by the German army[602].

The *Standard Oil of New Jersey* had a representation in the Nazi government through other subsidiaries such as the *Deutsche-Amerikanische Petroleum A.G.* or *DAPAG*, whose capital controlled the American company by 94%. Two of its directors, Karl Lindemann and Emil Helfrich, were linked to high-level Nazism. Lindemann was President of the *International Chamber of Commerce*, and director at several banks including *Dresdner Bank* or private bank *Carl Melchior & Co.* The two directors of *DAPAG* were part of the Keppler Circle, the most important funding body of the Nazi Party[603].

The unconditional support of *Standard Oil* to *I.G. Farben* gave the German company the monopoly of fuel production to Germany in the years before the war, and possibly this American corporation contributed more than any other foreign company to the Nazi military development.

* * *

The third most important German cartel, *Allgemeine Elektrizitats-Gesellschaft*, *A.E.G.* or the "General Society of Electricity" was one of the companies that most benefited by American loans with 35 million dollars. In 1930, *General Electric* controlled 30% of the stock of *A.E.G.*, which gave it majority control over the German company[604]. It also held a 16% of *Osram*'s stock. *G.E.* placed several American directors in the board of the German Company, such as Clark Minor and Gerard

---

[602] *Elimination of German Resources*, p.p. 952, 993. The transfer of hidrogenation, tetraethyl and synthetic rubber technologies were also mentioned in *Nuremberg Military Trials*, p.p. 1201-1308.

[603] Anthony Sutton, *Wall Street & the Rise of Hitler*, p.p. 75, 76.

[604] Anthony Sutton, *Wall Street and the Rise of Hitler*, p. 53, quoting the New York Times, May 11, 1930, *World Truce Seen in Electrical Line; General Electric's Part in Financing German Group is Called.*

Swope. *A.E.G.* contributed to the Nazi campaign with 60,000 German marks, and its subsidiary *Osram,* where it held the majority stock, contributed 40,000 German marks[605]. In total, the two German subsidiaries of *General Electric* contributed 100,000 marks to the Nazi campaign. In fact *G.E.* acquired stock in *Siemens* through the bank *Dillon & Read & Co.*, but Americans met with an outright rejection of *Siemens,* a fully-German controlled enterprise, to include its directors in the board. As Professor Sutton points out, companies like *A.E.G.*, and *Osram*, under partial or total American control, contributed substantially to Hitler's political campaign, while others like *Siemens*, under German control, did not.

The man at the head of *A.E.G.*, Walter Rathenau, was at the beginning of the twentieth century director in more than a hundred corporations. He was the Minister of Reparations, the man in charge of the fulfillment of the German payments of the Dawes Plan, while his company *A.E.G.* was one of the cartels that got the most money from American loans. From a position of high political level Rathenau was an ardent defender of the corporate state, in which he himself was one of the greatest beneficiaries.

Gerard Swope, President *General Electric* in the United States, and Rathenau himself, in charge of his subsidiary *A.E.G.* in Germany, shared the belief that large companies such as those they managed should acquire a greater role in society. The Swope Plan proposed by the President of *General Electric* was the first corporate Socialism project in the United States, and that Project re-emerged under the presidency of Franklin D. Roosevelt as the New Deal. Senator James A. Reed, once one of FDR's first supporters, remarked in 1936 that the Roosevelt family was "[606]one of the largest stockholders in the General Electric Company." The economic model of German National

---

[605] Anthony Sutton, *Wall Street and the Rise of Hitler*, p. 58.

[606] Anthony Sutton, *Wall Street and the Rise of Hitler*, p. 49. quoting the New York Times, October 6, 1936, *New Deal Called Tyranny by Reed; Former Democratic Senator Says in Newark That It Would Lead to Despotism.*

Socialism was no different from the American corporate Socialism of the New Deal: In both cases a handful of cartels or trusts, protected under the structure of the State, sought to obtain privileges such as fixed prices, restricted competition and great inflows of public money.

In Germany, corporate Socialism started with Walter Rathenau at the beginning of the Weimar Republic and flourished with the arrival of the Nazis in power. It was driven by the same American capital behind the New Deal because both systems met many of the expectations of the big monopolists and bankers. Measures such as the *National Industrial Recovery Act*, the fields of civil conservation, the fixing of tariffs and salaries and others aimed at favoring certain corporations were identical to those set in motion by fascist Italy or Nazi Germany. In fact, several of the measures of the New Deal were declared unconstitutional by the Supreme Court and the system eventually shut down. Some Wall Street interests in the United States promoted a fascist line harder than the New Deal, trying to impose a military in front of the White House. In Germany Wall Street tycoons worked with identical objectives.

* * *

It is well known, from the testimonies of the protagonists of this story, that all the decisions that led to the Second World War were not taken by the heads of state of the countries that participated in the war, but rather informally and privately by a group of bankers mainly related to two North American corporations, *J.P. Morgan* and *General Electric*. Reparations and other relevant economic issues at the Paris Conference of 1918 were the exclusive domain of bankers like Davis and Lamont. Years later, in 1923 and 1929 *General Electric*, the American electricity conglomerate formed by old Morgan led the negotiations of the Dawes and Young plans. The head of the American delegation was Owen Young, president of *G.E.* and banker of the Federal Reserve. Young, surrounded by Morgan bankers -including the junior Morgan- agreed to issue more than eight hundred million dollars in loans to Germany. The counterpart to Germany's interests was headed by Schacht, the son of an accountant of the Equitable Trust in Berlin, and by the Minister of Reparations Walther Rathenau, the son of the founder of *A.E.G.*, the German subsidiary of *G.E.* A lasting peace in Europe was not an object of the banker's interest, they only cared about the equitable split of the different sectors of the German economy. The Allied observer warnings about German rearmament and the systematic breaches of the Paris terms were ignored while interest money flowed into their pockets. Not everything went as they planned, and when Germany stopped paying the bankers began to worry.

The Money of the Nazi Party

The origin of the funds of the Nazism was a subject of research in the trials of Nuremberg and the Kilgore Committee of the American Senate. Although an important part of the funding sources of Nazism remain a mystery, it is known that the Keppler Circle was one of the main economic instruments of the Nazi Party before the elections of 1932. The Circle was born in a meeting between the German businessman Wilhelm Keppler and Adolf Hitler in December 1931. Keppler was president of *Braunkhole Benzine AG*, the subsidiary of *IG Farben* who exploited the patent for synthetic fuel from *Standard Oil*[607]. Several of the most outstanding characters of the Circle were bankers like the ex President of the *Reichsbank* Hjalmar Schacht, the Baron Kurt von Schroder of the *J.H. Stein Bankhaus*, Emil Helfferich of *DAPAG*, Friedrich Reinhardt of *Commerzbank* or Fritz Kranefuss of *Dresdner Bank*. After the elections Keppler lost his leadership in the economic area and moved into the sphere of influence of Heinrich Himmler, the head of the SS and one of the most important Nazis within the party. The Keppler Circle was renamed as the Circle of Friends of Heinrich Himmler. Three years later, Keppler was relieved as head of the economic area in favor of the banker Hjalmar Schacht, who would

---

[607] Anthony Sutton, *Wall Street and the Rise of Hitler*, p.p. 75-76, 80-83.

constantly struggle with the Nazi officer Hermann Goering for the control of the German financial apparatus.

In order to deposit the funds for the Nazi Party election campaign in 1933, Hjalmar Schacht opened the "Nationale Treuhand", a trust at the *Delbrück Schickler & Co.* bank in Berlin. The trust managed to obtain contributions over two million German marks, being Schacht its trustee[608]. Much of the party's contributions before the elections were made directly to the Nationale Treuhand, the Keppler Circle fund. For the most part the money came from the cartels created by the Dawes Plan, such as the steel trust *Vereinigte Stahlwerke*, the chemical trust of *I.G. Farben* and the electric trust *A.E.G.*

The real promoters of Nazism, those who decidedly committed to Hitler, were those who lent their support *before* his arrival in power. Many of the industrialists who contributed to Nazism after the elections simply did so out of necessity or fear. The largest contributor to Hitler's trust was *I.G. Farben*, who, as we already know, contributed 400,000 marks. Three of the eleven directors of the American branch of *I.G. Farben* were found guilty in Nuremberg for war crimes.

No evidence of financial support for the Nazis was found in relation with the controversial businessman Henry Ford or his company *Ford Motor Company of Detroit*, although the Ford family allowed its German subsidiary *Ford A.G.* to be acquired by *I.G. Farben*, leaving Edsel B. Ford as one of the directors of *I.G. Farben* in the United States.

Also it is remarkable that *A.E.G.* (*General Electric*) directly contributed 60,000 marks to the trust through other companies with significant cross-shareholdings (40,000 *Osram* and 25,000 *Acumulatoren Fabrik A.G.*). Friedrich Flick, one of the directors at *A.E.G.* and *I.G. Farben*, and also involved with *Vereinigte Stahlwerke*, personally contributed 100,000 German marks directly to the party[609]. In total about 225,000 German marks.

---

608 *Nuremberg Military Trials* vol. VII, p.p. 567, 568.

609 Anthony Sutton, *Wall Street and the Rise of Hitler*, p.p. 126, 130.

A very peculiar case was Eberhard Oppenheim, responsible for the banking firm *Sal. Oppenheim Jr. & Cie.* in Cologne. The family bank of the Oppenheimers in Germany was "Aryanized" in 1936 with the inclusion of Robert Pferdmenges and in 1938 changed its name to *Robert Pferdmenges & Co.* Both Eberhard and his new partner exercised a notable influence of German industry to through participations in various companies[610]. Pferdmenges for example was one of the directors of *A.E.G.* and *Acumulatoren Fabrik*[611]. The case of Eberhard Oppenheim was very striking because being a banker of Jewish origin - an Oppenheim, no less- he obtained the status of honorary Nazi after making a personal contribution of 200,000 marks to the Nazi party in 1934, perhaps in a desperate attempt to save his family and his business from the Nazis[612]. Eberhard remained very close to the Nazi financial circle until Goebbels and Hitler sent him to Stockholm in the spring of 1942, with the mission to appease the Allies. His failure in the peace mission discredited him within the party.

Fritz Thyssen, the German steel magnate who contributed personally with at least 250,000 marks[613], was probably the best-known economic supporter of Nazism. This amount could amount to one million marks according to his own biography, a book he later repudiated, entitled "I paid Hitler[614]." Thyssen was the owner of 26% of *Vereinigte Stahlwerke AG*[615], the most favored company by the Dawes Plan, receiving 70 million dollars, and although he refused to preside over it, Thyssen was in charge of its board of supervisors.

Emil Kirdoff, the coal tycoon of Germany and owner of the Rhine-Westphalia Coal Syndicate contributed 600,000 marks to the

---

[610] Elimination of German Resources, p. 857.

[611] Anthony Sutton, *Wall Street and the Rise of Hitler*, p. 55.

[612] William E. Dodd, *Diaries of Ambassador Dodd*, p. 73.

[613] Anthony Sutton, *Wall Street and the Rise of Hitler*, p.p. 104-105.

[614] Anthony Sutton, *Wall Street and the Rise of Hitler*, p. 106., quoting Thyssen's autobiography.

[615] "Fritz Thyssen", Thyssen Krupp website retrieved in 2015.

Nationale Treuhand trust. Kirdoff, the Managing Director of a company called *GBAG*, also had significant shareholding control over *Vereinigte Stahlwerke*.

The third great tycoon of metallurgy and mining in Germany was Gustav Krupp. He always refused to lend any support to Hitler until he finally rose to the chancellery. After the National Socialist victory he contributed about 5 million German marks, mostly paid to a fund called "Hitler spende[616]" through the matrix of his group *Krupp Gussstahlfabrik* or "Krupp Cast Steelworks". Krupp was not involved in the conglomerate of companies that formed *Vereinigte Stahlwerke*, and although he has always been considered one of the most ardent Nazi industrialists, it is possible that after his initial disdain for Hitler he was forced to prove his "unconditional loyalty" to the Reich. Gustav Krupp was not tried in Nuremberg because at the end of the war he was senile and incapacitated.

With regard to other German contributions to Hitler's election campaign we find old acquaintances; *Deutsche Bank-Disconto-Gesellschaft* made the first entry into the trust worth 200,000 marks, and Hjalmar Schacht personally contributed 125,000 marks. Most of the Nationale Treuhand funds were withdrawn by Rudolf Hess, Hitler's most trusted confidant. Schacht was the protagonist of the brilliant rise of Hitler and the only man in Germany capable of bringing together so many economic supporters around the National Socialism.

* * *

Fritz Thyssen, the individual who most heavily contributed to Hitler's election campaign in 1933, employed his personal bank, the

---

[616] The "Adolf Hitler Industry and Commerce Fund" or "Hitler spende" was created in June 1933 to facilitate the contribution of German enterprises to the Nazism. In exchange for their support, Hitler promised the eliminiation of the syndicates. What initially was a fund to gather donations from businessmen proggresively end up being a mandatory tax.

August Thyssen Bank, to finance the National Socialist Party, camouflaging the origin of the funds through its Dutch subsidiary, the *Bank voor Handel Scheepvaart NV*.

The steel tycoon forged his steel empire thanks to its privileged position during the rearmament of Germany and within the Nazi government. Then, during the war, he secured his estate out of Germany with the help of the Harrimans and Bushes. The bankers who made the most business in Bolshevik Russia also worked to hide the fortunes of some prominent Nazis.

Thyssen used the *August Thyssen Bank* also to hide his fortune: From Germany the money went to the *Union Banking Corporation* in the United States, possibly through the *Bank voor Handel Scheepvaart N.V.* in the Netherlands[617].

When the *Union Banking Corporation* or *UBC* opened its doors in 1924 its board had C. Livense as president and its directors were E. Roland Harriman, J.P. Ripley and J.D. Sawyer (*W.A. Harriman & Co.*), Hendrik Jozef Kouwenhoven (*Bank voor Handel Scheepvaart* and *Vereinigte Stahlwerke*), J.E. Groeningen (*Vereinigte Stahlwerke*) and Samuel F. Pryor (Chairman of the executive committee of du Pont's *Remington Arms*) [618].

The issue went public when the *New York Herald Tribune* published in its cover in July 1941 that the industrial Fritz Thyssen, had 3 million in the American bank *UBC*. Files declassified years later by the American government show that between 1931 and 1933 *UBC* made purchases of gold of more than eight million dollars, of which five million were international transactions and three million more were delivered to the Federal Reserve in 1934[619]. 3,991 out of the 4,000 shares of *UBC* belonged to E. Roland Harriman. One of the nine

[617] Anthony Sutton, *Wall Street and the Rise of Hitler*, p.p. 103, 106.

[618] New York Times, September 10, 1924, *New International Bank. Union Banking Corporation Opens Offices in Lower Broadway.*

[619] Desclassified document NND9108103, August 18, 1941. Web revised in 2015 in History News Network. See also chapter VII of Sutton, *Wall Street and the Rise of Hitler.*

remaining shares was owned by Prescott Bush, the patriarch of the Bush presidential dynasty.

UBC's assets were confiscated in 1942 under the *Trading with the Enemy Act*, along with various assets and rights of Thyssen and the *Bank voor Handel Scheepvaart*, Thyssen's financial vehicle in the Netherlands. No charges were filed against the directors of *UBC* and their assets were returned to them after the war. The incident thwarted the presidential aspirations of Averell Harriman and Prescott Bush, although Averell became Governor of the State of New York (a hunting ground reserved for the protégés of international bankers), and Prescott Bush was a Connecticut senator in 1952. Prescott Bush also had interests in the *Consolidated Silesian Steel Company*, a company that employed prisoners in German concentration camps, and in the *Silesian-American Company*, both companies being intervened under the law of trade with the enemy, under the vesting order 248[620].

* * *

Another person of interest linked to the financial establishment of New York was Baron Kurt von Schroeder, the banker who organized the historic meeting of 1932 in which Hitler and von Papen sealed their alliance. Von Schroeder was a member of the S.S. and an early support of Hitler. This opened many doors for him in the Nazi government, becoming the financial agent of Germany in the United Kingdom, and a member of the *Bank for International Settlements*. He was director and partner in several banks, the most important was the *J.H. Stein Bank of Cologne*[621].

---

620 Records of the Office of Alien Property (Record Group 113), Vesting Order Case Files, V.O. 341 and 6804, U.S. National Archives and Records Administration. The Guardian September 25, 2004, Ben Aris and Duncan Campbell, *How Bush's grandfather helped Hitler's rise to power*.

621 *Elimination of German Resources*, p.p. 870-881.

The banking house of the Schroder family had offices in London, New York and Cologne. When in 1936 the New York firm *J. Henry Schroder Banking Co.* merged with *Schroder, Rockefeller & Company, Inc.*, Carlton P. Fuller of *Schroder Banking Co.* was named President and Avery Rockefeller, nephew of John D. Rockefeller, its Vice President. Avery Rockefeller had previously worked with *J. Henry Schroder Banking*, the British firm of the Schroder[622]. The New York Times pointed out in 1944 the relationship of John Foster Dulles, lawyer of the Rockefellers with the interests of the Schroders[623]:

> «Senator Claude Pepper criticized John Foster Dulles, Gov. Dewey's foreign relations advisor for his connection with the law firm of Sullivan and Cromwell and having aided Hitler financially in 1933. Pepper described the January 4, 1933 meeting of Franz von Papen and Hitler in Baron Schroeder's home in Cologne, and from that time on the Nazis were able to continue their march to power. »

John Foster Dulles and Allen W. Dulles worked at a New York law firm called *Sullivan & Cromwell*, which represented *Schroder Bank* and the Rockefellers. The Dulles brothers were advisers to the United States in Paris in 1919. John would die as Secretary of State under President Eisenhower. Allen, a board member of *Schroders Inc.*, ran the CIA for years and was one of the members of the Warren Commission that investigated the assassination of President Kennedy[624].

In the Nuremberg trials large numbers of German officers and members of the National Socialist Party were executed, but the masterminds behind the rise of Hitler, many of them of American origin, emerged unscathed after the war. Kurt von Schroder, Hitler's

---

[622] Anthony Sutton, *Wall Street and the Rise of Hitler*, p . 81.

[623] New York Times, October 11, 1941, *Dulles is Accused of Breaking Faith*.

[624] The forensic examination of JFK, where it's brain dissapeared, was done in the Bethseda hospital, the place where James Forrestal allegedly committed suicide.

personal banker, spent three months in prison and paid a fine of 1,500 marks. Thyssen was condemned by a German court to pay a portion of his fortune as compensation for the victims. Krupp was not judged for his decayed physical and mental health. Von Papen came out unscathed once more. The Harrimans' assets were restored to them after the war. And then there is a case that deserves an in-depth analysis: Hjalmar Schacht. The president of the *Reichsbank* spent several months in a Nazi concentration camp and then two years in a denazification prison.

CHRONOLOGY OF THE SCHRODERS[625]

1800 Johann Friedrich Schroder founded *J. F. Schröder & Co.* in London. His brother Johann Heinrich Schröder associates in 1804.
1818 *J. Henry Schröder & Co.* is founded by Johann Heinrich Schröder.
1895 Baron Bruno Schröder joins the company.
1923 A branch is founded in New York, *J. Henry Schröder Banking Corporation.*
1936 Avery Rockefeller, nephew of John D. Rockefeller I, founded with Helmut Schroder *Schroder, Rockefeller & Company.*
1950 *J. Henry Schroder Co.* changed his name to *Schroders Ltd.*
1967 *Schroders Ltd.* absorbed *Schroder, Rockefeller & Company.*

[625] New York Times, May 23, 1986, *Avery Rockefeller, Investment Banker and Conservationist* and *Schroders* website, revised in June 2015.

ADOLF HITLER AND HJALMAR SCHACHT

The German Führer flanked by the President of the *Reichsbank*, Hjalmar Schacht.

Hjalmar Schacht

In the '20s Hitler was a corporal of the German army, the leader of a coup in the failed *Putsch* in Munich, who wrote a book called "My struggle" during his stay in prison. In the '30s he would become Chancellor of Germany. This transition would never have been possible without the aid of very influential German men. His first support was Erich Ludendorff, the retired general of the German General Staff who gave him the accolade before the military and veterans of the first war, participating in his premature coup of 1923. His second support was one of the great German spies of the First World War and its predecessor in the chancellery. The eternal conspirator Franz von Papen was the main political grip of Hitler in his ascent to the presidency. But long before the elections another figure of first order opened for Hitler the doors of all the financial and business circles of Germany and became the fundamental economic pillar for the National Socialist Party. The third pillar for the rise of National Socialism was the financier who managed to carry forward the Belgian "humanitarian" bonds. The same man that stopped the German hyperinflation of 1923. The one that led the request of the German industrialists to von Hindenburg to appoint Hitler as Chancellor. The President of the *Reichsbank*, Hjalmar Schacht, was the ideal man to carry out the plans of the General Staff to start a revolution in Germany.

* * *

A man of Danish origin, Horace Greeley Hjalmar Schacht was an extremely cultivated man; He studied Medicine, Philology and Political Sciences, doing his PhD in Economics in 1899. According to his autobiography[626], his parents decided to give him an Anglo-Saxon name

[626] Hjalmar Schacht, *My first seventy-six years. The autobiography of Hjalmar Schacht*, Ed. Allan Wingate, 1955, London. Most information contained here belongs to that source.

-Horace Greeley- and another Germanic -Hjalmar-. The Anglo-Saxon name was given to him due to the admiration his father had for Horace Greeley, an American Democrat and founder of the *New York Herald Tribune*, a major newspaper of the United States[627]. Greeley was by the way known to be the main economic support to Karl Marx, the father of Communism. Marx was a correspondent in London for the Tribune for ten years, a period in which he wrote more than 500 articles. Marx, like Trotsky, found in American capitalism his main source of sustenance. But Schacht was not a proletarian but the son of Baroness Constanze von Eggers, and his father was William Leonhard Ludwig Maximillian Schacht, an accountant in *Equitable Life Insurance* for thirty years, becoming Secretary General of the *J.P. Morgan* firm in Berlin[628].

In the early years of the twentieth century, Hjalmar Schacht mingled with the great German financiers and soon he got acquainted with Georg von Siemens[629]. Georg was a German banker nephew of the inventors Werner William and Carl von Siemens, the last was the co-founder of the *Deutsche Bank* and member of the board of directors of the *Dresdner Bank*. The father of Georg von Siemens provided most of the funds to create *Siemens AG*. The Siemens family successfully combined their industrial and financial activities in Germany, as did the Rockefellers or J.P. Morgan in the United States.

In 1903 Schacht made contact with Emil Rathenau who invited him to join the company he had founded, *A.E.G.* but Schacht declined his offer in favor of *Dresdner Bank*. The contact of Schacht with Georg von Siemens remained active in time, and this opened him the doors of the big banking industry.

By 1905 Schacht was already a prominent figure in German economic life. That year he traveled to New York with the *Dresdner Bank*, where he met the president of the United States, Theodore Roosevelt. Three decades later, in 1933, he had the opportunity to meet

[627] Hjalmar Schacht, *My first seventy-six years*, p.p. 14-15.
[628] Hjalmar Schacht, *My first seventy-six years*, p. 32.
[629] Hjalmar Schacht, *My First Seventy Six Years*, p. 96.

with Teddy's nephew and by that time also President, Franklin Delano Roosevelt. On his first trip to the United States he met John Pierpont Morgan when he was at the height of his fame. Schacht remembered it that way;

> «[630]A particularly happy occurrence — so far as I was concerned — was the conclusion or a deal in 1905 between the Dresdner Bank and the New York banking firm of Morgan & Co…
>
> Schuster devoted one day to going to Washington to pay his respects to President Theodore Roosevelt, and I was invited to accompany him. Then, on the occasion of my trip to Washington in 1933, I was able to tell President Franklin Roosevelt that I had visited his uncle in these same rooms twenty- eight years previously… »

Schuster and Schacht spent a full week at the offices of *J.P. Morgan & Co.,* where he worked closely with the legendary Morgan, with his son Jack and his right hand, Thomas Lamont. Schacht always spoke with great admiration of the old "corsair" J.P. Morgan:

> «[631]In outward appearance he was a giant, broad-shouldered and of Herculean stature. His son Jack inherited his figure. His somewhat rough-hewn face was characterized by an unusually large, fleshy nose. I have only seen one other nose like it and that was August Thyssen's before he had it operated on. The contrast between that Cyrano-like nose and the wise, kind eyes was all the more astonishing. Everyone who talked with Morgan came under their spell. »

---

[630] Hjalmar Schacht, *My First Seventy-Six Years*, p.p. 107-108.
[631] Hjalmar Schacht, *My First Seventy-Six Years*, p.109.

Of course, there was a special harmony between Schacht, the son of a senior officer of *Equitable Life* in Germany, with the American Morgans. His son Jens Schacht followed the family tradition and worked at the *First National Bank of Chicago* and at *Mendelssohn & Co.* [632] in Berlin[633]. Years later, in 1929, Schacht spent four months with the son of J.P. Morgan, Jack, in the Young Plan negotiations. Schacht said he last saw Jack in 1930 and Thomas Lamont in 1934[634].

Schacht was connected with all the pieces of Morgan's circle: John Pierpont and Jack Morgan, Young, the Roosevelts, Lamont and Rathenau. In Vienna he met Averell Harriman[635], and he was also a good friend of Benjamin Strong, the first Governor of the Federal Reserve. He knew Albert Ballin and Max Warburg from *HAPAG*. Schacht also maintained a lasting friendship with Montagu Norman, the Governor of the Bank of England for more than 20 years. The man who was supposed to watch over Germany's interests during the Dawes and Young plans was another pawn of the brotherhood of international bankers. He was the one who brought Hitler to the doors of the German chancellery.

* * *

In 1908 the Nazi banker Hjalmar Schacht joined freemasonry, a secular institution to which Trotsky, the Communist revolutionary, also belonged. Both Trotsky and Schacht seemed to share the vision of Freemasonry as an institution with an important political influence, linked to revolutions in various countries[636].

---

[632] A banking firm established in 1795 by Joseph Mendelssohn in Berlin, eldest son of Moses Mendelssohn, creator of the Haskala or "Jewish Enlightenment." In 1938 the bank was "Aryanized" and sold its assets to *Deutsche Bank*.

[633] Hjalmar Schacht, *My First Seventy Six Years*, p. 121.

[634] Hjalmar Schacht, *My First Seventy Six Years*, p. 118.

[635] Hjalmar Schacht, *My First Seventy Six Years*, p.p. 223, 263 and 46.

[636] Hjalmar Schacht, *My First Seventy Six Years*, p. 116.

«In 1908 I had joined a Freemasons' Lodge. Freemasonry runs in my family. My father belonged to an American Lodge. My great-grandfather Christian Ulrich Detlev von Eggers, was one of the Masonic notables of the Age of Enlightenment.

Neither the ceremonies of admission to the old Prussian Lodge *Urania sur Vitsterblichkeit* in Berlin, nor my later experiences in Freemasonry have ever been able to convince me that my German Lodge was a dangerous international organization which compelled its members to submit to some satanic ritual. That kind of thing is part of that unpleasant gossip invented by certain people who gamble on the stupidity of the masses and their love of creepy stories. The Freemasons were once a community — a community which set its face against any kind of religious intolerance. Their warlike actions date back to the Age of Enlightenment[637]. When the struggle was over, the importance of the Freemasons also diminished. What the Lodges preserved was the law of humanity and of friendly social activity.

That the Freemasons in other countries did undoubtedly sometimes take an active part in politics I learnt during a trip to Turkey with Rohrbach and Ernst Jakh in 1909. My Berlin Lodge had given me the address of a chemist who was a Freemason and lived in Salonika. As I could not get my bearings, I went into a shop in the main street and asked the way to the chemist's house. In less than ten minutes the shop was full of dozens of men, all of them Freemasons, who asked what they could do for me. At one stroke I had made contact with numerous inhabitants of this foreign city.

[637] In order to explore the anticlericalism of Freemasonry you can read my first book (in Spanish) "Las Revoluciones Masónicas". It is somehow true that the influence of Freemasonry has diluted, as its main aim of establishing a secular society has been accomplished in the western world.

This turned out to be very useful; my new friends initiated me into the background of the Young Turks Movement and their war against the absolute Sultanship of the Porte.

In this way I learnt that all the leaders of the Young Turks[638] were Freemasons and their secret meetings took place under the protection of the Lodge — the only place where they were safe from spies.

The incident made me thoughtful. I recognized that Freemasonry -not, admittedly, in Germany but in other countries — is sometimes used for politick purposes and I understood the reason for the dislike of Freemasonry in certain circles. Nevertheless I must once again emphasize that conditions in Germany are different. The Freemasons in the Old Prussian Lodges supported the idea of the preservation of the State through the monarchy. »

Contrary to what the freemasons usually deny, Schacht recognizes the political influence of freemasonry and its subversive role against the "old order" -represented by the clergy and the monarchy-. That role was not limited to ideological support, but it also included "warlike actions" carried out since the end of the 18th century. Some of these actions included the American Revolution of 1776, the Bavarian Illuminati of 1785 or the French Revolution of 1789, as Trotsky pointed out before in this chapter: "In the eighteenth century, Freemasonry became expressive of a militant policy of enlightenment, as in the case of the Illuminati, who were the forerunners of revolution."

---

638 The Young Turks were a political Group that in 1908 overthrew the monarchy of Sultan Abdul Hamid II in the Ottoman Empire, giving birth to the constitutional republic of Turkey. Mustafa Kemal Ataturk, founder of the modern Turkey and member of the Young Turks was a cryptojew from Thessaloniki, as he recognized in the Jewish journal *Forward* in January 28, 1994. Shacht and Helphand had a close political relation with this group in those years.

Prominent men in European politics as dissimilar as Prime Minister Churchill, Hitler's banker and a Bolshevik leader linked Freemasonry and Illuminism to the revolutions of the Enlightenment era and to later revolutions such as the Turkish Revolution of 1908 or the Russian Revolution of 1917. In regards to the persecution to which the Nazis subjected the freemasons, we discover that one of the most important members of the Third Reich, Hjalmar Schacht, was a freemason and did not see the need to hide it before the Nazi officers. When Hitler's Minister of Interior Wilhelm Frick, warned Hjalmar Schacht about the formal prohibition on hiring or maintaining freemasons in positions of responsibility, Schacht didn't take Frick's threats very seriously:

> «[639]Then I had to cope with a bit of general unpleasantness on the part of Herr Frick, the Minister of the Interior. He sent over an order one day according to which no employee who had been a Freemason was to be promoted or appointed to any position of trust. My reply, as always, was brief and to the point. I informed Herr Frick that I was not in a position to apply this order to my subordinate staff so long as a Freemason was head of the Reichsbank (I myself was a Freemason). My refusal created no repercussions. Henceforth, too, I graded and used all Freemasons on my staff according to their qualifications and character. »

Quite often freemansons complain (and boast) about the Nazi prohibition of Freemasonry, and the persecution they suffered in Germany after 1933, but apparently this did not affect all of them equally. In fact there are certain links between Nazism and some philo-masonic societies such as the Theosophical Society or the Thule Society[640].

---

[639] Hjalmar Schacht, *My First Seventy Six Years*, p.p. 325-326.

[640] Hitler dedicated his book, *Mein Kampf,* to Dietrich Eckhart, a politician and writer involved with the Foundation of the Thule Society. This group of occult study was founded by the Freemason Rudolf von Sebottendorff, and shared with

After the ban of Freemasonry, Heinrich Himmler tried to refound it as the "New Freemasons" [641]. Finally Hitler ceased his fight against this ancient and mysterious institution by promulgating a decree in 1939 that guaranteed a general amnesty to all freemasons[642].

* * *

During the First World War, Schacht worked under General von Lumm, the commissioner for occupied Belgium, managing the financing of German purchases in Belgium. Schacht was forced to leave public service when it was discovered that he had used his previous employer, *Dresdner Bank*, to channel remittances to Germany of some 500 million francs in Belgian bonds. This was money that then issued the bank *Société Générale de Belgique*, led by Emile Francqui, which at the time was operating as a central bank in Belgium:

> «[643]With the introduction of the new bank-notes (von Lumm's idea) the burden of their distribution (i.e. their exchange for German marks) fell on the military commissariat. The Deutsche Bank had a branch in Brussels and applied for a very considerable delivery of these notes, which came in very handy in their dealings with their Belgian customers. Whereupon the Dresdner Bank asked me to procure a supply of Belgian notes for them so that they might not be behind when doing business with their customers.

---

the Theosophists and the Nazis ideological elements such as Aryanism, Anti Semitism, Neo Paganism and Sun Worshipping, as well as iconographic elements such as the runes or the Swastika. Anton Drexler, co founder and President of the *Deutsche Arbeiterpartei* (DAP), the germ of the German National Socialist Party (NSDAP), was also a member of the Thule Society.

641 *Elimination of German Resources*, p. 826.

642 Nuremberg Military Trials, "The I.G. Farben Case", p.p. 636-637.

643 Hjalmar Schacht, *My First Seventy Six Years*, p. 137.

I submitted this request in person to the chief of the commissariat who agreed without further ado.

All this had happened in February 1915 and Lumm, of course, knew about it. Now, in July, he suddenly brought the matter up again. It was, he said, an improper action on my part to represent the interests of the bank that had sent me to Belgium. I replied that if I had been guilty of improper action I would request that a disciplinary enquiry be instituted against me. That, unfortunately, was not possible, retorted Herr von Lumm with a spiteful smile, as I had resigned two days previously. »

After leaving the public service with dishonor, Schacht rejoined his former employer *Dresdner Bank*, for some time.

* * *

In 1923, Schacht applied for his candidacy to head the *Reichsbank* or German Central Bank[644], which was dismissed largely for what happened while he was under von Lumm. He would still have to wait a while. In November of 1923 Schacht was appointed Currency Commissioner in the Republic of Weimar, according to his memories without earning a penny for it. The reparations to the Allies paid in gold dried the German reserves, and a currency not backed by precious metals the German mark was worth only the paper in which it was printed. Schacht remembered hyperinflation:

«[645]At the end of the war the mark was worth about half as much as at the beginning of hostilities. A gold mark (the standard

[644] German central bank. It's origings can be traced to *Royal Giro and Loan Bank* founded by Frederick the Great in Prussia in 1765. In 1846 it was re founded as the *Prussian Bank*, and afterwards the *Reichsbank,* which was active from 1876 to 1945. In 1957 it was replaced by *Bundesbank*.

[645] Hjalmar Schacht, *My First Seventy Six Years*, p. 163.

on which the paper currency was based) was worth 2.02 paper marks. But in November 1923 a gold mark was worth one billion paper marks. This is how it appeared in figures: — 1, 000,000,000,000. »

At the height of hyperinflation, in 1923, Finance Minister Karl Helfferich and Hjalmar Schacht conceived a plan to bring the German currency afloat. They decided to create a strong German mark or *rentenmark*, which in contrast to the "weak" mark was backed by Germany's land and real estate. Fiduciary money actually remained and remains a piece of paper, with no value other than trust in the government that issued it, but the financial acrobatics of Helfferich and Schacht had the desired effect and both managed to stabilize the currency.

Schacht seemed to be the King Midas of the banking industry, succeeding where others failed; the Helfferich Plan or the Belgian bonds were another example of his financial genius. Schacht presumed to be the accused with a higher IQ during the Nuremberg Trials, but there is also a different interpretation that could explain his endless success: He had the approval and complicity of international financiers, who would not accept a plan that did not come from one of the members of his exclusive brotherhood. We know also that Schacht was not the architect of the miraculous German economic recovery, as it has already been explained, the Dawes loans and the German decision of ceasing the payment of reparations in 1933 were far more effective than any of his financial or monetary policies. President Ebert agreed to appoint Schacht President of the *Reichsbank* from 1923 to 1930. One of Hitler's first steps when he came to power was to restore his sponsor at the head of the *Reichsbank*.

* * *

On January 5, 1931 Schacht was invited to dinner with prominent German industrialists who later would be relevant supporters for Hitler like Fritz Thyssen and some members of the National Socialist Party, which was already the second political force in Germany, like Goering and Goebbels. The banker Emile von Strauss introduced Schacht into the Nazi circles by introducing him to Goering[646]:

> In December 1930 von Strauss[647] a friend of many years' standing who had been on the board of the Deutsche Bank since 191 5, asked me to a dinner one evening to which he had also invited Hermann Goering. I was naturally very pleased to have the opportunity of meeting one of the foremost leaders of the National-Socialist movement. This dinner party of three discussed the universally burning topics of the economic situation, the rise in unemployment figures, the timidity of German foreign policy and all the other relevant questions. Goering turned out to be a pleasant, urbane companion, though he did not give me the impression of being especially conversant with any one subject. I could not possibly have deduced from the conversation anything that might have been described as an irreconcilable or intolerable political radicalism.
>
> Consequently when, not long afterwards, I received an invitation to dinner from Hermann Goering and his wife I had no scruples about accepting, particularly as the invitation was accompanied by a note to the effect that Adolf Hitler would be there. »

Adolf Hitler appeared at the end of the dinner, and apparently Schacht found no reasons to suspect the Nazis. Schacht had been one

[646] *My First Seventy Six Years*, p.p. 279-280. Goering was one of the main Nazi leaders, the natural heir of Hitler. In Nuremberg he was sentenced to death by hanging, but he committed suicide before that ingesting cyanide.

[647] Emil Georg von Strauss was General Director of *Deutsche Bank* and member of the board of 30 of the main German big business, like *Daimler-Benz AG, Lufthansa* and *BMW*.

of the founders and sponsors of the German Democratic Party[648], but in 1926 he left it. Years later he began supporting the National Socialist German Workers Party (NSDAP), especially between 1930 and 1932, although he was never affiliated with it.

* * *

Contrary to the image of ignorance and even dislike of Hitler's policies that Schacht alleged in his memoirs, the diaries of Ambassador Dodd proved that Schacht did know an important part of Hitler's plan since at least 1934[649]:

> «He [Schacht] said: "All the world is combining against us body is attacking Germany and trying to boycott her." Yes, I replied, but you know the way to stop such things is not to arm to the teeth If you went to war and won, you would lose more than you could gain. Everybody would lose. When he declared that the Germans are not arming so intensively, I said last January and February Germany bought from American aircraft people $1,000,000 worth of high class war flying machinery and paid in gold. He looked embarrassed and was about to deny it, but as he saw I was going to produce a document, he said "Yes, I suppose you know all about it, but we must arm."
>
> He then acknowledged that the Hitler Party is absolutely committed to war, and the people, too, are ready and willing. »

Schacht knew everything about the rearmament of Germany as was one of its main architects and promoters. In his conversation with Ambassador Dodd, Schacht was opposed to the war but he described Hitler as a "very great man". As von Papen did, Schacht simply staged a couple of public disagreements with Hitler, but both remained at the

---

648 Hjalmar Schacht, *My First Seventy Six Years*, p.151.
649 William Dodd, *Ambassador Dodd's Diaries,* p. 166.

heart of the Nazi government almost till the end. After revealing their differences with the *führer,* von Papen was relocated by the Nazi government as an ambassador in Vienna at the end of 1934, and Schacht remained several years as a minister without a portfolio, receiving a salary from the Reich.

Schacht, who in his memoirs and in the Nuremberg trials presented himself as a fervent friend and defender of the Jews, was perfectly aware of Hitler's anti-Semitism. He publicly condemned the events that took place during the Night of the Broken Glass of 1938, but could not pretend his ignorance. Hitler's hatred for the Jews was evident in his book *Mein Kampf.* In 1933 one of Hitler's first steps was to erect a monument to Rathenau's assassins[650] but Schacht did not seem to care and remained in his cabinet. A year earlier, Finance Minister Matthias Erzberger, who signed the Armistice of 1918, was assassinated. Both were seen by some Germans as traitors for collaborating with the Allies in peace and in payment of reparations.

Schacht was not affiliated with the Nazi party, he was one of the most important members of Hitler's cabinet, especially in its first stage. He led the German economy until 1937 and according to the Schacht and Dodd diaries the German banker often developed the functions usually reserved for a Minister of Finance and Foreign Affairs, although Goering and von Neurath were then the nominal owners of the aforementioned offices. Schacht did not abandon his position on the front line of German politics because he was frightened by the brutality of the Nazis: The disagreement actually arose from Hitler's refusal to adopt his economic positions, and he favoured Goering's, as it is clearly reflected in his memoirs.

The policy of fascist Germany was structured by four-year economic plans organized since 1936 by the Nazi Hermann Goering[651]. Its main executors were a number of private industrial cartels that operated as oligopolies within the state apparatus. This central planned

---

[650] See the Works quoted by Dodd, p. 311, and Schacht p. 97.

[651] Hjalmar Schacht, *My First Seventy Six Years*, p. 326.

economy established in Nazi Germany was almost identical to that of Stalin's communist Russia, which had established its five-year plans since 1928. Again we find the striking resemblance between the two totalitarian regimes. When Hitler put Goering at the forefront of the four-year plans, Schacht wrote resignation a letter to Hitler that showed his rivalry with Goering for the economic control of Germany. The letter is quoted by Schacht himself in his memoirs[652]:

October 8, 1937

«Mein *Führer*!

My dear Chancellor,

Following our conversation of the 6th inst., I beg to point out that a successful German economic policy can only be achieved under a central authority. In. view of the immense importance of our economy in relation to the preparedness of our defence force, it is impossible to tolerate the proximity of a heterogeneous crowd of business officials, the continual intervention by outside elements, or the permanent jamming of economic activities by the Deutsche Arbeitsfront. [653]»

Schacht did not conceive an economic policy in which there were several economic actors in equilibrium, instead he insisted on a "central authority", that is, a planned economy. Schacht had already renounced the economic direction of the Third Reich as a result of Goering's appointment as head of the four-year plans, but his leave did not become effective until two months later: "Being determined that my request to resign should stand I departed on leave on the 5th

[652] Hjalmar Schacht, *My First Seventy Six Years*, p. 375.

[653] "German Labour Front". Those were labor unions integrated inside the government. Free unions were prohibited.

September; nor did I return to the Ministry of Economic Affairs. Since no decision was taken on my above-mentioned letter mentioned, I gave notice to Hitler of my resignation, the two months having meanwhile elapsed." Even so, Schacht was appointed Minister without portfolio from 1939 to 1943, in what was possibly an appeasement gesture from the Nazis to the international financial powers.

In July 1944 Hitler seemed to lose confidence in Hjalmar Schacht. He was arrested by the Gestapo and sent to a concentration camp. He was not a Nazi but he was one of the most important man of the Reich and received several honors from Hitler's government. Schacht played a unique role in the rise of Hitler, even more important than von Papen. He was the main organizer of the Nazi financial apparatus in 1932 through the Keppler circle, and he opened him the doors to the group of the most important businessmen and industrialists in Germany. The *Industrielleneingabe*, the letter of 1934 that a group of German industrialists addressed to President Von Hindenburg, pushing him to appoint Hitler as Chancellor, was his own idea. Probably Hitler thought Schacht was about to change sides and escape with vital information.

When the Allies won the war Hitler's banker was tried in Nuremberg and sentenced again to two years of denazification for crimes against peace. He was acquitted of the accusations of war crimes and crimes against humanity. Schacht and von Papen avoided death by hanging for two reasons; they were not military officers and they never affiliated the Nazi party. But their role was far more tragic for the history of Europe and the Jews than that any Nazi or military officer.

* * *

Schacht describes in his biography some curious connections with Zionism. In Nuremberg he claimed that the first time he heard about the "Jewish question" was from the mouth of a banker from the Speyer house[654]:

---

[654] Hjalmar Schacht, *My First Seventy Six Years*, p. 468.

« "The Jewish Question," I said, "arose as early as 1933 when James Speyer, the New York banker (who has since died), announced his visit. I went to Hitler and told him: "Mr. James Speyer, one of the most respected of New York bankers and a great benefactor of his former country, is coming to see me and I intend to give a banquet in his honour. I take it that you have no objection." Whereupon he replied, in very decided and striking fashion: "Herr Schacht, you may do anything you like." From this I gathered that he gave me full liberty to associate with my Jewish friends as hitherto, which I did. And the banquet took place. »

In fact, neither "the Jewish question" nor "the final solution" were concepts born out of Hitler's discourse, as it is believed, those but appear much earlier in Zionist sources. The Jews had, or they thought they had a problem; they were a People without a State. An important part of Jewish politicians and personalities did not find it acceptable to integrate into the countries in which their population lived. The solution of the Zionists went through the creation of the State of Israel and the insane final solution of Hitler was a genocide.

In June 1933 Hjalmar Schacht met Stephen S. Wise, during a visit to Franklin Delano Roosevelt[655]. The Zionist rabbi Wise always seemed to be orbiting around the Democratic Party, giving his opinion on every diplomatic issue in the United States.

Schacht was granted the most extravagant privileges within the Nazi party; he freely practiced Freemasonry and was surrounded by freemasons, he organized lunches with Jewish American bankers like James Speyer and even met with Zionists like Wise. Hjalmar Schacht was the last diplomatic tie of the Nazis with the banking Anglo-Saxon establishment, and also with the Jewish world after Max Warburg exiled in the United States. As some other characters depicted in this book, Schacht probably played a dangerous three-way game, working primarily for the international bankers brotherhood.

---

655 Hjalmar Schacht, *My First Seventy Six Years*, p. 311.

George F. Kennan

Averell Harriman

George S. Patton

Dwight "Ike" Eisenhower

James Forrestal

Wilhelm Franz Canaris

EUROPE AND THE COMMUNISM

The Betrayal of Europe

At the Teheran Conference in November 1943 the three Allied leaders, Roosevelt, Churchill and Stalin reached a series of agreements on their joint strategy against Germany. This was the information that was made public, although privately discussed matters of another nature, relate not only to the war, but also the postwar, and more specifically the distribution of European frontiers. After the defeat of Germany in 1945 the new "big three" met again at the Yalta Conference.

The Russia of Josef Stalin emerged from Yalta as a great power, and as strange as it may seem, everything suggests that the United States and England, deliberately gave away Europe to Communism. Historians blamed the concessions that were made to Stalin on the state of physical weakness of the American President. FDR died on his desk a few weeks after the end of the war, victim of a disease as sudden and untimely as that suffered by Woodrow Wilson after the First World War.

The betrayal of Europe could respond to a plan drawn up by international bankers long before Tehran, and Hitler would be the necessary prelude to a Soviet Europe. Ambassador Dodd warned Hjalmar Schacht in the summer of 1936 that the war would mean the collapse of civilization, to which the banker replied that "[656]a general war would mean world-wide Communism and total economic collapse" It was a premonition, and a surprising statement coming from the banker of the Third Reich. The misery of war created in Europe the perfect ground for the Marxist utopia to flourish.

Only two factors prevented Russia from occupying almost all of continental Europe at the end of World War II. The first was the unexpected suicide attack from Germany to Russia in Operation Barbarossa. It was evident that Russia was preparing to invade the country and the German strategists decided that it would be better to

---

656 William Dodd, *Ambassador Dodd's Diares*, p. 345.

take the initiative and take Russia by surprise. Had the German invasion of Russia not occurred, the landing of Normandy might not have happened and the Allies would have only had to wait for Stalin's troops to "liberate" all of Europe.

The second factor was the genius of the greatest American military strategist of the Second World War, General George S. Patton. The Patton papers are one of the most important documents to understand the rise of communism as a superpower in the 20th century. Patton shone on all fronts; in Italy, North Africa and in France. His strategy was to attack without truce, preventing the enemy had time to reorganize their lines of defense. Often the general and his army advanced much faster than expected by the Allies, and their diaries and letters raise suspicions that certain forces within the Allies were trying to stop his advance. These doubts first arose timidly after the Normandy landings and later during the conquest of Germany, when he was about to cross the Meuse River:

> «[657]While at XII Corps, I found that, for unknown reasons, we had not been given our share of gas -140,000 gallons short. This may be an attempt to stop me in a backhanded manner, but I doubt it. »

The initial doubts progressively became certainties when he received orders from his superiors to stop his advance just as he was about to take up targets of high military value. In France he said "I have to battle for every yard but it is not the enemy who is trying to stop me, it is "They"". In Germany, before entering the Ruhr, he would write "At the moment I am being attacked on both flanks, but not by the Germans. But I may yet make my getaway." And again before the Rhine River "They did not want me to take Trier nor go to the Rhine, nor to cross the Moselle southwest of Koblenz, and now, if we don't cross the Rhine, we might be halted again[658]." Patton understood some

[657] Martin Blumenson, *The Patton Papers 1940-1945*, p. 530.

of the motives of his superiors in April 1945 when General Dwight Eisenhower -the future president of the United States- explained to him that the Allies had decided that it would be the Soviet Union and not the Anglo-American army that would take Berlin and Vienna:

> «[659]From a tactical point of view, it was highly inadvisable for the American Army to take Berlin, and he hoped political influence would not cause him to take the city. It had no tactical or strategical value, and would place upon American forces the burden of caring for thousands and thousands of Germans, displaced persons, Allied prisoners of war, etc. General Patton replied, "Ike, I don't see how you figure that one. We had better take Berlin and quick, and [then go eastward] on to the Oder [River]." »

Where had all the great American humanitarian like Hoover gone? The excuse must have been implausible for Patton, a man very cultivated and educated in military history from the times of Alexander the Great until his day. A few months later, in August 1945, Patton flew to Frankfurt where he dined privately with Eisenhower. His superior was honest and explained in detail the real reasons why the Allies constantly held him back:

> «[660]I learnt some interesting facts, particularly what impelled him to order us to halt short of the Moldau River when we could so easily have advanced that far… The same hold order of course applied also to the Ninth and First Armies.
>
> It seems that when Churchill, Roosevelt and Stalin were in Teheran in the fall of 1943, Churchill was convinced that even in the unlikely event of the Allies being able to make a landing on the

[658] Martin Blumenson, *The Patton Papers 1940-1945*, p.p. 531, 553 and 658.
[659] Martin Blumenson, *The Patton Papers 1940-1945*, p. 685.
[660] Martin Blumenson, *The Patton Papers 1940-1945*, p. 732.

Continent, they would never be able to cross the Rhine River, and he therefore persuaded FDR to go along with him in asking Stalin to have the Russian capture Berlin and Vienna and gave the Russians a line about a hundred miles west of Berlin. Later when we were going along well and could easily have taken Berlin, Churchill asked Ike to do it, and Ike replied by stating that it was Churchill's fault that the line had been established where it was. I believe this was a great mistake on his part because, had we taken the country to the Moldau River and Berlin, we would have saved a great deal of agricultural Germany and prevented what I believe historians will consider a horrid crime and great loss of prestige in letting the Russians take the two leading capitals of Europe.»

American Defense Secretary James Forrestal corroborated in his private notes the betrayal of Germany. In 1945 the head of the German General Staff, Alfred Jodl, tried to negotiate a separate peace with the Allies on the Eastern Front, excluding the Russians. That was the last hope to save Germany from the yoke of Communism. But Germany had been sentenced; Churchill and Roosevelt rejected peace attempts because they had already divided the European territory at the Tehran conference, some years before the war ended. The terms agreed with Stalin included the partition of Germany and probably of other territories, and Jodl was executed in Nuremberg.

> «After Hitler's death in 1945, Jodl made a final attempt to persuade the Allies to make a separate peace with Germany....The Russians were always terrified of this and they were equally terrified that we might push on through beyond Berlin and the Stettin-Trieste line. In 1945 Churchill wept when he was informed that we proposed to withdraw from territory we had conquered. The difficulty was that we were already committed by previous agreements arrived at between Mr. Roosevelt and Stalin, with Churchill the reluctant partner, to divide occupation responsibility on lines that suited the Russians. [661]»

On several occasions, Patton expressed his opinion that the United States had the responsibility to finish what it had begun, and that included liberating Europe from communist Russia, which he considered an even greater threat to the world than the dying Nazi Germany;

> «[662]Russia knows what she wants (domination of the world) and is laying her plans accordingly. We, on the other hand, and England and France to a lesser extent, don't know what we want. We get less than nothing as a result... Under the present system all that has been produced is a hot bed of anarchy and hopelessness which is an ideal germinating ground for Communism. »

The lack of American leadership in the London negotiations in 1944 became evident to diplomats such as George F. Kennan, a man who spent much of his career in Russia and who eventually became an American ambassador there:

> «[663]The British, who were well prepared, at once laid on the table a draft surrender instrument and detailed proposals for future zones of occupation in Germany… We Americans, of course, had no instruction on either subject –or, for the matter, on any other. We forwarded the British proposals to Washington and waited for a reaction.
>
> Several weeks went by. No word from Washington. Repeated telegraphic appeals for instructions went unanswered. Our British colleagues became restive, we ourselves acutely embarrassed.

---

[661] James Forrestal, *The Forrestal Diaries*, p. 496.
[662] Martin Blumenson, *The Patton Papers*, p. 768.
[663] George F. Kennan, *Memoirs*, 1925-1950, Little, Brown and Company, Toronto, 1967, p.p. 167-168.

On February 18 the Soviet delegate put forward his government's reaction to the British initiative. The Russians submitted their own alternative draft of the surrender terms. The British proposals on zones of occupation, on the other hand, accepted practically *in toto*. We Americans still had no instructions and could only inform Washington what the Russians had done.

We were, however, puzzled by the Russian action. We were not officially informed as to what had taken place at the Tehran Conference (Neither was the Department of State, for that matter)…

The British Proposals, as I was to learn many years later, had been drawn up some months before within the British government and had been made known to our military authorities at the time of the President's departure for Cairo in mid-November 1943. They had been discussed between the President and the American Joint Chiefs of Staff on the way to Cairo. They had been discussed at Cairo in the Combined (Anglo-American) Chiefs of Staff. Of all this, no one in the White House or in the Military establishment gave to us, or apparently even to the State Department, at any time the slightest inkling of official information, despite the fact that we were now supposed to negotiate with the British and Soviet governments on precisely this subject.

We in the American delegation in London continued therefore, during the remainder of February, to stumble along in total darkness… Then on March 8 came a most curious communication on the subject of zones of occupation… It consisted, to my present recollection, of a single sentence purporting to describe in rough geographic terms the zone of the United States proposed to occupy in northern Germany. »

Given the lack of answers Kennan traveled thousands of miles from London to Washington in a military plane only to speak personally with Roosevelt. The President listened to him, and somehow surprised and amused, he explained that indeed the only guideline of the American legation in the postwar period was no more than a diffuse dividing line on a map that he had sketched on the back of an envelope. Probably Treasury Secretary Henry Morgenthau would draw it to Roosevelt during a luncheon and he would have delivered it as it was to one of his aides.

Kennan ignored then the truth that Patton and Forrestal knew; Roosevelt's strategy was the same of the British, and it was as simple as complying with all Stalin's wishes. In a conversation in 1947 with former Secretary of State James F. Byrnes, Forrestal criticized Roosevelt's complacent attitude to all Stalin's claims:

> «[664]Lunched today with Jimmy Byrnes. We talked about Russia and American policy from 1943 on. He said one of the difficulties, he thought, after Roosevelt's death, was that Stalin did not like Truman and had told him (Byrnes) so. I made the observation that Mr. Truman was the first one who had ever said "no" to anything Stalin asked — that he had good reason for liking FDR because he got out of him the Yalta Agreement, anything he asked for during the war, and finally an opportunity to push Communist propaganda in the United States and throughout the world.»

From a purely strategic point of view, it is incomprehensible that the United States, which already had the world hegemony, would allow Russia to grow until it almost overshadowed the American empire. What motives guided Roosevelt and Churchill? The common denominator to understand both statesman was their debt to Colonel House, the agent of international bankers. Roosevelt knew that House could elevate presidents or depose them since the times of Woodrow Wilson. As for Churchill, House forced the United States to enter the First World War with the Lusitania incident, which was something that the British would have to repay in both wars.

---

[664] James Forrestal, *The Forrestal Diaries*, p. 318.

The group of international bankers opted for a Bolshevik Russia from the beginning: they financed the revolution, they were the first to reap benefits in the country and they took every opportunity to demand the recognition and international support of the communist regime. Schiff, Baruch, the Warburgs, Morgan, Rockefeller and Harriman exerted all their influence on the government to persuade the successive presidents to support the communist government in Russia. The Germans, who had marched thousands of kilometers into the Soviet soil and saw the atrocities that the communists committed with their own people, and wanted to avoid at all costs that Russia took Germany, which finally happened. They would accept a surrender in the West if they were saved from Bolshevik barbarism, but again in World War II there would be no honorable peace for Germany.

Pretty much against the consensus of the Allies to favor Stalin's Russia, General Patton repeatedly stressed the need for a strong Germany as the only way to contain the communist advance in Europe and throughout the world. His strategic vision proved as accurate on the battlefield as it was the postwar period.

> «[665]It is vitally necessary for us to build Germany up now as a buffer state against Russia. In fact, I am afraid we have waited too long. If we let Germany and the German people be completely disintegrated and starved, they will certainly fall for Communism and the fall of Germany for Communism will write the epitaph of Democracy in the United States.»

Pretty much against his opinion it prevailed that of prominent Zionists within the Roosevelt administration such as Bernard Baruch and Henry Morgenthau, who on numerous occasions expressed their predilection for Communism and their desire to see Germany annihilated.

---

665 Martin Blumenson, *The Patton Papers 1940-1945*, p. 766.

Much to his displeasure, Patton was part of the German occupation, where he was forced to implement some measures that were not to his liking, such as arresting citizens without trial, keep in prison any German who had ever been part of it of the Nazi party, to expel German citizens from their homes to be occupied by war refugees, or to send Germans to France to carry out forced labor. Patton considered that these tasks entrusted to the American occupation army were anti-democratic and shameful for the military:

> «[666]I attended the Military Government meeting at Frankfurt. There were a number of speeches by General Eisenhower and his various assistants, all of which were unrealistic and in every case the chief interest of the speaker was to say nothing which could be used against him. It is very patent that what the Military Government is trying to do is undemocratic and follows practically Gestapo methods. It is very probable, to me it seems evident, that the doctrines being executed or attempted are those promulgated by Morgenthau at the Quebec Conference which were not approved by either the Secretary of War [Forrestal] or the Secretary of State. It was the meeting in which Morgenthau and later Roosevelt, copying him, stated that Germany was to be [de-industrialized and demilitarized and] made into an agricultural state. It is patently impossible for Germany to be an agricultural state. First, because there Is not enough [food] in Germany for the country to feed itself on such a basis and, second, because if Germany has no purchasing power, we will not be able to sell our goods to her and, therefore, our markets will be very considerably restricted…
>
> I stated that in my opinion Germany was so completely blacked out that so far as military resistance was concerned, they were not a menace and that what we had to look out for was Russia. This caused considerable furore. »

[666] Martin Blumenson, *The Patton Papers 1940-1945*, p. 742.

In 1944, a year before the end of the war, Henry Morgenthau proposed to Roosevelt a plan for the dismemberment of Germany in various parts; the country would be divided into three large zones that would form two independent states and the third zone under international control. Other smaller territories, which included the most industrialized areas of Germany, would be delivered to France and Poland. The idea of splitting Germany and creating an "international zone" in its territory was not new at all. Colonel House had already proposed it at the Paris Conference of 1919!

> «[667]"A buffer state" he wrote "should be created [in Germany] for a period of five years, and then the League of Nations should decide whether the buffer state should exercise self-determination or should continue for another five-year period."»

The Morgenthau Plan, when it was known by the Germans, was used as a Nazi propaganda weapon that made the soldiers fight until the last breath to defend their country. Although the Morgenthau project was not carried out in all its terms, the final result did not differ much from the initial plan, with Germany divided into four occupation zones and subsequently into two, East Germany and West Germany. The eastern half was abandoned to its fate in the hands of communist Russia.

---

[667] Charles Seymour, *The Intimate Papers of Colonel House, vol. IV*, p. 383

HENRY MORGENTHAU JR. AND FRANKLIN DELANO ROOSEVELT

Secretary of the Treasury (1934-1945) with President of the United States (1933-1945).

Forrestal, a rather uncomfortable character within the postwar American administration, recalled how Roosevelt established his policy for occupied Germany, strongly influenced by Morgenthau:

> «[668]The Secretary of the Treasury [Henry Morgenthau, Jr.] came in with the President, with whom he had had lunch. The President said he had been talking with the Secretary of the Treasury on the general question of the control of Germany after the end of the war. He said that he had just heard about a paper prepared by the Army and that he was not at all satisfied with the severity of the measures proposed. He said that the Germans should have simply a subsistence level of food—as he put it, soup kitchens would be ample to sustain life—that otherwise they should be stripped clean and should not have a level of subsistence above the lowest level of the people they had conquered. »

Former Secretary of State James Byrnes told Forrestal at another meeting that the new secretary Cordell Hull was so disgusted with the criticism he received for his softness with the Germans, and by the appointment of Morgenthau as head of the committee for German affairs, that decided not to attend the Quebec Conference and he even thought about resigning from his position. He explained Forrestal that Morgenthau's policies had the backing of Roosevelt and Churchill.

The dividing lines of Europe were drawn in Tehran in 1943, before the Morgenthau Plan of 1945, and the spoils of Germany were distributed. The best proof of this is that the American military was forced to retreat over the conquered territory in order to fulfill the agreements previously made with Stalin.

Not only Morgenthau was in favor of the economic and civil annihilation of Germany. Bernard Baruch was one of the staunchest defenders of this policy, proposing his deindustrialization of the

---

[668] James Forrestal, *The Forrestal Diaries*, p.p. 10, 11.

country to turn it into an agricultural economy[669]. Patton referred to the policies of these Zionists as a "Semitic revenge of Morgenthau and Baruch[670]" on Germany, and criticized his influence on the administration of occupied Germany.

> «[671]I also wrote a letter to Secretary of War Mr. Stimson, on the question of pro-Jewish influence in the Military Government of Germany. I dared do this because when I was in Washington, he showed me a great deal of correspondence he had had with the Secretary of State and Mr. Morgenthau prior to the Quebec Conference. »

Patton admired the German people and its gallantry on the battlefield while he deeply despised the Nazis. The General disapproved of the abusive behavior that the American army was forced to exercise on the civilian population. Patton, like Forrestal, criticized the excessive influence of Zionism in the American government, and for that reason he was accused of taking extreme positions or even too close to the Germans. His opposition to Zionism and his temperamental character caused him to be accused of anti-Semitism in some media, and some of his statements and actions in the past were magnified. Patton was one of the first generals to know about the existence of concentration camps. When he liberated the Buchenwald camp[672], horrified by what he saw, he sent photos to Washington to document it and forced German civilians to visit them to understand the extent of Nazism. He

---

669 In his statement during the Kilgore Committee (*Elimination of German Resources* vol. I, p. 2-28) Baruch supported the same policies of other Zionist in the government; to dismantle the German industry, to turn it into a country of peasants, strengthen ties with the Soviet government, etc.

670 *Patton Papers*, p. 751.

671 *Patton Papers*, p. 745.

672 *Patton Papers*, p.p. 686, 709.

privately recorded in his diaries his concerns about the growing Zionist influence in the government:

> «[673]There is a very apparent Semitic influence in the press[674]. They are trying to do two things: First, implement Communism, and second, see that all business men of German ancestry and non-Jewish antecedents are thrown out of their jobs. They have utterly lost the Anglo Saxon conception of justice and feel that a man can be kicked out [of his house or job] because somebody else says he is a Nazi. They were evidently quite shocked when I told them I would kick nobody out without the successful proof of guilt…
>
> The attitude of the American people as evinced by the press and the radio is such [that] I am inclined to think I made a great mistake in serving them for nearly forty years, although I had a very good time doing it…
>
> The more I see of people I regret that I survived the war. »

Patton did not survive long after the war. Being close to his discharge, he died in a traffic accident while he was still serving in the American Army. The general could have reached the presidency thanks to his popularity among the American people, and his feats at the battlefront. George S. Patton was the most prominent figure among the Allies in World War II, and his untimely death allowed his superior, Commander in Chief of the Allies Dwight Eisenhower, to be the 34th President of the United States.

Patton and Forrestal held similar views on three important postwar issues such as the future of Germany, the partition of Palestine and the danger of Communism for world stability. These three closely related questions converged into one; the influence of certain elements of financial Zionism in the US administration. Both characters were

[673] *Patton Papers*, p. 766.

[674] He was probably speaking of the aforementioned Ochs Sulzberger (*New York Times*) and Meyer families (*Washington Post*).

relegated by the American government, Patton was reprimanded and Forrestal was dismissed during the Truman administration. An administration where domestic and foreign politics were carried out by sinister characters such as Morgenthau, Frankfurter, Baruch, Wise, House, the Harrimans and the Dulles.

Was the propagation of Communism all over Europe part of the plan? Did it really happen as a succession of unplanned events or was it agreed upon even before the war began? What about the foundation of the State of Israel on Palestinian land? Curtis B. Dall, a *Lehman Brothers* stockbroker and son-in-law of FDR gave a very similar testimony to that of Patton and Forrestal. Dall was working on a book about his former father-in-law Roosevelt, and a friend recommended him to visit George Earle, a retired politician who had information that would not leave him indifferent. Earle, attracted by the charisma of Roosevelt was one of the first *new-dealers* in 1933, and also one of the first to warn of the dangers of the rise of Nazism. During the First World War Earle was a decorated naval officer in charge of a submarine fighter ship. From 1933 to 1934 he was American Ambassador to Austria, from 1935 to 1939 Governor of Pennsylvania and from 1940 to 1942 Ambassador to Bulgaria. In 1943 he held the position of United States naval attaché in Turkey. George Earle explained to a stupefied Curtis Dall that at that time he received an unexpected visit from the head of German intelligence, Wilhelm Canaris, who made a peace proposal leaving Hitler behind[675]:

> «He [Governor Earle] arrived in Istanbul, Turkey, in the spring of 1943…
>
> The Governor told me that one morning there was a knock on his hotel room door. He opened it and there stood a broad shouldered, medium-sized man in civilian clothes, who requested an informal conference. He presented himself as Admiral Wilhelm Canaris, head of the German Secret Service [The *Abwehr*].

---

[675] Curtis B. Dall, *FDR. My Exploited Father-In-Law*, p.p. 148-151.

The gist of his conversation was there were many sensible German people who loved their Fatherland and who greatly disliked Adolph Hitler, feeling that Hitler was leading their nation down a destructive path. Admiral Canaris, continued, saying that the "unconditional surrender" policy recently announced by Roosevelt and Churchill at Casablanca was something the German generals could never swallow. He said, however, that if President Roosevelt would *merely indicate* he would accept a *honorable surrender* from the German Army, tendered to the American Forces, such an event could be arranged; that the real enemy of western civilization (the Soviets) could then be stopped. The German Army, if so directed, would move to the Eastern Front to protect the West against the crunching drive of the Soviet Army coming from the East, powered, fed and armed by Roosevelt's land-lease equipment[676]. The Soviets aimed to establish themselves as the supreme power in Europe and were obviously deceiving the American people, aided by their many high-level agents placed in the U.S.

The Governor remarked that at first he was staggered, but was extremely cautious in his reaction to the Admiral and to his startling proposal.

Then followed a meeting with the German Ambassador, Fritz [Franz?] von Papen, a devout Roman Catholic, and strongly anti-Hitler in his feelings.

A secret rendezvous was arranged late at night at a lonely site under some trees, five or six miles outside of Istanbul. There the Governor and the German Ambassador talked alone for several hours.

---

676 The "Lend-Lease" program of Roosevelt gave weapons, supplies, planes and ships to the Allies between 1941 and 1945, in exchange for setting military bases in their countries. Averell Harriman was in charge of delivering substantial amounts of military equipment to Russia that was never returned. This is another fact illustrative on how concerned were the Americans about pleasing Stalin.

The Governor told me that he soon became convinced of the sincerity manifested by the anti-Nazi Germans.

Becoming further informed concerning the hidden designs of the Soviet-led Russian Forces, he promptly dispatched a coded message to FDR in Washington, via the Diplomatic Pouch, reporting the whole matter.

He then waited for the requested prompt reply. *None came!*

Thirty days later, as agreed, Admiral Canaris phoned him and asked, "Have you any news?"

The Governor replied, "I am waiting for news, but have none today."

The Admiral said, "I am *very sorry*, indeed." Then there was silence….

Again, the Governor said, he dispatched an urgent coded message to the White House, pleading with President Franklin Roosevelt to explore what the anti-Nazis had to offer. Still *no reply* came back to him!

Governor Earle said he then prepared and sent a most urgent message to President Roosevelt in Washington, not only via the Diplomatic Pouch, but through Army-Navy channels this time to make *sure* the important message *got through* to FDR…

He continued, saying he felt sure that strong White House "influence" had the President's "ear", willing to see all the German people wiped out, regardless of how many American soldiers' lives would be sacrificed on the battlefield, on the sea, and in the air, to achieve that monstrous objective…

Finally, in effect, a purported answer did come. It was that he should take up with the Field Commander in Europe any proposals for a negotiated peace. Could any procedure have been more impractical or tragic? »

The disdain received by Admiral Canaris' failed armistice in 1943 was comparable to that received by Alfred Jodl in 1945, who was hanged by the Allies at the end of the war, after his desperate attempt to save Germany from the clutches of Stalin.

The story told by Earle is consistent with the story we know. Franz Wilhelm Canaris, the man who since 1935 headed the *Abwehr*, the intelligence and counterintelligence office of Germany, would never allow a communist Germany. Canaris ordered the execution of the Spartacists Rosa Luxemburg and Karl Liebknecht. Canaris, with the certainty that the Allies had turned his back on Germany in 1943, still participated in the last desperate attempt to kill Adolf Hitler, the bombing of Claus von Stauffenberg in 1944, in the so-called "Operation Valkyrie". The attack failed and von Stauffenberg, Canaris and other Germans who tried to kill Hitler were shot or hanged. Canaris himself was not allowed a quick and painless death. He was hanged with an iron collar, suffering agonizingly for almost half an hour before dying.

The American refusal to grant an honorable peace to Germany, as happened in the previous war, was also consistent with the policy of total annihilation proposed on numerous occasions by Morgenthau and Baruch. Roosevelt's Zionist advisors, who possibly were the same "influence" that Earle alludes to, had shown a predilection for the Soviet Union. Would their support go so far as to deliver Europe to Stalin on a silver tray? The betrayal of Europe is incomprehensible if it is only sustained on Roosevelt's political myopia. If the war had ended in 1943 and not in 1945, millions of lives would have been saved, many of them were American. Not only on the battlefield, but also many Jews would have saved their lives in the concentration camps, which were particularly active towards the end of the war. Dall lamented:

> «Only the Lord knows how many lives could have been saved if FDR had had the desire and the ability to have cabled, "George, tell them, yes; send details. FDR."»

Another disturbing conclusion is that the Americans unnecessarily prolonged the war in the same way as they did before with the Belgian Commission and the Russian Revolution.

The German attempts to sign a peace with his enemies were numerous. The first arrived as early as 1941. The declaration of war of the Allies to Germany two years before took Hitler by surprise, and he later learned that Stalin was preparing to invade Germany, repeating the German nightmare of the First World War fight in two fronts. Adolf Hitler sent his most trusted man, Rudolf Hess, on a desperate flight to Scotland with the sole purpose of contacting the Duke of Hamilton to negotiate a peace with Britain. Both the British and the Germans publicly reported that Hess's diplomatic mission was unknown to Hitler and it lacked any consistency, because the only possible choice for both sides. Germany would never formally recognize having initiated a peace mission, as it would sink the morale of his army, and Churchill would find it very embarrassing to explain to a country besieged by bombings that he was not willing to negotiate peace with Germany, and that the war I had to continue for several more years. In the armistice of Rudolf Hess, Germany accepted to renounce to its conquests on the Eastern front restoring practically all of the occupied territories with the exception of Alsace, Lorraine and Luxembourg[677]. Hess's pacification attempt of 1941 was evidently ignored by the Allies, and so were discarded those of Eberhard Oppenheim in 1942, Canaris in 1943 and Jodl in 1945. Needless to say, the Allied did not provide any support either for von Stauffenberg failed attempt to assassinate Hitler in 1944. Rudolf Hess was taken prisoner immediately, and after the Nuremberg trials he was confined as the only prisoner in the prison of Spandau, a

---

[677] Mark Weber, *The Inside Story of the Hess Flight*, Institute for Historical Review, The Journal of Historical Review, Atumn of 1982 (Vol. 3, No. 3), p. 291.
Mark Weber, *The Legacy of Rudolf Hess*, Institute for Historical Review, The Journal of Historical Review, Jan.-Feb. 1993 (Vol. 13, No. 1), p.p. 20-23.
Jan Friedmann and Klaus Wiegrefe, Der Spiegel, May 30, 2011, *Document Suggests Hitler Knew of Hess' British Flight Plans*.

place designed to accommodate up to six hundred occupants. Hess spent almost half his life in total isolation -46 years- and the guards referred to him as "Prisoner No. 7". Hess committed suicide there at age 93. What did he knew that made him so dangerous to the Allies?

Hess, Oppenheimer, Canaris, von Stauffenberg and Jodl tried to end the war, and some of them also wanted to end Nazism. All of them were abandoned by the Allies and had a tragic end. Why? Because the plan from the beginning was to deliver Europe to Communism. Some senior officials within the administration and the American military knew the plan. Curtis Dall, after reading George Earle's private correspondence, stated:

> «[678]General Patton knew the score but he died "early." Secretary James Forrestal knew the score, and he also died "early". General Douglas MacArthur certainly knew the score. Harry Truman, apparently did not; perhaps he did not want to know it.
>
> A copy of his letter of February 28, 1947, to Governor Earle, appearing at the end of this chapter with some other letters, could have been better signed "Alice-in-Wonderland", than by a President of the United States. »

The peace of World War II was not forged in a single conference as happened in the previous war, but in a series of conferences and meetings, during the war and at the end of the war, although its terms were even more tragic than those of Paris. Wilson failed in the peace of 1919, but Roosevelt did not even try. He simply agreed to everything Stalin asked.

Prominent experts in Russian political affairs within the American administration, including the ambassadors Kennan and Harriman, were forced to recognize the dangers of Communism from 1945 on, changing their policies of collaboration with the Soviet Union to one of containment. What history presented as an involuntary political myopia

---

[678] Curtis B. Dall, *FDR. My Exploited Father-In-Law*, p. 153.

of the United States, was the calculated decision of Roosevelt, strongly influenced by some obscure characters embedded within his administration. The reasons, only they knew: The political desire to develop an Anglo-American world supremacy, the economic interest of making Europe a pan-Soviet colony or the benefits reaped by the military industrial complex. Whatever the reason, the creation of the Soviet Union gave rise to the greatest war-like escalation known in the world and to the fifty years of greatest world tension that we remember, the Cold War.

The Banking Revolutions

Following the trail of capital it is possible to find the origin of revolutions. The banking fraternity influenced during the 20th century in the election of presidents, delivered victories and defeats in the battlefield and established dictatorships in the East and the West, promoting opposing regimes such as Fascism and Communism. There is no contradiction in this: Political logic encompasses ideological, social and territorial components, while the economic logic is as simple as maximizing profits. In the last century, financial logic prevailed over political logic.

Take the *Kuhn & Loeb & Co.* group as an example. In the First World War Jacob Schiff in the United States economically asphyxiated the Russian Empire and promoted Bolshevism among Russian prisoners. Max Warburg in Germany worked towards the same end, collaborating with Helphand and the German Ministry of Foreign Affairs. The two bankers weakened the Entente, lengthened the conflict for several years and caused the loss of many lives. And when the communist victory came, the bankers reaped benefits. Max and Felix Warburg were also involved with the Kaiser's spies through *HAPAG*, although it would be difficult to say if they helped Germany, because they rather landed the country a mortal blow as America entered the war.

Apparently on the opposite side, his brother Paul Warburg was fighting against the Germans, as an advisor to Wilson, a Director in the Federal Reserve and the War Finance Corporation. Another partner of *Kuhn & Loeb*, Otto Kahn, was also fanning the flames against his native country. Germany was the country of origin Kahn himself and other partners of *Kuhn & Loeb* as the Warburg, Schiff, Kuhn, Wolff and Loeb, but that did not seem to cause him any moral conflicts[679]:

> «A subsequent condemnation of "the outlaw among nations" delivered at a Red Cross mass meeting at the Hippodrome Theatre in New York, was heavy with invective and blazing with anger. He called the Germans the architects of war, murderers, perfidious plotters, violators of international law, perpetrators of "crime heaped upon crime in hideous defiance of the laws of God and man."»

Kahn was an example of economic logic in practice, flying the flags of Socialism and Fascism simultaneously. International bankers were pleased with totalitarianisms as the most profitable forms of government to secure their interests:

> «[680]He [Kahn] actually spoke out in praise of certain aspects of Socialist doctrine, which he had absorbed from the London Fabians[681] thirty years before:
>
> "Not a little [in Socialism] is high and noble; some things too are achievable and desirable. And to the extent that Socialism is an antidote to and a check upon excessive individualism... it is a force distinctly for good." »

---

679 Mary Jane Matz, *The Many Lives of Otto Kahn*, p. 182.

680 Mary Jane Matz, *The Many Lives of Otto Kahn*, p. 231.

681 The goal of the Fabian Society, founded in London in 1884, was the advance ot the Marxist theses, silently and gradually, not by means of a revolution. It's coat of arms was a wolf in sheep's clothing.

To the same extent, Kahn had a favorable view on fascism. He affirmed about his meeting with the *duce*, Benito Mussolini:

> «"I have never seen a government work with the intensity of application which characterizes the present Ministry of Italy, from Mussolini down," he said. "[He is] a fascinating, wholly sincere and immensely forceful personality."»

Otto Kahn spared no praise for Mussolini publicly or privately, and in a letter of 1923 he alluded to a new meeting:

> «[682]"I had a long talk with Mussolini and was again profoundly impressed by the greatness and irresistible personality of that wonderful man."»

Several Jewish bankers also supported Hitler from his beginnings in politics. Ambassador Dodd noted in his diaries his meeting with George Solmssen:

> «[683]Bank Director Solmssen of the great Disconto Gesellschaft spent a half hour with me. He reviewed the Nazi uprising of last spring with approval. It was necessary, he indicated. »

But shortly before the war the banker seemed less convinced of the suitability of the Nazis to direct the destiny of Germany:

> «[684]Dr. George Solmssen, long time president of the Deutsche Bank-Disconto Gesellschaft and one of the rich Jews of Germany, called a second time. He had told me a good deal of his sad story a

---

[682] This citation and the former on in Mary Jane Matz, *The Many Lives of Otto Kahn*, p. 250.
[683] William E. Dodd, *Diaries of Ambassador Dodd*, p. 50.
[684] William E. Dodd, *Diaries of Ambassador Dodd*, p. 183.

year ago, soon after my Chamber of Commerce address He now seems somewhat reconciled to the Hitler regime and wishes to spend a month in New York, Chicago and Washington Since he knows the European financial situation so well, I gave him letters of introduction to Henry Morgenthau, Jr., and Daniel Roper. I suspect his real mission is to pacify the American Jews, as he said he was having conferences with Dr. Schacht. He will find Morgenthau, father and son, most impatient with the German regime. »

Deutsche Bank and *Disconto-Gesellschaft*, the banks leading the German espionage during the first war, were later heralds of the Nazi revolution. The bank chaired by Solmssen made the first contribution to the trust of the Keppler Circle *before* the arrival of Hitler to power. And Solmssen was not the only Jewish-German banker to join the Nazi cause. Eberhard von Oppenheim of *Sal. Oppenheimer & Cie.* Also made a generous personal contribution:

«[685]My wife and family attended a party of Baron Eberhard von Oppenheim who is a Jew still living in style near us. Many Nazi Germans were present. It is reported that Oppenheim has given the Nazi Party 200,000 marks and has been given a special Party dispensation which declared him as Aryan. »

Another notable case is that of Max Warburg. The biography of the Warburgs published by Ron Chernow, which cannot be classified as a critical work in excess, points out his ambivalence towards Nazism. In 1933, for example, Max expressed a naive opinion to his nephew James Paul about the Nazi regime[686]:

---

685 William E. Dodd, *Diaries of Ambassador Dodd*, p. 73.

686 Ron Chernow, *The Warburgs*, p. 371.

> «It is a pity that this movement, which has so much good in it, is encumbered by so much rubbish and that the anti-Semitism makes it impossible to line up in formation with this movement". »

Max deceived himself by only seeing the economic advantages of a fascist regime and underestimated the dangers for his people. Max, concludes his biographer, believed that Schacht could provide him and some of his Jewish friends with political protection, and so it was for a time:

> «[687]Being ignorant of financial matters, Hitler granted Schacht unusual autonomy in Nazi officialdom… As his policies lift Germany from Depression, Schacht enjoyed immunity from party criticism. In May 1933, he shielded the bankers' trade association from party meddling and it confirmed Max and other Jews as board members.
>
> The most startling proof of Schacht's freedom from party structures was seen in the Reich Loan Consortium, the august bank syndicate that marketed German government issues. Of fifty member banks when the Nazis seized power, a third were Jewish, and Schacht resisted the party's efforts to expel some of them. Gradually almost all Jewish banks were pruned and only three managed to stay until 1938, including M.M. Warburg & Co. »

Max depended on Schacht to ensure his own personal safety, and his bank, *M.M. Warburg & Co*, depended on the *Reichsbank*, which then controlled despotically the supply of foreign currency. Max's relationship with Schacht, as Chernow explains, "gave him access to the high-level Nazi bureaucracy, a class that very few Jews enjoyed[688]". This position of privilege allowed the family bank to keep on business giving profits even in such a turbulent years as 1936 and 1938.

---

[687] Ron Chernow, *The Warburgs*, p. 378.

[688] Ron Chernow, *The Warburgs*, p. 378.

Schacht's help was not disinterested and he was not a lover of the Jewish people, he owed a favor to Max. In 1918 Max became part of the Central Committee of the *Reichsbank*, and when Schacht was proposed to head the central bank in 1933 the support of Germany's most powerful industrialist and banker, Max, was decisive[689]. Max and Schacht undertook a dangerous journey together financing Hitler's political campaign, Max through *I.G. Farben* and Schacht through the Keppler Circle, where Max was also present:

> «[690]Keppler circle provided a bridge between the business world and the Nazis… Few Jewish businessmen had better access to the Keppler circle than the Warburgs… the Warburg partners held 108 seats on corporate boards, reflecting the close ties between German banks and industry. As they were expelled from boards and lost customers through subtle nazi pressures, the Warburgs turned to the Keppler Circle.»

On the eve of the arrival of the Nazis to power Max and his partners of *M.M. Warburg & Co.* enjoyed unparalleled power in Germany, leading the German *Money Trust.* The man who stood as the representative of the Jewish people in Germany, turned out to be one of the main springs of Nazism. Max, founder and director of the German Jewish Aid Society, spoke of himself as a "God of the Jews"[691], but like other patriarchs such as Wise, Schiff or the Rothschilds he was never chosen by his people, but rather he bought his political influence by financing foundations, interest groups and academic institutions of the Jewish world.

Stephen S. Wise explained in a letter to Albert Einstein "[692]When I saw Brandeis he told me that President [Roosevelt] would have acted in

---

[689] Ron Chernow, *The Warburgs*, p.p. 377 and 218.

[690] Ron Chernow, *The Warburgs*, p.p. 378-379.

[691] Ron Chernow, *The Warburgs*, p. 441.

[692] Ron Chernow, *The Warburgs*, p. 387.

March 1933 had it not been for the Warburg family." The Warburg had their own economic interests in Germany intertwined with the Nazi government, and they expected some distinction within the regime. Years later it would be too late to act.

The friction between the Zionist group headed by Wise and that of the Jewish-German bankers led by the Warburgs was frequent, although their objectives were broadly similar. The goal of the Zionists was the founding of the State of Israel and the bankers paid more attention to the profits. The clearest example where both interests converged was the *Haavara* or "Transfer Agreements" of 1933. It was a pact between the Nazi government and the Jewish Agency that allowed the Jewish settlers who wanted to emigrate to Palestine -and only to Palestine, much to Zionist rejoicing- they could exchange their German marks for Palestinian pounds, provided that the money was used only for the purchase of German goods, machinery, fertilizers and the like. At that time it was practically impossible for any German to change German marks for any foreign currency. The anti natural deal between Zionists and Nazis allowed to escape to 52,000 Jews of Germany, something worth recognizing. The operation worked exclusively through the bank of Max, the new Moses of the Jewish people[693]:

> «To supervise the transfer agreement, German Jews set up Palestine Trust Company (Paltreu), and M.M. Warburg & Co. acted as conduit for three fourths of the money. The Palestinian end was handled by the Anglo-Palestine Bank, later called Bank Leumi. Considerable sums of money flowed through this pipeline –almost 140 million reichsmarks by the outbreak of the World War II –and it provided steady business for the Warburg bank in a grim season. »

The arrival of the Nazis to power caused Max Warburg to be gradually removed from the leadership of *HAPAG*, *I.G. Farben* and

---

693 Ron Chernow, *The Warburgs*, this quote and previous info, p.p. 400-401.

other companies, as it happened to Jews in such positions. He was able to leave the country to join his family in the United States.

The last case is that of *A.E.G.*, the company founded and directed by the Rathenau family, a company of purely Jewish capital that made one of the greatest economic contributions to Hitler's electoral campaign. None of these Jews seemed to have read the anti-Semitic theses of Hitler's *Mein Kampf*, published eight long years before he came to power.

But let's leave aside the Jewish-German bankers to observe the case of the Anglo-Saxon Protestant bankers, no less responsible in the rise of totalitarianism of the twentieth century. The partners of *J.P. Morgan & Co.* befriended fascists and communists. Boyce Thompson sponsored the Red Cross mission to Petrograd, also contributing one million dollars "for the purpose of spreading their doctrine in Germany and Austria."

Lamont, who was also involved in the rise of the Bolsheviks, secured a $ 100 million loan to Mussolini in 1926[694]. This is how Lamont referred to the dictator:

> «I leave it to the American people to judge from the facts. Italy, led by Mussolini, has succeeded in accomplishing feats which no other nation of Europe has been able to do[695]. »

His admiration was such that he even opened a propaganda office in New York to improve the public image of the *duce*[696]. His preeminence in the rise of fascism was twofold, as he calculated the German reparations after the first war and then handed over a fortune to Mussolini. All decisions made in Germany during the interwar period, including the peace of Paris, the Dawes and Young plans, and

---

694 New York Times, October 15, 2006, *The American Lamonts*.

695 Mary Jane Matz, *The Many Lives of Otto Kahn*, p. 250.

696 Ron Chernow, *The House of Morgan*, illustration 38 footnote.

the cartelization of their economy were attributable, in one way or another, to members of *J.P. Morgan & Co.*

The Harriman was another case of divided loyalty like that of the Warburgs. Averell Harriman was the American capitalist who did most business with Lenin and Stalin, thanks to his privileged position as ambassador to Russia. Meanwhile, his brother Roland partnered with Roosevelt in the postwar period to speculate with the German hyperinflation and hid the money from Nazis like Fritz Thyssen. The *Standard Oil* group, to which the Harrimans belonged, made incalculable technological and economic contributions to the Nazi regime, for the most part through *I.G. Farben.*

This story of international bankers in the twentieth century proves that Financial Capitalism does not know words such as loyalty, ideology, race or homeland. War, misery and human suffering are aspects that cannot be quantified in their economic terms, and thus are not taken in consideration. Financial Capitalism –or international banking, if this term is preferred- promoted any centralized economic system as the best means of maximizing profits. The Nazi four-year plans were not so different for their purposes from the Communism five-year plans. Before the Second World War it was usual to identify Fascism with other Socialist ideologies. Adolf Hitler was actually the leader of the National German *Socialist Workers* Party, a fact that points to his close ideological link with the great Marxist family. In the case of Benito Mussolini, the son of a second class radical socialist, the bond is even more evident[697]. Mussolini became active very early in the Italian Socialist Party, becoming part of the leadership before founding his National Fascist Party. The name chosen for his new political formation was also socialist in inspiration, and came from the Sicilian Fascios, a agrarian labor union that caused violent insurrections in Italy at the end of the 19th century, until it was stifled by executing its

---

[697] His father gave him the name of Benito Amilcare Andrea, in honor to Mexican President Benito Juarez and Italian socialists Andrea Costa and Amilcare Cipriani.

leaders. Finally, when the Allies occupied a part of Italy, he renamed it as the Italian *Social* Republic.

The good relations between communists and fascists became also evident in the Ribbentrop-Molotov non-aggression Pact of 1939, signed shortly before the war in which Hitler and Stalin divided Poland. The military confrontation between the two countries was not caused by ideological differences but to a simple question of necessity and opportunity. The main difference between the two totalitarian ideologies is that Communism lacks any nationalist component, a central element in Fascism, only because Communism aspires to be a universal movement, not a national one. Instead of the militaristic stance of Fascism, Communism used propaganda and political subversion as the most successful way to spread throughout the world. And Roosevelt's New Deal, which has been usually presented as the solution to the Great Depression, was not so different from Fascism either. It was only a small-scale replica of Italian and German policies, as Herbert Hoover pointed out in his memoirs.

Paraphrasing Professor Sutton, in spite of his humanistic and philanthropic pretensions, Socialism in its multiple aspects - Communism, Fascism, National Socialism or New Deal- have been ideologies promoted by Financial Capitalism throughout the world as the best instrument at its service. The international bankers knew well how to exploit the utopian promises for their own profit. Contrary to the spirit of *laissez-faire* and freedom imbued in the foundations of the United States, all these ideologies share the common Socialist idea of promoting a big government meddling in all economic and social aspects of life. All these ideologies restricted the civil liberties and oppressed the people, while favored a small group of companies an promoted militarism and foreign aggression. Yet no textbook will explain that these three ideologies are not ideologically confronted, but are instead different branches from the same tree of Socialim.

EPILOGUE: THE OTHER HISTORY

My first work published in Spanish, *The Masonic Revolutions*, began in 1776, a year of great revolutions. That year Freemasons such as Benjamin Franklin or George Washington led the United States towards independence. That year a professor from Ingolstadt named Adam Weishaupt founded the Bavarian Illuminati. And a few years later, in 1789, an army of freemasons led by the Duke of Orleans, Mirabeau, Lafayette and the Bonaparte brothers initiated a revolution that would shake the foundations of France. When revolutionaries separated Louis XVI's head from his shoulders, a brother freemason, the fratricidal struggle began. One by one they were killed by the fire they had started: Firstly his cousin the Duke of Orleans and then his peers in the revolution, Marat, Fauchet, Danton and Robespierre.

In 1776 another quite distinct revolution was taking place in England, an economic and industrial one. That year an economist named Adam Smith published his book *The Wealth of Nations*, where he argued that the personal interest and the desire of each individual to prosper are the true driving forces of economy and progress. Free competition in markets, *laissez-faire*, prevented sellers from forming communities of interests and monopolies to manipulate the market, allowing buyers to obtain better products at a better price. Excessive regulation discouraged entrepreneurs, reduced competition and favored undesirable monopolies. Smith left for the State only functions of public interest such as infrastructure, education or medical care. The work of Adam Smith led to the birth of capitalism, the socioeconomic system that had its heyday during the nineteenth century. It was an eminently industrial system, based on capital and the means of production.

In the 20th century, as I pointed out at the beginning of this book, the Golden Age of investment banking began, the time of the merchant bankers. Capitalism gave way to a new economic system that some authors have called *Financial Capitalism.* Although their names are similar, these are two very different economic systems. Capitalism is a model of productive economy, based on the creation of goods and the provision of services. On the contrary, credit is the cornerstone of the system in Financial Capitalism, and interest rates, currency, permanent inflation and speculation on the value of goods are central elements. It is a predatory model, where the main economic agents do not seek to maximize their profits by creating wealth, but its object is rather to deprive others of it. The credit of the economy caused that the great industries of the West to be at the mercy of the increasingly influential and powerful investment bankers, and the productive economy became subordinated to the high finance.

The Rothschilds initiated this new economic system by extending their family banking model throughout Europe, and opening the way to other large Jewish houses of international banking. *Kuhn & Loeb, Lehman Brothers, Goldman Sachs, Sal. Oppenheimer & Co., Lazard Freres*, and *Dillon & Read & Co.* were some pieces of this system. Some other houses were added to the list by men known by the surnames Warburg, Seligman, Speyer or Guggenheim. Several of these firms ended up disappearing from the banking landscape, some involving a large public scandal such as *Creditanstalt*, *L.F. Rothschild* or *Lehman Brothers*. Others, like *Goldman Sachs*, have soared. As it has been proven in this work, money and power change their names, but seldom changes hands.

Along came the Anglo-Saxon Protestant houses: In the United States the golden age of Financial Capitalism took place when J.P. Morgan disembarked in the country. By landing blow after blow on the economy the legendary corsair was able to change the direction of the country, imposing his own rule. The Morgans amassed their fortune by working hand in hand with the families of Frankfurt, and they ended up eclipsing the German Jews after enjoying several decades of a monopoly over American debt. The hand of John Pierpont Morgan was behind the formation of most of the American trusts existing today.

The last man to arrive was another great monopolist named John D. Rockefeller. He was not a banker from the cradle, but pedigree is not necessary when you have enough money to acquire several of the largest banks in the country.

The three banking houses, Rothschild, Morgan and Rockefeller shared a creed; Wealth could not be obtained by competing in equal conditions in a free market. The absence of rivals, monopolies, political influence and state money gave benefits that other businessmen could only dream of. Putting into practice this creed they undertook a common project to form the largest monopoly ever known, that of the issuance of the American dollar. The dollar is the currency on which the entire world economy, is based, the currency of international transactions, the denomination with which the price of gold or oil is fixed. The bankers tried to control the American money supply with the *First Bank* of Alexander Hamilton, and then with the *Second Bank* of Nicholas Biddle. Both institutions succumbed to the pressure of the people and to the determination of founding fathers of the country like Jefferson, Madison and Jackson. But the bankers were patient and astute. They had time on their side and a flock of complacent politicians.

In 1910 the banking elite of New York traveled to a private resort on Jekyll Island, where they planned the law that would allow them to set up a third and final central bank. The soul of the group was Henry P. Davison, who came on behalf of the legendary J.P. Morgan. He was accompanied by Senator Nelson Aldrich and Frank Vanderlip, respectively the son-in-law and the richest man's partner on the planet, John D. Rockefeller. And finally there was Paul Warburg, giving voice to the interests of Frankfurt. These men, agents of the greatest economic powers of the West, outlined a plan that Colonel House executed perfectly.

Edward House, a political adviser and discreet agent of the international financiers in the Democratic Party, sponsored Wilson before the banking elite and became his closest confidant. He was guiding the President along the path marked by bankers until in 1913 the Federal Reserve Law culminated the goals pursued by international financiers for more than two centuries. Paul Warburg, the great public defender of a centralized banking model, was appointed Vice-Governor of the institution, and Benjamin Strong, a Morgan partner, was elected Governor. On his first board of governors were William McAdoo, Wilson's son-in-law, and Frederick Delano, Roosevelt's uncle.

By the beginning of the twentieth century *merchant bankers* dominated banking, industry and politics in the United States, once a prosperous and free nation. Financial capitalism took control over the industry and every financial panic, every crisis, reinforced its dominant role in the economic and political life of the United States. And so began the decline of the American dream.

The history of our time is that of the United States, the last great empire. Its economy flourished during the First World War, a conflict of proportions never seen before, surpassing all the old disputes of the Prussian, French, British and Russian empires. The Federal Reserve and the newly created income tax financed its military campaign and allowed extending loans to countries in conflict, extending the European tragedy. The change from the gold standard to a fiduciary currency allowed the nations to grow its debt indefinitely and turned money into an inexhaustible resource, and so the war also extended in time indefinitely. With one hand the United States sold ammunition to the countries of the Entente, and with the other they sold food to Germany. Bankers and ammunition manufacturers set in motion the Comission for Relief in Belgium to keep an exhausted Germany fighting on the front, and thus be able to continue their lucrative business. Their success was so resounding that they decided to consolidate that humanitarian system by founding the International Red Cross with the money of the American people. Directed by members of Wall Street, and far from serving the noble purpose for which it was intended, the Red Cross became an ideal instrument to forward their international economic and political agenda. Operations such as the Petrograd mission of 1917, in which Morgan bankers delivered no less than a million dollars to the Bolsheviks, are a good example.

The war brought consequences for the old Russian Empire, which ended up falling apart from within. In 1905 Schiff and Wise cracked the government of the Tsars by planting the seed of Bolshevism, and in 1917 the Germans culminated the revolution that the Americans initiated. The money of the Kaiser and the machinations of Israel Helphand and Max Warburg allowed the strikes to spread throughout Russia. Even before the Bolsheviks won the war for control of the country, Schiff, Baruch, the Harrimans and the Warburgs demanded international recognition of the new regime. Wilson did not seem concerned about the fall of his ally Nicholas II, but rather congratulated himself publicly.

Socialism turned out to be the most successful formula of economic colonialism. The bankers managed to get the proletariat to fight their revolution for them and to shackle themselves, believing that so they were more free and equal. Like the French Jacobins, the Russian Bolsheviks were not impoverished sans-culottes but educated bourgeois. The "Communist Manifesto" of Lenin meant the social regression to a regime of servitude based on a tax system more typical of a feudal regime than of a modern day country (points 1, 2, 3 and 4). It also satisfied the most unspeakable desires of an investment banker; "The centralization of credit in the State through a national bank with state capital and monopoly regime (point 5)".

During the war the banks of New York placed their people in key positions in the American government. *J.P. Morgan, Kuhn & Loeb*, the *Chase Bank* or the *City Bank of New York* were the Entente's financial agents, putting their men at the forefront of intelligence services, diplomacy, military purchases and in the humanitarian apparatus. Max Warburg performed the same tasks on the enemy side, in the Central Powers. Men such as the Warburgs and Colonel House played a triple game with the governments of the United States, Germany and Great Britain, always in their own interests. The new Copernican reality of the twentieth century is that high finance did not orbit around the heads of state, but that the heads of state were forced to seek the favor of high finance to be elected and survive in politics. The collapse of Russia, the operations of *HAPAG* in America and the Commission for Relief in Belgium were sold to the Kaiser as great victories of the Warburgs, he but ignored that the astute Colonel House planned to attract the United States into war based on the errors of his spies and the sinking of the ship *RMS Lusitania*. The Germans and the Americans believed that the Frankfurt bankers were their best card for victory, but both were deceived. The bankers won and the countries at war lost.

Wilson was re-elected thanks to his promise to keep the country out of the war but succumbed to the influence of the small Texas Colonel. The President put Bernard Baruch, a Wall Street broker in charge of the military industries, was allowed to freely make purchases as never seen before in history. Baruch surrounded himself with speculators like himself, with one foot in the arms industry and another in public administration. Wilson was awarded the Nobel Peace Prize for the United States entering in the war and today he is regarded as one of the greatest American statesmen, but we know that neither the Federal Reserve, nor the entry into the war, the League of Nations, not even the peace plan for Paris, his "fourteen points of Wilson", were merits of Wilson. Maybe Colonel House should have been awarded the Nobel instead.

The war left behind millions of dead and wounded. In Paris in 1919 the "big four" of the Entente met to establish more than peace; a *new world order*. But the full weight of the negotiations fell on the shoulders of Colonel House. A Wilson in his lowest hours delegated his powers to him, as he always did. So did Lloyd George, in eternal debt to him for the Lusitania incident. Clemenceau came out alive from Paris just miraculously, and nobody paid too much attention to the distraught Prime Minister Orlando. House and his entourage of bankers were the silent protagonists of Paris, and as advisers, they drafted the borders of several continents, established reparations and signed the humiliation that would push Germany, Japan and Italy to the next war.

The First World War accomplished many of the objectives set by the banking fraternity to achieve its world supremacy. Parallel to the Paris conference new centers of influence were set up so that high finance could dictate the Anglo-Saxon political lines of thought, such as the *Council of Foreign Relations*, a non-partisan institution that functions as an extension of the *Rockefeller Foundation*. However, some projects such as the League of Nations did not obtain the expected popular support.

The peace agreements of 1919 created innumerable foci of conflict in the world that still remain one century later; Africa, the Balkans and the Middle East are the best examples. His policies also strengthened the communist presence in the world. This was the legacy of Wilson and the international bankers. What has often been explained as a series of random events, or a confluence of clumsiness by statesmen in Paris, was neither one nor the other. The United States was the most benefited country in terms of economy and influence. They entered the conflict when both sides were exhausted and became reinforced as the first world power, laureate as champions of freedom. As it happened in the next war. As hinted by Ludendorff, it is possible that the Anglo-American establishment, concerned about the rise of Russia and Prussia, was behind the strange succession of events that began with the assassination of the Austro-Hungarian heir in Sarajevo. France and England won a pyrrhic victory at the cost of many lives and a continent in ruins. The Middle East was promised a united Arabia for its military support, but it was broken into several states in permanent conflict. The disintegration of the Ottoman Empire was a necessary step for the creation of the State of Israel, which would hardly have existed with a united Arab world after the Peace of 1919. The Zionist delegation of Stephen Wise came out exultant from Paris, after achieving the British mandate on Palestine and the first Jewish colonies. These were founded with money from the Rothschilds and the taxes from the Americans.

The architects of the war realized that success could be ephemeral and they thought that a second conflict would be indispensable to consolidate their achievements and obtain new revenues. The central banks of the West, which allowed the almost infinite expansion of the money supply during the war, reduced it at the end of the war, in order to recover the total value of the money lent. The resulting brutal monetary contraction caused the Great Depression and created the perfect ecosystem for totalitarian regimes such as Communism, Fascism, and to a lesser extent the American "New Deal" to flourish.

After the peace of Paris a new war just a matter of time. The German General Staff, even before signing the terms of their surrender, was working for the next war. Neither France, nor England nor the United States moved a finger to avoid the rearmament that began in the Weimar Republic, long before the Nazis even existed. The indignity with which Germany was treated made General Erich Ludendorff, unable to overcome the defeat, and he was able to gather around him a large group of industrialists with the purpose of secretly breaching the provisions established in Paris to restore to Germany its greatness. The war did not end in 1918 in Paris for the General Staff and the German industrialists. The country never abandoned its military economy and all its productive efforts were directed towards rearmament and reducing the dependence on materials considered strategic by the General Staff. Neither the artificial hyperinflation of 1923, nor the staged bankruptcy of the country stopped the plans of the General Staff, but rather accelerated those.

The New York banks led by the Morgan group designed tailor-made plans for the payment of the debt. It was a pyramid system whose fundamental idea was to make the Americans issue new loans that would allow the repayment of the previous debt. It was an incomprehensible system from the perspective of the Allies and the Germans, but for the international bankers, the promoters of this system, its benefits were expressed in terms of interests, commissions and political influence. The Dawes and Young plans earned the bankers a lot of money and cartelized the German economy according to the needs of the General Staff.

Kaiser Wilhelm, fearing the same fate as his cousin the Tsar, had to part into exile and the chiefs of the General Staff, Ludendorff and von Hindenburg, remained at the helm of the unofficial government. The chancellors came and went, but two men remained. In 1923 Ludendorff found in Hitler the leader who had long sought and supported him in his failed coup d'état, but the country was not yet ready. Von Hindenburg, who was also a participant in Germany's remilitarization project, promptly pardoned the coup plotters. The ideas and the speech of Hitler in 1933 were those of Ludendorff in 1918, which blamed the German failure in the first war on a Judeo-Masonic, Communist and Jesuit confabulation.

Hitler was not a political accident but the instrument to execute the plans of the shadow government headed by the military, and the German industrialists. Some of the protagonists of the first war paved the way for Adolf Hitler; The political support of Von Papen, the military backing of Ludendorff, the patronage of Hjalmar Schacht and the support of Germany's most influential businessmen, brought him to power.

The German cartels, dominated by North American capital, were the most important economic supporters of National Socialism before the elections. Was Hitler aware that a substantial part of the credit that allowed German rearmament was of Jewish origin? Almost 41% of the Dawes Plan money came from three banks: *Dillon & Read & Co.*, *Speyer & Co.* and *Kuhn & Loeb & Co.* It is difficult to know if Hitler was informed about the economic forces behind his own rise, probably he got a clearer image towards the end of the war. Schacht knew better than anyone the origin of party funds. Some Jewish bankers, who emerged as community leaders thanks to their economic successes, did not hesitate to put their people in Russia and Germany in grave danger to achieve their goals. These Jewish "leaders" did not seem to mind the rise of Hitler until he repudiated the debt incurred. The masses of innocent Jews had nothing to do with their games at the highest levels of politics and finance. Hitler, perhaps involuntarily, did more than anyone to fulfill the main political prerogative of Zionism: to unify the Jewish world in the land of Israel. The Haavara agreements could explain the unnatural contribution of prominent Jewish funds to the Nazi campaign. And after the war the new Jewish exodus had as its preferred destination the new State of Israel.

The second war not as unexpected for Germany as the previous one. The lack of interest in taking England at the beginning of the war, when Germans still had the advantage, suggests that Hitler believed an armistice was possible, and there are numerous German attempts to conclude the war in a negotiated manner. The Allies turned their backs on all peace attempts. Only the total defeat of Germany could satisfy the Allies.

Some important voices within the US administration such as Patton and Forrestal were very critical of post-war management. They were the first to raise the alarm voice in the face of the dangers of Communism and the Zionist influence in the American government. Men like Baruch and Morgenthau exerted all the pressure they were capable of in the Roosevelt government to erase even the memory of Germany, while they openly demanded support for the Stalin government. In addition to the sympathy of the banking community in general, Communism had from the beginning the support of Wall Street members such as the Warburg, Schiff or Untermeyer, and Zionists such as Rabbi Wise, judges Brandeis, Lehman and Frankfurter. The Zionist leaders possibly thought that Russia could be an alternative to establish a homeland for their people, but Stalin soon made them see how wrong they were.

The territorial appetites of the communists were insatiable, and their hand was already seen in the failed Soviet of Munich in 1918, the revolution of Hungary in 1919 and the Soviet of Asturias in 1934. And after the war the Allies agreed to deliver to Stalin half continent: Poland, Romania, half of Germany and several Baltic republics, many more territories than Hitler would have dreamed of. Then came the Chinese Revolution of 1949. At the height of the cold war the communist bloc occupied much of Asia, Europe and Latin America. Did the West thought the Communism was more acceptable than Fascism?

Freemasonry, a secret society object of study in my previous book, served as a transmission belt to spread diverse currents of revolutionary thought; anti-monarchical, socialist, zionist, humanist and secular ideas. Prominent characters like Churchill, Trotsky and Hjalmar Schacht even suggest some kind of continuity between the revolutions of the eighteenth century -the French Revolution, the American War of Independence and the failed revolution of the Bavarian Illuminati- with those of the twentieth century, - the revolution Communist or that of the Young Turks. The obsession of fascist regimes with Freemasonry does not seem to be accidental. Franco in Spain published a book contrary to Freemasonry under a pseudonym, Ludendorff dedicated several works to Freemasonry, and Hitler also knew the internationalist and revolutionary significance of Freemasonry, two elements very present in the communist revolution. It is paradoxical that a bourgeois institution like Freemasonry was in the origin of several revolutions that annihilated the bourgeoisie itself as a social class. Ludendorff, Trotsky, Schacht and Churchill were possibly the best-informed men in their time on the ins and outs of international power, so we must give them some credit.

The Second World War culminated all the claims of international bankers, even those they left incomplete in the previous war. Europe was rebuilt with American money from the Marshall Plan, a conditional loan, subject as usual, to comply with the lender's guidelines. Financial capitalism, which already completely dominated the real economy, established a new global economic architecture based on credit at the Bretton Woods monetary and financial conference. Two essential elements for the new order were the United Nations and the founding of the State of Israel, which became one of the main foci of conflicts in the world until today. The Rockefeller family donated the land of Manhattan where the United Nations is based today, and the Rothschilds financed the first colonies of the State of Israel. James Armand de Rothschild contributed six million Israeli liras for the construction of his Parliament, the *Knesset*[698].

After the failure of the Soviet Union, and aware that absolute power was almost impossible to achieve, the brotherhood of investment bankers opted for a polycentric system of control composed of several groups of international bureaucrats who acted under his instructions. That did not mean giving up his initial plan to control every sovereign state on the planet through the coercive use of debt,

698 Website of Knesset, revised in 2012.

and by military means when necessary. The American government became its armed wing, relying also on the *UN* and *NATO*, two institutions designed for international aggression and not for peace. They organized the world economy in commercial blocks such as the EU or NAFTA and then concentrated more power in institutions like the G8 or the G20. The *Bank of International Settlements* was joined by economic institutions such as the *World Bank*, the IMF, the WTO and many other acronyms tailored to their interests. They created new informal groups of political influence such as the Trilateral Commission and the Bilderberg Club. All these institutions contributed to disseminate their political agenda, which promulgated as nonnegotiable policies international Socialism, inedbtedness, globalization, tariff disarmament, the disappearance of borders and the end of nation-states. Investment bankers and their political protégés were always in the origin and management of these institutions.

They designed a centrally planned economy on a planetary scale, where the Anglo-Saxon world would organize international finance, Asia would be the factory of the world, the Mediterranean countries would become recreational areas for tourism, the Middle East would provide oil, Latin America food and Africa raw materials. The new world order was born, but that is another story.

GENEALOGICAL RESEARCH AND BANKING HISTORY

Below there are some genealogical studies to help the reader understand the family relationships of the circle of international bankers. Also I included some diagrams with the history of mergers and acquisitions of some of the banking houses described here.

The Peabody Family

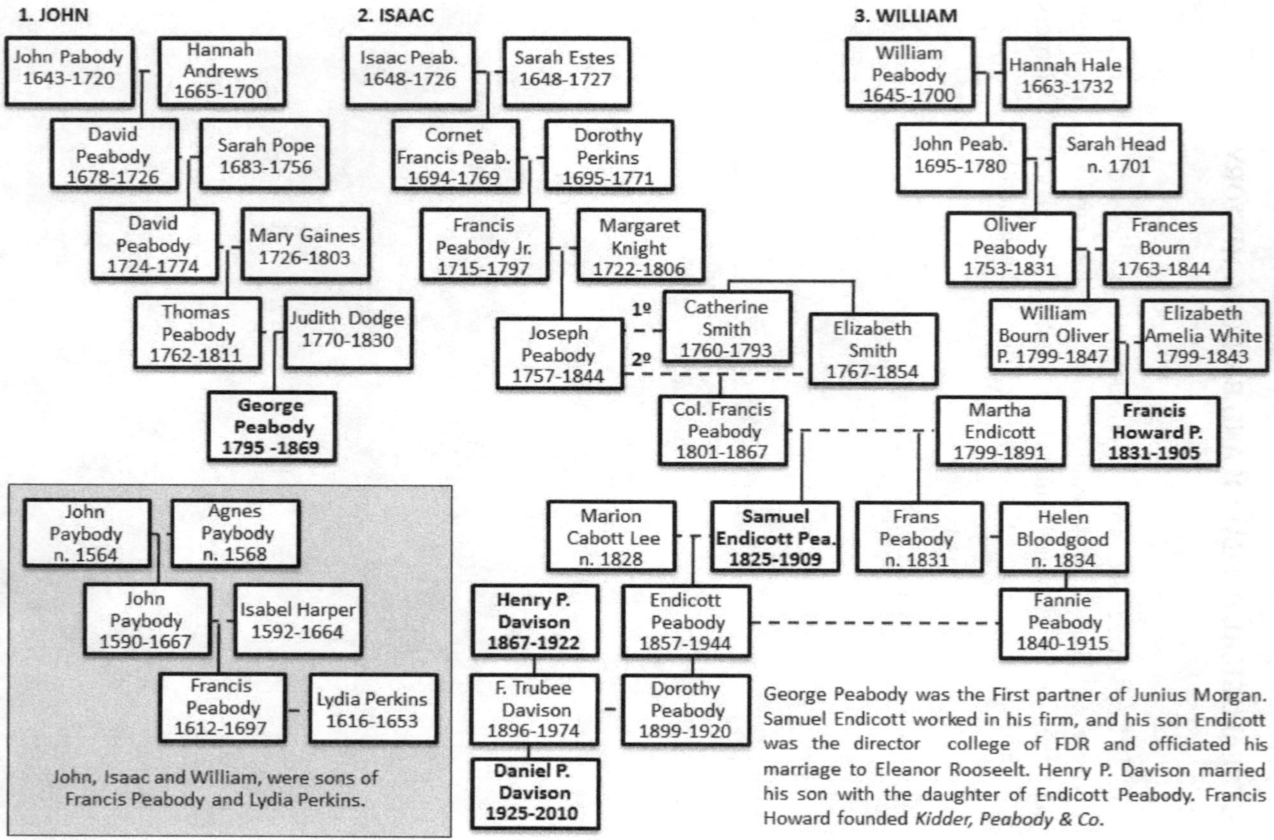

George Peabody was the First partner of Junius Morgan. Samuel Endicott worked in his firm, and his son Endicott was the director college of FDR and officiated his marriage to Eleanor Rooseelt. Henry P. Davison married his son with the daughter of Endicott Peabody. Francis Howard founded *Kidder, Peabody & Co.*

The Drexel-Biddle Family

Drexels and Biddles are among the most illustrious Banking families in the History of Philadelphia. Nicholas Biddle was the President of the *Second Bank* and his brother Thomas Biddle founded one of the first merchant banks of the United States, *Thomas Biddle & Co.*

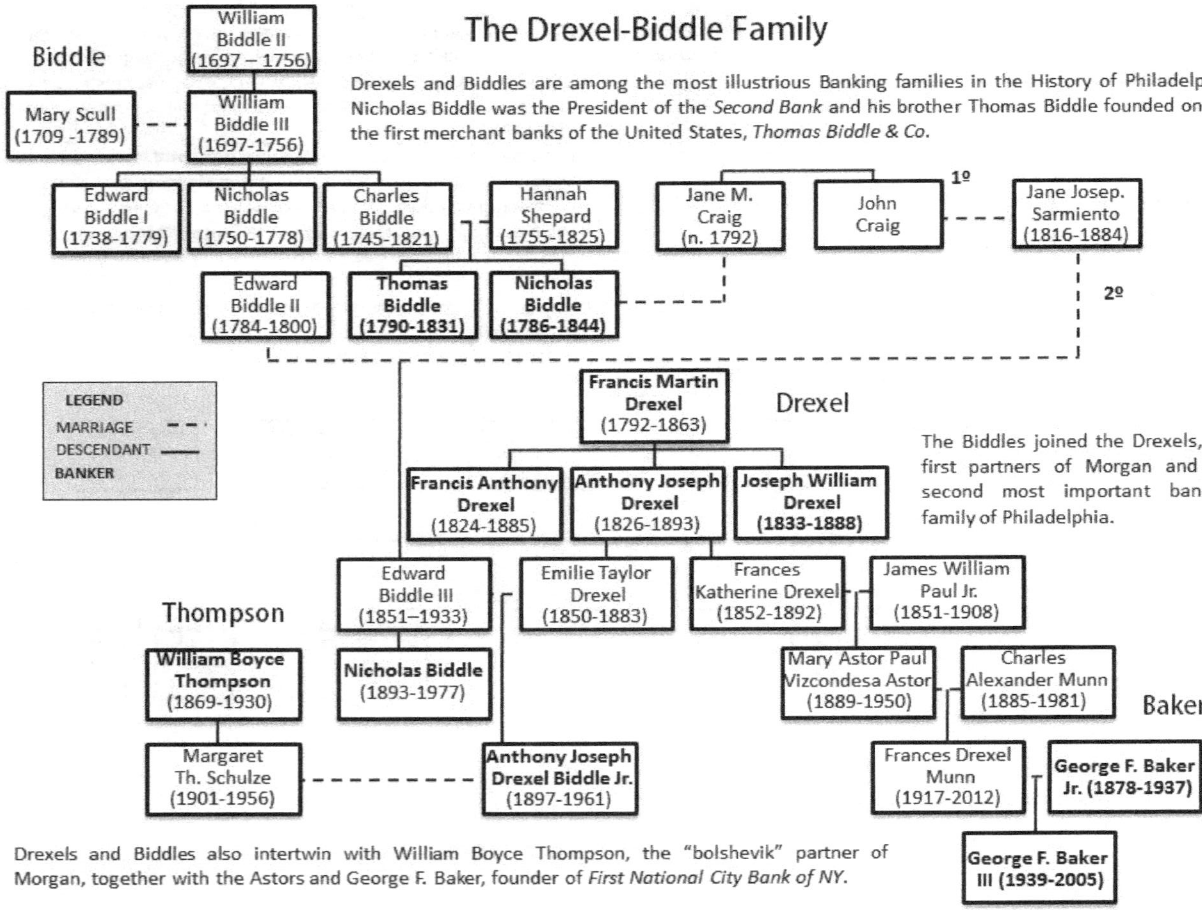

The Biddles joined the Drexels, the first partners of Morgan and the second most important banking family of Philadelphia.

Drexels and Biddles also intertwin with William Boyce Thompson, the "bolshevik" partner of Morgan, together with the Astors and George F. Baker, founder of *First National City Bank of NY*.

The Delano-Brown Family

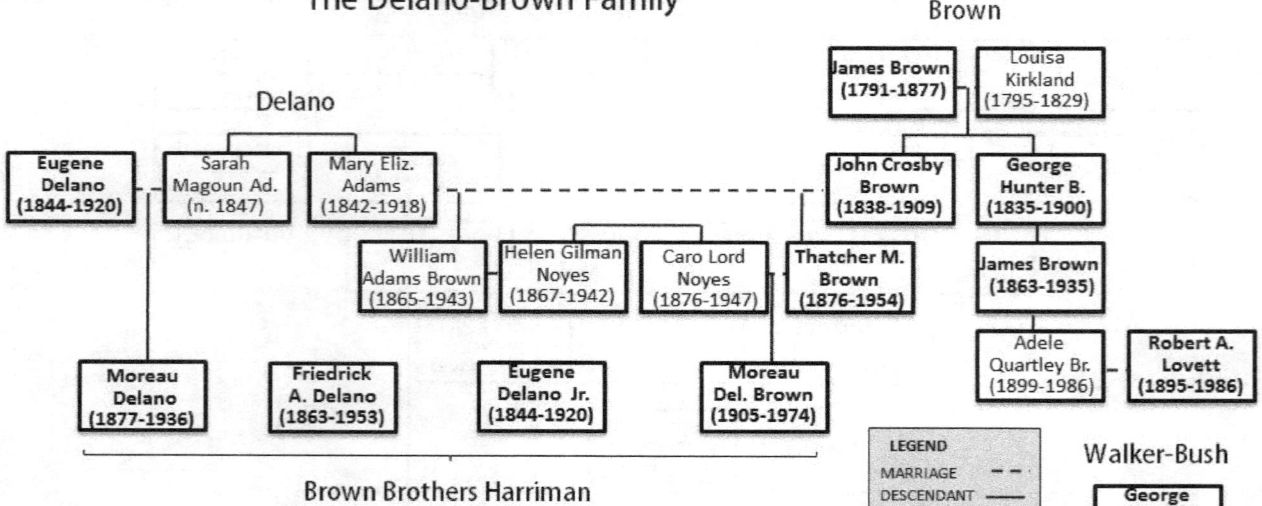

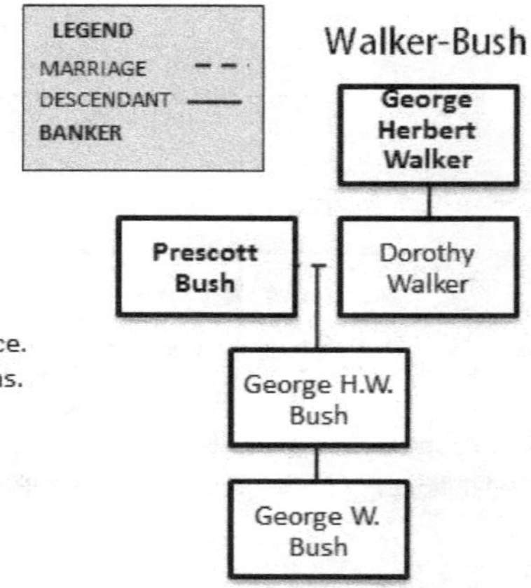

Delanos were closely related to several presidents of the United States:

* **Ulises S. Grant**: great-grandson of Noah Grant and Susannah Delano.
* **Calvin Coolidge**: a fifth generation descendant of Elizabeth Delano.
* **Franklin Delano Roosevelt**: was a son of Sara Ann Delano.
* **Franklin D. Roosevelt**: fifht cousin once removed of Theodore Roosevelt, married to his niece.
* **John Adams and John Quincy Adams**: they were ancestors of Sara and Mary Elizabeth Adams.

Some American illustrious characters worked for *Brown Brothers*:
*James Stillman Rockefeller worked six years in *Brown Brothers*.
*Four members of the Delano family were partners in *Brown Brothers Harriman*.
*George Herbert Walker and Prescott Bush, father and grandfather of the George Bush presidential saga, worked in *BBH*.

Some Familiar Relations I

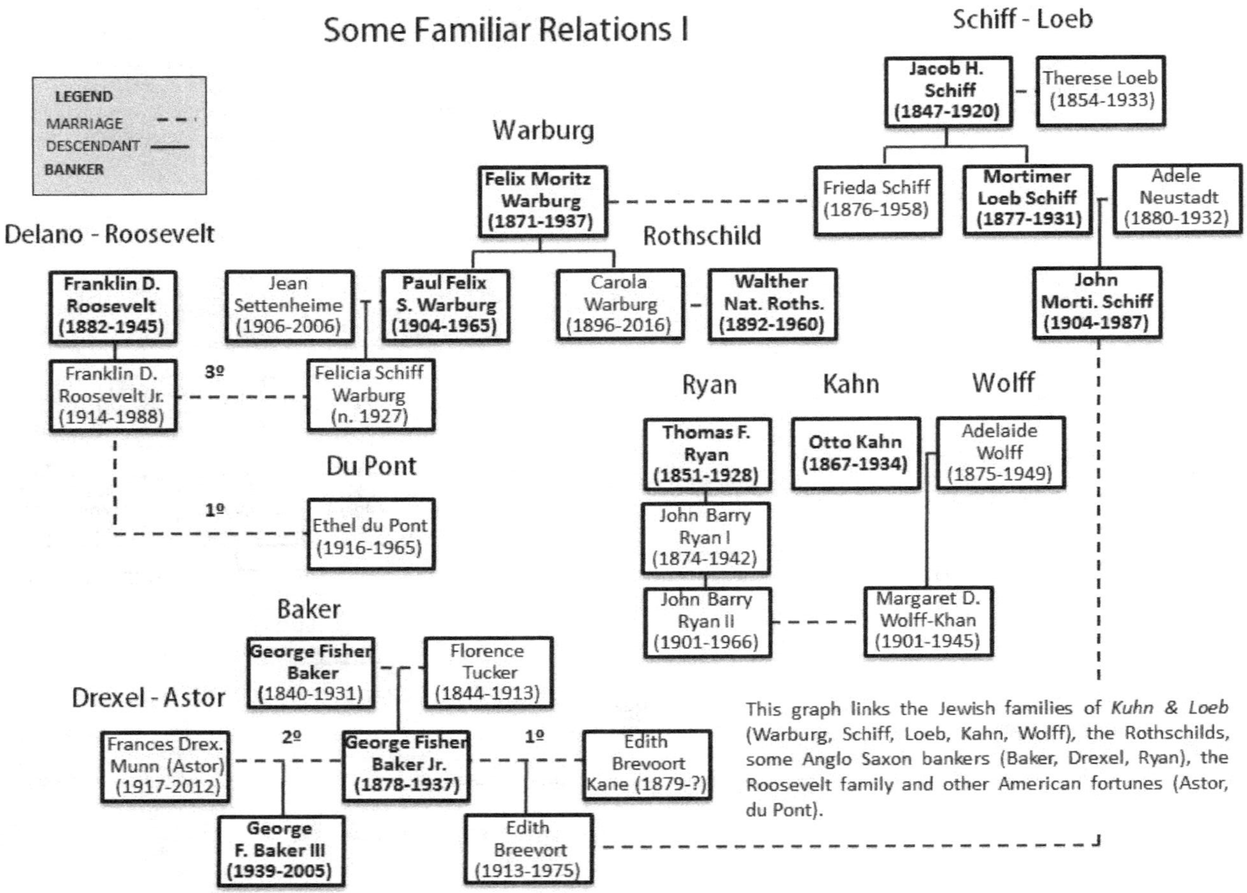

This graph links the Jewish families of *Kuhn & Loeb* (Warburg, Schiff, Loeb, Kahn, Wolff), the Rothschilds, some Anglo Saxon bankers (Baker, Drexel, Ryan), the Roosevelt family and other American fortunes (Astor, du Pont).

Some Familiar Relations II

The Relations of some German Jewish families are described here (Oppenheim, Guggenheim, Mendelssohn, Wolff, Seligman)

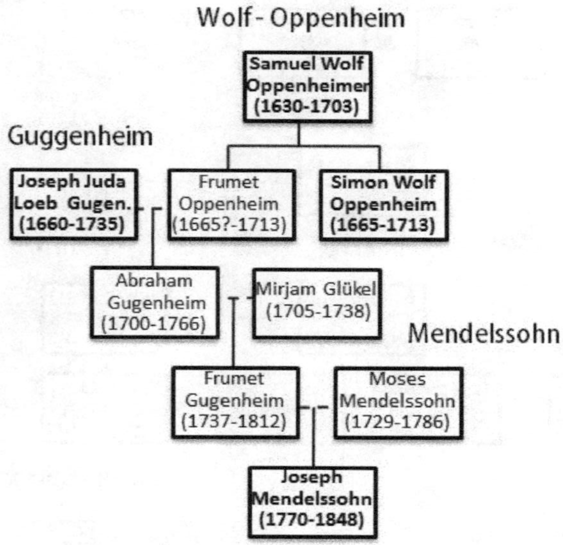

Moses Mendelssohn was the father of the Haskala or Jewish Enlightment. His son Joseph Mendelssohn founded in 1795 the bank *Mendelssohn & Co.* This firm acted as private banker of the Tsars during the first half of the Twentienth century. It remained in the hands of the Mendelssohn family until the Nazis "Aryanized" their assets, which went to the *Deutsche Bank*.

Samuel Wolf Oppenheimer (1630-1703) was the Imperial banker, diplomatic and military supplier for Leopold I, the Emperor of the Holy Roman Empire. His son, Simon Wolf Oppenheimer, was also a banker and founded a banking house in Hannover, where Mayer Amschel Rothschild learnt the banking business.

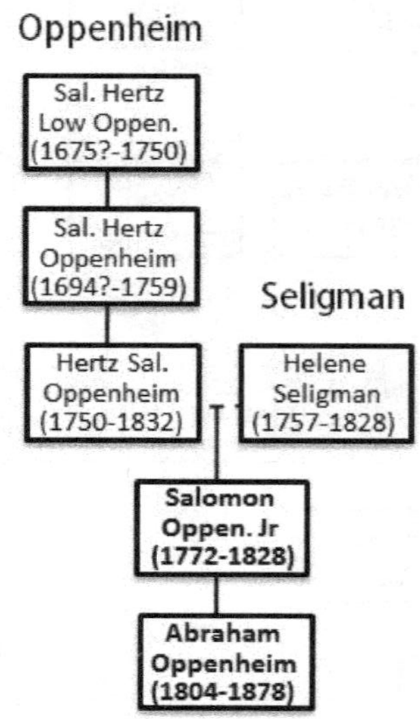

Salomon Oppenheimer Jr. (1772-1828) was a banker and tax collector for the Frenchmen occupying the Rhine area. He founded *Sal. Oppenheim & Cie.* in 1789 in Cologne. In 1938 the bank was "Aryanized" under the name of his new partner, *Robert Pferdmenges & Co.* The bank was acquired in 2010 by *Deutsche Bank*.

His son Abraham Oppenheim founded in 1853 the *Danatbank* with Gustav von Mevissen.

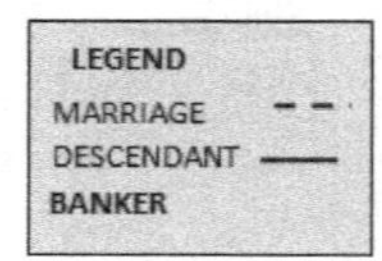

Some Familiar Relations III

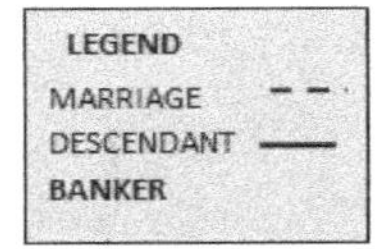

Some Relations of the Anglo-Saxon tycoons; Carnegie, Rockefeller, Stillman, Davison and Peabody.

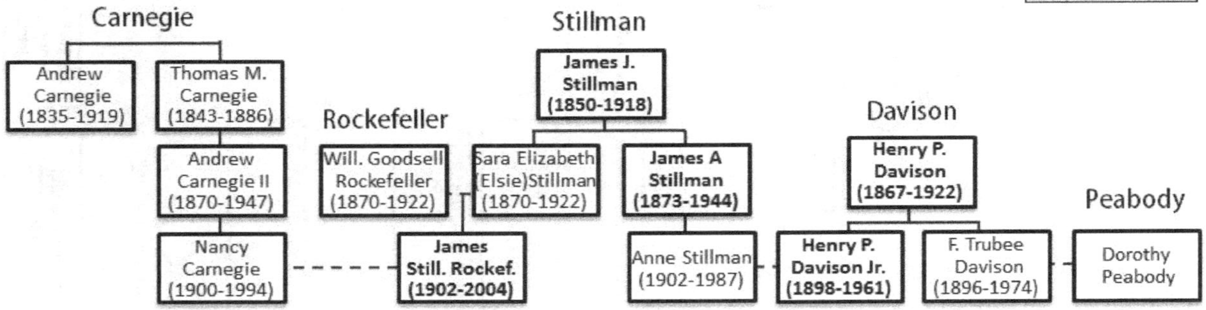

Below, some images of characters mentioned in this book:

ANDREW CARNEGIE

MAX WARBURG

MOSES TAYLOR

GEORGE PEABODY

The House of Morgan

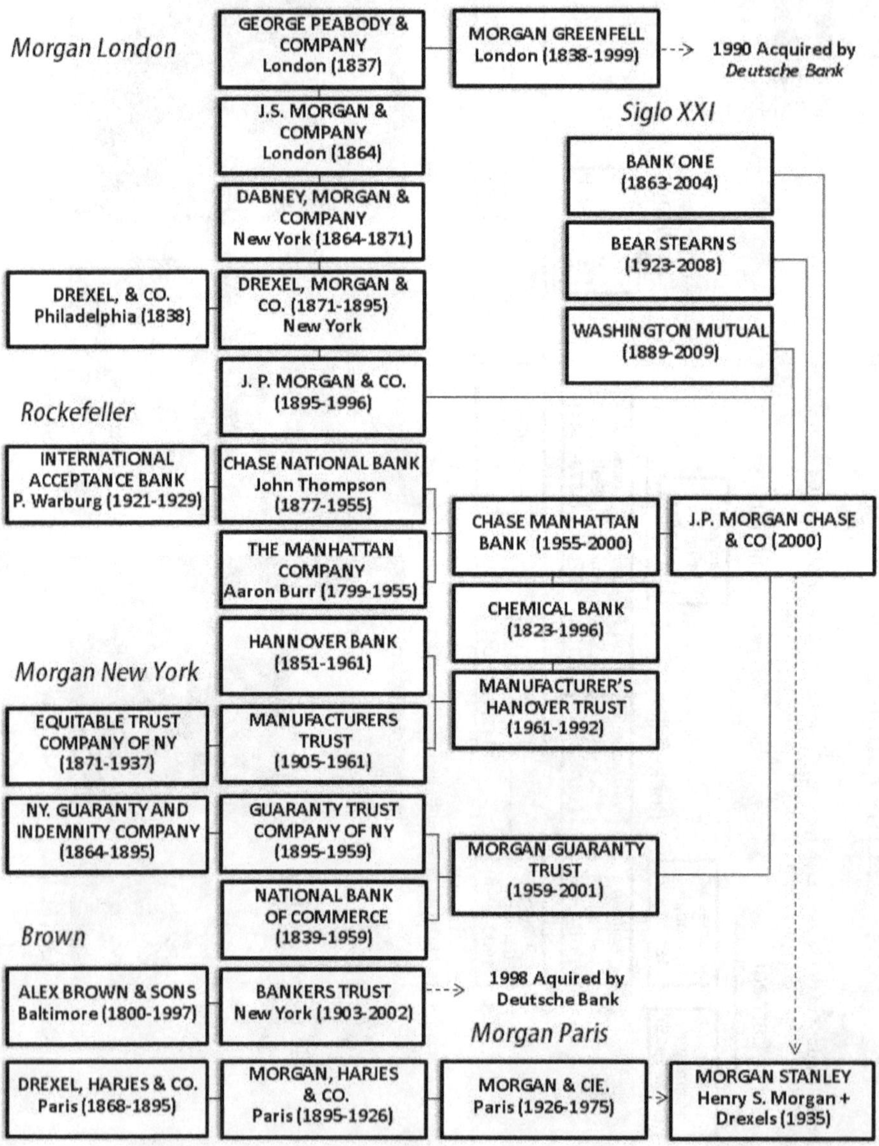

The House of Rockefeller

The House of Morgan aquired some banks of the Rockefeller Group, as *Chase Manhattan Bank* en 1955, while the Rockefeller purchased assets of Morgan like the *First National Bank* in 1863.

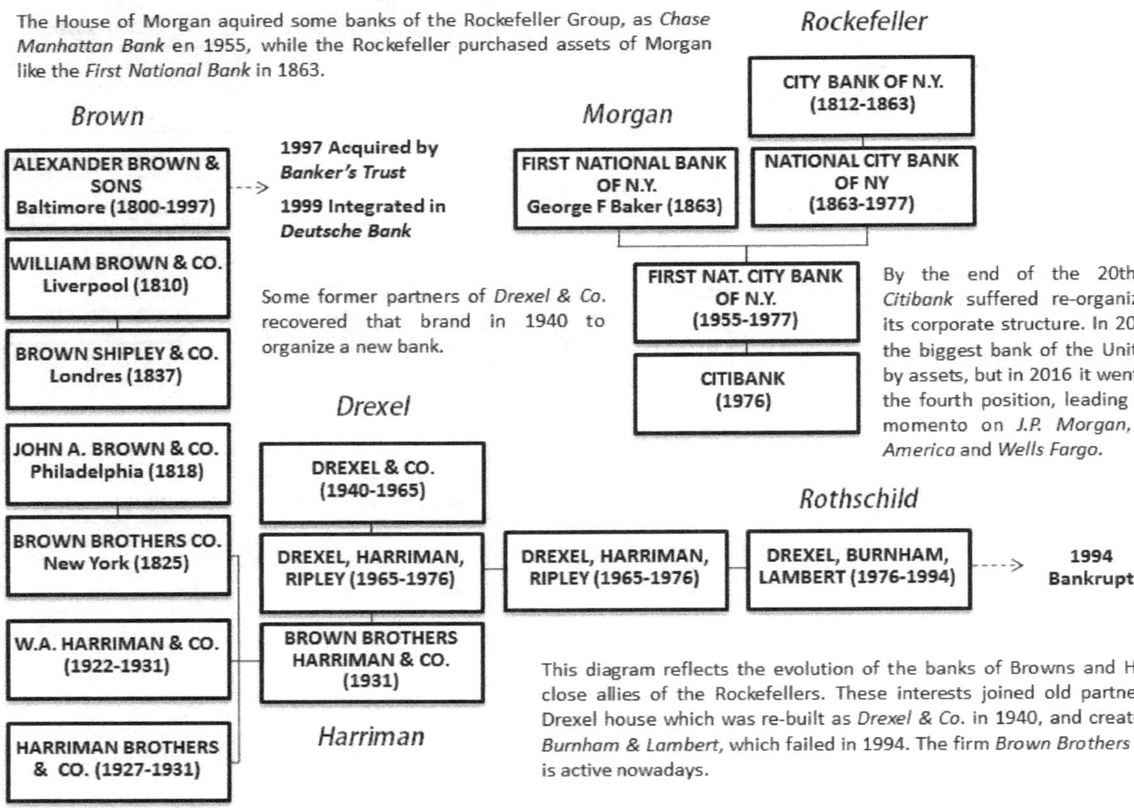

By the end of the 20th century *Citibank* suffered re-organizations in its corporate structure. In 2008 it was the biggest bank of the United States by assets, but in 2016 it went down to the fourth position, leading from that momento on *J.P. Morgan*, *Bank of America* and *Wells Fargo*.

This diagram reflects the evolution of the banks of Browns and Harrimans, close allies of the Rockefellers. These interests joined old partners of the Drexel house which was re-built as *Drexel & Co.* in 1940, and created *Drexel, Burnham & Lambert*, which failed in 1994. The firm *Brown Brothers Harriman* is active nowadays.

The Frankfurt Syndicate I: The Houses of Nueva York

We find in this graph some of the most important banks of the Frankfurt Syndicate. *Kuhn & Loeb* eventually was absorbed by another Jewish German firm, *Lehman Brothers,* whose bankrupcity shocked the world economy in the year 2000.

Goldman Sachs took the lead at the end of the 20th century, exercising the economic and political leadership that *Kuhn & Loeb* held in the first half of the 19th century.

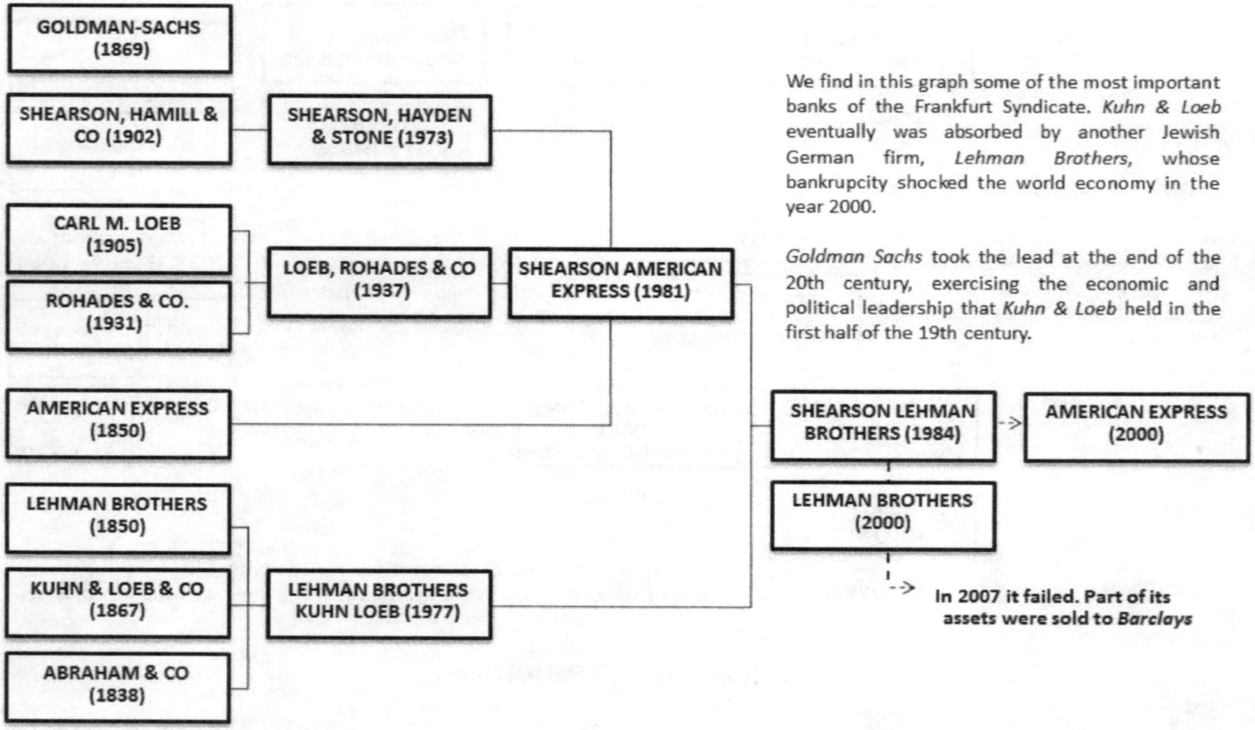

The Frankfurt Syndicate II: Germany

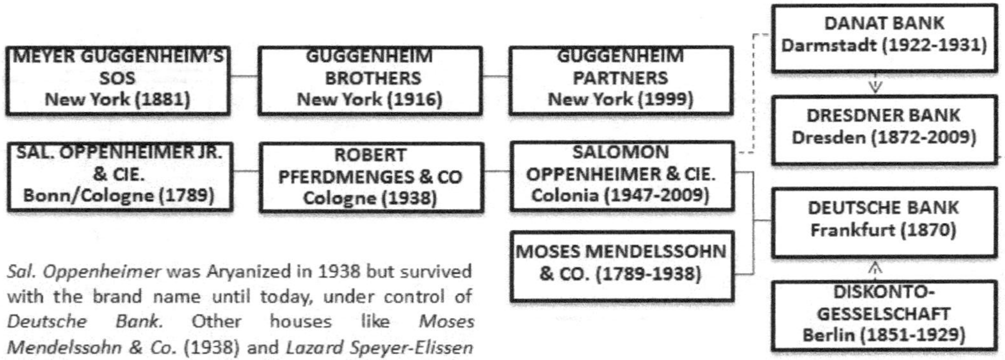

Four of the big German banks before WWII were the so called "4D":

-Danatbank

-Dresdner Bank

-Deutsche Bank

-Diskonto-Gesselschaft.

---> **2009 Aquired by *Commerzbank***

Commerzbank absorbed the four non-Jewish banks, except for *Deutsche Bank.* Since 2008 there has been rumours in press about the possible absorption of *Deutsche* by *Commerzbank* due to economic issues.

Sal. Oppenheimer was Aryanized in 1938 but survived with the brand name until today, under control of *Deutsche Bank.* Other houses like *Moses Mendelssohn & Co.* (1938) and *Lazard Speyer-Elissen* (1934) never reopened again. *Sal. Oppenheim* is nowadays the first familiar bank of Europe, being *M.M. Warburg* the second.

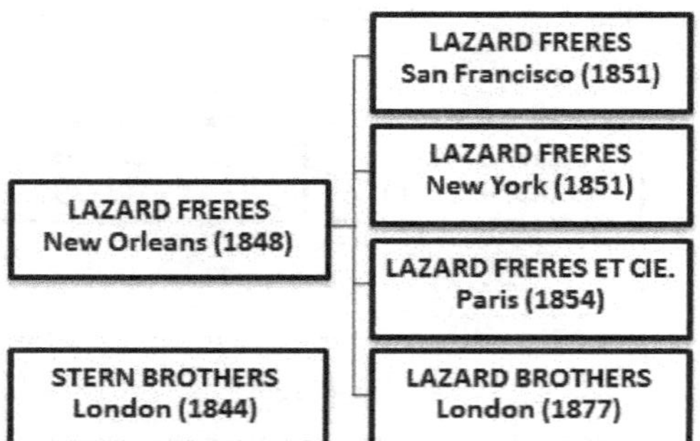

In the year 2000 al the banks of the brand Lazard unified under the name *Lazard LLC,* which in 2005 went public in the stock exchange.

When James Speyer retired in 1938, he decided to cease business of all Speyer firms.

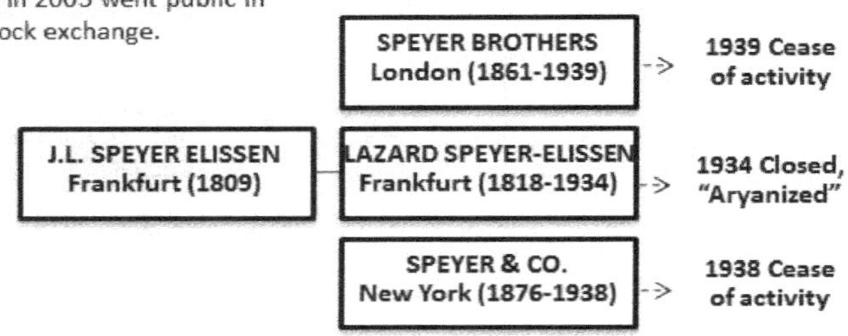

The Frankfurt Syndicate III: Rothschilds in Europe and USA

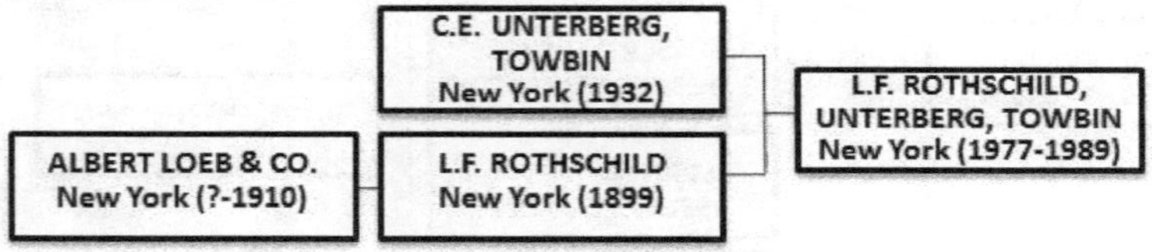

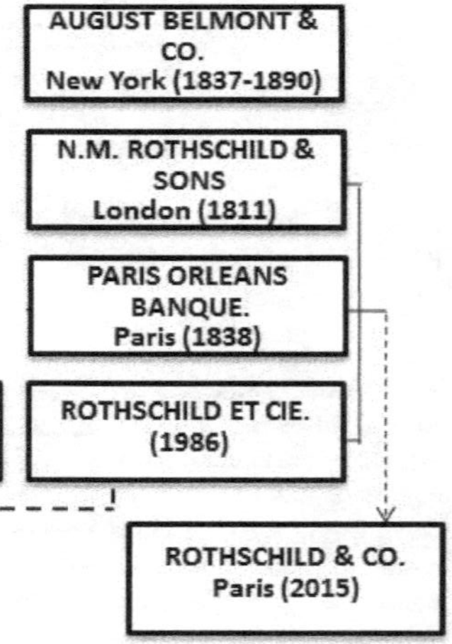

The Rothschilds centralized their European activities in the French railroad group *Chemins de Fer Paris-Orléans* (later *París Orléans Banque*). *París Orleans* changed the name to *Rothschild & Co.* in 2015.

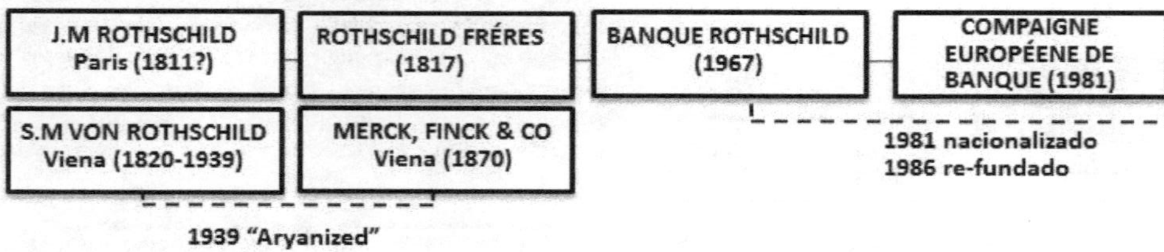

Nowadays two houses of Rothschild remain active. The first is *Rothschild & Co.*, where they grouped their familiar activities. Most of their business are integrated into a "special purpose vehicle" firm in Netherlands named *Concordia BV*. The second house, more recent, opened doors in 1953 and it's named after his founder, *Edmond de Rothschild Group*.

In 1855 Anselm von Rothschild founded in Viena *Creditansalt*, the most important bank of Austro-Hungary until it's default in 1931. The state tried to nationalize it in 1934 but finally it was forced into a merger with *Wiener Bankverein*. In 1946 it was nationalized, and in 1956 privatized again. In 2002 it became the *Bank of Austria-Creditanstalt*. In 2005 it was sold to *Unicredit* and stopped operating with it's original brand.

The Frankfurt Syndicate IV: Rothschilds France and Benelux

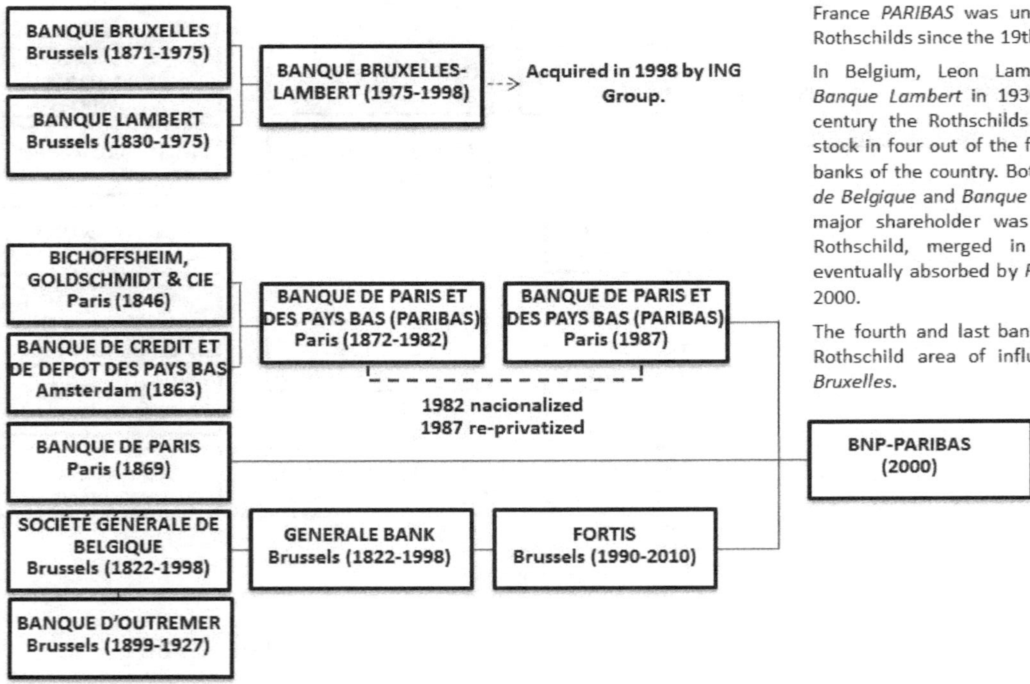

We include a brief history of the banks in the Rothschild's sphere of influence in France and former BENELUX countries (Belgium, Netherlands, Luxembourg). In France *PARIBAS* was under control of the Rothschilds since the 19th century.

In Belgium, Leon Lambert founded the *Banque Lambert* in 1930. During the 19th century the Rothschilds had an important stock in four out of the five most important banks of the country. Both *Société Générale de Belgique* and *Banque d'Outremer*, whose major shareholder was Leon Lambert de Rothschild, merged in 1927. This were eventually absorbed by *PARIBAS* in the year 2000.

The fourth and last bank to enter into the Rothschild area of influence was *Banque Bruxelles*.

The Frankfurt Syndicate V: Warburg, Schroder, Seligman and others

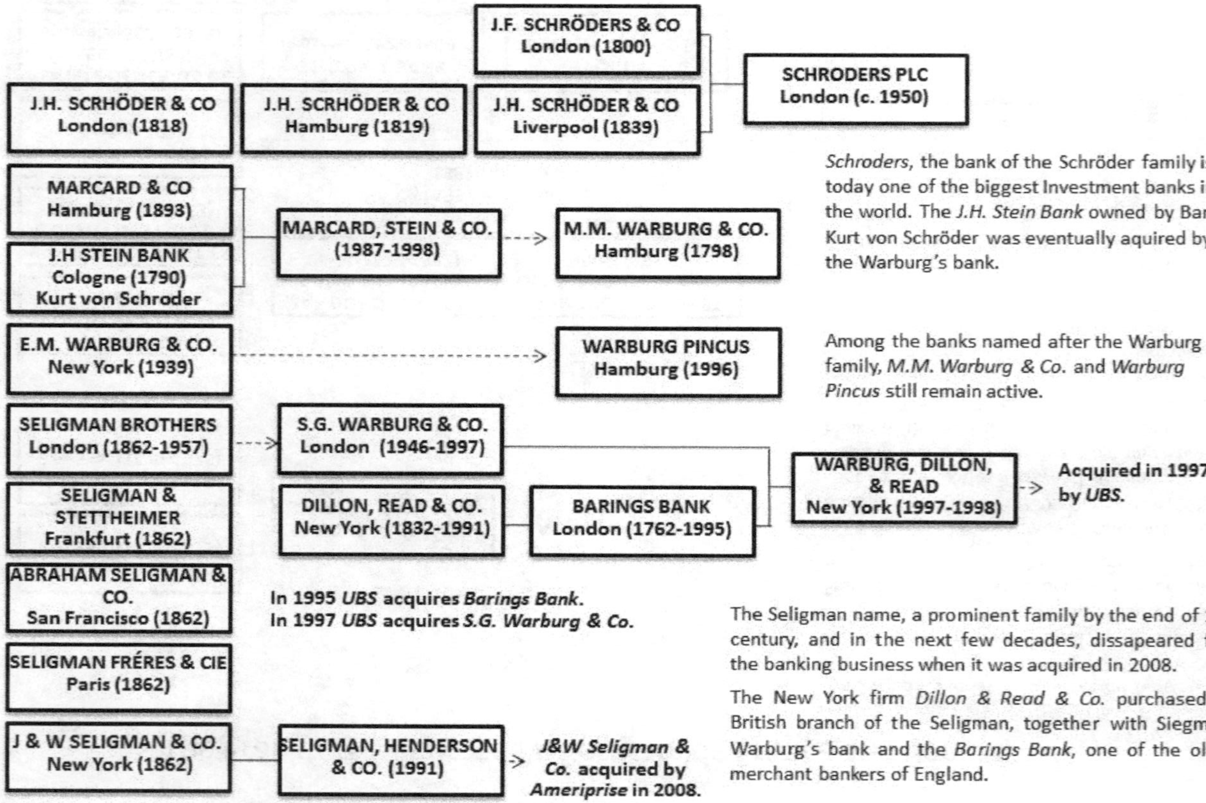

Schroders, the bank of the Schröder family is today one of the biggest Investment banks in the world. The *J.H. Stein Bank* owned by Baron Kurt von Schröder was eventually aquired by the Warburg's bank.

Among the banks named after the Warburg family, *M.M. Warburg & Co.* and *Warburg Pincus* still remain active.

The Seligman name, a prominent family by the end of 19th century, and in the next few decades, dissapeared from the banking business when it was acquired in 2008.

The New York firm *Dillon & Read & Co.* purchased the British branch of the Seligman, together with Siegmund Warburg's bank and the *Barings Bank*, one of the oldest merchant bankers of England.

ANNEXES

Annex I: The Comunist Manifesto

«The proletariat will use its political supremacy to wrest, by degree, all capital from the bourgeoisie, to centralize all instruments of production in the hands of the State, i.e., of the proletariat organized as the ruling class; and to increase the total productive forces as rapidly as possible.

Of course, in the beginning, this cannot be effected except by means of despotic inroads on the rights of property, and on the conditions of bourgeois production; by means of measures, therefore, which appear economically insufficient and untenable, but which, in the course of the movement, outstrip themselves, necessitate further inroads upon the old social order, and are unavoidable as a means of entirely revolutionizing the mode of production. These measures will, of course, be different in different countries. Nevertheless, in most advanced countries, the following will be pretty generally applicable.

1. Abolition of property in land and application of all rents of land to public purposes.
2. A heavy progressive or graduated income tax.
3. Abolition of all rights of inheritance.
4. Confiscation of the property of all emigrants and rebels.
5. Centralization of credit in the hands of the state, by means of a national bank with State capital and an exclusive monopoly.
6. Centralization of the means of communication and transport in the hands of the State.
7. Extension of factories and instruments of production owned by the State; the bringing into cultivation of waste-lands, and the improvement of the soil generally in accordance with a common plan.
8. Equal liability of all to work. Establishment of industrial armies, especially for agriculture.
9. Combination of agriculture with manufacturing industries; gradual abolition of all the distinction between town and country by a more equable distribution of the populace over the country.
10. Free education for all children in public schools. Abolition of children's factory labor in its present form. Combination of education with industrial production, etc.»

Karl Marx and Friedrich Engels, *the Communist Manifesto*, 1848

Annex II: The Letter of German Industrials "Industrielleneingabe" to President Paul von Hindenburg, 1932

After the victory of the National Socialist Party in November 1932, a group of German industrialists sent a letter to the German president requesting the appointment of Adolf Hitler as Chancellor of Germany. The initiative was headed by the banker and former president of the *Reichsbank*, Hjalmar Schacht. This was the request of the German industrialists to Paul von Hindenburg, I apologize for any possible error in the translation from German:

«[699]Your Excellency, November 1932

Very dear President of the Reich!

Your Excellency, imbued with ardent love for the German people and the fatherland, the undersigned have welcomed with hope the fundamental change that has paved the way for Your Excellency in the management of public affairs.

As your Excellency, we affirm the need for a government independent of the parliamentary system of parties, such as the opinion that Your Excellency has formulated on a presidential cabinet. The result of the parliamentary elections of November 6 has shown that the current cabinet, whose honesty no one doubts among the German people, does not in any way have enough popular support. But the objective raised by Your Excellency has an absolute majority in the German people, if it excludes - as is natural - the Communist Party, which is privative of the State. Faced with the previous parliamentary regime of parties, not only the National Party of the German People[700] and its small affiliated groups, but also the National Socialist German Workers Party, has stated the objective of Your Excellency. We believe that this is a desirable outcome and we cannot imagine that the achievement of this objective may now fail to maintain an ineffective [governance] system.

---

[699] Letter of the Industrialists to Paul von Hindenburg, Bavarian State Center for Political Education, website revised in May 2015.

[700] A conservative party leaded by Alfred Hugenberg which supported the Nazis.

It is clear that the frequent dissolutions of the parliament that follow each other, [and] the frequent struggles between the parties that worsen with each new election, must be counteracted with political and economical tranquility and consolidation. But it is also clear that any constitutional amendment that is not compatible with the broader group of people will cause even worse economic, political and psychological effects.

We consider that, therefore, it is our moral duty to ask Your Excellency respectfully, that, in order to achieve the objective supported by all of us, Your Excellency allows us to carry out the remodeling of the [government] cabinet in a way that brings the greatest popular strength to it.

We declare ourselves free of commitments to any closed partisan environment. We recognize the national movement that passes through our people as the auspicious beginning of a time that creates the necessary bases for the resurgence of the German economy, only through the overcoming of class antagonisms. We know that this growth still requires many sacrifices. We believe that these sacrifices will only be carried out voluntarily if the larger group of this national movement leads the government.

Transferring the responsibility of leading the presidential cabinet to the leader of the largest national group, endowed with the best material and personal resources, will eliminate the weaknesses and errors that will necessarily suffer any mass movement, and will drag the millions of men who have remained outside, before an affirmative force.

Entirely trusting in the wisdom of Your Excellency and Your Excellency's national sense, we welcome you with the greatest reverence.»

The document included the following signatures:

1. Hjalmar Schacht: former president of the *Reichsbank*, member of the Keppler Circle.
2. Friedrich Reinhart: Director of *Commerzbank*, member of the board of the *AEG*, president of the Chamber of Commerce of Berlin, member of the Keppler Circle.
3. August Rosterg: General Manager of *Wintershall AG*, member of the Keppler Circle.
4. Kurt von Schröder: banker in Cologne, member of the Keppler Circle.

5. Fritz Beindorff: owner of *Pelikan AG*, member of the Supervisory Board of *Deutsche Bank*.

6. Emil Helfferich: Chairman of the Board of Directors of *DAPAG*, member of the Keppler Circle.

7. Franz Heinrich Witthoefft: President of *Commerzbank*, President of the Chamber of Commerce of Hamburg, member of the Keppler Circle.

8. Ewald Hecker: President of the Chamber of Commerce of Hanover, member of the Keppler Circle.

9. Kurt Woermann: Hamburg shipowner and a member of the Nazi Party.

10. Karl Vincent Krogmann: co-owner of *Hamburger Bank*, and transport and trade company Hamburg, *Wachsmuth and Krogmann*, member of the board of the Hamburg National Club, from 1933 to 1945 Burgomaster of Hamburg, member of the Chamber of Commerce of Hamburg and member of the Keppler Circle.

11. Kurt von Eichborn: partner of *Breslauer Privatbank*.

12. Eberhard Graf von Kalckreuth: President of the National Rural League.

13. Erich Lübbert: General Manager of *Dywidag*, a construction company, President of *AG für Verkehrswesen*, a transport holding.

14. Erwin Merck: President of *HJ Merck & Co*, a bank in Hamburg.

15. Joachim von Oppen: President of the Chamber of Agriculture of Brandenburg.

16. Rudolf Ventzki: General Manager of *Maschinenfabrik Esslingen*, a railway and other vehicles manufacturing company.

In the copy of the letter, which is the file of the President's office, the following signatures were presented:

17. Fritz Thyssen: Chairman of the Board of Supervisors of *Vereinigte Stahlwerke*.

18. Robert Graf von Keyserlingk-Cammerau: member of the Council of Associations of Agricultural Employers.

19. Kurt Gustav Ernst von Rohr-Manze: landowner.

Annex III: The Balfour Declaration

In 1917 the British Minister of Foreign Affairs, Arthur James Balfour, sent a letter to Baron Lionel Walter Rothschild, conveying his sympathy with the cause of the Zionist Federation in England. This document is considered one of the most important founding documents in the creation of the State of Israel:

Foreign Office
November 2 1917

Dear Lord Rothschild, I have much pleasure in conveying to you on behalf of His Majesty's Government the following Declaration of sympathy with Jewish Zionist aspirations which have been submitted to and approved by the Cabinet:

"His Majesty's government view with favour the establishment in Palestine of a national home for the Jewish people, and will use their best endeavours to facilitate the achievement of this object, it being clearly understood that nothing shall be done which may prejudice the civil and religious rights of existing non-Jewish communities in Palestine, or the rights and political status enjoyed by Jews in any other country."

I should be grateful if you would bring this Declaration to the knowledge of the Zionist Federation.

Yours sincerely,

(Signed) ARTHUR JAMES BALFOUR

Annex IV: Excerpts from the The Case of Anti-Soviets "Bloc of Rights and Trotskyites

In March 1938 the People's Comissariat of Justice of the U.S.S.R. conducted hearings with former aides of Leon Trotsky to investigate an alleged conspiracy of Trotskyites in combination with foreign powers against the government of Joseph Stalin, the so called "The Case of Anti-Soviets "Bloc of Rights and Trotskyites".

Christian Rakovsky was the leader of a group of Bolshevik leaders suspicious of counterrevolutionary activities acting under Trotsky's orders in exile. Rakovsky was a man linked both to Trotsky and Helphand, the true architects of the revolution in Russia in 1917. Helphand and Rakovsky were, as it has already been proven, in the payroll of the Kaiser, who spent millions of German marks in the Bolsheviks to drive Russia out of the First World War.

After Stalin became successful in the struggle to lead the Soviet Union, Trotsky and his followers conspired against him by any means, trying to overturn the situation and regain power for Trotsky.

The testimony of Rakovsky puts together some very interesting facts. Rakovsky admitted to State Prosecutor Vyshinsky that he had been working for the Japanese, British and German intelligence services, conspiring thus against Russia. According to the testimonies, Trotsky himself also worked for to the latter, British and German services. Of course a sworn testimony in a Communist trial is not exacty a very reliable document, but it perfectly complements the information provided by the German Ministry of Foreign Affairs and other sources and facts. It adds further evidence that the Bolsheviks worked for foreign powers and *against* the interests of Russia. The collaboration, according to the defendants, started after the revolution, around 1921, but we know it actually started before the Revolution of 1917. Trotsky was probably working with foreign intelligence services before even he came back to Russia, and that's why when he was detained in Canada in 1917 on the way back to Russia, and as Sutton explained, he had 10,000 dollars of German money and he was released thanks to a diplomatic cable of the British.

This is the confession of Christian Rakovsky explaining how he became a spy for the Japanese, the British and the German[701]:

---

[701] People's Comissariat of Justice of the U.S.S.R., Report on Court Proceedings in the Case of Anti-Soviet "Bloc of Rights and Trotskyites", heard before the Military Collegium of the Supreme Court of the U.S.S.R., Moscow, March 2-13, 1938.

RAKOVSKY: Yesterday I concluded with the statement that, after my conversation with the high personage who was close to the Japanese government, I had three talks with the public man of whom I have spoken, the man at the head of a big public organization in Japan.

During the second and third meeting with the public man who headed a big public organization in Japan we established the nature of the information which I promised to supply to the agents of the Japanese intelligence service in Moscow and also the technique of transmitting this information. While still in Tokyo, I drew into this work Dr. Naida, secretary of the Red Cross Delegation[702], of whom I already knew that he was a member of the underground counter-revolutionary terrorist organization… I wrote to Trotsky about all this about my negotiations in Tokyo…

We Trotskyites have to play three cards at the present moment: the German, Japanese and British. It was not quite clear to me, at that time at least, what the German card promised. Personally I thought that the possibility was not excluded that Hitler would seek a rapprochement with the government of the U.S.S.R. I cited the policy of Richelieu: in his own country he exterminated the Protestants, while in his foreign policy he concluded alliances with the Protestant German princes. The relations between Germany and Poland were still in the stage of their inception at the time. Japan, on the other hand, was a potent aggressor against the U.S.S.R. For us Trotskyites the Japanese card was extremely important, but, on the other hand, we should not overrate the importance of Japan as our ally against the Soviet government. Even if Japanese aggression could force its way into the territory of the U.S.S.R., it would be lost in the vast spaces, and in the taiga. As for Great Britain, the situation was rather more serious. At that moment Great Britain was antagonistic to Japan. I am telling you about our private conversations which ought to show why we pursued one line or another. At the moment there was antagonism between ourselves and Japan, but it should not be forgotten that England once headed a coalition against the French Revolution and fought on for twenty-five years.

THE PRESIDENT: You should dwell less on the past and speak more about the Trotskyite organization[703].

RAKOVSKY: Thus, the conclusion was that it was necessary to maintain the connection with the British Intelligence Service, but to pay attention to the Japanese intelligence service at the present time.

---

702 Again, the Red Cross developing functions that have no relation with its purported humanitarian aims.

703 This is a shocking and off topic remark. Was Rakovsky suggesting the Russian Revolution was a sort of continuation of a process started by some group (like freemasons?) in the French Revolution?

VYSHINSKY: I did not quite get you. You say: it was necessary to maintain the connection with the British Intelligence Service and to pay attention to the Japanese intelligence service.

RAKOVSKY: To pay the main attention.

VYSHINSKY: Hence, to serve both the Japanese and British intelligence services, and in addition also the German.

RAKOVSKY: According to my personal opinion at the time, this latter was a mere prospect.

VYSHINSKY: From Krestinsky s evidence you saw that it was not a mere prospect.

What intelligence services were you personally connected with?

RAKOVSKY: The British and the Japanese.

VYSHINSKY: And Krestinsky? Accused Krestinsky, what intelligence service were you connected with?

KRESTINSKY: The German.

VYSHINSKY: Prospectively or actually?

KRESTINSKY: Actually.

VYSHINSKY: Actually? Proceed, please.

RAKOVSKY: I returned from Tokyo with the credentials of a Japanese spy in my pocket... Trotskyism passed through a period of passive defeatism when it was maliciously gleeful over every mistake, every failure in the sphere of Party development and every failure of the Soviet government in the sphere of Socialist construction. Even during that period there had already been certain links, and in my person too, with one intelligence service or another... The second period was the period of active defeatism, a period when one does not wait for mistakes or failures, for mistakes in internal work, but begins to cause them by wrecking activities carried on according to a definite system and program... Now we became a school of espionage, wrecking, treason, terrorism. We were the vanguard of foreign aggression, of international fascism, and not only in the U.S.S.R., but also in Spain, China, throughout the world. Clearly, there was some kind of inner connection here with our past... Radek informed me of the negotiations between the Germans and Trotsky, and asked for my co-operation. In his opinion it was necessary to support Trotsky in Moscow, that is to say, with the representatives of the German intelligence service in Moscow.

VYSHINSKY: How did it come about that you were recruited by the British Intelligence Service? This is what interests us. This is what we accuse you of... you were already enlisted as an agent of the Intelligence Service in 1924. Is that so?

RAKOVSKY: It is.

VYSHINSKY: Tell us under what circumstances you were enlisted, under what circumstances you became an agent of the Intelligence Service in 1924...

RAKOVSKY: Armstrong [An English intelligence agent] said: "We have great sympathy for you, we want to warn you of a danger which is threatening you." He took out from his pocket a slip of paper which he showed me.

VYSHINSKY: What kind of a slip of paper?

RAKOVSKY: It was a letter, typewritten and bearing my forged signature.

VYSHINSKY: Was it really forged?

RAKOVSKY: It was.

VYSHINSKY: For whom was this letter intended?...

RAKOVSKY: It followed from the contents that it was intended for the German government.

VYSHINSKY: For the German intelligence service?

RAKOVSKY: Possibly.

VYSHINSKY: What did the letter say?

RAKOVSKY: The letter said approximately the following: "I am enclosing a list of Rumanian commercial firms and newspaper offices which should be won over to the side of Germany in order to draw Rumania itself into the war on the side of Germany."

VYSHINSKY: What is the meaning of these contents of the letter?

RAKOVSKY: The contents of the letter meant that there existed a connection between me and the German intelligence service, the German government, or some German organization.

VYSHINSKY: And you helped Germany in enlisting Rumanian citizens on Rumanian territory to aid Germany?

RAKOVSKY: Yes.[704]

VYSHINSKY. Was that what it was about?

RAKOVSKY. Yes.

VYSHINSKY. And tell us, were you in Rumania at the time to which this letter refers?

RAKOVSKY: At the time to which this letter refers?

VYSHINSKY: Yes.

RAKOVSKY: The letter was dated Berne, October 1915, but at that time I was not at Berne.

VYSHINSKY: But were you in Rumania?

RAKOVSKY: Yes, of course, I was connected with the labour movement.

---

[704] Rakovsky states he joined the British services because he was blackmailed by them with a false letter he allegedly wrote that proved he has been an agent for the Germans before the Revolution of 1917. He denies he was an agent of Germany before the Russian Revolution but later he states he "helped Germany in enlisting Rumanian citizens on Rumanian territory to aid Germany".

VYSHINSKY: You leave the labour movement out of this; I am not speaking of the labour movement, which, according to your own evidence, you betrayed in 1924. Did you say that you became an agent of the British Intelligence Service in 1924?

RAKOVSKY: I did.

VYSHINSKY: Is that betrayal of the working class? We may as well clarify this point once we have touched on this question.

RAKOVSKY: I did betray.

VYSHINSKY: Therefore speak less of the labour movement and dwell on the questions which are more closely related to this trial. In what year were you in Rumania?

RAKOVSKY: I was in Rumania from 1904 to 1907 and from 1912 to 1917.

VYSHINSKY: Were you in Rumania during the war?

RAKOVSKY: I was.

VYSHINSKY: What was your official occupation in Rumania? What were your means of existence?

RAKOVSKY: My father was a landlord.

VYSHINSKY: A landlord?

RAKOVSKY: My means of existence were the income I received from my father's property…

VYSHINSKY: Hence, it was not only your father who was a landlord, but you also were a landlord, an exploiter?

RAKOVSKY: Well, of course I was an exploiter. The fact is I lived on an income; and income, as is well known, accrues from surplus value…

VYSHINSKY: But you lived in Rumania all through the war?

RAKOVSKY: Yes.

VYSHINSKY: I want to put the question bluntly: I have a grave suspicion that your signature on the letter which Armstrong presented to you, a letter addressed to the German intelligence service, was not forged but was actually signed by you, because you were then already an agent of the German intelligence service. Is this right or wrong?

RAKOVSKY: Absolutely wrong...[705]

VYSHINSKY: Let us pass on to the further business…

RAKOVSKY: I admit that beginning with 1924 I became a traitor to the Soviet Socialist fatherland.

VYSHINSKY: And your activity at first factional, then counter-revolutionary underground Trotskyite criminal activity began in what year?

---

[705] Of course it would not be very smart to provide a complete confession that put at stake the very foundations of the Communist Revolution, suggesting the Bolshevik revolutionists were traitors working for the Kaiser.

RAKOVSKY: I have been personally acquainted with Trotsky since 1903. This acquaintance grew closer and I was his intimate friend…

VYSHINSKY: Consequently, for nearly thirty-five years you have been bound to Trotsky by political and personal friendship.

RAKOVSKY: Yes…

VYSHINSKY: Consequently, if you had managed to seize power it would inevitably have fallen into the hands of the fascists?

RAKOVSKY: I share this estimate entirely.

VYSHINSKY: So you wanted to seize power with the help of the fascists?

RAKOVSKY: With the help of the fascists…

VYSHINSKY: No? On whose help was the "bloc of Rights and Trotskyites" relying for the seizure of power? Whose help?

RAKOVSKY: The help of an aggressor, a fascist aggressor[706].-

---

[706] These "fascists" were probably those who financed the original Bolshevik Revolution of 1917 and wanted to harvest the interests of their investments on Russia: The German government and the Morgans, Rockefellers, Warburgs and Harrimans. They might have considered Stalin an "outsider" leading the country, a man who left these capitalists deprived of their expected return on investment.

BIOGRAPHICAL GLOSSARY

This glossary refers to characters, companies and authors mentioned in this work. The authors whose works are quoted are marked with an asterisk "*".

* **Adler, Cyrus**: An intellectual and leader of the Jewish community born in Arkansas in 1863. He graduated from the University of Pennsylvania and earned his doctorate at John Hopkins University, where he was professor of Semitic languages for several years. Adler was employed by the *Smithsonian Institution* for several years, and became an influential character in the Jewish world. Dean of the *Jewish Theological Seminary of America*, and President of the *Center for Advanced Judaic Studies*, he participated in the creation of the *Jewish Welfare Board* founded in 1917. After the First World War was invited to speak in the Paris Peace Conference of 1919. He was editor of the *Encyclopedia Judaica* 1901 a work in twelve volumes that is still considered one of the most complete references in the field of Judaism. It is a work very quoted here along with some biographical works composed by him.

Aldrich, Nelson: A banker and senator from New York who participated in the creation of two plans to establish a central bank in the United States, the Aldrich Plan and the Federal Reserve. His daughter Abby married the son of John D. Rockefeller.

Baring (family): Family of Christian bankers founded by an English wool merchant, Sir Francis Baring.

Bethmann (family): Family of Christian bankers in Frankfurt.

Baruch, Bernard: A Wall Street Jewish Broker, he financed the election campaigns of Wilson and Roosevelt and became an influential figure within the Democratic Party. During the First World War he headed the War Industries Board, the agency that centralized all the military purchases of the American government, and also played a leading role in the government during the Second World War.

Belmont, August: The principal agent of the Rothschild family in the United States until the arrival of *Kuhn & Loeb & Co.*

*** Birmingham, Stephen**: Birmingham was a renowned chronicler of New York high society. Some of the genealogies elaborated in this book have been based on his work.

Brown, Alexander: English merchant and patriarch of the Brown dynasty, the origin of important banking houses such as *Brown & Shipley* in England and *Brown Brothers Harriman* in the United States.

Biddle, Nicholas: President of the second central bank of the United States, the *Second Bank of the United States.*

Bush, Prescott: Banker and patriarch of the Bush family. Prescott Bush was professionally and politically linked to the Harriman and Rockefeller, being one of the partners of *Brown Brothers Harriman.* His political career suffered a considerable setback when he got involved in the *UBC* scandal.

Butler, Smedley Darlington: One of the most decorated generals in the United States. He exposed a plot that included characters close to the Morgan group to establish a fascist dictatorship in the United States.

Carnegie, Andrew: American steel magnate who sold his *Carnegie Steel* empire to John Pierpont Morgan. Known simultaneously for his many philanthropic works and the inhumane working conditions in his factories.

* **Chernow, Ron**: American writer and journalist who won the Pulitzer Prize. Along with Niall Ferguson, Chernow is the most important modern author specialized in the lives of investment bankers. Among his most famous titles are the biographies of the Warburg family, John D. Rockefeller, Morgan and Alexander Hamilton.

Davison, Henry P.: Banker affiliated with the Morgan group; *Bankers Trust, J.P. Morgan* and *First National Bank.* He was one of the bankers of Jekyll Island in 1910, and with Thomas Lamont he succeeded Morgan at the head of his empire.

*** Dall, Curtis Bean**: Franklin Delano Roosevelt's son-in-law, married to his daughter Anna Eleanor Roosevelt since 1926. Colonel of the air forces, he worked as a manager at *Lehman Brothers.* In 1934 he divorced his wife and in 1968 he published a very critical biography with Roosevelt.

*** Dodd, William E.**: A Doctor in History from the University of Leipzig, Professor at the University of Chicago and President of the American Historical Association. He collaborated with Ray Stannard Baker in the compilation of *The Public Papers of Woodrow Wilson.* He was an American Ambassador in Nazi Germany before the war.

Drexel (family): A family of German immigrants. The brothers Anthony Joseph and Joseph William Drexel were the first partners of Morgan and the Rothschilds in the United States in *Drexel, Morgan & Co.* They made their fortune in the sale of American public bonds.

Du Pont (family): A family that finds the origin of his fortune in Éleuthère Irénée du Pont, a chemist who emigrated during the French Revolution to the United States, where he founded *E.I. Dupont de Nemours*. Its small gunpowder factory became a chemical and armament giant in the 20th century. The *Du Pont* family held the majority shareholding in this company and also in *General Motors*.

Earle, George H: A naval officer during the two great wars. He was ambassador in Austria, a Governor of the State of Pennsylvania, Ambassador in Bulgaria and Deputy Naval in Istanbul.

Engels, Friedrich: Along with Marx, father of scientific socialism and co-author of the Communist Manifesto.

Eugene Isaac Meyer: A banker of *Lazard Frères*. In 1918 Wilson placed him at the head of the War Finance Corporation. In 1930 President of the Board of Governors of the Federal Reserve, and in 1946 of the *World Bank*. The Meyer family has owned the *Washington Post* since 1933.

*** Ferguson, Niall:** A professor of History at Harvard and author specialized in finance. Highlights include his biographies of Siegmund Warburg and his history of the Rothschild House.

Ford, Henry: Billionaire founder of the automobile brand that bears his name. A declared anti-Semite, he sponsored the creation of *The International Jew*, the story of an alleged international Jewish conspiracy. His portrait was prominently displayed in Adolf Hitler's office.

*** Forrestal, James**: Banker at *Dillon, Read & Co.*, the firm that led the Dawes and Young banking union and first Secretary of Defense of the United States. After the Second World War, he showed his concers of Communism and the Zionist influence in the American government.

Francqui, Emile: A Belgian banker. Partner of Herbert Hoover and representative of the interests of Baron Leon Lambert de Rothschild in China, in the Congo and in Belgium.

*** Giannini, Amadeo Pietro**: An Italo-American banker who made *Bank of America* the largest financial institution in the country.

Goldman (family): Marcus Goldman and Samuel Sachs founded *Goldman Sachs* in 1869, the most influential investment bank in the 21st century. That bank manages assets worth around 900,000 million dollars and has placed its members in governments and institutions around the world.

Guggenheim (family): Stephen Birmingham notes that before 1696 there was a Jew in Langnau called Maran Guggenheimb, whose family could come from a German city called Guggenheimb-today Jugenheim (Our Crowd, p.53). Born in 1828, Meyer Guggenheim initiated the saga of mining magnates and bankers established in the United States, owners of the Guggenheim museums. Their children were married in the Rothschild, Loeb and Seligman families. The family firm *Guggenheim Partners* provides financial services and manages 240,000 million dollars in assets.

Hamilton, Alexander: A man of humble origins, Alexander Hamilton was one of the fathers of the Constitution of the United States and first Secretary of the Treasury in 1789. He was promoter and President of the first central bank of the country, the *First Bank of the United States.*

Harriman, Averell W.: One of the founding partners of the investment bank *Brown Brothers Harriman.* He held several public offices, the most remarkable of which was ambassador in the Russia of Stalin.

Harriman, Edward H.: American railways tycoon. He was an agent of the Rockefeller family and was also associated with the banking firm *Kuhn & Loeb & Co.* The father of Roland and Averell Harriman.

Harriman, Roland: A member of the *Brown Brothers Harriman* family firm. Partner with Franklin Delano Roosevelt at the *International Germanic Trust*, a fund that he speculated in Germany during hyperinflation. He held various positions of responsibility within the Red Cross. He was embroiled in the *UBC* scandal.

Helphand, Israel Alexander: One of the leaders of the Russian Revolution of 1905, and author of the "Financial Manifesto". A successful businessman, was the link between the German government and the Bolsheviks, obtaining large sums to carry out the revolution.

Herzl, Theodor: A Hungarian Jew, founder of the Zionist movement.

Hindenburg, Paul von: Field marshal and member of the General Staff during the First War. German President between 1925 and 1934.

*** Hoover, Herbert**: A mining promoter in various parts of the world. Partner of Emile Francqui and Baron León Lambert de Rothschild in the Commission for Relief in Belgium and other companies. His memoirs are briefly cited.

*** House, Edward Mandell**: A close collaborator to President Wilson, his campaign advisor, and one of the main economic contributors to his campaign. Although he never held any public office, Stephen S. Wise rightly defined him as "the unofficial Secretary of State of Woodrow Wilson." His private documents are an important part of the material used in this work.

* **Jackson, Andrew**: 7th president of the United States. Hero of the war of independence against the British. His presidency stood out for his fight against the *Second Bank of the United States.*

*** Kahn, Otto**: A member of *Kuhn & Loeb*, and successor of E.H. Harriman at the head of the railroad business. Maecenas and director of the Metropolitan Opera of New York. Parts of a biography authorized by his daughter are cited.

*** Koestler, Arthur**: Jewish author born in 1905 in Budapest, he studied Science and Psychology, and was a foreign correspondent for several European newspapers. Member of the Communist Party since 1931, he turned his back on Hungarian Communism after the Stalinist purge of 1938. Detained by in the side of General Franco while covering the Spanish Civil War, and in France occupied by Hitler. In 1968 he received the "Sonning Prize" from the University of Copenhagen, in 1974 named "Companion of Literature" by the Royal Society of Literature. In 1972 he was appointed Commander of the Order of the British Empire. Some parts of his work *The 13th Tribe*, are quoted here.

Kerensky, Alexander: Russian politician member of the Social Revolutionary Party. His government amnestied thousands of Russian revolutionaries and eventually transferred power to the Bolshevik government.

Lamont, Thomas W: Banker of the Morgan group, and one of the founder's successors.

Lazard (family): A dynasty founded by Abraham Lazard, born in 1745 in Bohemia. Brothers Alexandre, Lazare and Simon founded *Lazard Frères* in 1848 in New Orleans. In 1851 they moved to San Francisco and opened an office in New York, in 1854 in Paris and in 1870 London.

Lehman (family): The brothers Mayer and Emanuel founded one of the largest investment banks in the United States, *Lehman Brothers* in 1850. This Jewish family is closely linked by matrimonial and business ties with *Kuhn & Loeb*, whose business they would eventually absorb in 1977.

Lehman, Herbert H: He was a partner of *Lehman Brothers* and son of one of the founders in that bank. One of the main contributors to the Franklin Delano Roosevelt campaign, designated by him as his successor as Governor of the State of New York.

Lenin, Vladimir Ilich: The Bolshevik leader born as Alexander Ulyanov. His older brother had been executed for the attempted murder of the Tsar. In his mandate as the first leader of Bolshevik Russia, the entire Romanov royal family, including women and children, were executed.

*** Ludendorff, Erich**: German General, member of the General Staff and military officer in charge of the Eastern Front in the First World War.

Marx, Karl: German Jew, father of communism and coauthor with Engels of the *Communist Manifesto.*

*** Moody, John**: A financial analyst and founder of the Moody's rating agency. His work *The Masters of Capital*, a reference work in the study of the great American fortunes, is frequently cited.

Morgan, John Pierpont: The son of Junius Spencer Morgan, George Peabody's partner in London. John Pierpont Morgan was the most prominent banker in history and founded the banking house that bears his name. The Morgans are among the first American partners of the Rothschilds.

*** Mullins, Eustace**: A veteran of the Air Force of the United States during the Second World War. He went to the universities of Washington, Lee, New York, Ohio and North Dakota, the School of Fine Arts of Salvador Allende in Mexico and the Institute of Contemporary Arts in Washington. He was the last protégé of Ezra Pound, one of the greatest writers of the 20th century, who edited four Nobel prizes in literature; T.S. Eliot, James Joyce, Ernest Hemingway and William Butler Yeats. Pound asked his last disciple to study about a different subject, the Federal Reserve. No book dealt with the history of the Federal Reserve or the secret meeting of Jekyll Island until the appearance of *Secrets of the Federal Reserve* of Mullins in 1952. Even today it is the best work published on the subject.

*** Myers, Gustavus**: Historian and journalist, author of *History of the Great American Fortunes.* Like John Moody, he told the story of the great magnates of the United States, although on a much more critical stance.

Norman, Montagu: Member of the firm *Brown & Shipley* and Governor of the Bank of England for 24 years. Montagu Norman maintained an excellent relationship with other central bankers such as Benjamin Strong of the Federal Reserve and Hjalmar Schacht of the Reichsbank.

Oppenheim (family): A Jewish family of Friedberg, located about 27 kilometers from Frankfurt. Its fortune began when Salomon Oppenheim Jr. founded the family bank in 1789, *Sal. Oppenheim Jr. & Cie.* Like the Rothschilds and Guggenheims, the Oppenheims were great mining magnates, mainly related to the *De Beers* diamond company. Maternal lineage of the Warburg brothers.

* **Papen, Franz von**: During the First World War he was Military Attaché of Germany in the United States, and the man in charge for the German espionage on American soil. Because of his diplomatic status he avoided prison, but he was reproved and expelled from the country. Later he was appointed chancellor of Germany and responsible for the rise of Adolf Hitler to power, occupying various positions in Nazi Germany. Despite this, he was acquitted in the Nuremberg trials.

* **Patman, J. W. Wright**: Chairman of the Banking and Currency Committee in Congress from 1965 to 1975. Patman was very critical of banking industry and the Federal Reserve. In 1932 he led the impeachment of Secretary of the Treasury Andrew Mellon, one of the wealthiest bankers in history.

* **Patton, George S.:** This controversial General was the most prominent military figure of the Allies during World War II.

Peabody, George: A representative of the Rothschilds in England. He established ties with the Morgans, who after his death continued the business.

* **Quigley, Carroll**: Author known for his history of civilizations titled *Tragedy and Hope*. Quigley was a professor at Harvard University, where he earned his doctorate in History, at Princeton and Georgetown. He was an advisor to various government institutions in the United States such as the Ministry of Defense, the Navy or the Smithsonian. In the 1992 Democratic Party primaries, the candidate Bill Clinton recognized him as a powerful influence for him in his university days[707].

* **Rakovsky, Christian**: A socialist leader of the Balkans, one of the most trusted characters of Leon Trotsky and Israel Helphand. His confession is cited during the Great Stalinist Purge as well as a text attributed also to him.

Rockefeller, John Davison: The patriarch of the Rockefeller dynasty obtained his fantastic patrimony thanks to the monopoly of the petroleum industry. He was considered the greatest non inherited fortune in history. His

---

[707] Bill Clinton's speech in the National Democrat Convention of 1992, Youtube.

company, the *Standard Oil of New Jersey*, was fragmented into other smaller companies for violating the anti-trust laws. He entered in the banking acquiring participations in the *National City Bank*.

Romanov, Alexander II: Penultimate Tsar of Russia. Its mandate stood out as one of the most progressive, culminating in the liberation of the serfs and proposing a parliament for Russia on its own initiative. He was killed by the Marxist group *Narodnaya Volia*.

Romanov, Nicholas II: The last tsar of Russia. At the end of the revolution he was executed with all his family at the hands of the Bolsheviks.

Roosevelt, Theodore: 26th President of the United States, from 1901 to 1909, his term is best remembered for his anti-trust policies. In 1912 he left the Republican Party and founded the short-lived Progressive Party or "Bull Moose."

Roosevelt, Franklin Delano: 32nd President of the United States and the only one to win four elections in a row between 1932 and 1945. A distant relative of President Theodore Roosevelt, he contended for the elections with the rival party, the Democratic Party. Their mandates stood out for the New Deal and the entry of the United States in World War II.

Rothschild (family): A banking dynasty founded by Mayer Amschel Rothschild, who sent his five children to the most important financial capitals of Europe. The Rothschilds were also mining and industrial tycoons.

Rothschild, León Lambert de: One of the most powerful men in Belgium, along with Ernest Solvay and Emile Francqui. The three of them managed the Commission for Relief in Belgium.

Rothschild, Nathan Mayer: One of the five children of Mayer Amschel, he continued the family saga in England with *N.M. Rothschild & Sons*, whose offices have set the world price of gold until a few years ago. Nathan was elected for the House of Parliament for several terms.

Rothschild, James Mayer: Son of Mayer Amschel and head of the family saga in France.

Sachs (family): see 'Goldman'.

Seligman (family): Established in Frankfurt in the sixteenth century, the eight brothers of the Seligman saga founded in 1862 the banking houses *Seligman Frères* in Paris, *Abraham Seligman & Co.* in San Francisco, *Seligman Brothers* in London, *Seligman & Stettheimer* in Frankfurt, and *J. & W. Seligman & Co.* of New York.

* **Schacht, Hjalmar**: The son of an accountant of *Equitable Trust Company*. He was President of the *Reichsbank*, the German central bank and German representative in the Dawes and Young plans. He was a key support for the rise of Hitler and went through several years of denazification after the Nuremberg trials. His memoirs are cited several times.

Schroder (family): In 1800 Johann Friedrich Schröder founded *J. F. Schröder & Co.* in London. His brother Johann Heinrich joined the company and founded his own firm in London in 1918, *J. Henry Schröder & Co.* Baron Kurt von Schröder, a prominent Nazi, led the *J.H. Stein Bank* in Cologne. The group *Schroders plc.* is today one of the most important investment banks in England and manages assets worth almost 416,000 million dollars. Gordon Richardson, President of *Schroders* was Governor of the *Bank of Engla*nd (1973-1983). James Wolfensohn, Deputy Chairman of *Schroders* in London, was appointed President of the *World Bank* (1995-2005).

Schiff, Jacob: A Jewish banker and agent of the Rothschilds. Appointed director of investment banking firm *Kuhn & Loeb* and President of *Wells Fargo.* Schiff served as treasurer of the Red Cross and financed the fall of the Tsars.

Speyer (family): The Speyer brothers founded *Speyer Brothers* in London, *Speyer & Co.* in New York and *Lazard-Speyer Ellissen* in Frankfurt, (E.J. vol.XI, p.505.)

Stern (family): Baron Hermann de Stern and Viscount David de Stern founded *Stern Brothers* in London in 1844. They granted loans to the governments of Spain, France and Portugal, where their titles of nobility were granted. David de Stern was also Director of the *Imperial Bank, Bank of Romania* and the *London & San Francisco Bank.* (E.J. vol.XI, p.505)

Stalin, Joseph: One of Lenin's men, he took advantage over Trotsky in succession, becoming a dictator with an iron hand in the U.R.S.S.

Strauss (family): The Strauss have their origins in the Rhineland, on the border between Germany and France. Some famous bankers in this saga are Albert Strauss, who succeeded Paul Warburg as Deputy Governor of the Federal Reserve board, Dominique Strauss-Kahn, director of the *IMF*, or Emil George von Strauss, Managing Director at *Deutsche Bank.*

Strong, Benjamin: A partner of *Banker's Trust*, and a Governor of the Federal Reserve for fourteen years, until his death.

* **Sutton, Anthony Cyril**: A British economist and historian. He studied at the universities of London, Gottingen and California, receiving his Doctorate in Science from the University of Southampton. Professor of

Economics at the California State University and the University of Los Angeles. Researcher at the *Hoover Institution* at Stanford University.

In his trilogy *Western Technology and Soviet Economic Development* he proved that the economic, technological and productive development of the Soviet Union would never have been possible without the cooperation of the West. Its publication caused his expulsion from the *Hoover Institution.*

In his *Wall Street* trilogy he documented the relationship between a small American financial elite and the communist revolution in Russia, the rise of National Socialism in Germany and the corporate Socialism of the New Deal. His central thesis was that this elite promoted different types of totalitarian Marxist states, sometimes confronted with each other, to obtain economic benefits such as captive markets, fixed prices and state monopolies.

* **Trotsky, Leon**: One of the Bolshevik leaders, who eventually led the Petrograd Soviet. He was exiled to U.R.S.S. and murdered in Mexico at the hands of an agent of Stalin. His memoirs are cited here.

Warburg, Felix Moritz: One of the three Warburg brothers, a Jewish family linked to other powerful German families immigrated to New York as the Rothschilds, Oppenheimers, Loebs or Schiffs. Felix was American director of *Hamburg-America Line*, a company directly linked to the German espionage in the United States during the First World War.

Warburg, Max: The representative of the Warburg in Hamburg. Max was an advisor to Kaiser Wilhelm II and German director in *Hamburg-America Line.* Max was also one of the main shareholders of *Deutsche-Russian Transport*, the transportation monopoly established with the Harriman in Russia, and Director of *I.G. Farben*, a German chemical cartel linked to high level Nazism.

Warburg, Paul: A Jewish-German Banker, partner of *Kuhn & Loeb & Co.*, President of *Wells Fargo*, the intellectual father and first Vice Chairman of the Federal Reserve, co-founder of the *International Acceptance Bank* and President of the *Manhattan Bank*. In the First World War he created the agency that centralized the American war finances, the *War Finance Corporation.* Paul was a Director of the American subsidiary of *I.G. Farben.*

Warburg (family): A family of Jewish-German bankers whose surname comes from the German city of Warburg. Its origins can be traced back to the Del Banco family in Italy at the beginning of the 16th century. The houses formed by the Warburg were:

- In 1798 Moses Marcus Warburg and Gerson Warburg formed *M.M. Warburg & Co.* in Hamburg, which manages 8,000 million euros in assets.

- In 1946 Siegmund Warburg founded *S.G. Warburg & Co.* in London, which ended up integrating in 1995 with the Swiss bank *UBS*.

- In 1939 Eric, the son of Max Warburg, formed E.M. Warburg & Co. at 52 William Street, in the *Kuhn & Loeb* building. After Eric Warburg associated with Lionel Pincus, in 1966 it became *Warburg Pincus LLC.*, which currently manages assets worth 45,000 million dollars.

*** Wilson, Woodrow**: Wilson was the President of the prestigious Princeton University, a post he left to become Governor of the State of New Jersey. He became the 28th President in office, from 1913 to 1921. His presidency stood out for the creation of the Federal Reserve, the introduction of Income Tax and the entry of the United States in the First World War. He was a Nobel Peace Prize in 1919. Several documents and speeches are quoted here.

Wise, Stephen S: A Rabbi and Zionist leader. He participated in the creation of the Federation of American Zionists. He was a delegate in the Second Zionist Congress of Basel and creator of the World Jewish Congress -directed since 2013 by David René de Rothschild-. He pressed for the creation of a mandate in Palestine in the Peace of Versailles and exerted a powerful influence in various North American presidential administrations.

LEGAL GLOSSARY

Sherman Antitrust Act (1890): Its main purpose was to limit the power of the trust and to promote free competition in the American industry.

Sherman Silver Purchase Act (1890): Law that established the minimum monthly amounts of silver that the American government should purchase. Its main objective was to protect the stability of the dollar.

Aldrich Vreeland Act (1908): Approved after the panic of 1907, it established the National Monetary Commission. This institution prepared several reports favorable to the creation of a central bank.

Sixteenth Amendment to the Constitution of the United States (1913): This amendment allowed Congress to set taxes on personal income such as *Income Tax*.

Owen Glass Act or Federal Reserve Act (1913): Act in virtue of which the Federal Reserve System was established in 1913.

Clayton Antitrust Act (1914): It complemented and developed several of the provisions of the Sherman Antitrust Act on free competition.

Trading with the Enemy Act (1917): A Law designed to restrict trade with countries declared hostile to the United States.

Espionage Act (1917): That Law intended to reinforce the powers of the Executive branch in times of war, punishing with severe penalties those who interfered in military operations, recruitment, or who lent support to the enemy. This included anyone who refused to be enlisted, who promoted conscientious objection or publicly opposed war.

National Industrial Recovery Act or NIRA (1933): One of the most important laws of Roosevelt's New Deal, it influenced almost every field of the American economy; It allowed the government to set prices and salaries, encouraged the creation of trust and oligopolies, promoted state spending on public works and established regulations on trade union matters.

Glass Steagall Act or Banking Law (1933): Law signed after the Crash of 29 comprising several banking reforms, the main one being the separation between investment banking and deposit banking.

Gold Reserve Act (1934): This law completed Roosevelt's Executive Order 6102 and the Emergency Banking Relief Act, both signed in 1933. By virtue of the same, Americans were prohibited from holding physical gold or in the form of titles. Every citizen should change all the gold that would keep the American Treasury at the fixed price. The penalties for non-compliance were up to $ 10,000 and ten years in prison.

Decree of the Reich President for the Protection of People and State (1933): Known as the Reichstag Fire Decree, and together with the Enabling Act of the same year, it suppressed all individual rights of Germans and de facto eliminated democracy in the country, by granting full powers to Chancellor Adolf Hitler.

Executive Order 11110 (1963): It was signed by President Kennedy months before his assassination. It allowed the American Treasury to issue silver certificates. Some have seen it as an attempt to substitute the Federal Reserve notes (dollars) for money issued by the Treasury and backed by silver.

CPSIA information can be obtained
at www.ICGtesting.com
Printed in the USA
LVHW111445140720
660686LV00001B/7

9 781096 898320